Active Vision

Active Vision

edited by
Andrew Blake and Alan Yuille

The MIT Press
Cambridge, Massachusetts
London, England

This book was set in LaTeX by the authors. Camera-ready copy was produced by Chiron, Inc.

This book was printed and bound in the United States of America.

Library of Congress Cataloging-in-Publication Data

Active vision / edited by Andrew Blake and Alan Yuille.
    p.   cm. — (Artificial intelligence)
    Includes bibliographical references and index.
    ISBN 0-262-02351-2
    1. Computer vision. 2. Image processing—Digital techniques.   I. Blake, Andrew.   II. Yuille, A. L. (Alan L.)   III. Series: Artificial intelligence (Cambridge, Mass.)
TA1632.A255   1993
006.3'7—dc20   92-22427
                                                        CIP

Contents

Series Foreword   vii

Foreword by Rodney A. Brooks   ix

Preface   xiii

Introduction   xv

I Tracking

1 **Tracking with Kalman Snakes**   3
   Demetri Terzopoulos and Richard Szeliski

2 **Deformable Templates**   21
   Alan Yuille and Peter Hallinan

3 **Dynamic Contours: Real-time Active Splines**   39
   Rupert Curwen and Andrew Blake

4 **Tracking with Rigid Models**   59
   Chris Harris

5 **Tracking Nonrigid 3D Objects**   75
   Demetri Terzopoulos and Dimitri Metaxas

6 **Data Association Methods for Tracking Systems**   91
   Bobby Rao

7 **Color Region Tracking for Vehicle Guidance**   107
   Jill D. Crisman

II Control of Vision Heads

8 **Real-time Smooth Pursuit Tracking**   123
   Christopher Brown, David Coombs and John Soong

9 **Attentive Visual Servoing**   137
   James J. Clark and Nicola J. Ferrier

10 **Design of Stereo Heads**   155
   David W. Murray, Fenglei Du, Philip F. McLauchlan,
   Ian D. Reid, Paul M. Sharkey and Michael Brady

III Geometric and Task Planning

11 **Visual Exploration of Free-space**   175
   Andrew Blake, Andrew Zisserman and Roberto Cipolla

**12 Motion Planning Using Image Divergence and
     Deformation**   189
     Roberto Cipolla and Andrew Blake

13 Adaptive Local Navigation   203
     Tony Prescott and John Mayhew

14 Task-oriented Vision with Multiple Bayes Nets   217
     Raymond Rimey and Christopher Brown

IV Architectures and Applications

15 A Parallel 3D Vision System   239
     Michael Rygol, Stephen Pollard, Chris Brown and John
     Mayhew

16 Geometry from Visual Motion   263
     Chris Harris

17 Medical Image Tracking   285
     Nicholas Ayache, Isaac Cohen and Isabelle Herlin

**18 Expectation-based Dynamic Scene
     Understanding**   303
     Ernst D. Dickmanns

     Acknowledgements   337

     References   341

     Contributors   357

     Index   360

Series Foreword

Artificial intelligence is the study of intelligence using the ideas and methods of computation. Unfortunately, a definition of intelligence seems impossible at the moment because intelligence appears to be an amalgam of so many information processing and information representation abilities.

Of course psychology, philosophy, linguistics, and related disciplines offer various perspectives and methodologies for studying intelligence. For the most part, however, the theories proposed in these fields are too incomplete and too vaguely stated to be realized in computational terms. Something more is needed, even though valuable ideas, relationships, and constraints can be gleaned from traditional studies of what are, after all, impressive existence proofs that intelligence is in fact possible.

Artificial intelligence offers a new perspective and a new methodology. Its central goal is to make computers intelligent, both to make them more useful and to understand the principles that make intelligence possible. That intelligent computers will be extremely useful is obvious. The more profound point is that artificial intelligence aims to understand intelligence using the ideas and methods of computation, thus offering a radically new and different basis for theory formation. Most of the people doing work in artificial intelligence believe that these theories will apply to any intelligent information processor, whether biological or solid state.

There are side effects that deserve attention, too. Any program that will successfully model even a small part of intelligence will be inherently massive and complex. Consequently, artificial intelligence continually confronts the limits of computer science technology. The problems encountered have been hard enough and interesting enough to seduce artificial intelligence people into working on them with enthusiasm. It is natural, then, that there has been a steady flow of ideas from artificial intelligence to computer science, and the flow shows no sign of abating.

The purpose of this series in artificial intelligence is to provide people in many areas, both professionals and students, with timely, detailed information about what is happening on the frontiers in research centers all over the world.

J. Michael Brady
Daniel Bobrow
Randall Davis

Foreword

Computer Vision has been an identifiable discipline for over twenty five years. To a large extent it has been concerned with the passive inversion of the image formation process[1] either to produce three dimensional reconstructions of the world or, at a higher level, to identify objects and their locations and orientations.

This book represents a recent change in emphasis within the discipline. In the new approach, vision is an active participant in the world. Participation changes what the vision system is capable of perceiving and changes the nature of the requirements on what needs to be perceived. A change in scientific and philosphical viewpoint such as this is rarely a step function; it comes on rather gradually at first, followed by a rapid change in primary perspective. If we think of the change in intellectual perspective as a standard sigmoid function of time, then this book comes out around the $t = 0$ point, right in the thick of the change, but still with opportunity for further radical change in the future.

In the sixties it was discovered that simulating human vision with computers was much harder than many people intuitively imagined relative to other skills that humans possessed. Our own vision seems effortless. We cannot help but see identifiable objects around us. The world offers us a stable panorama as we move our heads and bodies. Objects have a constancy of appearance in our minds and to a large extent a constancy of color as lighting changes from natural daylight to unnatural indoor light. And it all occurs without us consciously thinking. Perception just happens. Other tasks such as playing chess, solving crypto-arithmetic problems, and integrating algebraic expressions seem much harder. We, as humans, really need to "think" about these problems, and need to have been explicitly taught quite a bit in order to handle them. They do not just happen.

It was a surprise therefore, when the apparently harder problems fell rather simply, but computer vision made very little progress. However, simplifying the scenes to be viewed, essentially to a world of blocks with uniformly colored faces, did allow for rapid progress. And in two landmark projects from the late sixties, the *copy demo* at MIT and the robot *Shakey* at Stanford Research Institute, such restrictions led to vision systems which could identify objects and their locations, and feed their descriptions to intelligent programs which then made plans for real physical robots which acted in the world.

An intellectual trap had been sprung, and it ensnared computer vision researchers for the next twenty years. As with other aspects of Artificial Intelligence success came by considering what seems to go on in humans at a conscious level, and the conscious manifestation of vision was the ability to name recognized objects, and their relative positions. The shape of an object seemed the natural way to describe a particular object. Success had been

---

[1] This has been done from single images and from sequences of closely temporally spaced images.

achieved in simple worlds, so all that remained was to generalize the worlds. This required some more sophisticated early vision processing, and so we soon saw work on such topics as shape from shading, stereo vision, shape from motion, and, as always, edge detection, which supposedly would provide the input to many of the recognition programs that worked in simplified worlds.

This approach to computer vision was accepted impicitly, and at the same time made explicit by a number of writers. One of the most influential documents in computer vision is the book by Marr (1982). In the first paragraph he states that

> *vision is the* process *of discovering from images what is present in the world, and where it is.*

The tenor of the whole book is not *what should be done* with computations in vision, but *what should be computed.* In particular his $2\frac{1}{2}$D sketch emphasizes the recovery of shape and orientation information in the general case; an inversion of the image formation process.

As a result of this nearly uniform reality shared by vision researchers, outsiders from the computer vision field have viewed it as a well defined sub-area of Artificial Intelligence, one of the few areas which has a clearly circumscribed goal. For instance, Charniak and McDermott (1985) in their introductory AI text state that the problem which vision must solve is:

> *Given a two-dimensional image, infer the objects that produced it, including their shapes, positions, colors, and sizes.*

The emphasis is on recognition and pose determination from a single two dimensional image. It implies a knowledge based system which has models, at the object level, of all that is to be perceived. For instance Tanimoto (1990), as a vision researcher writing for a general AI audience, portrays vision as a mostly bottom up process culminating in a description of what an image contains. Image sequences are considered, but only as an extra source of constraint in determining what is in the images, either at the surface level or the object level. The vision system is a passive observer.

Horn (1986), in a technical book on computer vision, is careful not to make recognition the primary purpose of vision, preferring instead to define it in terms of some task, and embedding vision within a feedback loop. However, he still maintains that the central issue of machine vision is:

> *generating a symbolic description from one or more images.*

In contrast, the current volume, *Active Vision*, represents a clear turning point for both the tasks and the processes of computer vision. The term *active vision* is used in at least two senses herein:

- active operation in the world in order to change the images that are being collected in a way which enhances task achievement

- active autonomous processes (e.g., snakes) which exploit the coherence of images in a sequence in order to efficiently and reliably track aspects of interest over time

Both uses of the term rely on constraints that the world provides in order to make the problem tractable. In moving a stereo head or a vehicle around in the world, there is constraint provided by the fact that the world itself does not change too much in the time interval between images, so that much of the change that is observed can be attributed to camera motion. In using active processes to track aspects of deformable or articulated objects, there is a constraint that the objects are changing smoothly rather than switching modes of appearance completely between frames.

Several of the vision systems described in this book produce outputs which are not symbolic at all. Rather they are themselves control signals which can be used directly in the furtherance of some task. In some cases that task is control of the vision system itself—Horn's feedback loops being realized at tens of Hertz. In many cases the tasks are not recognition *per se*, but things like grasping and navigation. It is the task that is important, not the results of conscious-like querying of the vision system.

To be sure, the papers in this book do not represent a complete break with traditional work in computer vision. There are clear continuities with the work of the last twenty years. Three dimensional models and symbolic descriptions still play a role in many of the papers. The book does, however, represent a change in emphasis; vision is no longer a passive process, instead it interacts with the dynamics of the world, becoming an active participant.

Much of the work reported here has been made possible by advances in computer hardware. Many of the techniques presented will be refined and extended as new hardware options become available. In particular the availability of a well foveated camera will have a great impact upon the field, both in terms of requirements it will place on active vision systems and in terms of the opportunities it will provide for those able to implement appropriate active vision algorithms.

We can expect this change in emphasis to be extended over the next few years as a new orthodoxy arises for computer vision research. Lest we feel too self satisfied that we now really understand what we are doing, we should take note of the history of science. It teaches us that the new approach will itself be only transient in nature, and eventually it too will be supplanted by new perspectives.

Rodney A. Brooks

Preface

This book arose out of a workshop held by the *Rank Prize Funds* at Grasmere, England, in the summer of 1991. Within the *Active Vision* paradigm, only lately establishing itself within the field of machine vision, some clear themes were emerging. First, common technologies were being developed, namely machinery for directing visual attention and control architectures for stereoscopic heads. Secondly the new paradigm was achieving something that had always been hard to achieve in machine vision — systems that really worked. These include visually guided robots, both mobile robots and robot arms, and also spin-offs in areas such as medical imaging and visual surveillance.

The reason for the success seems to be threefold. Partly, research goals are focussed onto particular tasks, and hence better defined, so that it is clear when some success has been achieved. Partly, moving images from an active robot contain more information and hence are, in many respects, easier to analyse than the still ones which were most commonly studied in machine vision a decade ago. Partly, the Active Vision approach is inherently economical because the visual processes themselves are focussed — the "selfish eye"[2] obdurately ignores superfluous detail. The old paradigm was a natural child of the hippy era — visual systems were supposed to relax and take in the scene. The new paradigm is born of the eighties, a robot yuppy that makes straight for its goal, immune to distraction

Active Vision is a sufficiently recent development that no definitive textbook, to our knowledge, yet exists. Whilst a textbook treatment is clearly ideal, it seemed to us worthwhile to compile a multi-authored volume that laid out what seemed to be the emerging coherent themes. We have tried therefore, as far as possible, to achieve continuity and coherence. If not actually a textbook, we sincerely hope that it is a passable simulation of one. And in the meantime, until the definitive work appears, we hope that readers will be caught up in the excitement of this latest era in the development of Machine Vision.

We would like to thank the Rank Prize Funds for providing the workshop in the first place. Thanks are due to T. Ehling of MIT Press, to P. Winder, C-S. Fu, M. Nitzberg and Y. Yang for their invaluable assistance with typesetting, and to P. Beardsley, I. Reid, L. Shapiro, D. Sinclair and W. Triggs for proof-reading. Further acknowledgements for contributions to individual chapters are listed towards the end of the book.

---

[2]Shameless plagiarism from the title of Richard Dawkins' influential book "The Selfish Gene".

Introduction

Why?

Why has the study of Active Vision become important? Partly it is a matter of technological opportunity and partly because of traditional approaches to vision running aground. Until the mid-eighties, the limitations of computing power restricted experimentation in Computer Vision to the analysis of static scenes. In the last five years, powerful general-purpose processors have become relatively cheap and, in particular, parallel-processors can be assembled in modular fashion and harnessed to analyze images. The result is that researchers are now able to experiment with the links between perception and action.

The success of this approach has lead to a re-evaluation of the goals of Computer Vision itself. As Brooks pointed out in his foreword, previous theories suggested that the visual system should reconstruct a map of the visible surface, aiming literally to invert the imaging process. A slogan from Marr (1982) puts it like this:

> Vision is knowing what is where by looking.

In contrast an active vision system is far more selfish. It picks out the properties of images which it needs to perform its assigned task, and ignores the rest. There is no need for a detailed reconstruction of the visible world. To adapt J.F. Kennedy, an active vision system asks what the image can do for it, rather than what it can do for the image.

What?

What is Active Vision? A short answer is, in the absence of agreed international standards, you should go ahead and read the book! One thing that we certainly do *not* mean by an "active" system is one that contains its own source of radiation (as opposed to a passive imaging system). Vision sensors which are active in that older sense include "structured light" systems and scanning laser range-sensors (Shirai, 1972; Jarvis, 1983; Besl & Jain, 1982). More recently the term *Active Vision* has been justifiably[1] hijacked to refer to something quite different and rather broader in concept.

Active Vision refers not to sensing technology but to strategies for observation. As Aloimonos et al. (1987) explain in their seminal paper, it is the *observer* that is active. Rather than processing snapshots, or sequences of snapshots treated individually, the observer and sensor continually interact. Visual sensory data is analysed purposefully, in order to answer specific queries posed by the observer. The observer constantly adjusts its vantage point in order to allow the sensor to uncover the piece of information that

---

[1] Justifiably, at least, in our view — a similar thing happened to the term "Computational Geometry" which once referred to modelling smooth surfaces for CAD and Graphics but was taken over by complexity theorists.

is immediately most pressing. This parsimonious, opportunistic, mobile observer operates at a distinct advantage for several reasons.

Structure from controlled motion   Over the last decade or so, the theory of the computation of egomotion and surface structure from optic flow has been extensively developed (Koenderink & Van Doorn, 1975; Koenderink & Van Doorn, 1978; Ullman, 1979; Longuet-Higgins & Pradzny, 1980; Huang & Tsai, 1981; Waxman & Ullman, 1985; Maybank, 1985; Faugeras *et al.*, 1987; Murray & Buxton, 1990). It seems natural to expect that if the analysis of single images is hard then the analysis of sequences of images should be harder but, as a consequence of the richness of geometric information in image flow, the opposite is actually true. A robot is able, therefore, to perceive *more* while it (or its eye (Geiger & Yuille, 1987)) is moving. It is often worthwhile for the robot to generate deliberate exploratory motions precisely in order to induce motion of the image.

Tracking   The complexity of the structure from motion problem is considerably reduced by tracking — fixating a point on a moving object and measuring optic flow in a frame in which the fixated point is at rest (Aloimonos *et al.*, 1987). This is closely related to the advantages of *parallax* or relative image motion in removing the effects of the observer's rotational velocity on measurements of depth (Koenderink & Van Doorn, 1975; Longuet-Higgins & Pradzny, 1980) and of curvature (Blake & Cipolla, 1990). Furthermore, exploiting the temporal continuity of features tracked over time yields the accuracy enjoyed when large baselines are used in binocular stereo (Matthies & Shafer, 1987) but without the computationally complex correspondence problem (Pollard *et al.*, 1985a; Ohta & Kanade, 1985). Tracking is a valuable competence in its own right, quite apart from application to structure from motion. Applications include automated surveillance and traffic monitoring (Sullivan, 1992), hand-eye coordination for robots (Anderson, 1988; Blake, 1992) and road-following (see chapter 18) This has motivated much of the work described here on tracking mechanisms in section I.

Focussed attention   Attention mechanisms are well known in human vision (Treisman & Gelade, 1980) and it is reasonable to expect that they might be needed in machine vision systems too (Ullman, 1984; Hurlbert & Poggio, 1986). An autonomous low-level mechanism for tracking low-level features (Inoue & Mizoguchi, 1985) liberates higher level processes to analyse the features relevant to a particular task, switching freely between them as required. This is particularly effective in binocular vision (Ballard & Ozcandarli, 1988; Olson & Coombs, 1991) where tracking fixates a region not merely of an image but of 3D space. Control of fixation in binocular vision heads is discussed extensively in section II.

Prediction   A compelling reason for a temporal image sequence to be *easier* to process than a single image is that the images in the sequence are not mutually independent. Features found in one image are strongly correlated with those in the image immediately previous. A weak form of this correlation is the temporal continuity mentioned in the context of tracking above. A stronger form can be invoked if prior models of 3D motion are available. The Kalman filter (Gelb, 1974) is the classical mechanism for doing this, capable of combining a deterministic temporal model with a stochastic allowance for uncertainty. The Kalman filter makes frequent appearances in each of the four sections of the book and is an underlies the very impressive vehicle navigation system of chapter 18.

Sensing strategies A major opportunity for the active observer is to plan sensor-actions in real-time, incrementally on the basis of cumulatively acquired information. The aim of each sensing step is to maximise the information acquired during the step, with respect to the goal task. Information theoretic measures of relevant information have been used in machine learning (J.R.Quinlan, 1986). Rigorously Bayesian measures can been used in sensory planning problems involving simple sensors (Cameron & Durrant-Whyte, 1990). Section III of the book explains recent progress in harnessing both deterministic and probabilistic schemes for sensory planning with vision.

Real tasks The acid test of the Active Vision paradigm has been its effectiveness in helping to build seeing systems. Section IV exhibits some of the early successes. Systems are demonstrated, in several cases operating at real-time rates, that perform navigation, recognition and surface analysis. Of course these systems are nowhere near the general-purpose vision systems that researchers were dreaming of 10 or 15 years ago. They are somewhat cosseted and protected, performing well defined tasks in insulated environments. Clearly, much remains to be done in enhancing versatility and generality, and this is beginning to happen. Nonetheless, we believe that the discipline of studying complete perception-action tasks, and implementing machines to perform them, is already leading to a significant advance in vision research.

Where next?

As Brooks indicates in the foreword, we can expect that the Active Vision viewpoint will evolve and change considerably. It represents a paradigm shift (Kuhn, 1962), a radical change of emphasis on what is considered important in vision. Such shifts of emphasis require the development of new technical tools and, initially, pose more problems than they solve. As the chapters in this book illustrate, there are technical problems to be solved to do with designing simulated elastic mechanisms, algorithms for feature search and efficient control systems. Nevertheless the "evolutionary idea", central to Active Vision, of building systems to perform simple tasks and gradually making the tasks more difficult, as illustrated in Section IV, has been highly successful and is extremely promising.

The chapters in this book raise a number of broad issues. First there is the relationship between the mechanical and probabilistic models for trackers. This is somewhat reminiscent of the alternative mechanical/probabilistic views of visual reconstruction problems (Blake & Zisserman, 1987), known to be formally equivalent as a consequence of the Hammersley-Clifford theorem (Besag, 1974). The probabilistic, or Bayesian, view is very attractive for modelling vision (Szeliski, 1989; Clark & Yuille, 1990) and has the advantage that system parameters could be automatically set by statistical means. The mechanical view made available powerful tools of continuous analysis, notably variational calculus. The same advantages apply here, to spatio-temporal problems. It remains to establish an appropriately general equivalence between the two views.

Another general issue is the acquisition of control strategies and systems. On the one hand there is the idea that complex behaviours can arise in relatively simple systems (Simon, 1969) with a self-organising mechanism (Braitenberg, 1986). This is what lies behind the innovative exploration in chapter 13. In other chapters, planning and control strategies are programmed manually, making use of explicit geometrical and dynamical concepts. So far, the explicit approach has achieved the more sophisticated behaviours. The prospect is, however, that they may run out of steam and force the development of implicit programming, by application of punishment and reward.

One final question is whether the relatively low-level vision methods described in this book can be integrated, at last, with Artificial Intelligence. Once robot vision was part of Artificial Intelligence — a part which, reputedly, a certain renowned researcher considered should be solvable in a few months. After mathematical and algorithmic excursions lasting a couple of decades, is the time now right for a re-marriage with the school of symbolic computation? The experiments of chapter 14 into control of visual search by probabilistic planning give some reason to hope so.

I Tracking

Considerable advances have been made in the technology that lies at the heart of Active Vision systems — real-time visual tracking. A spectrum of techniques has been developed, from the general method with considerable tolerance for uncertainty, to the model-based tracker seeking evidence for some sharply tuned hypothesis or hypotheses. A highly influential piece of work here has been the paper of Kass *et al.* (1987a) which laid down the mechanical framework for the *snake* tracker. This is an elastic, graphic simulation, programmable for the nature of its internal stiffness and dynamics and its external attraction to image features. Chapter 1 reviews the basis of the snake in Lagrangian dynamics which allows the spatially distributed mechanical structure to be programmed in terms of energy functions. A Lagrangian dynamics formalism then acts as a machine for turning energy functions into dynamical equations. The link is also made between snakes and the Kalman filter which is a standard tool that has been used for some time in robotic sensing applications (see e.g. Hallam (1983) and chapter 18 by Dickmanns). The distributed mechanical system becomes a linear recursive filter with a large state-space consisting of a chain of finite elements.

The *deformable template* of chapter 2, in contrast, is at the model-based end of the spectrum of techniques. It is an assembly of articulated rigid limbs with programmable geometry and affinity for image features which constitutes a prior object model. The principle is illustrated via the worked example of a face template. The emphasis here is on recognition and capture. In that respect it is complementary to most of the other chapters in this section which develop tracking mechanisms. Tracking has to be initiated and the deformable template is a mechanism for doing exactly that. The *dynamic contour* of chapter 3 is, in some respects, a synthesis of the snake and the deformable template. Like the snake, it is elastic but it incorporates a rigid template which defines the resting state of the contour. In addition, it uses a sparse curve representation, the B-spline, which, coupled with efficient image search and parallel architecture, leads to a real-time (25 Hz) spatiotemporal tracker.

Faster tracking yet (50 Hz) is attainable even from a single processor when a strict, rigid prior model is available. Chapter 4 uses the machinery of the Extended Kalman Filter to update, over time, the mapping of a rigid 3D structure onto an image. This technique is sufficiently powerful to keep up with an object rotating in front of the camera at almost 2 revolutions per second. The model based tracking theme is continued in chapter 5, now extended to flexible bodies and retaining the Kalman Filter apparatus. Superquadrics are used as the model primitives and these are sufficient to represent, for instance, a finger and track its motions in a stereoscopic image pair.

So far, only the tracking of single targets has been dealt with and, where articulated bodies are involved, this is already hard enough. Chapter 6 addresses the problem of tracking multiple bodies — how can the tracker disentangle the crossed paths of two moving bodies? The difficulty is to maintain the continuity of each path in the presence of uncertainty. Effective solutions to this problem are demonstrated in the case of point objects (as opposed to the spatially distributed objects of previous chapters) observed in a multiple camera surveillance system. Finally, chapter 7 addresses model-based tracking using probabilistic prior knowledge about surface colour. Road and non-road surfaces are classified by a maximum likelihood estimator and the results have been used to guide a mobile vehicle, even in the presence of shadows and clutter on the road surface.

1 Tracking with Kalman Snakes

Demetri Terzopoulos and Richard Szeliski

Snakes (a.k.a. active contour models) are deformable contours that have been used in many image analysis applications, including the image-based tracking of rigid and nonrigid objects. Deformable contours and their multidimensional generalizations conform to object shapes and motions by numerically integrating differential equations of Lagrangian elastodynamics. The snake equations of motion provide flexible tracking mechanisms that are driven by simulated forces derived from time-varying images.

This chapter first reviews the physically motivated formulation of snake models. It then proposes a probabilistic interpretation of the approach that leads to optimal estimation as a means of extracting reliable information from noisy observations. For the purposes of real-time tracking, it is essential that the estimation proceed sequentially as new observations become available. This is the premise of Kalman filtering theory. We show how to construct continuous Kalman filters that incorporate the dynamic snake into their system and prior models. These *Kalman snakes* are a promising technique for image-based tracking of rigid and, especially, nonrigid objects; they forge a link between the physical and probabilistic modeling approaches to active vision.

Snakes were introduced in (Kass *et al.*, 1987b; Terzopoulos, 1987). The idea of edge and curve detection by optimizing models of curve contrast and smoothness can be traced back to (Montanari, 1971) and (Martelli, 1972). The snake model generalizes this notion through the use of elastodynamic models and applied forces. This chapter builds upon the dynamical systems point of view and its connections to estimation theory. For simplicity we consider the original snake model formulated using controlled-continuity variational splines. There exist several noteworthy variants, however, including snakes based on the Fourier (Scott, 1987; Staib & Duncan, 1989), B-spline (Menet *et al.*, 1990; Leitner *et al.*, 1990; Curwen *et al.*, 1991) (also see Chapter 4), finite element (Cohen & Cohen, 1990; Cohen, 1991), and discrete representations (Terzopoulos & Waters, 1990; Carlbom *et al.*, 1991).[1] Snakes and their variants have been applied to static images requiring edge, curve, and boundary detection, as well as region segmentation and skeletonization (Kass *et al.*, 1987b; Zucker *et al.*, 1988; Ferrie *et al.*, 1989; Fua & Leclerc, 1990; David & Zucker, 1990; Amini *et al.*, 1990; Pavlidis & Liow, 1990). Since snakes conform readily to complex biological structures, many applications have been in the area of biomedical image interpretation (Ayache *et al.*, 1989; Leymaire & Levine, 1989; Cohen & Cohen, 1990; Leitner *et al.*, 1990; Berger, 1990; Cohen, 1991; Carlbom *et al.*, 1991).[2] The idea of tracking objects in time-varying images using snakes was orig-

---

[1] Chapter 3 considers parameterized models akin to snakes, known as deformable templates (Lipson *et al.*, 1990).

[2] Deformable contours are also applicable to problems unrelated to vision (Durbin & Willshaw, 1987; Durbin *et al.*, 1989).

inally proposed in (Kass *et al.*, 1987b), where it was applied to track a speaker's lips through dynamic forces generated from the images. A more thorough tracking of articulate facial features using multiple snakes is described in (Terzopoulos & Waters, 1990). In (Leymaire, 1990), closed snakes are applied to track amorphously deforming living cells that locomote using pseudopods. In (Cipolla & Blake, 1990; Curwen *et al.*, 1991), real-time snakes are used to track the occluding contours of 3D objects as seen from a camera attached to a moving robot arm. These applications have demonstrated that snakes are very well suited to tracking rigid and nonrigid objects. As it tracks an object of interest, a snake can provide detailed quantitative information about its position, velocity, acceleration, and its evolving shape in the image plane.

Another popular approach to tracking, particularly in the context of active vision, is based on Kalman filtering theory (Gelb, 1974) (see also chapters 4, 5, 6, 16, 18, 17). The Kalman filtering approach was first applied to the incremental estimation of rigid object motion (Hallam, 1983; Broida & Chellappa, 1986; Schick & Dickmanns, 1991) and to the tracking of sparse rigid features such as points and lines (Faugeras *et al.*, 1986; Matthies & Shafer, 1987). More recently, the approach has been extended to more complex representations, such as the depth maps obtained when a camera moves through a static scene (Matthies *et al.*, 1989).

Dynamic deformable models, such as snakes, can serve as system models for Kalman filter trackers (Szeliski & Terzopoulos, 1991; Metaxas & Terzopoulos, 1991a; Metaxas & Terzopoulos, 1991b). The resulting shape and motion estimators are able to deal very effectively with the complex motions of nonrigid objects, because deformable models are governed by the principles of nonrigid dynamics. This chapter formulates image-plane Kalman filter trackers using snakes, while Chapter 6 considers the more general case of three dimensional tracking using 3D deformable models that are related to snakes.

1.1   Snakes: Dynamics and Tracking

Snakes are planar deformable contours that move under the influence of image forces. We can define a deformable contour by constructing a suitable deformation energy $\mathcal{E}_s(\mathbf{v})$, where $\mathbf{v}$ represents the contour as a mapping from the unit parametric domain $s \in [0,1]$ into the image plane $\Re^2$.[3] The components of the mapping $\mathbf{v}(s) = (x(s), y(s))$ are the contour's coordinate functions. It is convenient to think of the external forces on the contour as deriving from a potential $\mathcal{P}$. A snake is a deformable contour that minimizes the energy

---

[3]For the purposes of this paper, we can think of an image intensity function as being defined over all of $\Re^2$, albeit with a value of zero outside some finite bounded region.

$$\mathcal{E}(\mathbf{v}) = \mathcal{E}_s(\mathbf{v}) + \mathcal{P}(\mathbf{v}). \tag{1.1}$$

For a simple (linear) snake, the internal deformation energy is

$$\mathcal{E}_s = \int_0^1 w_1(s)|\mathbf{v}_s|^2 + w_2(s)|\mathbf{v}_{ss}|^2 \, ds, \tag{1.2}$$

where the subscripts on $\mathbf{v}$ denote differentiation with respect to s. The energy models the deformation of a stretchy, flexible contour $\mathbf{v}(s)$ and includes two physical parameter functions: $w_1(s)$ controls the "tension" and $w_2(s)$ controls the "rigidity" of the contour. These functions are useful for manipulating the physical behavior and local continuity of the model. In particular, setting $w_1(s_0) = w_2(s_0) = 0$ permits a position discontinuity and setting $w_2(s_0) = 0$ permits a tangent discontinuity to occur at s_0.

To apply snakes to images $I(x, y)$, we specify external potentials $\mathcal{P}$ which attract the snake to intensity extrema, edges, or other perhaps more complex features of interest, depending on the application. We define

$$\mathcal{P}(\mathbf{v}) = \int_0^1 P(\mathbf{v}(s)) \, ds \tag{1.3}$$

where $P(x, y)$ is a scalar potential function defined over the image plane and which is typically computed through image processing.[4] It is natural to interpret the local minima of P as snake "attractors." The snake will have an affinity for darkness or brightness if $P(x, y) = \pm c[G_\sigma * I(x, y)]$, depending on the sign, and for intensity edges if $P(x, y) = -c|\nabla[G_\sigma * I(x, y)]|$, where c controls the magnitude of the potential. $G_\sigma * I$ denotes the image convolved with a (Gaussian) smoothing filter whose characteristic width σ controls the spatial extent of the attractive "depression" of P. Kass et al. (Kass et al., 1987b) discuss some of the motivations and issues surrounding the smoothing operation.

Figure 1.1 shows a snake, the closed white contour, which has been attracted by the dark membrane of a cell in an EM photomicrograph (see (Carlbom et al., 1991) for details). In the figure, $P = c[G_\sigma * I]$ where I is the EM image and σ is about 1 pixel.

1.1.1 Lagrangian Dynamics

It is natural to view energy minimization as a static problem. More generally, however, one can construct a dynamical system and allow it to arrive at a minimal energy state as it achieves equilibrium. Suitable dynamic models with intuitively appealing physical behaviors may be derived by applying the principles of Lagrangian mechanics. This approach leads to dynamic

---

[4]It makes sense to compute $P(x, y)$ at all image points only if dedicated hardware is available that can do so in real time. According to (1.3), however, P need only be computed along the deformable contour $\mathbf{v}(s)$, which presents an opportunity for improving efficiency when such hardware is unavailable (see Chapter 4).

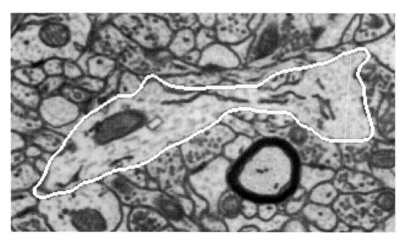

Figure 1.1
Snake attracted to cell membrane in an EM photomicrograph.

snakes which offer a variety of interesting possible behaviours that are not necessarily evident from the static energy minimization point of view. For example, a dynamic model may be guided by an adaptive control system or interactively by the user as it minimizes its energy. To visualize a dynamic snake in an image potential, think of P as slippery terrain and the deformable contour as having a tendency to slide downhill into the depressions in the terrain, conforming to their shapes as it does so. In Figure 1.1, for example, the snake has slid into the ravine associated with the dark membrane that surrounds the large cell. The snake minimizes the total energy $\mathcal{E}$ when it attains the equilibrium state shown in the figure.

The Lagrangian formulation of snakes was first presented in (Terzopoulos, 1987). We can represent a dynamic snake by introducing a time-varying mapping $\mathbf{v}(s,t)$ and a kinetic energy $\int_0^1 \mu |\mathbf{v}_t|^2 \, ds$, where $\mu(s)$ is the mass density, and the subscript t denotes a time derivative. We combine the kinetic energy and the deformation potential energy functional $\mathcal{E}(\mathbf{v})$ to define the Lagrangian

$$\mathcal{L}(\mathbf{v}) = \frac{1}{2} \int_0^1 \mu |\mathbf{v}_t|^2 \, ds - \frac{1}{2}\mathcal{E}(\mathbf{v}). \qquad (1.4)$$

If the initial and final configurations are $\mathbf{v}(s,t_0)$ and $\mathbf{v}(s,t_1)$, then Hamilton's principle dictates that the deformable model's motion $\mathbf{v}(s,t)$ from $t = t_0$ to $t = t_1$ is such that the action integral $\int_{t_0}^{t_1} \mathcal{L}(\mathbf{v}) \, dt$ is stationary, which implies that its variation with respect to $\mathbf{v}$ vanishes:

$$\delta_{\mathbf{v}} \left(\frac{1}{2} \int_{t_0}^{t_1} \int_0^1 \mu |\mathbf{v}_t|^2 - w_1(s)|\mathbf{v}_s|^2 - w_2(s)|\mathbf{v}_{ss}|^2 - P(\mathbf{v}) \, ds \, dt \right) = \mathbf{0}. \qquad (1.5)$$

The condition leads to Lagrange's equations of motion for the model (Courant & Hilbert, 1953). Once set in motion, a snake with a mass distribution will move perpetually, unless kinetic energy is dissipated. To dampen the snake so that it can achieve static equilibrium, we incorporate the Rayleigh dissipation functional $\mathcal{D}(\mathbf{v}_t) = \frac{1}{2} \int_0^1 \gamma |\mathbf{v}_t|^2 \, ds$ where $\gamma(s)$ is the damping density. Evaluating the appropriate variational derivatives of the integrands L in (1.5) and D in the dissipation functional, the Lagrange equations are

$$\frac{d}{dt}\left(\frac{\partial L}{\partial \mathbf{v}_t}\right) + \frac{\partial D}{\partial \mathbf{v}_t} - \frac{\partial L}{\partial \mathbf{v}} + \frac{\partial}{\partial s}\left(\frac{\partial L}{\partial \mathbf{v}_s}\right) - \frac{\partial}{\partial s^2}\left(\frac{\partial L}{\partial \mathbf{v}_{ss}}\right) = \mathbf{0}. \tag{1.6}$$

Assuming constant mass density $\mu(s) = \mu$ and constant dissipation $\gamma(s) = \gamma$, the equations of motion for the snake may be written as

$$\mu \mathbf{v}_{tt} + \gamma \mathbf{v}_t - \frac{\partial}{\partial s}(w_1 \mathbf{v}_s) + \frac{\partial^2}{\partial s^2}(w_2 \mathbf{v}_{ss}) = -\nabla P(\mathbf{v}(s,t)) \tag{1.7}$$

with appropriate initial and boundary conditions. This can be interpreted as a force balance relationship. On the left hand side are inertial, damping, stretching, and bending forces. These forces balance the negative gradient of the potential on the right hand side, which may be interpreted physically as generalized external forces coupling the snake to the image data.

1.1.2 Force-Based Tracking

The equation of motion (1.7) suggests a straightforward force-based mechanism for tracking dynamic data where the model maintains dynamic equilibrium in a time-varying potential (Kass *et al.*, 1987b).

If the image varies as a function of time, the potential $P(x, y, t)$ will also be time-varying. If the potential $P(x, y, t)$ changes after a snake has achieved static equilibrium, potential energy is converted to kinetic energy and the snake will move nonrigidly to achieve a new equilibrium. Thinking in terms of the force balance relationship in (1.7), the model will track the dynamic data as it attempts to maintain the generalized forces $-\nabla P$ in dynamic equilibrium against the inertial, damping, and deformation forces.

One way to visualize the tracking scheme on a discrete, frame-by-frame basis is to imagine once again the potential energy surface $P(x, y, t_k)$ for a given image frame k as a slippery terrain. Suppose that a deformable contour is at rest at the bottom of an extended depression in the terrain. The next frame $k + 1$ will induce a potential $P(x, y, t_{k+1})$ which is a perturbation of $P(x, y, t_k)$ such that the depression will have shifted. If the shift is not too great, the snake will now find itself somewhere up on a slope and will slide downhill into the shifted depression, moving (and deforming) appropriately as it does so. In this way, they are convected over the image by the moving depressions of the potential surface.

Figure 1.2 illustrates the force based tracking procedure. At the top are three frames from an image sequence of a surprise expression. In the middle

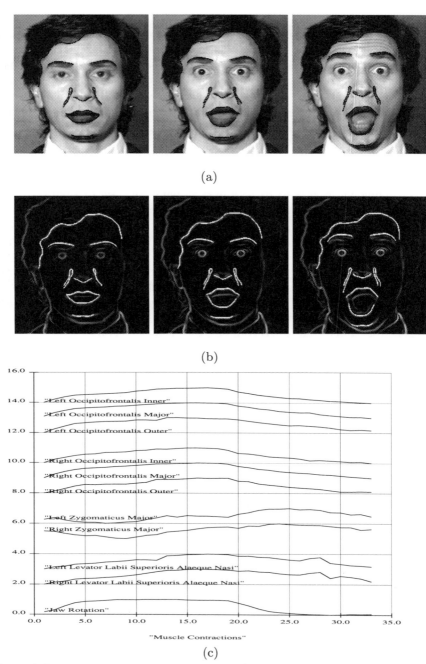

(a)

(b)

(c)

Figure 1.2
Tracking facial features using snakes. (a) Three frames from an image sequence with
snakes (black contours) tracking hairline, eyebrows, nose, mouth, and chin. (b) Snakes
(white contours) on negative potential function. (c) Estimated facial muscle contractions
plotted as time series.

are the negative potential functions $-P = c|\nabla[G_\sigma * I]|$. The snakes track the nonrigidly moving image features, making it possible to glean useful information about the face. For example, it is possible to derive dynamic estimates of facial muscle contractions shown in the plotted traces (see (Terzopoulos & Waters, 1990) for details).

In Section 1.3, we will identify force driven tracking as a special case of a general framework for sequential estimation of dynamic data. The framework is capable of dealing with uncertainties in image data and modeling them in an optimal way.

1.1.3   Discretization and Numerical Simulation

In order to numerically compute a minimal energy solution, it is necessary to discretize the energy $\mathcal{E}(\mathbf{v})$. A general approach to discretizing energies $\mathcal{E}(\mathbf{v})$ is to represent the function of interest $\mathbf{v}$ in approximate form as a linear superposition of basis functions weighted by *nodal variables* $\mathbf{u}_i$. The nodal variables may be collected into a vector $\mathbf{u}$ to be computed. The local-support polynomial basis functions prescribed by the finite element method are convenient for most applications. An alternative to the finite element method is to apply the finite difference method to the continuous Euler equations, such as (1.7), associated with the model.

The discrete form of quadratic energies such as (1.1) may be written as

$$E(\mathbf{u}) = \tfrac{1}{2}\mathbf{u}^\top \mathbf{K}\mathbf{u} + \mathrm{P}(\mathbf{u}), \tag{1.8}$$

where $\mathbf{K}$ is called the *stiffness matrix*, and $\mathrm{P}(\mathbf{u})$ is the discrete version of the external potential. The minimum energy (equilibrium) solution can be found by setting the gradient of (1.8) to $\mathbf{0}$, which is equivalent to solving the set of algebraic equations

$$\mathbf{K}\mathbf{u} = -\nabla\mathrm{P} = \mathbf{f} \tag{1.9}$$

where $\mathbf{f}$ is the generalized external force vector.

Finite elements and finite differences generate local discretizations of the continuous snake model, hence the stiffness matrix will have a sparse and banded structure. To illustrate the discretization process, suppose we apply the finite difference method to discretize the energy (1.2) on a set of nodes $\mathbf{u}_i = \mathbf{v}(ih)$ for $i = 0, \ldots, N-1$ where $h = 1/(N-1)$. Suppose we use the finite differences $\mathbf{v}_s \approx (\mathbf{u}_{i+1} - \mathbf{u}_i)/h$ and $\mathbf{v}_{ss} \approx (\mathbf{u}_{i+1} - 2\mathbf{u}_i + \mathbf{u}_{i-1})/h^2$. For cyclic boundary conditions (i.e., a closed contour), we obtain the following symmetric pentadiagonal matrix (unspecified entries are 0):

$$\mathbf{K} = \begin{bmatrix} a_0 & b_0 & c_0 & & & & c_{N-2} & b_{N-1} \\ b_0 & a_1 & b_1 & c_1 & & & & c_{N-1} \\ c_0 & b_1 & a_2 & b_2 & c_2 & & & \\ & c_1 & b_2 & a_3 & b_3 & c_3 & & \\ & & \ddots & \ddots & \ddots & \ddots & \ddots & \\ & & & c_{N-5} & b_{N-4} & a_{N-3} & b_{N-3} & c_{N-3} \\ c_{N-2} & & & & c_{N-4} & b_{N-3} & a_{N-2} & b_{N-2} \\ b_{N-1} & c_{N-1} & & & & c_{N-3} & b_{N-2} & a_{N-1} \end{bmatrix}, \qquad (1.10)$$

where

$$a_i = (w_{1i-1} + w_{1i})/h^2 + (w_{2i-1} + 4w_{2i} + w_{2i+1})/h^4, \qquad (1.11)$$

$$b_i = -w_{1i}/h^2 - 2(w_{2i} + w_{2i+1})/h^4, \qquad (1.12)$$

$$c_i = w_{2i+1}/h^4, \qquad (1.13)$$

assuming that $w_{1i} = w_1(ih)$ and $w_{2i} = w_2(ih)$ are sampled at the same nodes. All indices in these expressions are interpreted modulo N.

The discretized version of the Lagrangian dynamics equation (1.7) may be written as a set of second order ordinary differential equations for $\mathbf{u}(t)$:

$$\mathbf{M\ddot{u}} + \mathbf{C\dot{u}} + \mathbf{Ku} = \mathbf{f}, \qquad (1.14)$$

where $\mathbf{M}$ is the mass matrix, $\mathbf{C}$ is a damping matrix; both matrices are typically also sparse and banded. In the simple case of a finite difference discretization where we assume that mass is lumped at the nodes, $\mathbf{M}$ and $\mathbf{C}$ will be diagonal matrices. Note that for static $\mathbf{f}$, the dynamic equilibrium condition $\mathbf{\ddot{u}} = \mathbf{\dot{u}} = \mathbf{0}$ leads to the static solution (1.9), as expected.

To simulate the snake dynamics, this system of ordinary differential equations must be integrated forward through time. The finite element literature offers several suitable explicit and implicit direct integration methods, including the central difference, Houbolt, Newmark, or Wilson methods (Bathe & Wilson, 1976). We can illustrate the basic idea with a semi-implicit Euler method that takes time steps Δt. We replace the time derivatives of $\mathbf{u}$ with the backward finite differences $\mathbf{\ddot{u}} \approx (\mathbf{u}^{(t+\Delta t)} - 2\mathbf{u}^{(t)} + \mathbf{u}^{(t-\Delta t)})/(\Delta t)^2$, and $\mathbf{\dot{u}} \approx (\mathbf{u}^{(t+\Delta t)} - \mathbf{u}^{(t-\Delta t)})/2\Delta t$, where the superscripts denote the quantity evaluated at the time given in parentheses. This yields the update formula

$$\mathbf{Au}^{(t+\Delta t)} = \mathbf{b}^{(t)}, \qquad (1.15)$$

where $\mathbf{A} = \mathbf{M}/(\Delta t)^2 + \mathbf{C}/2\Delta t + \mathbf{K}$ is a pentadiagonal matrix and $\mathbf{b} = (2\mathbf{M}/(\Delta t)^2)\mathbf{u}^{(t)} - (\mathbf{M}/(\Delta t)^2 - \mathbf{C}/2\Delta t)\mathbf{u}^{(t-1)} + \mathbf{f}^{(t)}$.

The pentadiagonal system can be solved very efficiently ($O(N)$ complexity) by factorizing $\mathbf{A}$ into lower and upper triangular matrices, then solving the two resulting sparse triangular systems. We compute the unique normalized factorization $\mathbf{A} = \mathbf{LDU}$ where $\mathbf{L}$ is a lower triangular matrix, $\mathbf{D}$ is a diagonal matrix, and $\mathbf{U} = \mathbf{L}^{\top}$ is an upper triangular matrix (Bathe &

Wilson, 1976). The solution $\mathbf{u}^{(t+\Delta t)}$ to (1.15) is obtained by first solving $\mathbf{Ls} = \mathbf{b}^{(t)}$ by forward substitution, then $\mathbf{Uu} = \mathbf{D}^{-1}\mathbf{s}$ by backward substitution. For the linear snakes described above, only a single factorization is necessary, since $\mathbf{A}$ is constant. Note that the LDU factorization and forward/backward substitutions are inherently sequential, recursive operations.

Researchers have investigated alternative approaches to numerically simulating snake models, including dynamic programming (Amini *et al.*, 1990) and greedy (Williams & Shah, 1992) algorithms.

1.2   Snakes and Bayesian Estimation

The dynamic response of snakes to forces computed from images addresses the problem of inferring the image-based shapes and motions of rigid or nonrigid objects. An alternative to this physical point of view is to cast the inference task in a probabilistic framework and to view it as an estimation problem. Snake models may then be interpreted in terms of Bayesian estimation, where the posterior distribution $p(\mathbf{u} \mid \mathbf{d})$ of the unknown quantity $\mathbf{u}$ conditioned on the data $\mathbf{d}$ is computed using Bayes' rule

$$p(\mathbf{u} \mid \mathbf{d}) = \frac{p(\mathbf{d} \mid \mathbf{u})\, p(\mathbf{u})}{p(\mathbf{d})} \tag{1.16}$$

with the normalizing denominator

$$p(\mathbf{d}) = \sum_{\mathbf{u}} p(\mathbf{d} \mid \mathbf{u}).$$

The *prior model* $p(\mathbf{u})$ is a probabilistic description of the state we are trying to estimate before any sensor data is collected. The *sensor model* $p(\mathbf{d} \mid \mathbf{u})$ is a description of the noisy or stochastic processes that relate the original (unknown) state $\mathbf{u}$ to the sampled input image or sensor values $\mathbf{d}$. Bayes' rule combines these two probabilistic models to form a *posterior model* $p(\mathbf{u} \mid \mathbf{d})$ which describes probabilistically the best estimate of $\mathbf{u}$ given the data $\mathbf{d}$ (Meyer, 1970).

The snake serves as a prior model of the shapes and nonrigid motions of features of interest in the image. Intuitively, it should yield prior distributions that bias Bayesian estimates towards low energy configurations as measured by the deformation energy $\mathcal{E}_s$ in (1.2). The trick is to convert an energy which elastically restores the deformable model to its natural shape into a prior distribution over expected shapes, with lower energy shapes being the more likely. This is done conveniently using a Gibbs (or Boltzmann) distribution of the form

$$p(\mathbf{u}) = \frac{1}{Z_{\mathrm{p}}} \exp\left[-E_{\mathrm{p}}(\mathbf{u})\right], \tag{1.17}$$

where $E_p(\mathbf{u})$ is a discrete version of $\mathcal{E}_s$, and Z_p is a normalizing constant (called the partition function). When $E_p(\mathbf{u})$ stems from a finite element or finite difference discretization, it can be written as a sum of local energy terms, and the distribution (1.17) reduces to a Markov random field. Since, according to (1.8), $E_p(\mathbf{u})$ is a quadratic energy of the form

$$E_p(\mathbf{u}) = \tfrac{1}{2}\mathbf{u}^\top \mathbf{K} \mathbf{u}, \tag{1.18}$$

the prior distribution is a correlated zero-mean Gaussian with a covariance matrix $\mathbf{P} = \mathbf{K}^{-1}$. Although, $\mathbf{K}$ is sparse and banded, $\mathbf{P}$ will not be.

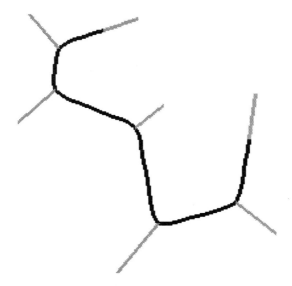

Figure 1.3
Snake (black) constrained with spring (grey) forces.

The external potential applied to the snake is equivalent to a sensor model. We can see this by examining a linear sensor model involving Gaussian uncertainty. For simplicity, consider the physical situation depicted in Figure 1.3, where a snake is constrained by a set of zero-length "springs" with stiffnesses c_i. The springs couple the snake to "nails" $\mathbf{d}_i$ in the plane which represent data points with independent additive Gaussian noise. If spring i is attached to the snake at s_i, it is stretched by an amount $|\mathbf{v}(s_i) - \mathbf{d}_i|$. Hence the continuous potential energy functional of all the stretched springs is

$$\mathcal{P}(\mathbf{v}) = \sum_i c_i [\mathbf{v}(s_i) - \mathbf{d}_i]^2. \tag{1.19}$$

The discrete version of this potential may be written as the quadratic form

$$P(\mathbf{u}) = E_d(\mathbf{u}, \mathbf{d}) = \tfrac{1}{2}(\mathbf{Hu} - \mathbf{d})^\top \mathbf{R}^{-1}(\mathbf{Hu} - \mathbf{d}). \tag{1.20}$$

The associated spring forces (cf. (1.9)) are expressed by the linear form

$$-\nabla P = \mathbf{f} = \mathbf{H}^\top \mathbf{R}^{-1}(\mathbf{d} - \mathbf{Hu}). \tag{1.21}$$

Here, $\mathbf{H}$, known as the interpolation or measurement matrix, maps nodal variables to the nails which are interpreted as measurement data $\mathbf{d}$.[5] [6] The entries of $\mathbf{R}^{-1}$ are spring stiffnesses c_i. Using the Gibbs distribution once again, we arrive at the sensor model

$$p(\mathbf{d} \mid \mathbf{u}) = \frac{1}{Z_d} \exp\left[-E_d(\mathbf{u}, \mathbf{d})\right], \tag{1.22}$$

This implies that the sensor distribution is a correlated Gaussian with covariance matrix $\mathbf{R}^{-1}$. Hence, if each dataipoint has independent noise with standard deviation σ_i^2, the optimal spring stiffnesses for estimation are $c_i = 1/\sigma_i^2$.

Combining the prior (1.17) and the sensor (1.22) models using Bayes' rule, we obtain the posterior distribution

$$p(\mathbf{u} \mid \mathbf{d}) = \frac{p(\mathbf{d} \mid \mathbf{u})\, p(\mathbf{u})}{p(\mathbf{d})} = \frac{1}{Z} \exp\left[-E(\mathbf{u})\right], \tag{1.23}$$

where

$$E(\mathbf{u}) = E_p(\mathbf{u}) + E_d(\mathbf{u}, \mathbf{d}). \tag{1.24}$$

Note that this is the same energy equation as (1.8), which describes the energy of a discrete snake. Thus, computing the *maximum a posteriori* (MAP) estimate (Geman & Geman, 1984), i.e., the value of $\mathbf{u}$ that maximizes the conditional probability $p(\mathbf{u} \mid \mathbf{d})$, provides the same result as finding the minimum energy configuration of the snake.

Although in this case both the physical and the Bayesian models may be used to produce the same solution, there are several advantages to the probabilistic approach (Szeliski, 1989). Most importantly, the external force fields (data constraints) can be derived in a principled fashion taking into account the known noise characteristics of the sensors and the uncertainty in the posterior model can be quantified and used by higher level stages of processing.

---

[5] In general, (e.g., for nonlinear snake models) the measurements $\mathbf{d}$ may be related to the state variables $\mathbf{u}$ through a non-linear function $\mathbf{d} = \mathbf{h}(\mathbf{u})$. The *extended Kalman filter* formulation is applicable in this case, although the resulting estimator may be sub-optimal (Gelb, 1974). The extended Kalman filter formulation is necessary for the 3D physical models described in Chapter 6.

[6] Note that if the dimensionality of $\mathbf{d}$ is smaller than that of $\mathbf{u}$, the snake will approximate the data using the deformation energy as a smoothness constraint to constrain the extra degrees of freedom. On the other hand, if the dimensionality of $\mathbf{d}$ is greater than that of $\mathbf{u}$, the snake will provide a least squares fit to the data. Both cases are handled by the same measurement equation.

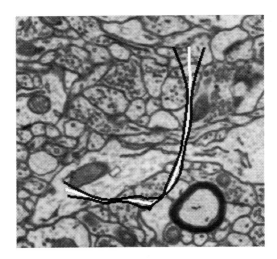

Figure 1.4
Confidence envelope of snake estimate. The snake is shown in white, and the confidence
envelope in black.

As an example of quantifying the uncertainty of a snake, we can compute it
in equilibrium by generating random samples from the posterior distribution
and accumulating the desired statistics. In general, generating good random
samples can be tricky (Szeliski, 1989). However, for a snake with spring
constraints, the posterior energy is quadratic

$$E(\mathbf{u}) = \tfrac{1}{2}(\mathbf{u} - \mathbf{u}^*)^\top \mathbf{A}(\mathbf{u} - \mathbf{u}^*) + k, \qquad (1.25)$$

where $\mathbf{u}^* = \mathbf{A}^{-1}\mathbf{b}$ is the minimum energy solution. The Gibbs distribution
(1.23) corresponding to this quadratic form is a multivariate Gaussian with
mean $\mathbf{u}^*$ and covariance $\mathbf{A}^{-1}$. It is straightforward to generate an unbiased
random sample because the discrete snake energy factorizes into LDU form.
Substituting $\mathbf{u} = \mathbf{L}^\top \mathbf{v}$ into (1.25), we obtain

$$E(\mathbf{v}) = \tfrac{1}{2}(\mathbf{v} - \mathbf{v}^*)^\top \mathbf{D}(\mathbf{v} - \mathbf{v}^*) + k, \qquad (1.26)$$

where $\mathbf{v}^* = \mathbf{D}^{-1}\mathbf{L}^{-1}\mathbf{b}$ is the intermediate solution in the LDU solution of
the banded snake system $\mathbf{L}\mathbf{D}\mathbf{L}^\top \mathbf{u} = \mathbf{b}$. Thus, to generate a random sample,
we simply add white Gaussian noise with variance $\mathbf{D}^{-1}$ to $\mathbf{v}^*$ and continue
with the solution for $\mathbf{u}$. The resulting collection of random snakes are used to
compute the local variance at each point on the snake, and hence a confidence
envelope (Figure 1.4).

1.3   Sequential Estimation and Kalman Snakes

The probabilistic interpretation of snakes allows us to generalize and amelio-
rate the force-based tracking scheme. It enables us to design, in a principled

way, sequential estimation algorithms which integrate visual measurements over time to improve the accuracy of estimates. Such sequential estimation algorithms become even more potent when they are combined with the equations of motion of a physical model. The resulting estimation algorithm is known as the continuous Kalman filter (Gelb, 1974).

1.3.1 The Kalman Filter

The Kalman filter is formulated by adding a *system model* to the prior and sensor models of the Bayesian formulation. The system model describes the expected evolution of the vector of state variables $\mathbf{u}(t)$ over time.[7] The continuous Kalman filter assumes the system model

$$\frac{d}{dt}\mathbf{u} = \mathbf{Fu} + \mathbf{q}, \qquad \mathbf{q} \sim N(\mathbf{0}, \mathbf{Q}), \tag{1.27}$$

where $\mathbf{F}$ is the system matrix and $\mathbf{q}$ is a white Gaussian noise process with covariance $\mathbf{Q}$. The system noise is used to model unknown disturbances or uncertainty about the true system dynamics.

The sensor model component $p(\mathbf{d} \mid \mathbf{u})$ of the Bayesian formulation is rewritten as

$$\mathbf{d} = \mathbf{Hu} + \mathbf{r}, \qquad \mathbf{r} \sim N(\mathbf{0}, \mathbf{R}), \tag{1.28}$$

where each measurement is assumed to be corrupted by a Gaussian noise vector $\mathbf{r}$ whose covariance $\mathbf{R}$ is known.

The Kalman filter operates by continuously updating an estimated state vector $\hat{\mathbf{u}}$ and an error covariance matrix $\mathbf{P}$. The state estimate equation

$$\dot{\hat{\mathbf{u}}} = \mathbf{F}\hat{\mathbf{u}} + \mathbf{S}^{-1}\mathbf{H}^{\top}\mathbf{R}^{-1}(\mathbf{d} - \mathbf{H}\hat{\mathbf{u}}) \tag{1.29}$$

consists of two terms. The first term predicts the estimate using the system model, while the second term updates the estimate using the residual error $(\mathbf{d} - \mathbf{Hu})$ weighted by the *Kalman filter gain matrix* $\mathbf{G} = \mathbf{S}^{-1}\mathbf{H}^{\top}\mathbf{R}^{-1}$, where $\mathbf{S} = \mathbf{P}^{-1}$ is the inverse covariance (or *information matrix*) of the current estimate. The size of the Kalman gain depends on the relative sizes of the $\mathbf{S}$ and the noise measurement covariance $\mathbf{R}$. As long as the measurements are relatively accurate compared to the state estimate, the Kalman gain is high and new data measurements are weighted heavily. Once the system has stabilized, the state estimate covariance becomes smaller than the measurement noise, and the Kalman filter gain is reduced.

The information matrix $\mathbf{S}$ is updated over time using the *matrix Riccati equation* expressed in terms of inverse covariance

$$\dot{\mathbf{S}} = -\mathbf{SF} - \mathbf{F}^{\top}\mathbf{S} - \mathbf{SQS} + \mathbf{H}^{\top}\mathbf{R}^{-1}\mathbf{H}. \tag{1.30}$$

---

[7]In the remainder of this paper, we will assume that all quantities are continuous functions of time, and we will omit (t).

This equation is derived from the standard matrix Riccati equation (Gelb, 1974, p. 122) using simple matrix algebra.[8] Here again, we see the competing influences of the system and measurement noise processes. As long as the measurement noise $\mathbf{R}$ is small or the Kalman filter gain $\mathbf{G}$ is high, the information (or certainty) $\mathbf{S}$ will continue to increase. As the system begins to reach steady state, the relative influence of the system noise $\mathbf{Q}$, which decreases the certainty, and the measurement inverse covariance $\mathbf{R}^{-1}$, which increases it, counterbalance each other. Of course the absence of new measurements or sudden bursts of new or accurate information can cause fluctuations in this certainty. The inverse covariance formulation of the matrix Riccati equation $\mathbf{S}$ has been more appropriate here than the commonly used covariance formulation involving $\mathbf{P}$. This has to do with the nature of the prior distributions that arise from the snake model's elastic energy. As we showed in Section 1.2, the prior distribution is a multivariate Gaussian with a covariance matrix $\mathbf{P}(0) = \mathbf{K}^{-1}$, the inverse stiffness matrix. While $\mathbf{K}$ is sparse and banded, $\mathbf{P}(0)$ (and hence $\mathbf{P}(t)$) will not. For snake models with many nodal variables, it is impractical to store and update the dense covariance matrix.

1.3.2   The Kalman Snake

We create Kalman snakes by employing the snake equations of motion (1.14) as the system model of a continuous Kalman filter. To this end, we write these equations in the standard dynamical system form

$$\frac{d\mathbf{u}}{dt} = \mathbf{F}\mathbf{u} + \mathbf{g} \tag{1.33}$$

which corresponds to the system model (1.27) of the Kalman filter. For a massless snake (i.e., for $\mathbf{M} = \mathbf{0}$), (1.14) reduces to the first-order system

$$\frac{d}{dt}\mathbf{u} = -\mathbf{C}^{-1}\mathbf{K}\mathbf{u} + \mathbf{C}^{-1}\mathbf{f} \tag{1.34}$$

which is in standard form. To express the second-order system (1.14) similarly, we include the nodal velocities $d\mathbf{u}/dt = \dot{\mathbf{u}}$ as explicit state variables along with the positions $\mathbf{u}$ to obtain the set of coupled first order equations

---

[8]To convert the standard Riccati equation

$$\begin{aligned}
\dot{\mathbf{P}} &= \mathbf{F}\mathbf{P} + \mathbf{P}\mathbf{F}^\top + \mathbf{Q} - \mathbf{G}\mathbf{R}\mathbf{G}^\top \\
&= \mathbf{F}\mathbf{P} + \mathbf{P}\mathbf{F}^\top + \mathbf{Q} - \mathbf{P}\mathbf{H}^\top\mathbf{R}^{-1}\mathbf{H}\mathbf{P}
\end{aligned} \tag{1.31}$$

into the inverse covariance form, we use the lemma

$$\dot{\mathbf{S}} = -\mathbf{S}\dot{\mathbf{P}}\mathbf{S} \tag{1.32}$$

which can easily be derived from the identity $\mathbf{S}\mathbf{P} = \mathbf{I}$,

$$\frac{d}{dt}(\mathbf{S}\mathbf{P}) = \dot{\mathbf{S}}\mathbf{P} + \mathbf{S}\dot{\mathbf{P}} = \mathbf{0}.$$

Substituting (1.31) into (1.32), we obtain the desired result (1.30).

$$\frac{d}{dt}\begin{bmatrix} \dot{\mathbf{u}} \\ \mathbf{u} \end{bmatrix} = \begin{bmatrix} -\mathbf{M}^{-1}\mathbf{C} & -\mathbf{M}^{-1}\mathbf{K} \\ \mathbf{I} & \mathbf{0} \end{bmatrix}\begin{bmatrix} \dot{\mathbf{u}} \\ \mathbf{u} \end{bmatrix} + \begin{bmatrix} \mathbf{M}^{-1}\mathbf{f} \\ \mathbf{0} \end{bmatrix}. \tag{1.35}$$

We can then rewrite (1.35) in the standard form (1.33) by simply renaming the augmented state vector $[\dot{\mathbf{u}}^\top \quad \mathbf{u}^\top]^\top$ to $\mathbf{u}$.

We can relate the second term in (1.29) back to the physical snake model, thus arriving at a physical interpretation of the Kalman filter. The residual error $(\mathbf{d} - \mathbf{H}\hat{\mathbf{u}})$ can be interpreted as the deformations of springs coupling selected state variables $\mathbf{H}\mathbf{u}$ to the data $\mathbf{d}$, the matrix $\mathbf{R}^{-1}$ contains the spring stiffnesses (inversely proportional to the variances in the measurement noise), and $\mathbf{H}^\top$ converts the spring forces to generalized forces that can then be applied directly to the state variables of the model. The general idea is very similar to the simple force-based tracking scheme described in Section 1.1.2, but there is one significant difference. Before applying the generalized spring forces to the state variables of the model, the Kalman snake transforms them with the covariance matrix $\mathbf{S}^{-1} = \mathbf{P}$ which has accumulated the history of prior observations, their uncertainties, etc., through the evolving matrix Riccati equation. A simple way of describing the relationship is that force-based tracking amounts to "Kalman filtering" with a constant unit covariance/information matrix.

Both the first-order (1.34) and second-order (1.35) system models may be employed in Kalman snake trackers, but their behaviors will differ. Suppose a Kalman snake is tracking an object that is translating across the image and the object suddenly becomes temporarily occluded. The first-order Kalman snake, although simpler to compute, lacks an inertial term and it will therefore stop moving as soon as data forces vanish because of the occlusion. When the object reappears, it may have moved too far away for the first-order snake to recapture it. The inertial term of the second-order Kalman snake, however, will enable it to continue moving for a distance which will depend on the magnitude of the damping term, and it may stand a better chance of regaining its lock on the object when it reappears.

1.3.3 A Simplified Kalman Snake

We can derive a more convenient approximation to the Kalman snake equations if we assume that the inverse covariance matrix $\mathbf{S}$ can be partitioned into a time-invariant internal stiffness component $\mathbf{K}_s$ and a time-varying diagonal component $\mathbf{S}'$

$$\mathbf{S}(t) = \mathbf{K}_s + \mathbf{S}'(t). \tag{1.36}$$

We can set $\mathbf{K}_s = \mathbf{K}$, the snake stiffness matrix. We then apply the Riccati equation (1.30) directly to $\mathbf{S}'$, and ignore any off-diagonal terms that arise. The state update equation (1.29) becomes

$$\dot{\hat{\mathbf{u}}} = \mathbf{F}\hat{\mathbf{u}} + (\mathbf{K}_s + \mathbf{S}')^{-1}\mathbf{H}^\top\mathbf{R}^{-1}(\mathbf{d} - \mathbf{H}\hat{\mathbf{u}}). \tag{1.37}$$

The state update equation (1.37) changes the current state estimate according to both the dynamics of the system described by $\mathbf{F}$ and according to the filtered difference between the sampled state $\mathbf{Hu}$ and the data values $\mathbf{d}$ (these can be replaced by other external forces). The Kalman gain contains a weighting component $\mathbf{R}^{-1}$ which is inversely proportional to the noise in the new measurements, a weighting term $\mathbf{S}'$ which varies over time and represents the current (local) certainty in the estimate, and a spatial smoothing component corresponding to the internal stiffness matrix $\mathbf{K}_s$. Note that we do not explicitly compute $\mathbf{G}$. Instead, we solve the system of equations $(\mathbf{K}_s + \mathbf{S}')\tilde{\mathbf{u}} = \mathbf{H}^\top \mathbf{R}^{-1}(\mathbf{d} - \mathbf{Hu})$ for $\tilde{\mathbf{u}}$, and use this as the second term in (1.37).

Equation (1.37) employs the snake elasticity, as expressed through the stiffness matrix $\mathbf{K}$, in two places. The first is in the system dynamics $\mathbf{F}$, which result in the model returning to a rest state in the absence of new measurements. The second is through the "prior smoothness" $\mathbf{K}_s$, which filters the new measurements to ensure smoothness and interpolation, without destroying shape estimates that may already be built up.

We now demonstrate these two behaviors of Kalman snakes. Figure 1.5 (a)–(e), which shows several frames from an image sequence of a rotating dodecahedral puzzle in which a closed snake is tracking the left-to-right motion of the dark boundary of one of the pentagonal faces. If the model smoothness and shape structure are totally in the dynamics $\mathbf{F}$, then the snake will return to its natural, relaxed rest configuration when the image data is temporarily removed (such as when the object being tracked becomes occluded). For example, after the image data is removed from the snake in Figure 1.5(e) it relaxes to the equilibrium state in Figure 1.5(f).

If, on the other hand, the smoothness is totally in the prior, then the snake will retain its shape during occlusion, but will find it increasingly difficult to adapt to non-rigid motion because of its adherence to old measurements ("sticky data"). The latter behavior is illustrated in Figure 1.6. Compare the equilibrium shape of the Kalman snake in Figure 1.6(b) to Figure 1.5(f).

The right blend of the aforementioned sources of *a priori* knowledge is application specific and depends on what is known about the real-world physics of the objects being modeled and about the sensor characteristics. For example, a rigid object should have a system model $\mathbf{F}$ which only supports rigid transformations, whereas a nonrigid object should have a deformable system model. The advantage of the Kalman filter which incorporates the Lagrangian dynamics of snakes is that it gives us the flexibility to design tracking behaviors that are not possible with conventional snakes. Moreover, the model parameters, such as how much to weight new measurements versus old shape estimates could, in principle, be derived from statistical models of sensors, rather than being heuristically chosen, and they can vary over time.

(a)   (b)

(c)   (d)

(e)   (f)

Figure 1.5
Snake tracking a rotating object. (a)–(e): frames 0–16 (steps of 4), (f): image data is occluded.

(a)   (b)

Figure 1.6
Kalman snake. (a) snake at equilibrium in last frame of image sequence (b) snake retains
shape after image data is occluded.

1.4   Conclusion

The class of deformable models known as snakes has proven useful in several
image analysis tasks. When applied to static images, the physical behavior
of these models is useful mainly to support user interaction. The dynamical
nature of snakes has a much larger impact, however, when they are applied
to time-varying imagery. The dynamical system approach yields snakes and
other deformable models that can track nonstationary data using forces,
continuously adapting to images of complex rigidly or non-rigidly moving
objects. The probabilistic approach, especially the well-known techniques of
Bayesian estimation and Kalman filtering, has proven successful in dealing
with noisy measurements and integrating information from multiple sources
(sensor fusion) and over time (sequential estimation). This chapter realizes
the full potential of the dynamic and probabilistic approaches, by combining
them to create a new sequential motion estimator, the Kalman snake. The
Kalman snake uses snake dynamics as a system model to constrain and predict possible motions and, under the right conditions, it optimally acquires
new information from uncertain measurements in a sequential fashion and
optimally blends them with previous estimates. Chapter 5 will extend this
approach to more sophisticated deformable models.

2 Deformable Templates

Alan Yuille and Peter Hallinan

2.1 Introduction

A mobile robot that uses an active vision system needs to identify features in the world and track them. In current systems such features may be fairly simple (though not necessarily easy to detect) such as the boundaries of a road. In future systems, however, they could be more complicated. A theory is needed both to detect such features, ideally giving some confidence measure, and then to track them.

Deformable templates offer a promising approach to this problem. This paper will be based on prior work (Yuille *et al.*, 1989) and (Hallinan, 1991) on face recognition that investigated the detection of features such as eyes and mouths from single images. In this chapter we briefly show that these templates can be adapted to perform tracking.

We also describe an alternative formulation of deformable templates in terms of discrete matching units. This is illustrated by an application to the detection of particle tracks in high energy physics experiments (Yuille *et al.*, 1991; Ohlsson *et al.*, 1992). An attraction of this reformulation is that it provides a precise link between deformable templates and Hough transforms (Ballard & Brown, 1982).

Our work on deformable templates was influenced by snakes (Kass *et al.*, 1987a) (see also chapters 1 and 3) and by the elastic models (Fischler & Elschlager, 1973; Burr, 1981). It is closely related to work by Grenander and his collaborators (Grenander, 1989; Grenander *et al.*, 1991). The work on deformable templates with matching units is related to the elastic net model for the traveling salesman problem (Durbin & Willshaw, 1987; Durbin *et al.*, 1989) and generalizations to other matching problems (Yuille, 1990).

This chapter is organized as follows. In Section 2.2 we introduce deformable templates. Section 2.3 describes our first application to feature extraction (Yuille *et al.*, 1989) while Section 2.4 critiques this approach and describes a newer method for feature detection (Hallinan, 1991). In Section 2.5 we provide an example of tracking a moving feature with these templates. Section 2.6 concludes by describing an alternative formulation of deformable templates in terms of discrete matching (Yuille *et al.*, 1991; Ohlsson *et al.*, 1992).

2.2   Deformable Templates

Template matching is one of the classic approaches to feature detection (Ballard & Brown, 1982). In its most basic form it involves convolving an image with a mask corresponding to the feature to be detected. Large values of the convolved image, hence good matches between the template and the image, are interpreted as detected features.

This approach is very effective in certain domains but it has a number of drawbacks. It will fail if the object in the image is slightly deformed (possibly due to foreshortening) or if the lighting in the scene is very different from that used to generate the template. Thus one needs a template that is relatively invariant to geometric distortions and lighting variations. In addition one would like to have a confidence measure of detection that is also relatively invariant.

The deformable template approach attempts to solve these problems. It consists of three basic elements:

1.   A parameterized *Geometrical Model* for the feature including prior probabilities for the parameters. This corresponds to a geometric measure of fitness.

2.   An *Imaging Model* to specify how a deformable template of specific geometry will give rise to specific intensities in the image. This can be expressed as an imaging measure of fitness.

3.   An algorithm using the geometrical and imaging measures of fitness to match the template to the image.

It is attractive to formalize this definition in terms of probabilities. Suppose $T(\mathbf{g})$ specifies the geometrical model of the template with prior probability $P(\mathbf{g})$ on the template parameters $\mathbf{g}$. The imaging model $P(I \mid T(\mathbf{g}))$ gives the probability of producing an image I from a template $T(\mathbf{g})$. Thus $P(I \mid T(\mathbf{g}))P(\mathbf{g})$ can be used to synthesize features.

Bayes' theorem can be used to obtain a measure of fitness. We write

$$P(T(\mathbf{g}) \mid I) = \frac{P(I \mid T(\mathbf{g}))P(T(\mathbf{g}))}{P(I)}. \tag{2.1}$$

This gives us a probability of detection of a template, $P(T(\mathbf{g}) \mid I)$, in terms of the imaging model and the prior probabilities. By maximizing $P(T(\mathbf{g}) \mid I)$ with respect to $\mathbf{g}$ we can find locally optimal candidate matches. We can also use $P(T(\mathbf{g}) \mid I)$ as a confidence criterion for the matches.

2.3 Facial Feature Extraction by Deformable Templates

The following section is based on work described in (Yuille *et al.*, 1989). It gives the basic intuition for the deformable template approach.

This work is aimed at extracting facial features such as the eyes and mouth. It is motivated as follows: (i) the edges of these features are rarely step edges in the intensity and so standard edge detectors are poor at detecting them, (ii) valleys and peaks in the image intensity seem more salient than edges as cues for facial features.

This suggests: (i) building in as much prior knowledge as possible about the geometry of the feature to be detected, (ii) representing the feature by a parameterized model with as few parameters as possible (this is advantageous also for tracking — see chapter 3) (iii) making the template interact with intensity peaks and valleys.

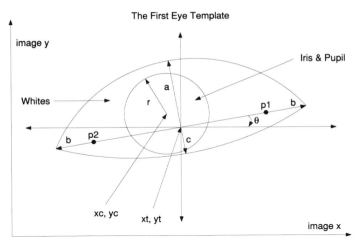

Figure 2.1
A human eye template for an "archetypal" eye, see Figure 2.2. It is parameterized by $a, b, c, x_t, y_t, x_c, y_c, r, \theta, p_1$, and p_2. R_w and R_b are intensity regions containing the whites and dark center of the eye respectively. R_w is bounded by parabolic curves ∂R_w specified by parameters a, b and c. R_b is bounded by a circle ∂R_b of radius r.

We first specify the eye template geometry – see Figure 2.1. It is represented by eleven parameters $\mathbf{g} = (\mathbf{x}_t, \mathbf{x}_c, r, a, b, c, \theta, p_1, p_2)$. The iris is modeled as a circle with center $\mathbf{x}_c$ and radius r. The template as a whole has center $\mathbf{x}_t$ and orientation θ which defines two directions $\mathbf{e}_1 = (\cos \theta, \sin \theta)$ and $\mathbf{e}_2 = (-\sin \theta, \cos \theta)$. It is bounded by two parabolae specified by parameters a, b, c: they correspond to $\mathbf{x}(\alpha) = \mathbf{x}_t + \alpha \mathbf{e}_1 + \{a - \frac{a}{b^2}\alpha^2\}\mathbf{e}_2$ and $\mathbf{x}(\alpha) = \mathbf{x}_t + \alpha \mathbf{e}_1 - \{c - \frac{c}{b^2}\alpha^2\}\mathbf{e}_2$ for $|\alpha| \leq b$. In addition two parameters p_1 and p_2 are given to determine the positions of the centers of the peaks

$\mathbf{x}_t + p_1\mathbf{e}_1$ and $\mathbf{x}_t + p_2\mathbf{e}_2$ (p_2 will be a negative number).

An energy term is used to impose relations between different parameters, such that the center of the eye is close to the center of the iris. It will be shown later that, by using the Gibbs distribution (Parisi, 1988), we can transform this into prior probabilities on the parameter values.

$$E_{prior} = \frac{k_1}{2}\|\mathbf{x}_t - \mathbf{x}_c\|^2 + \frac{k_2}{2}(p_1 - p_2 - \{r + b\})^2 + \frac{k_3}{2}(b - 2r)^2$$
$$+ k_4\{(2c - a)^2 + (b - 2a)^2\}. \tag{2.2}$$

The imaging model assumes that the iris corresponds to a valley in the image intensity, the whites to peaks and the boundaries to edges, so we must extract edge, valley and peak fields from the intensity data. In (Yuille et al., 1989) these fields are computed by using morphological filters (Maragos, 1987; Serra, 1982). These filter responses are then smoothed by convolving with a filter, $e^{-\rho(x^2+y^2)^{1/2}}$, to give edge, valley and peak fields $\Psi_e(x,y)$, $\Psi_v(x,y)$ and $\Psi_p(x,y)$. Figure 2.2 shows potential fields for an "archetypal" eye. In Section 4 we describe an alternative way to compute these fields.

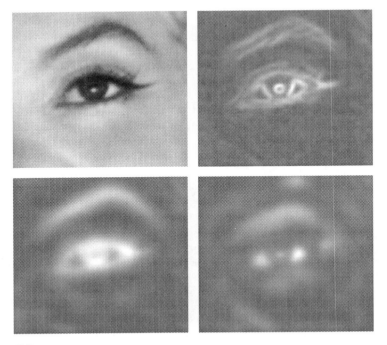

Figure 2.2
The potential fields for an "archetypal" eye. The eye, top left, has edge, valley and peak fields shown top right, bottom left and bottom right.

The potential fields are designed for coarse-scale matching. They will select salient regions of the image and guide the template towards them.

The imaging model will also include intensity terms which are useful for fine scale matching.

We now define the interaction energy between the deformable template and the image. This has contributions from the valley (the iris), peaks (the whites of the eyes) and edges (boundaries of the iris and the eyes). More specifically

$$E_v \quad = \quad -\frac{c_1}{|R_b|} \int_{R_b} \Psi_v(\mathbf{x}) dA \tag{2.3}$$

$$E_e \quad = \quad -\frac{c_2}{|\partial R_b|} \int_{\partial R_b} \Psi_e(\mathbf{x}) ds - \frac{c_3}{|\partial R_w|} \int_{\partial R_w} \Psi_e(\mathbf{x}) ds \tag{2.4}$$

$$E_I \quad = \quad \frac{c_4}{|R_b|} \int_{R_b} I(\mathbf{x}) dA - \frac{c_5}{|R_w|} \int_{R_w} I(\mathbf{x}) dA \tag{2.5}$$

$$E_p \quad = \quad -c_6 \left[\Psi_p(\mathbf{x}_e + p_1 \mathbf{e}_1) + \Psi_p(\mathbf{x}_e + p_2 \mathbf{e}_1) \right]. \tag{2.6}$$

Here R_b, R_w, ∂R_b and ∂R_w correspond to the iris, the whites of the eye, and their boundaries – see Figure 2.1. Their areas, or lengths, are given by $|R_w|$, $|R_b|$, $|\partial R_w|$, and $|\partial R_b|$. A and s correspond to area and arc-length respectively.

The algorithm uses a search strategy based on steepest descent that attempts to find the most salient parts of the eye in order. It first uses the valley potential to find the iris, then the peaks to orient the template, and so on.

To implement this strategy we divide the search into a number of epochs with different values of the parameters $\{c_i\}$ and $\{k_i\}$. The updating in each epoch is done by steepest descent in the total energy

$$E = E_v + E_p + E_e + E_I + E_{prior} \tag{2.7}$$

i.e. $\frac{dr}{dt} = -\frac{\partial E}{\partial r}$.

In the first epoch c_1 is the only non-zero parameter and hence only the valley forces act on the template. The center of the eye $\mathbf{x}_t$ is set equal to the center of the iris $\mathbf{x}_c$. During this epoch the iris drags the eye-template towards the eye. In the next epoch the parameters c_2 and c_4 are switched on to tune the position and size of the iris. After this stage the position and size of the iris are considered fixed and an inertia term

$$E_{inertia} = \frac{k_5}{2}(r - r_{old})^2 + \frac{k_6}{2} \left|\left| \mathbf{x}_t^{old} - \mathbf{x}_t \right|\right|^2 \tag{2.8}$$

is added to the energy. This destroys the symmetry in the E_{prior} to ensure that the parameter values of the iris can influence the parameter values of the remainder of the template, but not *vice-versa*. Finally, the remainder of the template is activated. c_6 is turned on to enable the peak fields to orient the template and c_3 and c_5 are switched on to make fine scale adjustments. The system changes epoch automatically when the rate of change of variables appropriate to that epoch remain below a cutoff for a sufficient number of iterations. Further details of the implementation can be found in (Yuille *et al.*, 1992).

Results from this template are shown in Figure 2.3. This result can

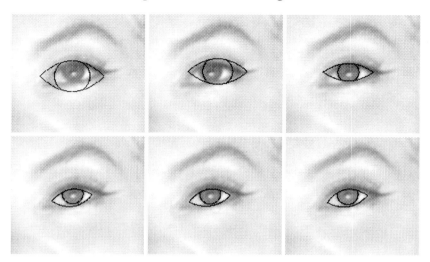

Figure 2.3
Eye template at different times during the minimization.

be interpreted in terms of probability by defining the Gibbs distribution $P(\mathbf{g}) = e^{-\beta E(\mathbf{g})}/Z$ where β is a positive constant, corresponding to the inverse temperature, and Z is a normalization factor. Maximizing $P(\mathbf{g})$, with respect to $\mathbf{g}$, is equivalent to minimizing $E(\mathbf{g})$.

The eye templates can also be modified to extract mouths (Yuille *et al.*, 1989). See Figure 2.4.

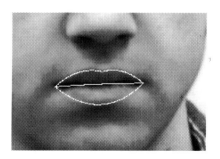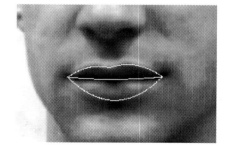

Figure 2.4
Two different mouths fit by a template for closed mouths.

2.4   Robust Deformable Templates

The preceding section described the basic properties of deformable templates and a system that implemented them. Though these templates worked reasonably well (Yuille *et al.*, 1989; Shackleton & Welsh, 1991; Bennett & Craw, 1991) and could be adapted to other problems (Lipson *et al.*, 1990) they had several unsatisfactory aspects:

1.   The use of morphological filters seems unaesthetic when instead we can extract the valleys and peaks by elementary deformable templates and then define the eye template as being composed of a set of these elementary templates.

2.   A fixed scale was used to detect valleys and peaks. This should be automated.

3.   The deformable templates fail when the feature is partially occluded or too degraded by noise. A more sophisticated measure of fitness is needed.

4.   The initialization of the templates was by hand. This should be automated.

These problems were dealt with in recent work reported in (Hallinan, 1991). The basic geometrical structure of the templates shown here is fairly similar (see figure 2.5) but the goodness of fit criterion and the algorithm are rather different.

The deformable templates for the eye are made out of deformable templates for peaks and valleys. These valley and peak templates are first run on the image at a variety of scales. Plausible valley and peak candidates are detected. Inhibition is used to prevent valley candidates at different scales from responding to the same image region. This gives a set of possible eye candidates which can be used as initial configurations for the full eye templates which are minimized by steepest descent.

The imaging model and the goodness of fit measure can be illustrated by considering the valley template. The geometrical model of a valley is a circle of radius r_b with a surround of radius r_w (where $r_w = 2r_b$ for this application), see Figure 2.6. The imaging model specifies that the intensities inside the valley and its surround be distributed normally with means μ_b and μ_w and standard deviations σ_b and σ_w respectively. Given such assumptions we derive a statistical measure (related to Fisher's linear discriminant) for determining the extent to which the valley and surround distributions differ, namely $M = (\mu_b - \mu_w)/\{h + \gamma\sqrt{(\tilde{n}_b\sigma_b^2 + \tilde{n}_w\sigma_w^2)}\}$ where n_b and n_w are the number of pixels in the valley and in the background. $\tilde{n}_b = n_b/(n_b + n_w)$, $\tilde{n}_w = n_w/(n_b + n_w)$ and γ is a positive dimensionless constant. $h = \max_{(x,y)}\{I(x,y)\} - \min_{(x,y)}\{I(x,y)\}$ is a factor to prevent this measure from blowing up for small σ_b and σ_w. Maximizing M will maximize the ratio of between class scatter to within class scatter.

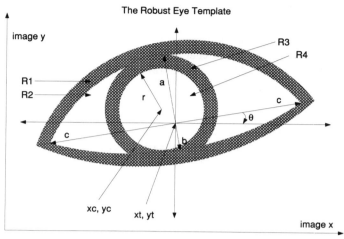

Figure 2.5
A human eye template parameterized by $a, b, c, x_t, y_t, x_c, y_c, r, \theta$. R_1 and R_3 are edge regions bounding the whites and iris respectively. Intensity data within these regions is ignored. R_2 and R_4 are intensity regions containing the whites and center of the eye respectively. Both prefer the absence of edges. R_1 and R_2 are bounded by parabolic curves and R_3 and R_4 by circles.

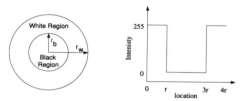

Figure 2.6
The blob geometry and a cross-section of the intensity model for an ideal valley.

We could use M as a measure of fitness between the valley template and the image. It is, however, unsatisfactory for two reasons: (i) the geometrical shape of the template may be inaccurate, i.e. if the valley is not perfectly round, and (ii) the valley, or the background, may contain salt and pepper noise, a highlight or be partially occluded. It is well known that the usual sample means and standard deviations are sensitive to contamination caused by such outliers.

These problems can be avoided by using robust estimators of the parameters (Huber, 1981). Hallinan (1991) uses α-trimmed estimators. The data values are ordered and the lowest α_1 percent and the highest α_2 percent of the data is removed. This removes the effect of outliers from the robust estimators $\hat{\mu}_b, \hat{\mu}_w, \hat{\sigma}_b, \hat{\sigma}_w$. Alpha-trimming also has the effect of enlarging the set of global minima of the template. When the data is corrupted, this enlarged set can contain the desired minimum whereas the set with no trimming does not. See Figure 2.7 for an example with owl eyes. For the human template, we set $\alpha_1 = 0$ for the valley and $\alpha_2 = 0$ for the surround since we assume that the outliers for the valley are bright and the outliers for the background are dark.

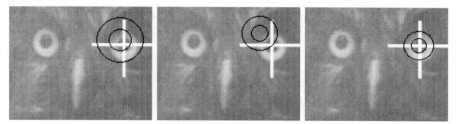

Figure 2.7
The valley template run on an owl's eye occluded by two white bars. Left: the starting position of the template. Middle: the final fit when no trimming is performed. Right: the final fit when $\alpha = 49$. The color and large area of the occluding bars force α to be high.

This now yields a robust measure of fitness

$$M_R = \frac{\hat{\mu}_b - \hat{\mu}_w}{h + \gamma\sqrt{\tilde{n}_b(\hat{\sigma}_b)^2 + \tilde{n}_w(\hat{\sigma}_w)^2}}. \qquad (2.9)$$

The full system includes similar fitness measures for the peaks and the eye itself. This leads to a following strategy:

1.   Run the valley template over the image at all scales. Keep all possible candidates above threshold. Use nonmaximum suppression to eliminate multiple candidates with similar positions and scales.

2.   Repeat for the peak template.

3.   Find co-linear peak/valley/peak regions to obtain possible eye candidates.

4.   Run the full eye template at all possible eye candidates. Use steepest descent to adjust the template to the local best fits.

5.   Evaluate and rate the full eye templates.

2.4.1   The Cost Functional

The cost functional for the full template is divided into data and prior terms as above,

$$T_{template}[\mathbf{g}] = T_{data}[\mathbf{g}] + T_{prior}[\mathbf{g}] \qquad (2.10)$$

which correspond to log probabilities in a Bayesian interpretation. The data term acts both on the raw intensity and on an edge potential field Φ_E, generated adaptively in two steps. The first step is to create a binary edge map by thresholding the gradient magnitude $\|\nabla I\|$ at the β percentile of the histogram of $||\nabla I||$ over $\bigcup_{i=1}^{4} R_i$, see 2.5 where $\beta = \frac{n_1+n_3}{n_1+n_2+n_3+n_4}$ and n_i is the number of pixels in the region R_i ($i = 1, 2, 3, 4$). The second step is to smooth the binary edge map to get Φ_E using the kernel defined by $\exp(-\rho(x^2+y^2)^{\frac{1}{2}})$, ρ a scale factor. Without smoothing $||\nabla I||$, the attractive power of an edge can be as little as one or two pixels, making minimization much harder. The data term is thus

$$T_{data}[\mathbf{g}; I, \Phi_E, \alpha] = k_1 \frac{(\hat{\mu}_4 - \hat{\mu}_2)}{h + \gamma(\tilde{n}_4\hat{\sigma}_4^2 + \tilde{n}_2\hat{\sigma}_2^2)^{\frac{1}{2}}} + k_2 \frac{(\hat{e}_1 + \hat{e}_3) - (\hat{e}_2 + \hat{e}_4)}{\sum_{i=1}^{4}\hat{e}_i}. (2.11)$$

The k_i are non-negative constants chosen so that $T_{data} \in [-1, 1]$. Definitions of $h, \tilde{n}_i, \hat{\mu}_i, \hat{\sigma}_i^2$ are as in the valley template and $\hat{e}_i$ is the α-trimmed mean of Φ_E over R_i. Again, the side of the histogram trimmed depends on whether the intensity or edge strength is intended to be high or low. To summarize, the intensity term has the familiar structure from before, while the edge term is even simpler – just desiring the mean edge strength to be highest in the edgy regions R_2 and R_4.

The priors are derived from crudely approximating the empirical distributions obtained by hand-fitting the template twice to each of 30 different eyes. They are essentially similar to the priors used in the previous section. For more details see (Hallinan, 1991).

This system has been run on a large variety of eyes (more than 100). Table 2.1 presents the results of searching for candidate eyes with the robust valley and peak detectors on the two sets $\mathcal{T}$, 25 test eyes having various types of noise, and $\mathcal{P}$, 107 positive eyes (some very difficult). Approximately sixty five percent of the eyes in $\mathcal{P}$ were very accurately located in the robust case (hits), i.e. the scale, location, and orientation were all within about 5–10% of correct as estimated by eye. Another 15% were only slightly off, for example one peak might be located on an eyelid above the white, tipping the orientation by 10 or 15 degrees. The remaining eyes were clearly missed, often completely. The non-robust search had similar but distinctly worse results. To summarize, the overall hit rate of the first stage with trimming was about 80%, an increase of about 15% over the non-trimming version. From this we conclude that even the very simple robustness we have introduced here has a beneficial effect.

The results of minimizing the eye template energy suggest that given a hit or near hit from stage 3, a good fit can nearly always be found. More detailed results are being summarized in Hallinan (1992). It is important to note though, that there is no unique best fit as judged by a human observer, i.e. there are always several plausible ways in which to manually fit the template to the data. This is to be distinguished from the possibly unique fit provided by a particular template; thus there is some flexibility in actually specifying the weights, priors, and minimization schedule of the template.

The present limitations of the system are:

1. The system almost always finds the correct eyes as plausible eye candidates, but does not always rate them more highly than false alarms.

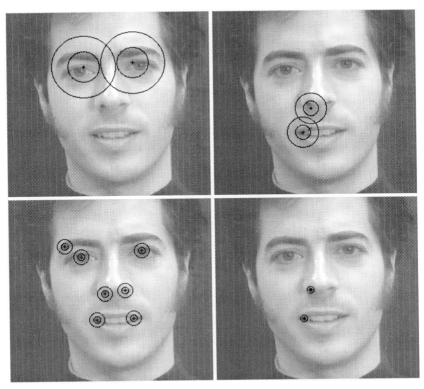

Figure 2.8
Results of the valley detector after thresholding and non-maximum suppression. Resolution increases by 3 octaves from left to right.

2. It displays a limited ability to deal with occlusion.

3. Minimization is more difficult than with the template of Section 2.2, partially because of the trimming, which adds global minima to the set of minima. Depending on the value of α, it can transpire that the desired minimum is added to a set that did not previously contain it or that minima are added that effectively push the desired fit into the interior of the set of minima and thus out of reach of a gradient descent algorithm. Such over-trimming can be cured by adaptive methods for setting α.

2.5   Tracking

It is straightforward to adapt the deformable templates for tracking. Here we describe an implementation that tracks eyes automatically given an initial position and a set of potential fields. This system merges aspects of both eye templates described above to create a hybrid tracking system that is more robust than the first template but easier to minimize than the second. The

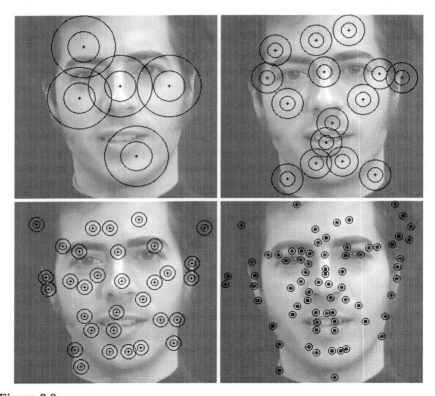

Figure 2.9
Results of the peak detector after thresholding and non-maximum suppression. The scales
match those above.

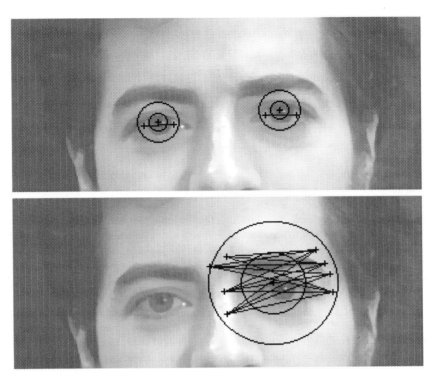

Figure 2.10
Candidate eyes at 2 scales. Each circle represents a valley. Each line connects two peaks
and thus represents a single candidate. No other candidates appear either in the truncated
image or at different scales.

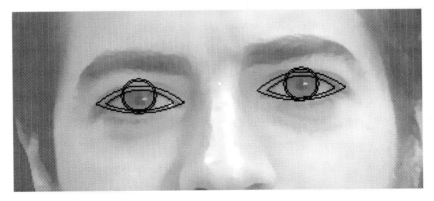

Figure 2.11
The two final fits of the robust eye template.

α_v	α_p		$\mathcal{T}$	$\mathcal{P}$
0.00	0.00	% Hits	72	56
		% Near Hits	8	10
		% Misses	20	34
0.25	0.25	% Hits	72	65
		% Near Hits	20	13
		% Misses	8	22
		Total Eyes	27	107

Table 2.1
Evaluation of the quality of the candidate eyes as judged by eye.

algorithm is straightforward. For the first frame, we initialize the template by hand as before, but for succeeding frames, we use as the initial position the best fit of the preceding frame.

This method obviously succeeds only as long as the best fit at time $t - 1$ lies in the basin of attraction of the system at time t. In turn this will be true only if: (i) the deformations and movements of the eye are small (e.g. on the order of the diameter of the iris) and (ii) the potential fields are sufficiently clean and accurate, e.g. eyebrows are not marked as valleys and the smoothing scale ρ is long enough to pull in templates from far away.

The first criterion is met by using a high enough frame rate. The second criterion is met by constructing potential fields in the following way: (i) choose a scale for the potential fields, (ii) construct peak and valley energy fields by running the robust peak and valley templates over each frame with $\alpha = 10\%$, (iii) perform nonmaximum suppression on the resulting energy fields, and (iv) suppress peaks that do not appear within the surround of any valley. Edge fields are generated by thresholding the gradient magnitude. The results are smoothed as before with an exponential decay kernel. However, because valleys and peaks appear as single points in the results, the smoothing scale is set longer for valleys and shorter for peaks to improve tracking by valleys and to minimize conflicts between intensity peaks on the skin and those on the whites. To these clean potential fields we then apply the template of Section 2.3 since it is easier to minimize.

A final point is that since the acquisition stage provides a close fit to the eye and since the deformation is not expected to be great from frame to frame, we can economize on computation by relaxing the convergence criteria and by turning on the valley radius momentum term in the first epoch.

Results of this system for a real eye are shown in Figure 2.12. Note that a completely automatic system could be built by incorporating the automatic acquisition of Section 2.4. Also, robust potential fields could be generated on the fly using as a scale estimate the radius of the iris in the previous frame.

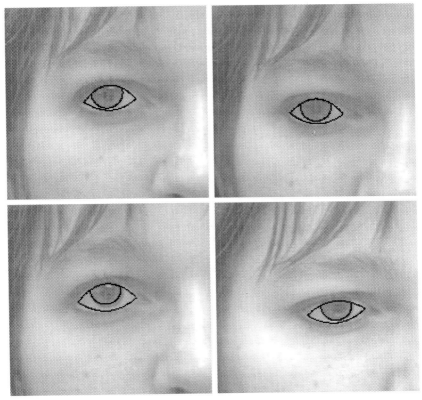

Figure 2.12
A sequence of images of eyes being tracked. Both the subject's head orientation and direction of gaze are varying.

2.6 Discrete Matching

An alternative formulation (Yuille, 1990) of deformable templates works on discrete problems, or on continuous problems that have been discretized. It is similar to the elastic net model for solving the traveling salesman problem (Durbin & Willshaw, 1987).

It assumes that the we have a set of image measurements $\{I_i(\mathbf{x}_i)\}$ at positions $\{\mathbf{x}_i\}$ for $i = 1, \ldots, N$. The deformable template has a geometrical structure $\{\mathbf{y}_a(\mathbf{g})\}$, where $\mathbf{g}$ is a set of parameters characterizing the geometry of the template, and each $\mathbf{y}_a$ for $a = 1, \ldots, n$ is associated with a property J_a, which could indicate, for example, whether the structure matches intensity or edges. Let $M_{im}(I_i, J_a)$ be a compatibility measure of fitness between I_i

and J_a. Similarly let $M_{geom}(\mathbf{y}_a, \mathbf{x}_i)$ be a geometric measure of fit between the $\{\mathbf{y}_a\}$ and $\{\mathbf{x}_i\}$.

For example, suppose the $\{\mathbf{x}_i\}$ are the points of an image and I_i is the modulus of the gradient of the intensity at that point. Then the deformable template could be the two parabolae bounding the whites of the eyes, $n = 2$. $\mathbf{g}$ would correspond to the parameters $a, b, c, \mathbf{x}_t, \theta$. $\mathbf{y}_1(\mathbf{g})$ and $\mathbf{y}_2(\mathbf{g})$ would represent the upper and lower parabolae. We could define $M_{im}(I_i, J_a) = I_i$ for $a = 1, 2$ (i.e. points in the image attract the parabolae with a strength depending on the modulus of the gradient of the intensity) and $M_{geom}(\mathbf{x}_i, \mathbf{y}_a)$ could be the shortest distance between the point $\mathbf{x}_i$ and the parabola labeled by a.

Then we can define a matching criterion

$$E[V, g] = \sum_{i,a=1}^{N,n} V_{ia} M_{im}(I_a, J_i) M_{geom}(\mathbf{y}_i, \mathbf{x}_a) + E_{prior}[\mathbf{g}] + E_{prior}[V] \quad (2.12)$$

where the $\{V_{ia}\}$ are binary decision units so that $V_{ia} = 1$ means that i is matched to a and $V_{ia} = 0$ otherwise. $E_{prior}[\mathbf{g}]$ and $E_{prior}[V]$ give prior terms.

To make this more concrete we describe an application to the detection of particles in high energy physics experiments (Yuille et al., 1991; Ohlsson et al., 1992). Here the inputs to the system are the binary outputs of sensors, so $M_{im}(I_a, J_i) = 1 \ \forall a, i$.

We assume that the tracks are helices centered at the point of collision. The tracks can be described by parameters $\mathbf{g} = (\kappa_a, \theta_a, \gamma_a)$ where κ_a is the curvature, θ_a the initial angle of orientation θ_a, and γ_a is a measure of the speed in the longitudinal direction. The cost function becomes

$$E[V, \kappa, \theta, \gamma] = \sum_{i,a=1}^{N,n} V_{ia} M_{geom}(\mathbf{x}_i, \kappa_a, \theta_a, \gamma_a) + \lambda \sum_{i=1}^{N} \left(1 - \sum_{a=1}^{n} V_{ia}\right) \quad (2.13)$$

where we require that each sensor measurement i is either matched to a single track a or to no track at all. Equivalently $\forall i$, $\sum_a V_{ia} = 0 \ or \ 1$. λ corresponds to the penalty paid for not matching a data point. $M(\mathbf{x}_i, \kappa_a, \theta_a, \gamma_a)$ is a measure of distance between the sensor point $\mathbf{x}_i$ and the curve parameterized by $\kappa_a, \theta_a, \gamma_a$. Typically we choose M to be the square of the shortest distance from $\mathbf{x}_i$ to the curve.

This can be given a probabilistic formulation by introducing the Gibbs distribution

$$P[V, \theta, \kappa, \gamma] = \frac{1}{Z} e^{-\beta E[V, \theta, \kappa, \gamma]} \quad (2.14)$$

where β is the inverse of the temperature of the system and Z is a normalization constant.

We can compute the marginal distribution of $\{\kappa_a\}$ $\{\theta_a\}$ and $\{\gamma_a\}$ by summing over the possible configurations of the $\{V_{ia}\}$. It can be shown (Yuille et al., 1991) that

$$P[\theta, \kappa, \gamma] = \frac{1}{Z} e^{-\beta E_{\text{eff}}[\theta, \kappa, \gamma]}, \tag{2.15}$$

where the effective energy is

$$E_{\text{eff}}[\theta, \kappa, \gamma] = \frac{-1}{\beta} \sum_{i=1}^{N} \log \left[e^{-\beta \lambda} + \sum_{a=1}^{n} e^{-\beta M(\mathbf{x}_i, \kappa_a, \theta_a, \gamma_a)} \right]. \tag{2.16}$$

There are two main advantages to this probabilistic formulation. The first is that we can interpret the deformable template as performing the maximal likelihood estimation of a mixture of distributions. This corresponds in this case to a mixture of error distributions for a regression model and a uniform distribution. The particle tracks are assumed to be generated by the regression model while the false-positive responses and the cosmic rays are assumed generated by the uniform distribution. The uniform distribution gives a form of robustness by allowing us to throw away a certain amount of the data. The β parameter must now be interpreted as a measure of the inverse variance of the regression distribution.

The second advantage is that there is a good heuristic algorithm, deterministic annealing, for obtaining the estimators. This involves minimizing E_{eff} with respect to κ, θ and γ at high temperature (small β) and then tracking the solution down to low temperature (high β). Deterministic annealing can be shown to be a good approximation to simulated annealing and is typically considerably faster (Durbin & Willshaw, 1987; Peterson, 1990).

Variants of the Hough transforms (Ballard & Brown, 1982) are used to estimate the number of structures of the template and their initial positions. Interestingly the Hough transform can be directly related to deformable template models (Yuille *et al.*, 1991) in the limit as $\beta \to \infty$ and $\lambda \to 0$.

2.7   Conclusion

We have described the deformable template approach to feature recognition and shown how such templates can be applied to tracking. The key ingredients are the flexible geometrical model and the imaging model which together allow us to detect a variety of examples of the same basic feature under different lighting conditions. We have used examples of eye detection and high energy particle detection, but the principles involved can be applied directly to other domains.

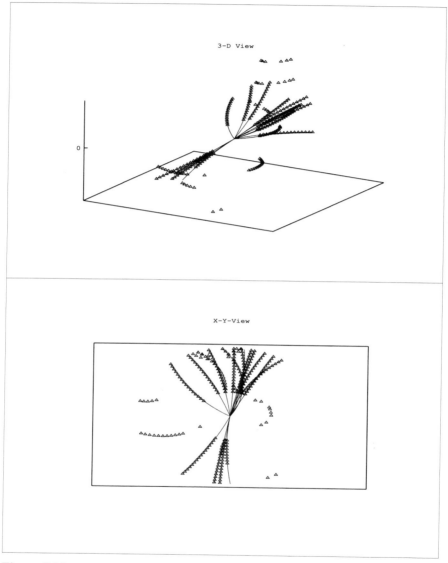

Figure 2.13
Deformable Template finding particle tracks. The triangles correspond to sensor events, i.e. data points $\mathbf{x}_i$. The solid lines represent the template structures given by $\{y_a\}, a = 1, \ldots, n$ where n was estimated and fixed before the fitting process (see text). The unmatched points are due to false positive responses from the sensors sometimes corresponding to cosmic rays. Figure taken from (Ohlsson *et al.*, 1992) with permission.

3 Dynamic Contours: Real-time Active Splines

Rupert Curwen and Andrew Blake

We describe the design of real-time **Dynamic Contours** that run at video rates. Dynamic contours have evolved from the principles of the snake (see (Kass *et al.*, 1987a) and chapter 1) with the purpose of achieving high-speed, real-time tracking together with shape selectivity. Dynamic contours are elastic, as snakes are, but defined parametrically, using B-splines (Curwen *et al.*, 1991; Cipolla & Blake, 1990). The compact parametric representation leads to efficient state-space equations for the contour. When this is combined with parallel computing in the form of a small Transputer network (11 processors), video-rate tracking performance is achievable for several contours simultaneously (figure 3.1). We have demonstrated the applications of

Figure 3.1
Dynamic contours tracking objects in a scene (raster order). All contours are "coupled" (see text). The top left contour peels away from the tracked feature as it approaches the image boundary and is repelled by it.

such tracking in surveillance of people and vehicles, robotic path-planning (see chapter 11) and grasp-planning.

Two important developments are explored in this chapter: the use of **coupled contours** and analysis of **tracking dynamics**. Their combined effect is to achieve high-speed tracking with good rejection of distractors in the background texture.

3.0.1 Coupled contours

Unconstrained snakes relax back, typically, to a straight line configuration. Dynamic contours, if unconstrained, retain full degrees of freedom with no unique relaxed state. Frequently however, it is desirable to incorporate a strong tendency to a particular relaxed configuration. This is useful when the shape of the target feature is approximately known. Incorporating that prior knowledge greatly reduces, we have found, the tendency of the dynamic contour to be *distracted* when the tracked feature moves over background clutter. This is achieved by coupling the B-spline contour to a rigid B-spline *template.* The effect is to combine the elastic properties of the snake with those of a parametric template like the ones described in chapter 2. The template is "learnt" by allowing an unconstrained dynamic contour to lock onto a representative target feature. This contour is then "frozen" and becomes the template coupled elastically to a new dynamic contour.

3.0.2 Tracking dynamics

Substantial improvements in tracking performance are realised when the model incorporates distributed mass and a viscous medium (Curwen *et al.*, 1991). As with snakes and deformable models (chapter 5), we follow a Lagrangian formulation of the dynamics of the contour. The couplings of a dynamic contour with its template and with image features are determined by the elasticity and viscosity parameters. By applying *modal analysis* we have been able to characterise precisely the effect of these parameters on tracking behaviour. Contour motion is naturally decomposed into *modes* (eigenstates of the dynamical equations) each of which behaves as a second order control system. The tuning of each modal control system is different. However tuning is interdependent across modes and this limits tracking performance. The modal analysis has been done for single-span quadratic and cubic splines (i.e. Bezier curves). This is easily extended to higher order polynomials. It remains to extend the analysis for multiple spans. Nonetheless, the single-span analysis is sufficient to predict steady-state lag and transient effects which are consistent with our experimental findings.

3.1 The dynamical system

3.1.1 Feature search

Points along the B-spline contour are programmed to have an affinity for image features such as brightness or high intensity-gradient. This affinity, coupled with the intrinsic continuity and elasticity of the B-spline, produces the desired flexible tracking behaviour. This is the principle on which snakes work. The original proposal (Kass *et al.*, 1987a) stressed the importance of convolution as a means of artificial blurring, in order to control the acuteness of spatial tuning. This implies considerable computational power if real-time tracking is to be achieved. However, we have found that use of large blur is unnecessary, a crucial factor in achieving real-time performance. Instead a controlled-scale search is executed along linear search paths emanating from the contour. This is similar to the scheme used for tracking rigid 2D structures in chapter 4.

Search paths may be parallel lines in a fixed direction in the image. Alternatively, tracking along normals to $\mathbf{x}(s)$ has the advantage that no fixed tracking direction need be chosen; but it has certain theoretical disadvantages (see below) and also suffers from instability problems in which an "idle" contour gradually shrinks to a point, blows up, or tangles. Notwithstanding the theoretical problems, practical implementations of the normal search have been successful, stabilised satisfactorily by the coupled contour mechanism. A third alternative is to search radially from a fixed point. This allows a closed contour to grow radially outward from a point known to be in the interior of a closed image feature, and lock onto that feature. Again there are theoretical problems in this case, but in practice it has been made to work satisfactorily. In this paper we consider primarily the first case in which search, and consequently all motion of the contour, is along fixed parallel lines.

The feature search strategy is recursive, operating in a coarse-to-fine fashion. It works by approximating the image data by finite differences at successively finer scales of detail. At each scale, finite difference approximations to the image gradient are made at the search point and at points either side. The new search point is then the one with the largest calculated gradient, and the scale is halved. This is shown for a single scale in figure 3.2.

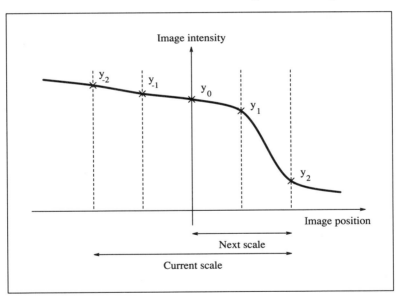

Figure 3.2
Coarse to fine search for an image feature. At each step the search bracket moves towards the largest value of $|y_0 - y_{-2}|$, $|y_1 - y_{-1}|$ and $|y_2 - y_0|$, and its scale is halved.

3.1.2 The Lagrangian

Contour dynamics are specified by energy terms chosen to achieve the desired tracking behaviour. This requires at least a kinetic energy, a potential energy (attraction towards feature) and a dissipative term (viscosity) which are

substituted into the Lagrangian Equation (Landau & Lifshitz, 1972) to give
the equations of motion of the dynamic contour.

The contour is described by a B-spline (quadratic or cubic) with L spans
(figure 3.3) in which the position in the ith span, $\mathbf{x}_i$, is a function of the

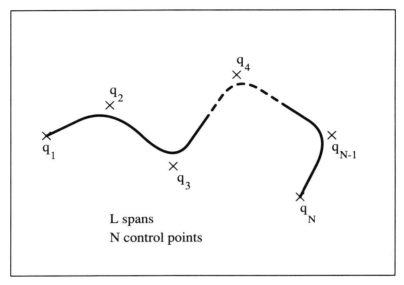

Figure 3.3
Dynamic contours are elastic, like snakes, but constructed from B-spline curves. The
parametric representation inherent in the B-spline leads to computational efficiency. This,
in turn, makes possible real-time, video-rate performance.

control points $\mathbf{Q}_i = (\mathbf{q}_i, \mathbf{q}_{i+1}, \mathbf{q}_{i+2})$, the shape matrix $\mathbf{M}_i$ and the parameter
vector $\mathbf{s} = (1, s, s^2)^\top$, where $0 \leq s \leq 1$ over each single span:

$$\mathbf{x}_i(s) = \mathbf{s}^\top \mathbf{M}_i \mathbf{Q}_i. \tag{3.1}$$

In this description, the shape matrix $\mathbf{M}$ for each span depends on the knot
positions for the B-spline (Bartels *et al.*, 1987).

In order to derive the equations of motion, via Lagrangian dynamics,
energy terms are required for each of the desired properties of the contour,
in terms of the global control point vector

$$\mathbf{Q} = (\mathbf{q}_1, \mathbf{q}_2, \cdots, \mathbf{q}_N)^\top.$$

When motion of control points $\mathbf{q}_i$ is constrained along parallel lines, we
can think of them as having one degree of freedom only, in the direction of
motion.

3.1.3   Inertia

The contour is assumed to have constant linear density ρ with respect to the
curve parameter s. For an element ds of a spline span, the kinetic energy

dT is:

$$dT = \frac{\rho}{2}\dot{\mathbf{x}}^2(s)ds. \tag{3.2}$$

Total kinetic energy T is found by integration of (3.2) along spans, and summation along the contour:

$$T = \frac{\rho}{2}\dot{\mathbf{Q}}^\top \mathbf{H}_0 \dot{\mathbf{Q}} \tag{3.3}$$

where

$$\mathbf{H}_0 = \sum_{i=1}^{L} \mathbf{G}_i^\top \mathbf{M}_i^\top \mathbf{S}_0 \mathbf{M}_i \mathbf{G}_i$$

$$\text{and } \mathbf{S}_0 = \int_0^1 \mathbf{s}\mathbf{s}^\top \, ds$$

$$\text{so that } (\mathbf{S}_0)_{ij} = \frac{1}{i+j-1}, \; 1 \le i, j \le 3.$$

The matrix $\mathbf{G}_i$ is defined such that $\mathbf{G}_i\mathbf{Q} = \mathbf{Q}_i$, transforming the global vector of control points into the control point vector for the ith span.

In our model, $\mathbf{x}_i(s)$ and $\mathbf{y}_i(s)$ are then attached by an elastic membrane of spring constant k so that the potential energy U is proportional to the square of the distance from the feature. For an element ds of a span:

$$dU = kds(\mathbf{x}(s) - \mathbf{y}(s))^2. \tag{3.4}$$

Thus by expanding the squared term and integrating along the contour, we get:

$$
\begin{aligned}
U &= k\int (\mathbf{x}(s) - \mathbf{y}(s))^2 \, ds \\
&= k\mathbf{Q}^\top \mathbf{H}_0 \mathbf{Q} - 2k\sum_{i=1}^{L}\int_0^1 (\mathbf{s}^\top \mathbf{M}_i\mathbf{Q}_i).\mathbf{y}_i(s) \, ds + \int \mathbf{y}(s)^2 \, ds. \tag{3.5}
\end{aligned}
$$

In the case that a *fixed* direction is used for feature tracking and contour motion, $\mathbf{y}(s)$ can be regarded as "constant" — that is, independent of $\mathbf{Q}$. Then the Euler-Lagrange equation can be applied (see below) to find the equations of motion. Unfortunately, tracking along radiating normals introduces a dependence of $\mathbf{y}(s)$ on $\mathbf{Q}$ because the parameterisation of $\mathbf{y}(s)$ is then a function of the shape of $\mathbf{x}(s)$. The dynamical equations then become more complex.

3.1.4 Velocity damping

The rate of frictional energy dissipation P is proportional to the square of velocity along the contour. If λ is the constant of proportionality, for an element of span ds we have:

$$dP = -\lambda \dot{\mathbf{x}}^2(s) \mathrm{d}s. \tag{3.6}$$

Thus by integration (3.6) along the contour we get:

$$P = -\lambda \dot{\mathbf{Q}}^\top \mathbf{H}_0 \dot{\mathbf{Q}}. \tag{3.7}$$

The frictional forces $\mathbf{f}$ which cause this energy loss can be written as the derivatives of a quadratic form F:

$$\mathbf{f} = -\frac{\partial F}{\partial \dot{\mathbf{Q}}}. \tag{3.8}$$

The dissipative function has physical significance as the rate of dissipation of energy in the system (Landau & Lifshitz, 1972):

$$P = \frac{dE}{dt} = -\frac{\partial F}{\partial \dot{\mathbf{Q}}} \cdot \dot{\mathbf{Q}}. \tag{3.9}$$

Comparing equations (3.7) and (3.9) we can see that:

$$\frac{\partial F}{\partial \dot{\mathbf{Q}}} = \lambda \mathbf{H}_0 \dot{\mathbf{Q}}. \tag{3.10}$$

3.1.5   Equations of motion

Using (3.3), (3.5) and (3.10) in Lagrange's equations (Landau & Lifshitz, 1972):

$$\frac{d}{dt}\left(\frac{\partial L}{\partial \dot{\mathbf{Q}}}\right) = \frac{\partial L}{\partial \mathbf{Q}} - \frac{\partial F}{\partial \dot{\mathbf{Q}}} \tag{3.11}$$

we get the governing second order differential equation of the contour:

$$\ddot{\mathbf{Q}} = \omega_0^2 \{\mathbf{Q}_f - \mathbf{Q}\} - 2\beta_0 \dot{\mathbf{Q}} \tag{3.12}$$

where

$$\omega_0^2 = \frac{2k}{\rho} \quad \text{and} \quad \beta_0 = \frac{\lambda}{2\rho}$$

and

$$\mathbf{Q}_f = \mathbf{H}_0^{-1} \sum_{i=1}^{L} \mathbf{G}_i^\top \mathbf{M}_i^\top \int_0^1 s \mathbf{y}_i(s)\, \mathrm{d}s,$$

which is simply the the B-spline approximation to $\mathbf{y}(s)$.

The equation of motion (3.12) can be integrated numerically (see later) to find the motion of the control points of the contour for a given set of feature samples $\mathbf{p}_{ij}$ and parameters ω_0, β_0. Optimal values for these parameters may be determined by control theoretic analysis. For example, it is shown later that setting $\beta_0 = \omega_0$ gives critical damping for rigid translational motion.

3.2 Coupled B-spline model

Defining a contour with inertia, as above, implies a model in which the image velocity of features is assumed uniform. However, stronger prior assumptions about the feature can be incorporated when appropriate, to considerable effect. This is done by making the further assumption that the feature shape will change only slowly. As an illustration, with no shape assumption, the contour flows *around* corners (figure 3.4a). When the shape assumption is incorporated it moves almost rigidly with the corner feature (figure 3.4b).

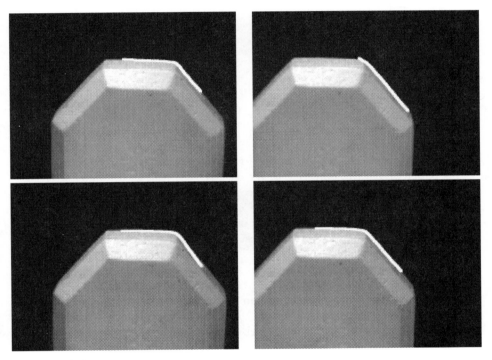

Figure 3.4
A dynamic contour tracking a corner. In (a) the contour is flexible, and slides round the corner as the object moves to the left, whereas the "coupled" B-spline contour in (b) follows the true motion of the corner.

The shape assumption is imposed by using a pair of coupled B-splines. The first can be trained by taking the original (uncoupled) contour and allowing it to relax onto a feature. Its shape is then frozen and becomes the "template" shape (see also (Yuille *et al.*, 1989) and chapter 2) in the new model. A second B-spline curve, initially an exact copy of the first, is then spawned and coupled to the template B-spline. The coupling is defined, naturally, by a new elastic energy term. Suppose the template has control point vector $\mathbf{Q}_s$, then the equations of motion, derived by an analysis similar to the previous uncoupled model (3.12), are:

$$\mathbf{H}_0\ddot{\mathbf{Q}} + 2\mathbf{B}\dot{\mathbf{Q}} + \mathbf{W}\mathbf{Q} = \mathbf{P} \tag{3.13}$$

where

$$\mathbf{B} = \sum_{n=0}^{N} \beta_n \mathbf{H}_n, \tag{3.14}$$

$$\mathbf{W} = \sum_{n=0}^{N} \omega_n^2 \mathbf{H}_n, \tag{3.15}$$

$$\mathbf{P} = \omega_0^2 \mathbf{H}_0 \mathbf{Q}_f + \sum_{n=1}^{N} \omega_n^2 \mathbf{H}_n \mathbf{Q}_s, \tag{3.16}$$

$$\mathbf{H}_n = \sum_{i=1}^{L} \mathbf{G}_i^\top \mathbf{M}_i^\top \mathbf{S}_n \mathbf{M}_i \mathbf{G}_i, \tag{3.17}$$

$$\mathbf{S}_n = \int_0^1 \frac{\mathrm{d}^n \mathbf{s}}{\mathrm{d}s^n} \cdot \frac{\mathrm{d}^n \mathbf{s}}{\mathrm{d}s^n}^\top \mathrm{d}s. \tag{3.18}$$

Here N is simply the upper limit on the *order* of the elastic couplings. In this paper we restrict ourselves to the case $N = 1$, that is, 0th and 1st order couplings. Thus the position of the contour is coupled with the position of the feature, and the gradient of the contour is coupled with the gradient of the template. In principle, higher order couplings are possible up to the order of the B-spline, the next highest being a curvature coupling between contour and template.

The entire scheme can be regarded as a dynamic polynomial fitting process. Indeed, in the steady state an uncoupled snake will relax exactly to the least squares spline approximation to the feature $\mathbf{y}(s)$. Not surprisingly then, $\mathbf{H}_0$ is the matrix in the *normal equations* for least squares linear spline fitting, and $\mathbf{H}_n$ is the equivalent matrix for fitting by least squares of the nth derivative. Matrices $\mathbf{S}_n$ are also matrices from normal equations for least squares fitting, but this time for polynomial fitting in the *power* basis.

3.3 Modal analysis of contour dynamics

The dynamics of the coupled system (3.13) can be split by modal analysis into independent 2nd order control systems. Each mode corresponds to a distinct distortion or motion of the contour and each has its own natural frequency and damping constant. We consider only 0th and 1st order couplings $(N = 1)$ in this section. In that case the natural frequencies and damping constants are a function of the relative eigenvalues of the normal equation matrices $\mathbf{H}_0$ and $\mathbf{H}_1$. Their relative eigenvectors give, in the B-spline basis, the spatial configuration of the modes. In the case of a single-span B-spline contour, the problem simplifies. Then the relative eigenvalues are also relative eigenvalues of $\mathbf{S}_0$ and $\mathbf{S}_1$ whose relative eigenvectors give the modes, but now in the power basis. Now $\mathbf{S}_0$ and $\mathbf{S}_1$ are well known to be ill-conditioned (Johnson & Reiss, 1982), a problem for polynomial fitting in the power basis. In the dynamic fitting context this leads to a wide range of relative eigenvalues and hence widely varying control characteristics for different modes. That makes it difficult satisfactorily to control all modes simultaneously.

3.3.1   Rigid translation

A complete modal analysis has only been done for single-span snakes. However, before embarking on that, there is one mode which is present for all B-spline contours — rigid translation. It corresponds to the eigenvector $\mathbf{U} = (1, 1, \ldots, 1)^{\top}$ in which all control point displacements are equal. Now it is easily shown that

$$\mathbf{H}_n \mathbf{U} = \mathbf{0} \quad \text{for } n \geq 1$$

so that for $\mathbf{Q}(t) = f(t)\mathbf{U}$ all terms in $\mathbf{H}_n$ for $n \geq 1$ drop out of equation (3.13) to give (using the fact that $\mathbf{H}_0$ is non-singular)

$$\ddot{\mathbf{Q}} + 2\beta_0 \dot{\mathbf{Q}} + \omega_0^2 \mathbf{Q} = \omega_0^2 \mathbf{Q}_f. \tag{3.19}$$

This is a simple second order forced oscillation with natural frequency ω_0 and damping constant β_0, critically damped when $\omega_0 = \beta_0$. Under constant motion there is a steady-state lag $\Delta\mathbf{Q}$, due to the viscous drag, of

$$\Delta\mathbf{Q} = \frac{2\beta_0}{\omega_0^2} \dot{\mathbf{Q}}_f. \tag{3.20}$$

Tracking, in our system, fails when that lag exceeds the radius of the tracking window.

Note that the template is entirely decoupled under rigid translation — there is no $\mathbf{Q}_s$ term in (3.19). This is not surprising since the template-contour coupling is 1st order and higher. It is also consistent with the aim of including the template which was to constrain the shape of the contour but not its mobility.

3.3.2   Polynomial modes

To find the other modes of the dynamic contour, we simply solve the equation

$$\mathbf{H}_1 \mathbf{U} = \lambda \mathbf{H}_0 \mathbf{U} \tag{3.21}$$

for the relative eigenvector $\mathbf{U}$ and eigenvalue λ. The lowest mode is always the translational one with $\lambda = 0$. For higher modes we restrict ourselves to the single-span (Bezier) case in which, from (3.17),

$$\mathbf{H}_n = \mathbf{M}_1^{\top} \mathbf{S}_n \mathbf{M}_1, \tag{3.22}$$

so that $\mathbf{H}_n$ is obtained from $\mathbf{S}_n$ simply by a change of basis from the polynomial power basis $\{1, s, s^2, ..\}$ to the B-spline (Bezier) basis. Thus each λ is also a relative eigenvalue of $\mathbf{S}_1$ and $\mathbf{S}_0$ and the corresponding eigenvalues give the modes, but expressed in the power basis. Having solved for λ, $\mathbf{U}$, substituting (3.21) into (3.13) and using the fact that $\mathbf{H}_0$ is non-singular we obtain the second order system for each mode as

$$\ddot{\mathbf{Q}} + 2\beta\dot{\mathbf{Q}} + \omega^2\mathbf{Q} = \omega_0^2\mathbf{Q}_f + \lambda\omega_1^2\mathbf{Q}_s \tag{3.23}$$

where the constants governing damping and resonance for the mode are:

$$\beta = \beta_0 + \lambda\beta_1 \tag{3.24}$$
$$\omega^2 = \omega_0^2 + \lambda\omega_1^2. \tag{3.25}$$

The table 3.1 below summarises the results for the quadratic and cubic cases. Modes are arranged in ascending order of eigenvalue λ and hence also of frequency ω and damping constant β.

One consequence of the relationship of damping factor (3.24) and frequency (3.25) on the modal eigenvector λ is that not all modes can simultaneously be critically damped. If $\omega_0 = \beta_0$ the first mode is critically damped and if also

$$\beta_1 = \frac{1}{\lambda}\left(\sqrt{\beta_0^2 + \lambda\omega_1^2} - \beta_0\right) \tag{3.26}$$

the second mode is critically damped. Higher modes will then be overdamped and hence slower than one would ideally like them to be. In principle, control over higher modes could be obtained by allowing higher order spatial coupling ($N > 1$).

3.3.3   Performance predictions

The modal analysis can be used to predict steady state and transient response of the dynamic contour. In the steady state, for a static feature, the configuration of the snake is a compromise between those of the feature and the template:

$$\mathbf{Q} = \frac{\omega_0^2\mathbf{Q}_f + \lambda\omega_1^2\mathbf{Q}_s}{\omega^2}, \tag{3.27}$$

with the relative influence of the template increasing for higher modes. Under steady state motion, the translational mode showed a constant lag (3.20) but higher modes exhibit a lag that increases over time due to the influence of the template. The amplitude of motion of the template is only a fraction ω_0^2/ω^2 of that of the image feature. Thus different modes lag by varying amounts leading to distortion effects like the one shown in figure 3.5. Rotation of the feature is tracked by a cubic spline contour. Pure rotation is not present as a single mode in the cubic case (table 3.1) so it is split into modes 3 and 4. Each mode is tracked at a different rate so that their inflections, which initially cancel exactly, are visible during tracking.

Quadratic Spline			
Mode	Eigenvalue λ	Eigenvector $\mathbf{U}$	Configuration
1	0	$\begin{pmatrix} 1 \\ 1 \\ 1 \end{pmatrix}$	
2	12	$\begin{pmatrix} 1 \\ 0 \\ -1 \end{pmatrix}$	
3	60	$\begin{pmatrix} -1 \\ 2 \\ -1 \end{pmatrix}$	

Cubic Spline			
Mode	Eigenvalue λ	Eigenvector $\mathbf{U}$	Configuration
1	0	$\begin{pmatrix} 1 \\ 1 \\ 1 \\ 1 \end{pmatrix}$	
2	9.88	$\begin{pmatrix} -1 \\ 1 \\ 1 \\ -1 \end{pmatrix}$	
3	60	$\begin{pmatrix} 0.232 \\ 0.244 \\ -0.244 \\ -0.232 \end{pmatrix}$	
4	170	$\begin{pmatrix} 0.054 \\ -0.149 \\ 0.149 \\ -0.054 \end{pmatrix}$	

Table 3.1
Modes for the single-span quadratic and cubic B-spline dynamic contours.
Frequency ω and damping factor β for each mode increase with the eigenvalue λ. Modes are shown in the B-spline (control-point) basis.

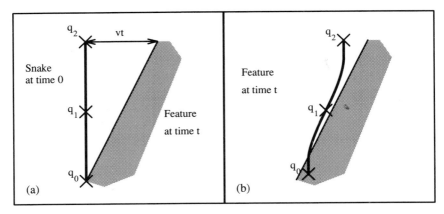

Figure 3.5
Cubic single-span dynamic contour with first derivative coupling, following a feature with rigid rotation. (a) Feature motion. (b) Steady-state distortion during tracking. (Feature search and contour motion here is along horizontal lines.)

3.4   The implicit Euler scheme

The equations of motion must be sampled both spatially and temporally.

3.4.1   Spatial sampling

Spatial sampling of the feature is achieved by measuring $\mathbf{y}_i(s)$ at M sample points $\mathbf{p}_i$ along each span, and approximate:

$$\mathbf{y}_i(s) = \mathbf{p}_{ij}, \text{ if } s_j < s < s_{j+1}.$$

and $\mathbf{Q}_f$ is then, approximately:

$$\mathbf{Q}_f = \mathbf{H}^{-1} \sum_{i=1}^{L} \mathbf{G}_i^{\top} \mathbf{M}_i^{\top} \mathbf{V} \mathbf{p}_i \tag{3.28}$$

where

$$\mathbf{V}_{kj} = \{(s_{j+1})^k - (s_j)^k\}/k.$$

3.4.2   Iterative algorithm

Since a dynamic contour is stiffened by coupling its shape to a template B-spline, its dynamical equations become numerically stiff. As we have seen from the modal analysis there are now three or more different implicit time scales for motion and the time constants cover a wide range. In an Euler scheme, the time step used to discretise the system must be small with respect to the highest frequency component of the expected solution if the result is not to diverge. One way to avoid this instability, but still retain the speed inherent in the simple Euler scheme, is to use implicit differencing. Rather than using the gradient at time step n to project to time step $n + 1$, the implicit Euler scheme uses the gradient at time step $n + 1$.

Equation (3.13) may be expressed in the first order form:

$$\dot{\mathbf{Q}}_1 = \mathbf{Q}_2 \tag{3.29}$$
$$\mathbf{H}_0 \dot{\mathbf{Q}}_2 = \mathbf{P} - 2\mathbf{B}\mathbf{Q}_2 - \mathbf{W}\mathbf{Q}_1. \tag{3.30}$$

The implicit differencing equations are:

$$\mathbf{Q}_1^{n+1} = \mathbf{Q}_1^n + h\dot{\mathbf{Q}}_1^{n+1} \tag{3.31}$$
$$\mathbf{Q}_2^{n+1} = \mathbf{Q}_2^n + h\dot{\mathbf{Q}}_2^{n+1}. \tag{3.32}$$

Here h is the discrete time step. Substituting equations (3.29) and (3.30) into the above and rearranging gives the implicit scheme:

$$\mathbf{H}_0 \mathbf{Q}_2^{n+1} = (h^2\mathbf{W} + 2h\mathbf{B} + \mathbf{I})^{-1} \left[\mathbf{H}_0 \mathbf{Q}_2^n - h(\mathbf{W}\mathbf{Q}_1^n - \mathbf{P}^{n+1}) \right] \tag{3.33}$$
$$\mathbf{Q}_1^{n+1} = \mathbf{Q}_1^n + h\mathbf{Q}_2^{n+1}. \tag{3.34}$$

The scheme represented in this set of equations does not exactly solve equation (3.13). As h becomes large compared to the time constants in the matrices $\mathbf{W}$ and $\mathbf{B}$, the implicit steps each include some significant error. However it can be shown that the scheme does still solve an equation of the same form as (3.13), but with different time constants. For example, it can be shown that, in the uncoupled case, the implicit scheme solves exactly an equation of the form:

$$\mathbf{H}_0 \ddot{\mathbf{Q}} = \omega_e^2 (\mathbf{P} - \mathbf{Q}) - 2\beta_e \dot{\mathbf{Q}}. \tag{3.35}$$

The relationship between the exact solution parameters ω_e and β_e, and the parameters ω_0 and β_0 used in the implicit scheme, is governed by:

$$e^{2\beta_e h} = (h\omega_0)^2 + 2h\beta_0 + 1 \tag{3.36}$$
$$\cos(\omega_e h) = \frac{1 + h\beta_0}{\sqrt{(h\omega_0)^2 + 2h\beta_0 + 1}}. \tag{3.37}$$

In the approximation that ω_0, β_0 are not too large, these relations show that the implicit scheme has additional damping and a lower effective natural frequency (ω_e, β_e) than the continuous scheme specified by ω_0, β_0. Thus to solve exactly for a case when damping is very small, it may even be necessary to use a negative damping constant β_0 in the implicit scheme. In general, by inverting the relations above, we can choose the parameters ω_0, β_0 for the implicit scheme which solve exactly the desired dynamics. However, the relations also give the condition for the scheme to be stable. In order that the solution does not diverge, we must have $\beta_e \geq 0$. Substituting this condition into (3.37) gives:

$$(h\omega_0)^2 + 2h\beta_0 \geq 0. \tag{3.38}$$

The solutions for ω_e in (3.37) are periodic. A unique solution for ω_e is obtained by assuming a band-limited signal, as in standard Nyquist sampling theory. This puts a practical limit on the size of ω_e:

$$\omega_e \leq \frac{\pi}{2h}, \tag{3.39}$$

the bound being attained when $\omega_0 = \beta_0$.

The foregoing analysis applies to the transient response of the system but it is incorrect to take β_e, ω_e also to apply for the steady state response. That is because the step and ramp inputs used to elicit steady state response are not band-limited. It can be shown however, that the *continuous* equation for steady state lag in the translational mode (3.20) remains valid for the implicit Euler scheme.

3.5   Parallel implementation

The equations of motion are integrated using an implicit Euler scheme for speed on a network of transputers. The configuration of the network is shown in figure 3.6. The bulk of calculation is involved in the evaluation

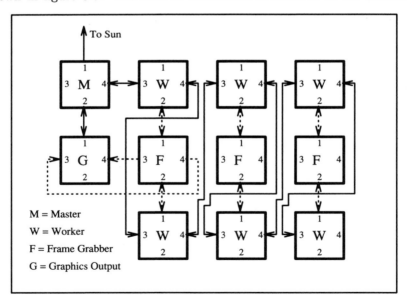

Figure 3.6
The configuration of the network of Transputers. Master controls scheduling; workers update spans.

of the term $\mathbf{Q}_f$. Here each span contributes to a B-spline estimate of the feature position. The steps involved in this estimation, for the ith span, are:

1. Sample the predicted position of the B-spline at a number of points along the span, x_i. The prediction is made based on the contour velocity, which is calculated during the Euler integration, and on the time interval between frames.

2. Allow each point to move along the corresponding spline normal vector to a local maximum of image gradient, p_i.

3. Multiply by the shape matrices for the span.

This analysis of the dynamical equations suggest a natural, span-based parallelization. For the transputer model of concurrency (Hoare, 1985), this translates into a separate *process* for each span. Figure 3.7 shows the processes comprising a four span contour, and indicates how the summation required to calculate Q_f is implemented by two running sums. Contours are

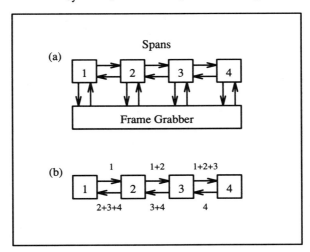

Figure 3.7
(a) A four span dynamic contour. (b) The summation in for Q_f.

allocated to worker transputers a span at a time. Individual spans communicate their contribution to Q_f to the rest of the contour at each Euler step. With six worker transputers, Euler steps can be performed at frame rate (25 Hz). The bandwidth of the transputer links is not sufficient to sustain communication of real-time image data. To overcome this problem, three separate frame grabbers are used, driven from a common video input. The transputer network resides within a standard Unix workstation, accessed via a library of routines written in the C programming language.

3.6 Results

The system will successfully track features whose velocity is such that the lag caused by viscous drag does not exceed the radius of the tracking window. With a tracking window radius of approximately 35 mrad in a field of view of 300 mrad, a sampling period of 1/25 second and $\beta_0 = \omega_0 = 50\text{s}^{-1}$, the theoretical maximum tracking velocity is 0.875 rad/sec for rigid translation. The effective frequency (3.37) is $\omega_e = 1/h$, just at the Nyquist limit. The effective damping constant (3.36) is $\beta_e = 1.1\omega_e$ so that the system is just overdamped. Experimental measurements for our system have given tracking velocities of up to 0.7 rad/sec in this case. The difference is due to transients: the result in (3.20) is for the steady state, but in practise it is difficult to achieve steady state conditions within a limited field of view. This performance can, of course, be further improved by decreasing the damping factor β_e, but at the expense of critical damping. Note that varying the tracking window radius is our mechanism for control of scale. For example, a large window is used during feature capture, getting smaller as the contour locks on.

Figure 3.8 shows the tracking of a small target on a moving remote controlled buggy. The buggy is moving at approximately 20 cm/s, at a distance of up to 0.5m, in a field of view of about 300 mrad. Parameters were set to $\omega_0 = \beta_0 = 50\text{s}^{-1}$ and $\omega_1 = \beta_1 = 10\text{s}^{-1}$. The angular tracking velocity is thus about 0.4 rad/s which is roughly half of the limiting value predicted in equation (3.20).

3.7 Incorporating uncertainty

Uncertainty can incorporated into tracking using a dynamical, stochastic model of feature motion in the form of a continuous Kalman filter (Gelb, 1974). This was done for snakes in chapter 1 and for parametric models in chapter 5. The resulting trackers take a similar form to ones derived via Lagrangian Dynamics, but with non-homogeneous, time-varying coefficients. Our dynamic contours, being B-splines, are a kind of parametric model and hence the Kalman filter model is more akin to the derivation of chapter 5 than that of chapter 1. A great advantage of this view, for dynamic contours, is that it provides a natural mechanism for control of the *scale* for feature-search, via the *range-gate* mechanism (Bar-Shalom & Fortmann, 1988). This is a form of the general notion of a validation gate that will be discussed in chapter 6.

The scale for feature search is derived from the covariance $\mathbf{P}(t)$ of the estimated state of the contour which, in turn, translates to the covariance $\mathbf{C}(s,t)$ of the point $\mathbf{x}(s,t)$ on the contour:

$$\mathbf{C}(s,t) = \mathbf{s}^\top \mathbf{M} \mathbf{P}(t) \mathbf{M}^\top \mathbf{s}. \tag{3.40}$$

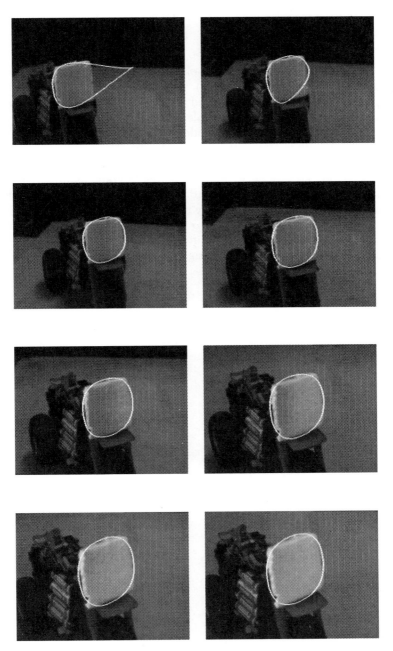

Figure 3.8
A dynamic contour tracking a moving buggy (raster order). It locks onto the front of the buggy, then follows it as it moves. The camera rotates to maintain the contour in the image centre.

Applying a fixed confidence limit of the form

$$\mathbf{x'}^\top \left(\mathbf{C}(s) + \mathbf{R}\right)^{-1} \mathbf{x'} = \text{const},$$

where $\mathbf{R}$ is the covariance of feature point measurements, then determines an elliptical search window around $\mathbf{x}(s)$. Since the dynamic contour searches along a line, search can be restricted to that portion of the line that lies within the ellipse at $\mathbf{x}(s)$. For example, figure 3.9(d) shows a contour where one section lies outside the search window. Position covariance in that region grows in the absence of measurements, enlarging the search window grows therefore, until it catches a feature, at which point it shrinks again. When a feature is "locked", lying within the search window along the length of the snake, covariance will decrease to a steady state. This is because the Kalman gain $\mathbf{K}(t)$ settles to a steady state value (Gelb, 1974). In this way the search window is made shrink to a minimum size during steady-state tracking. The development of this kind of uncertainty-driven controller for spatial scale is currently being investigated.

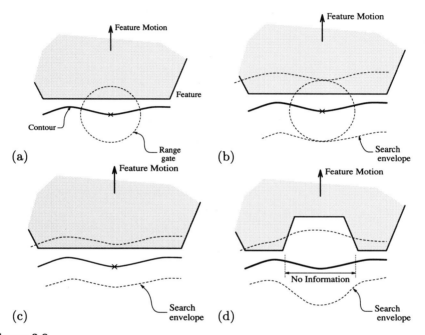

Figure 3.9
Continuous Kalman Filter. The advantage of the Kalman filter is that it provides
a natural mechanism for control of scale in feature-search. This arises from the well-
known *range-gate* mechanism. Where no feature lies inside the search window, positional
covariance increases, causing the search window to enlarge. In (a) a range gate is shown
for a single point on the snake. The range gates for the whole contour combine to form
the search window in (b). Given measurements for all points on the snake, the envelope
contracts over time, reaching a steady state, shown in (c), defined by the noise processes
of measurement and by the inherent system noise. In (d) no information is available about
the middle section of the feature as it has moved outside the search space. The positional
covariance estimates for the middle of the contour then increase, causing the search scale
to expand until the feature is recaptured.

4   Tracking with Rigid Models

Chris Harris

RAPiD (Real-time Attitude and Position Determination) is a model-based three-dimensional tracking algorithm for a known object executing arbitrary motion, and viewed by a standard video-camera. The 3D object model consists of selected control points on high contrast edges, which can be surface markings, folds or profile edges. The use of a Kalman filter permits rapid object motion to be tracked, and produces stable tracking results. The RAPiD tracker runs at video-rate on a standard minicomputer equipped with an image capture board.

4.1   Introduction

Three-dimensional (3D) Model-Based Vision is concerned with finding the occurrence of a known 3D object within an image, and obtaining a measure of the object's location in the image. The existence and location of the object can then be used for tasks such as robotic manipulation, process monitoring, vehicular control, etc. As only certain aspects of the object (such as the geometry of its edges) are utilised, these aspects are said to form a model of the object: it is the occurrence of the model that is sought. A geometric model is attractive to work with, because the strong geometric invariances under perspective projection can provide reliability and computational simplicity. Additionally, the results from a geometric model will be quantitative. The utility of a geometric model will be greatest for rigid objects, and for those that are simply jointed (e.g. a box with a hinged lid) or simply parameterised (e.g. a telescoping tube). The geometry of flexible, malleable and generically described objects is harder to use, but see chapter 5. Non-geometric models, utilising such attributes as colour and texture, may serve to reveal the existence of the object, but not a quantitative measure of its 3D location.

Model-Based Tracking is Model-Based Vision applied to a sequence of video images. It appears initially to be a much more difficult problem than Model-Based Vision, due to the high data-rate in an image sequence (up to 10 Mbyte.s^{-1} at video-rate). However, the continuity between successive images can lead to it being a much easier problem, because the motion of the object can be anticipated with some precision. It can thus be advantageous to process at the maximum rate, which is at field rate (50 Hz) for standard video cameras.

The geometric model features used for tracking must be simple to extract (i.e. computationally cheap) if processing is to proceed at near video-rate. They must also be reliably present in the images. Computationally expensive and unreliable model features, such as closed regions representing surfaces, cannot be afforded. This indicates the use of simple local features such as points (or "corners") and edges. Point features seem generally more difficult to extract cheaply and reliably from images than edges.

Straight edge segments can form good features, as linearity is invariant under perspective projection, and many strong geometric invariances can be used (Rothwell *et al.*, 1991). However, unless specialised image-processing hardware is used, such as the Esprit P940 DMA boards, straight edge extraction over the entire image will be much slower than video-rate. The breaking of edges due to drop-out or clutter, and their incomplete and variable termination at junctions, often mean that only the measurement perpendicular to the edge will provide reliable information. The information obtained along a straight edge may additionally be highly redundant, since a straight edge possessing end-points unreliably located along the edge is fully specified by just two (accurate) points on the edge. The above three considerations (speed, unreliable end-points, and redundancy) lead to point model features located on edges, with each point feature providing only a single measure of perpendicular distance to an edge. Each feature will individually suffer from the aperture problem, but given more (independent) features than degrees of freedom of motion for the object (e.g. six for a rigid body), or else some temporal filtering, a set of edge point features can provide the information needed for Model-Based Tracking. As only the perpendicular distance from the projected model point to the observed image edge is needed, edge detection can be performed very cheaply by looking along a line of pixels perpendicular to the projected model edge. Ideally, the model points should be located on straight edges, but edges of low curvature are also acceptable.

RAPiD uses these points situated on high-contrast object edges, such as surface markings, fold edges (such as edges of a cube), and profile edges (such as the outline of a sphere). These model points are simple to project onto the image, and the corresponding image edges simple to locate by searching the image pixels perpendicularly to the edge direction. The set of measured displacements of these edges are used to refine, or update, the estimate of model pose. Since the estimated model pose must be close to the true model pose for the correct image edges to be associated with the model points, the update equations can be safely linearised. RAPiD is primarily designed for tracking a rigid object with three translational and three rotational degrees of freedom: these comprise the pose of the object in camera coordinates. Alternatively, if the viewed scene is tracked as the camera moves, the pose of the camera is determined.

If the object is moving quickly across the image, the above method of updating the object pose will produce a result that lags behind the true pose. It is advantageous to counter this deficiency by predicting ahead. This predicting ahead is most simply achieved by using a position and velocity tracker, the so-called alpha-beta tracker (Harris & Stennett, 1990), or, with more sophistication, an Extended Kalman Filter (Evans, 1990).

The tracking of rigid and jointed objects has been performed by Lowe (1990) using straight edge segments extracted over the entire image area. This approach is computationally expensive and slow, and has been demonstrated at about 1 Hz using Datacube image-processing hardware. The strength of the approach is that a prior estimate of object pose is not necessary. Another full-image method is that of Bray (1989), who uses the discrepancies of the locations of extracted Canny edgels from the projected model to update the pose, and thus needs a good pose estimate. The approach of Stephens (1989) is closest to RAPiD, his model being control points on high-contrast edges, but determination of the pose change is performed using many iterations of a Hough transform. Stephens' system has been demonstrated in real-time (about 10 Hz) using a small Transputer array.

4.2 Applications

The RAPiD algorithms have been implemented on both a Sparc2 hosting Datacube cards, and a VAX3400 hosting an Imaging Technology FG100 card. The FG100 and Datacube cards merely perform image capture, storage and display, and are not otherwise used for processing. Standard monochrome video imagery is used, either live from a camera, or from video-tape. On the Sparc, processing is undertaken at field rate (50 Hz), while on the VAX only frame rate can be achieved. In uncluttered situations, object tracking can be maintained at object rotation rates of 10 rad s^{-1} and angular accelerations of 100 rad s^{-2}.

Figures 4.1 and 4.2 show RAPiD tracking respectively a model and a real F18 Hornet aircraft. Control points are shown as white dots, and some selected representative edges are shown as black lines. Note that self-obscured control points have been disabled. In the upper right of the image is shown a running display of the aircraft location and attitude.

Figure 4.3 shows the tracking of a primarily cylindrical object, with control points along the profile edge of the cylinder. Tracking of this object is successfully achieved both when it falls under gravity and throughout its impact with the floor.

Video imagery from a forward looking camera mounted in the nose of an unmanned aircraft has been used to determine the aircraft attitude and position for use in automatic landing approach. The model consists of surveyed points on both the runway and the ground. Figure 4.4 shows a view approaching the airfield. Control points are shown as white dots, and the outline of the runway is shown in black. The plan-view glide-path is shown black, with range markings every 1500 feet. The white box-like structure shows acceptable glide-paths, through which the plane is flying. The trajectory recovered by RAPiD is accurate to 0·5%, the errors principally arising from inaccuracies in the location of control points, and on occasion their insufficiency in the imagery.

Figure 4.1
Tracking of a model Hornet aircraft.

Figure 4.2
Tracking of a real F18 Hornet aircraft.

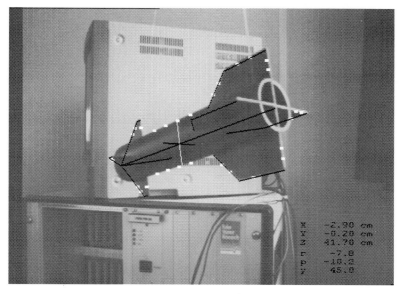

Figure 4.3
Tracking of a primarily cylindrical object.

Figure 4.4
A view approaching the airfield.

4.3 Algorithm

Define the (Cartesian) camera coordinate system, which has its origin at the camera pin-hole, Z-axis aligned along the optical axis of the camera, and X and Y axes aligned along the horizontal (rightward) and vertical (downward) image axes respectively, as shown in Figure 4.5. Imaging of points in 3D

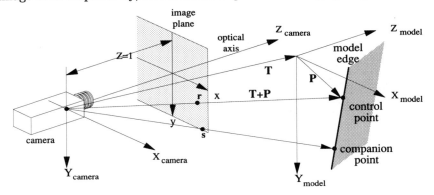

Figure 4.5
Camera and model coordinate systems.

will be handled by the introduction of a conceptual image-plane situated at unit distance in front of the camera pin-hole. The conversion to these coordinates from pixels is facilitated by the use of the geometric calibration of the camera, and henceforth all image locations will be expressed in these conceptual image-plane units, and not in pixels. A point at position $\mathbf{R} = (X, Y, Z)^\top$ in camera coordinates will project to image position $\mathbf{r} = (x, y)^\top = (X/Z, Y/Z)^\top$.

Define a model coordinate system, with origin located at $\mathbf{T}$ in camera coordinates, and with axes aligned with the camera coordinate system. Consider a control point on the model located at $\mathbf{P}$ in model coordinates, and situated on a prominent 3D edge. This control point will project onto the image at $\mathbf{r} = (T_x + P_x, T_y + P_y)^\top / (T_z + P_z)$. Let the tangent to the 3D edge on which the control point is located be called the control edge. The orientation control edge is defined by specifying a companion control point to $\mathbf{P}$, often located on the same physical edge, and projecting onto the image at $\mathbf{s}$. By considering the image displacement between $\mathbf{r}$ and $\mathbf{s}$, the expected orientation of the control edge on the image can be determined. Let this be an angle α from the image x-axis, so that

$$\cos\alpha = \frac{s_x - r_x}{|\mathbf{s} - \mathbf{r}|} \quad \text{and} \quad \sin\alpha = \frac{s_y - r_y}{|\mathbf{s} - \mathbf{r}|}. \tag{4.1}$$

We wish to find the perpendicular distance of $\mathbf{r}$ from the appropriate image edge. Assuming that the orientations of the image edge and the control edge are nearly the same, a one-dimensional search for the image edge can be conducted by looking perpendicularly to the expected control edge from **r**. However, to search perpendicular for the edge in the image to the edge at the control point would require finding the image intensity at non-pixel positions. To avoid this inconvenience and computational cost, the image edge is searched for in one of four directions: horizontally, vertically, or diagonally (that is, by simultaneous unit pixel displacements in both the horizontal and vertical directions). If the pixels are square, the diagonal direction will be at 45 degrees, but with different image aspect ratios, other angles will be traversed. The direction which is closest to being perpendicular to the control edge is chosen, and a row of pixel values centred on **r**, the projection of the control point, is read from the image.

Write the orientation of the row of pixels from the x-axis on the image-plane as the angle β, as shown in Figure 4.6. On the image-plane, let the

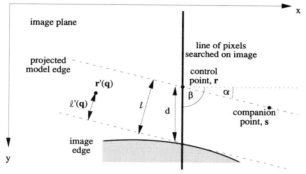

Figure 4.6
The perpendicular distance, ℓ, of a control point from its image edge.

dimensions of a pixel be k_x and k_y in the x and y directions respectively (thus k_x is the reciprocal of the focal length in pixels). Hence the orientation of the diagonal directions of the row of pixels will be $\beta = \pm\beta^*$, where $\tan\beta^* = k_y/k_x$. Let the image edge be encountered at a displacement from the control point **r** of n_x pixels in the x-direction and n_y pixels in the y-direction (for diagonal directions, $n_x = \pm n_y$, otherwise either n_x or n_y will be zero). Then the image-plane distance of **r** from the image edge along the row of pixels will be

$$d = \sqrt{n_x^2 k_x^2 + n_y^2 k_y^2} \tag{4.2}$$

and the perpendicular distance to the edge will be

$$\ell = d\sin(\beta - \alpha). \tag{4.3}$$

Let n be the number of pixel steps (horizontal, vertical or diagonal) traversed along the row of pixels before the edge is encountered. For the four permissible orientations of the row of pixels, the above equation for ℓ is explicitly:

Horizontal $(\beta = 0°)$	$\ell = -nk_x \sin \alpha$
Vertical $(\beta = 90°)$	$\ell = nk_y \cos \alpha$
Upward diagonal $(\beta = \beta^*)$	$\ell = n(k_y \cos \alpha - k_x \sin \alpha)$
Downward diagonal $(\beta = -\beta^*)$	$\ell = n(k_y \cos \alpha + k_x \sin \alpha)$.

Each control point will result in a measured perpendicular distance, ℓ, as illustrated in Figure 4.7. The set of these perpendicular distances will be

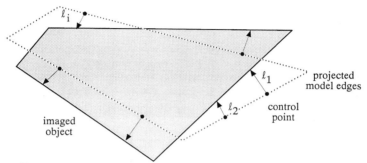

Figure 4.7
The set of perpendicular distances, $\{\ell_i\}$, used to estimate the model pose.

used to find the small change in the object pose that should minimise the perpendicular distances on the next frame processed.

Consider rotating the model about the model origin by a small angle $\boldsymbol{\theta}$, and translating it by a small distance $\boldsymbol{\Delta}$. Write these two small displacements as the "six-vector", $\mathbf{q}$. This will move the model point $\mathbf{P}$, located in model coordinates at $\mathbf{R} = \mathbf{P} + \mathbf{T}$, to $\mathbf{R}'$ in camera coordinates:

$$
\begin{aligned}
\mathbf{R}'(\mathbf{q}) &= (X', Y', Z')^\top \\
&= \mathbf{T} + \boldsymbol{\Delta} + \mathbf{P} + \boldsymbol{\theta} \times \mathbf{P} \\
&= \begin{pmatrix} T_x + \Delta_x + P_x + \theta_y P_z - \theta_z P_y \\ T_y + \Delta_y + P_y + \theta_z P_x - \theta_x P_z \\ T_z + \Delta_z + P_z + \theta_x P_y - \theta_y P_x \end{pmatrix} .
\end{aligned} \tag{4.4}
$$

This will project onto the image at

$$
\mathbf{r}'(\mathbf{q}) = (x', y')^\top = (X'/Z', Y'/Z')^\top . \tag{4.5}
$$

Expanding in small $\boldsymbol{\Delta}$ and $\boldsymbol{\theta}$, and retaining terms up to first order, gives

$$
x' = x + \frac{\Delta_x + \theta_y P_z - \theta_z P_y - x(\Delta_z + \theta_x P_y - \theta_y P_x)}{T_z + P_z} \tag{4.6}
$$

$$
y' = y + \frac{\Delta_y + \theta_z P_x - \theta_x P_z - y(\Delta_z + \theta_x P_y - \theta_y P_x)}{T_z + P_z} . \tag{4.7}
$$

Thus $\mathbf{r}'(\mathbf{q})$ can be written

$$
\mathbf{r}'(\mathbf{q}) = \mathbf{r} + (\mathbf{q} \cdot \mathbf{a}, \mathbf{q} \cdot \mathbf{b})^\top \tag{4.8}
$$

where

$$\mathbf{a} = (-xP_y, xP_x + P_z, -P_y, 1, 0, -x)^\top / (T_z + P_z) \tag{4.9}$$
$$\mathbf{b} = (-yP_y - P_z, yP_x, P_x, 0, 1, -y)^\top / (T_z + P_z). \tag{4.10}$$

Hence the perpendicular distance of the image edge from the control point is

$$\ell'(\mathbf{q}) = \ell + \mathbf{q} \cdot \mathbf{a} \sin \alpha - \mathbf{q} \cdot \mathbf{b} \cos \alpha$$
$$= \ell + \mathbf{q} \cdot \mathbf{c} \tag{4.11}$$

where $\mathbf{c} = \mathbf{a} \sin \alpha - \mathbf{b} \cos \alpha$, and ℓ is the measured distance to the edge.

Consider now not just one control point, but N control points, labelled $i = 1..N$. The perpendicular distance of the ith control point to its image edge is

$$\ell_i'(\mathbf{q}) = \ell_i + \mathbf{q} \cdot \mathbf{c}_i. \tag{4.12}$$

We would like to find the small change of pose, $\mathbf{q}$, that aligns the model edges precisely with the observed image edges, that is to make all $\ell_i'(\mathbf{q})$ zero. If the number of control points, N, is greater than 6, then this is not in general mathematically possible as the system is overdetermined. Instead, we choose to minimise an objective function, E, the sum of squares of the perpendicular distances:

$$E(\mathbf{q}) = \sum_{i=1}^{N} (\ell_i + \mathbf{q} \cdot \mathbf{c}_i)^2. \tag{4.13}$$

By setting to zero the differentials of E with respect to $\mathbf{q}$, the following equations are obtained

$$\sum_{i=1}^{N} \mathbf{c}_i \mathbf{c}_i^\top \mathbf{q} = -\sum_{i=1}^{N} \ell_i \mathbf{c}_i. \tag{4.14}$$

This is a set of 6 simultaneous linear equations, and so can be solved using standard linear algebra. The pose change, $\mathbf{q} = (\boldsymbol{\theta}, \boldsymbol{\Delta})^\top$, in the model pose specified by the above algorithm must now be applied to the model. Applying the change in model position is straightforward:

$$\mathbf{T} := \mathbf{T} + \boldsymbol{\Delta}. \tag{4.15}$$

The change in object attitude, however, causes some practical difficulties. Conceptually, the positions of the control points on the model should be updated thus

$$\mathbf{P}_i := \mathbf{P}_i + \boldsymbol{\theta} \times \mathbf{P}_i. \tag{4.16}$$

However, after numerous (thousands of) cycles of the algorithm, finite numerical precision and the approximation to rotation represented by the above equation, results in the control points no longer being correctly positioned with respect to each other, and thus the model distorts. To overcome this problem, the attitude of the model is represented by the rotation vector ϕ (a 3-vector whose direction is the axis of rotation and whose magnitude is the angle of rotation about this axis), which rotates the model from its reference attitude, in which the model has its axes aligned with the camera coordinate axes. From the rotation vector ϕ can be constructed the orthonormal rotation matrix $\mathbf{A}(\phi)$, which appropriately rotates any vector to which it is applied. Conceptually, the rotation matrix, $\mathbf{A}(\phi)$, should be updated by the model attitude change, θ, thus

$$\mathbf{A}(\phi) := \mathbf{A}(\theta)\mathbf{A}(\phi) \tag{4.17}$$

but doing this, the orthonormality of the rotation matrix may be lost in time due to rounding errors, since, even allowing for the symmetry of the rotation matrix, it is still redundantly specified. Instead, the rotation vector, ϕ, is updated directly by use of quaternions (Horn, 1986). If $\mathbf{A}(\phi)$ is the rotation matrix after the rotation vector has been updated, and the ith model point is located in some reference coordinates at $\mathbf{P}_i^{\text{ref}}$, then the position of this point in model coordinates at the beginning of the next cycle will be

$$\mathbf{P}_i = \mathbf{A}(\phi)\mathbf{P}_i^{\text{ref}}. \tag{4.18}$$

4.4   Kalman filter

It is, in principle, possible to use the pose estimate, calculated by processing one video frame, as the initial estimate of the object's pose in the next video frame. This approach to tracking a moving object has the disadvantage that the object's motion would be limited to small movements between frames since RAPiD searches for model edges in a limited region about the predicted position. This problem can be overcome by using a simple predictor, such as an $\alpha\beta$ tracker which also has the advantage of performing a temporal smoothing of pose estimates, to reduce measurement noise. In practice however, it has been found difficult to set the tracker parameters as the measurement noise depends on the number and position of edges found, and also on the current pose of the object. In some extreme cases, the edges detected in a particular frame may not define all the object's degrees of freedom; clearly a more sophisticated predictor/filter is required.

This paper describes the use of a Kalman filter (Kalman, 1960) for pose prediction and filtering. The next section outlines the formulation of a Kalman filter and the following sections describe how the required models are constructed for use in filtering pose estimates. Finally, we demonstrate the technique by applying RAPiD to a video sequence recorded in an unmanned aircraft during landing.

4.4.1   Kalman filter notation

The Kalman filter mechanism was reviewed briefly in chapter 1. There, the application was a two-dimensional spatially distributed system. Here the notation is set out for a three-dimensional Kalman filter to smooth out estimates of rigid motion from the algorithm described above.

Let $\hat{\mathbf{x}}_t$ be a vector that represents the estimated state of a system at time t. Given a new measurement, $\mathbf{y}_t$, made at that same instant, the state vector estimate is updated to $\hat{\mathbf{x}}_t'$, given by

$$\hat{\mathbf{x}}_t' = \hat{\mathbf{x}}_t + \mathbf{K}(\mathbf{y}_t - \mathbf{H}\hat{\mathbf{x}}_t), \tag{4.19}$$

where $\mathbf{K}$ is the Kalman gain matrix and $\mathbf{H}$ is a matrix which maps the estimated state to the corresponding expected observation. Between observations it is assumed that the true state of the system evolves according to

$$\mathbf{x}_{t+1} = \mathbf{A}\mathbf{x}_t + \mathbf{e}_t, \tag{4.20}$$

where $\mathbf{e}_t$ is a random variable of zero mean and covariance defined by the matrix $\mathbf{Q}_t$. Thus given $\hat{\mathbf{x}}_t'$, $\hat{\mathbf{x}}_{t+1} = \mathbf{A}\hat{\mathbf{x}}_t'$. If the error in the observation $\mathbf{y}_t$ has zero mean and covariance $\mathbf{R}_t$, and the error in $\mathbf{x}_t$ has zero mean and covariance $\mathbf{P}_t$, then the optimal choice of $\mathbf{K}$ (that which minimises the trace of $\mathbf{P}_t'$, the covariance of $\hat{\mathbf{x}}_t'$) is

$$\mathbf{K} = \mathbf{P}_t \mathbf{H}^\top \left(\mathbf{H}\mathbf{P}_t\mathbf{H}^\top + \mathbf{R}_t\right)^{-1}, \tag{4.21}$$

and

$$\mathbf{P}_t' = \mathbf{P}_t - \mathbf{K}\mathbf{H}\mathbf{P}_t. \tag{4.22}$$

In the time to the next observation, however, confidence in the state vector estimate worsens because of the uncertainty in evolution, thus

$$\mathbf{P}_{t+1} = \mathbf{A}\mathbf{P}_t'\mathbf{A}^\top + \mathbf{Q}_t. \tag{4.23}$$

4.4.2   The object model

In this application of Kalman filtering, the RAPiD pose estimate, $\mathbf{y}_t$, is the 6-vector change in pose found by the minimisation of $E(\mathbf{q})$. In the simplest moving object case we assume uniform motion, so the state vector contains both position and velocity terms. In particular we write,

$$\mathbf{x} = (\mathbf{r}, \boldsymbol{\theta}, \dot{\mathbf{r}}, \dot{\boldsymbol{\theta}})^\top, \tag{4.24}$$

where $\mathbf{r}$ is the object's position 3-vector (relative to the camera), and $\boldsymbol{\theta}$ is a rotation 3-vector defining its orientation

$$\mathbf{A} = \begin{pmatrix} \mathbf{I}_6 & \mathbf{I}_6 \\ \mathbf{0}_6 & \mathbf{I}_6 \end{pmatrix} \tag{4.25}$$

and

$$H = \begin{pmatrix} I_6 & 0_6 \end{pmatrix},\tag{4.26}$$

where I_6 and 0_6 are the 6×6 identity and zero matrices. We assume that the above motion model is accurate apart from a random fluctuation in velocities due to forces acting on the model making it accelerate, so that the state covariance is of the form

$$Q = \begin{pmatrix} 0_6 & 0_6 \\ 0_6 & Q_6 \end{pmatrix}.\tag{4.27}$$

The form of Q_6 will depend on the the dynamics of both the camera and the tracked object, and is discussed in (Evans, 1990).

4.4.3 The measurement model

If the object pose is in error by q, then the probability of getting the set of measurements $\{\ell_i\}$ is

$$P(\{\ell_i\} \mid q) \propto \prod_i \exp\left[-\frac{1}{2\sigma^2}(\ell_i + q \cdot c_i)^2\right]\tag{4.28}$$

where the measurement accuracies are assumed to be uncorrelated and of size σ. Using Bayes' theorem, the probability of the pose being in error by an amount q is

$$\begin{aligned} P(q \mid \{\ell_i\}) &\propto \exp\left[-\sum_i \frac{1}{2\sigma^2}(\ell_i + q \cdot c_i)^2\right] \\ &= \exp\left[-\tfrac{1}{2}(q - q_0)^\top R^{-1}(q - q_0)\right] \end{aligned}\tag{4.29}$$

where q_0 is the best estimate for the pose error, and the state covariance, R, is given by

$$R = \sigma^2 \left(\sum_i c_i c_i^\top\right)^{-1}.\tag{4.30}$$

Unfortunately, when less than 6 control points are detected, the matrix inverse cannot be calculated because of rank deficiency. This is also true in certain situations when the detected control points do not fully define the pose of the object. The formula defining the Kalman filter gain can be rearranged, however, to avoid the need to compute the inverse, thus

$$K = PH^\top R^{-1}(HPH^\top R^{-1} + I)^{-1}.\tag{4.31}$$

With this formulation for K, the filter gain can be calculated robustly for each filter cycle, weighting each measurement according to its expected accuracy.

4.5 Profile edges

The theory presented above is only able to track control points situated on edges which have an objective 3D existence, such as surface markings and folds. We wish to extend the theory to cater for profile edges, as they are often very prominent on images, and objective 3D edges may be deficient. The simplest case to consider is that of a surface of revolution, and fortunately, these are common in man-made objects.

Consider, for example, making use of the two profile edge points **P** and **P′** lying on the surface of revolution, R, as shown in Figure 4.8. These points

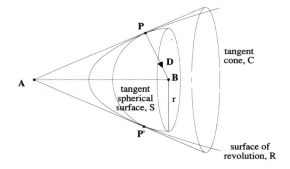

Figure 4.8
Profile edges.

lie on the circle of intersection of a plane that is perpendicular to the axis of revolution. The particular circle we want is specified by constructing a cone, C, and a sphere, S, which are both tangential to the surface of revolution along the circle of intersection. The tangent cone **C** will be coaxial with the surface and will have its apex, **A**, on axis. The tangent sphere S, of radius r, will have its centre point, **B**, on axis. Note that the 3D points **A** and **B** are both affixed to the surface and are independent of the camera location. The 3D vectors **A**, **B** and **P** are all expressed in camera coordinates. Define the vector from **P** to **B** to be **D**, and since **D** is a radius to the tangent sphere it will be of length r:

$$|\mathbf{D}|^2 = r^2. \tag{4.32}$$

The plane passing through the camera origin and points **A** and **P**, will be tangential to the cone, and to both the sphere and the surface of revolution at **P**. Since **D** is normal to the sphere at **P**, it will be perpendicular to the plane and all vectors lying in the plane, so that

$$\mathbf{D}\cdot\mathbf{P} = 0 \quad \text{and} \quad \mathbf{D}\cdot\mathbf{A} = 0. \tag{4.33}$$

Defining $\mathbf{C} = \mathbf{A}\times\mathbf{B}$, the above three equations can be solved for **D**, so allowing **P** to be written in terms of model parameters:

$$\mathbf{P} = \frac{1}{|\mathbf{C}|^2} \left[r^2 \mathbf{A}(\mathbf{A}.\mathbf{B}) + \mathbf{B}(|\mathbf{C}|^2 - r^2|\mathbf{A}|^2) \pm r\mathbf{C}\sqrt{|\mathbf{C}|^2 - r^2|\mathbf{A}|^2} \right]. \qquad (4.34)$$

Consider the 3D line passing through $\mathbf{A}$ and $\mathbf{P}$ which lies on the surface of the cone. To first order, changes in pose of the cone will leave this line lying on the profile edge. Thus by simply using $\mathbf{P}$ as a control point with companion point $\mathbf{A}$, the profile edge at $\mathbf{P}$ can be introduced into the formulation constructed for objective edges.

The above profile edge theory has been further generalised to cater for general conic surfaces (e.g. spheres, ellipsoids and hyperboloids), so permitting a large class of profile edges to be tracked using RAPiD.

4.6   Algorithm enhancements

When the tracked object moves, control points are often self-obscured, for example by rotating around to the back side of the object. Such control points need to be disabled as they become invisible, or else they will pick up on incorrect edges, and interfere with the tracking. To overcome this problem, a quantised "view-potential" table is constructed, each entry in the table corresponding to a different (distant) camera viewpoint with which the camera can view the object. In each table entry is stored whether or not each control point is obscured or visible. The view-potential table is based upon square bins on the faces of a distant cubical box surrounding the object. Assignment of the true/false visibility flags may be either from a CAD model using ray-casting, or else user-controlled as the object is moved.

It is dangerous to use an edge with a weak response for tracking, as it may subsequently incorrectly latch on to a stronger nearby clutter edge. For this reason a control point is automatically disabled when the edge response is small, and re-enabled when it becomes large. A useful attribute of an edge is its polarity, that is, whether it is a dark/light edge or a light/dark edge. The polarity of an edge is usually conserved, and so can act as a useful device to reject incorrect edges, as nearby edges on an image very often have opposite polarities.

4.7   Conclusions

Faced with up to 10 Mbyte of input data every second, the addressing and interpretation of full motion video constitutes an severe computational task for any processing system. If no attempt is made to focus the processing, the task remains beyond the abilities of general purpose mini and personal computers, even assuming a mathematical model of the object under observation.

This paper has presented a method of exploiting local geometric features of rigid models in order to compute object position in 3D and orientation from each field of a standard video stream. The approach uses selected control points on objective and profile edges. A comprehensive series of trials has demonstrated the method to be both robust and fast enough to be implemented at video-rate on general purpose computers.

The use of conventional video for precision non-contact 3D positioning has many practical applications and offers significant advantages of cost and complexity over alternative schemes in both analysis and real-time control tasks.

5 Tracking Nonrigid 3D Objects

Demetri Terzopoulos and Dimitri Metaxas

Tracking rigid and nonrigid objects using deformable models that are based on physical principles is a powerful idea. One outgrowth is the Kalman snake for tracking objects moving in the image plane (see chapters 1 and 3). In this chapter we consider the use of 3D deformable models to track nonrigid objects moving in three-dimensional space. We pay particular attention to an important category of nonrigid objects—articulated objects, such as the human body, which are composed of somewhat nonrigid parts constrained together at joints. The body can produce astonishingly complex motions not only because of the articulate skeleton, but also because of tissue deformations due to muscle actions and gravitational effects. The complexity of motion easily overwhelms the capabilities of purely geometric models and representations, especially when it is necessary to go beyond simple tracking to arrive at detailed estimates of the nonrigidly evolving shape. The challenge of nonrigid motion tracking, estimation, and analysis has prompted research into 3D physics-based models capable of synthesizing the shapes and motions of nonrigid objects and techniques that employ such models are beginning to appear in the literature (Terzopoulos *et al.*, 1988; Pentland & Horowitz, 1991; Metaxas & Terzopoulos, 1991a).

This chapter describes a class of dynamic modeling primitives that can deform locally and globally as they move freely in space (Terzopoulos & Metaxas, 1991). These primitives, which incorporate both the parameterized and free-form modeling paradigms, are suitable for representing natural object parts. Although the primitives are useful for nonrigid motion tracking *per se*, we enhance their capabilities by applying simulated physical constraints between them. These constraints enable us to automatically construct dynamic models of articulated objects with deformable parts. Differential equations of motion derived using Lagrangian dynamics make the models responsive to applied forces derived from visual data, such as images and sparse, noisy 3D observations.

Appealing to nonlinear Kalman filtering theory, we employ these differential equations as the system model of a recursive nonrigid motion estimator (Metaxas & Terzopoulos, 1991a; Metaxas & Terzopoulos, 1991b; Szeliski & Terzopoulos, 1991). A number of Kalman filter applications have appeared in the vision literature (Hallam, 1983; Broida & Chellappa, 1986; Faugeras *et al.*, 1986; Matthies *et al.*, 1989; Pentland & Horowitz, 1991; Schick & Dickmanns, 1991), but they typically employ simple constant velocity or constant acceleration system models, whereas the application described in this chapter employs a sophisticated model of nonrigid dynamics. The estimator synthesizes nonrigid motions using the system model. It expresses the discrepancy between the observations and the estimated model state as generalized forces that formally account for uncertainty in the observations. A Riccati procedure updates a covariance matrix that further transforms the forces due to the current observations in accordance with the system dynamics and the prior observation history.

5.1   Deformable Cylinders and Force-based Tracking

The deformable model approach to estimating the motions of nonrigid 3D objects was introduced in (Terzopoulos *et al.*, 1988). We review the approach as it is relevant to the ensuing development. A deformable cylinder model (a.k.a. symmetry-seeking model) was proposed which takes the form of an elastic tube encircling a deformable spine. Although its elastic generalized spline components make it fully deformable, internal forces coupling the spine and tube weakly constrain the model towards axial symmetry. Internal force and elasticity parameters analogous to the rigidity and tension of a snake afford control over the model's deformability and affinity for symmetry.

Analogous to snakes, the behavior of the model is governed by elastodynamics equations and the model is coupled to visual data through a force field computed from one or more input images; however, the force field computation is not as simple as it is in the case of snakes. The model feels forces by sampling the gradient of a 3D potential function that is defined over the entire ambient space surrounding the model. The potential is nonzero only within the volume defined by the union of the projective cones from assumed viewpoints, through each corresponding image, and outwards into space. The potential derives from processing each image and (implicitly) extruding the result outwards along its expanding projective cone. To create a potential which promotes consistency between a 3D model and the imaged profiles of a 3D object, each image is processed by applying blurring and gradient kernels. The deformable cylinder model samples the potential gradient near its occluding contour; i.e., where its surface normal vector is approximately perpendicular to lines of sight.

Figure 5.1 illustrates force-based object tracking with a deformable cylinder applied to dynamic stereo imagery of a moving finger. The forces position the model in depth and mold it so that its binocular projections conform maximally with the profiles of the finger in both images. The figure shows the initial model reconstructed with the force field obtained from the first stereo frame. As the finger moves in successive frames, the ambient potential changes over time. The model evolves by numerically integrating its differential equations of motion subject to driving forces from the changing potential. The forces induce a traction on the model, pulling it through space while continuously deforming it as necessary to maintain maximal consistency with the evolving image data. Note that the model's shape is updated as it tracks the nonrigidly moving finger and that as the finger tilts backwards in depth, the model follows suit. The force field encourages the model to project consistently into both images of each stereo-pair, thereby determining proper depth.

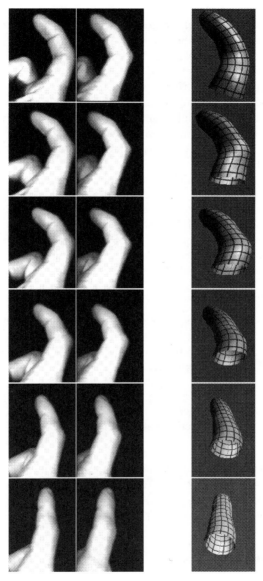

Figure 5.1
Force-based nonrigid motion tracking using a deformable cylinder. Frames from a dynamic
stereo image sequence of an articulating finger are shown (left). From the force field of
the first stereo-pair, the model reconstructs an initial shape estimate for the finger, then
tracks the finger in successive stereo-pairs, updating the shape and motion estimate in
response to the time-varying force field (right).

5.2   Dynamic Models with Global/Local Deformations

The distributed nature of the deformable cylinder model enhances its descriptive power and allows the representation of natural objects with asymmetries and fine detail. However, its generalized spline components do not explicitly provide an abstraction of the shape of an object in terms of a few parameters. That is to say, they do not provide a particularly efficient representation for describing natural parts, say, for the purposes of recognition. Significant effort has gone into the use of parameterized geometric models for this task. Some interesting results have been achieved with superquadric ellipsoids subject to global geometric deformations (Pentland, 1986; Gross & Boult, 1988; Ferrie *et al.*, 1989; Solina & Bajcsy, 1990).

We now present an approach for turning parameterized geometric models and global deformations into physical models that have a dynamic response to forces. We show how to combine these models with dynamic generalized splines to allow local deformations. As a concrete example of the approach, we will review the formulation of *deformable superquadrics*, a family of physics-based modeling primitives with fully dynamic global and local deformations (Terzopoulos & Metaxas, 1991; Metaxas & Terzopoulos, 1991a).

5.2.1   Geometry

We consider models which are closed surfaces in space whose intrinsic (material) coordinates are u = (u, v), defined on a domain Ω. The positions of points on the model relative to an inertial frame of reference Φ in space are given by a vector-valued, time varying function of u:

$$\mathbf{x}(\mathbf{u}, t) = (x_1(\mathbf{u}, t), x_2(\mathbf{u}, t), x_3(\mathbf{u}, t))^\top, \qquad (5.1)$$

where $^\top$ is the transpose operator. We set up a noninertial, model-centered reference frame ϕ, and express these positions as

$$\mathbf{x} = \mathbf{c} + \mathbf{R}\mathbf{p}, \qquad (5.2)$$

where $\mathbf{c}(t)$ is the origin of ϕ at the center of the model and the orientation of ϕ is given by the rotation matrix $\mathbf{R}(t)$. Thus, $\mathbf{p}(\mathbf{u}, t)$ denotes the positions of points on the model relative to the model frame. We further express $\mathbf{p}$ as the sum of a reference shape $\mathbf{s}(\mathbf{u}, t)$ and a displacement function $\mathbf{d}(\mathbf{u}, t)$:

$$\mathbf{p} = \mathbf{s} + \mathbf{d}. \qquad (5.3)$$

Figure 5.2 illustrates the model geometry.

5.2.2   Global Deformations

The ensuing formulation can be carried out for an arbitrary reference shape given as a differentiable parameterized function of u. For concreteness, however, we consider the case of superquadric ellipsoids with tapering and bending deformations (Pentland, 1986; Solina & Bajcsy, 1990).

The parametric equation of a superquadric ellipsoid $\mathbf{e} = (e_1, e_2, e_3)^\top$ is

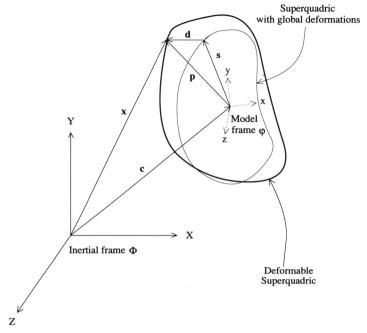

Figure 5.2
Geometry of deformable superquadric.

$$\mathbf{e} = a \begin{pmatrix} a_1 C_u{}^{\epsilon_1} C_v{}^{\epsilon_2} \\ a_2 C_u{}^{\epsilon_1} S_v{}^{\epsilon_2} \\ a_3 S_u{}^{\epsilon_1} \end{pmatrix}, \tag{5.4}$$

where $-\pi/2 \le u \le \pi/2$, $-\pi \le v < \pi$, $S_w{}^{\epsilon} = \text{sgn}(\sin w)|\sin w|^{\epsilon}$, and $C_w{}^{\epsilon} = \text{sgn}(\cos w)|\cos w|^{\epsilon}$ respectively. Here, $a \ge 0$ is a scale parameter, $0 \le a_1, a_2, a_3 \le 1$, are aspect ratio parameters, and $\epsilon_1, \epsilon_2 \ge 0$ are "squareness" parameters.

We combine linear tapering along the z axis and bending along the x axis of the superquadric into a single parameterized deformation $\mathbf{T}$, and express the reference shape as

$$\mathbf{s} = \mathbf{T}(\mathbf{e}) = \begin{pmatrix} \left(\frac{t_1 e_3}{a a_3} + 1\right) e_1 + b_1 \, \cos\left(\frac{e_3 + b_2}{a a_3} \pi b_3\right) \\ \left(\frac{t_2 e_3}{a a_3} + 1\right) e_2 \\ e_3 \end{pmatrix}, \tag{5.5}$$

where $-1 \le t_1, t_2 \le 1$ are the tapering parameters in the x and y axis, respectively, and where b_1 defines the magnitude of the bending and can be positive or negative, $-1 \le b_2 \le 1$ defines the location on the z axis where bending is applied and $0 < b_3 \le 1$ defines the region of influence of bending. Our method of incorporating global deformations is not restricted to only tapering and bending deformations. Any other deformation that can be expressed as a continuous function can be incorporated into our global deformations in a similar way.

We collect the parameters in s into the parameter vector

$$\mathbf{q}_s = (a, a_1, a_2, a_3, \epsilon_1, \epsilon_2, t_1, t_2, b_1, b_2, b_3)^\top. \tag{5.6}$$

5.2.3   Local Deformations

In general, we can express the displacement $\mathbf{d}$ as a linear combination of basis functions $\mathbf{b}_i(\mathbf{u})$

$$\mathbf{d} = \sum_i \text{diag}(\mathbf{b}_i)\mathbf{q}_i, \tag{5.7}$$

where $\text{diag}(\mathbf{b}_i)$ is a diagonal matrix formed from the basis functions while $\mathbf{q}_i$ depend only on time and are known as degrees of freedom or generalized coordinates. Local, finite element basis functions are the natural choice for representing local deformations. In (Terzopoulos & Metaxas, 1991) we employ bilinear quadrilateral elements and linear triangular elements (at the poles) to tessellate the surface of the model. The elements have a node at each of their corners. The generalized coordinates of the finite element basis functions are the nodal variables—a displacement vector $\mathbf{q}_i$ associated with each node i of the model. If we collect the generalized coordinates into a vector of degrees of freedom $\mathbf{q}_d = (\ldots, \mathbf{q}_i, \ldots)^\top$, we can write

$$\mathbf{d} = \mathbf{S}\mathbf{q}_d, \tag{5.8}$$

where $\mathbf{S}$ is the shape matrix whose entries are the finite element basis functions.

5.2.4   Kinematics and dynamics

The velocity of points on the model is given by,

$$\dot{\mathbf{x}} = \dot{\mathbf{c}} + \dot{\mathbf{R}}\mathbf{p} + \mathbf{R}\dot{\mathbf{p}} = \dot{\mathbf{c}} + \mathbf{B}\dot{\boldsymbol{\theta}} + \mathbf{R}\dot{\mathbf{s}} + \mathbf{R}\mathbf{S}\dot{\mathbf{q}}_d, \tag{5.9}$$

where $\boldsymbol{\theta} = (\ldots, \theta_i, \ldots)^\top$ is the vector of rotational coordinates of the model and $\mathbf{B} = [\ldots \partial(\mathbf{R}\mathbf{p})/\partial\theta_i \ldots]$. Furthermore, $\dot{\mathbf{s}} = [\partial\mathbf{s}/\partial\mathbf{q}_s]\dot{\mathbf{q}}_s = \mathbf{J}\dot{\mathbf{q}}_s$, where $\mathbf{J}$ is the Jacobian of the superquadric ellipsoid function. We can therefore write

$$\dot{\mathbf{x}} = [\mathbf{I} \ \mathbf{B} \ \mathbf{R}\mathbf{J} \ \mathbf{R}\mathbf{S}]\dot{\mathbf{q}} = \mathbf{L}\dot{\mathbf{q}}, \tag{5.10}$$

and

$$\mathbf{x} = \mathbf{h}(\mathbf{q}) = \mathbf{c} + \mathbf{R}(\mathbf{s} + \mathbf{d}), \tag{5.11}$$

where $\mathbf{q} = (\mathbf{q}_c^\top, \mathbf{q}_\theta^\top, \mathbf{q}_s^\top, \mathbf{q}_d^\top)^\top$, with $\mathbf{q}_c = \mathbf{c}$ and $\mathbf{q}_\theta = \boldsymbol{\theta}$.

Our goal when fitting the model to visual data is to recover the vector of degrees of freedom $\mathbf{q}$. Our approach carries out the coordinate fitting procedure in a physically-based way—by enabling the data to apply traction forces to the surface of the model. We can make our model dynamic in $\mathbf{q}$ by introducing mass, damping, and a deformation strain energy. Applying Lagrangian dynamics, we obtain equations of motion that take the general form (see Terzopoulos & Metaxas, 1991)

$$\mathbf{M}\ddot{\mathbf{q}} + \mathbf{D}\dot{\mathbf{q}} + \mathbf{K}\mathbf{q} = \mathbf{g}_q + \mathbf{f}_q, \tag{5.12}$$

where $\mathbf{M}$, $\mathbf{D}$, and $\mathbf{K}$ are the mass, damping, and stiffness matrices, respectively, where $\mathbf{g}_q$ are inertial centrifugal and Coriolis forces arising from the dynamic coupling between the local and global degrees of freedom, and where $\mathbf{f}_q(u, t)$ are the generalized external forces associated with the degrees of freedom of the model. The stiffness matrix $\mathbf{K}$ determines the elastic properties of the model. We derive $\mathbf{K}$ from a membrane deformation energy whose two parameters $w_0 \geq 0$ and $w_1 \geq 0$ control the local magnitude and the local variation of the deformation respectively. We discretize the membrane energy using the finite element basis functions in each elemental domain of the model's surface (Terzopoulos & Metaxas, 1991).

For tracking applications in the event of temporary but significant occlusion of the object, the second-order dynamical model (5.12) may be more desirable, since its inertia prolongs motion in the absence of data forces. The model therefore has an improved chance of regaining its lock on the object which is temporarily obscured. When fitting models to static data, however, it makes sense to simplify the motion equations, while preserving useful dynamics, by setting the mass density $\mu(u)$ to zero to obtain the first-order model

$$\mathbf{D}\dot{\mathbf{q}} + \mathbf{K}\mathbf{q} = \mathbf{f}_q, \tag{5.13}$$

which has no inertia and comes to rest as soon as all the forces equilibrate.

5.3   Constrained Nonrigid Motion

We can extend (5.12) and (5.13) to account for the motion of objects consisting of interconnected parts which are constrained not to separate. The augmented equations of motion of such objects take the form

$$\mathbf{M}\ddot{\mathbf{q}} + \mathbf{D}\dot{\mathbf{q}} + \mathbf{K}\mathbf{q} = \mathbf{g}_\mathbf{q} + \mathbf{f}_\mathbf{q} + \mathbf{f}_{\mathbf{g}_c} \tag{5.14}$$

in second order systems and

$$\mathbf{D}\dot{\mathbf{q}} + \mathbf{K}\mathbf{q} = \mathbf{f}_\mathbf{q} + \mathbf{f}_{\mathbf{g}_c} \tag{5.15}$$

in first order systems, where $\mathbf{q}$ is the vector of each objects' generalized coordinates or degrees of freedom while $\mathbf{f_q}$, $\mathbf{f_{g_c}}$ and $\mathbf{g_q}$ are the vectors of the applied generalized external, constraint and inertial forces respectively.

Shabana (1989) formulates the equations of motion of objects consisting of interconnected rigid and deformable parts. He augments the equations of motion of each part with a set of nonlinear algebraic equations to account for the holonomic constraints among the parts. We can write these nonlinear algebraic equations in a compact vector form as

$$\mathbf{C}(\overline{\mathbf{q}}, t) = \mathbf{0}, \tag{5.16}$$

where $\mathbf{C} = [\mathbf{C}_1^\top, \mathbf{C}_2^\top, \ldots, \mathbf{C}_k^\top]^\top$ is the vector of k linearly independent constraint equations for the n parts of the object and $\overline{\mathbf{q}} = (\mathbf{q}_1^\top, \mathbf{q}_2^\top, \ldots, \mathbf{q}_n^\top)^\top$ is the total vector of all of the parts' generalized coordinates or degrees of freedom. Combining (5.12) and (5.16), we arrive at the system of differential algebraic equations

$$\begin{aligned} \mathbf{M}_i\ddot{\mathbf{q}}_i + \mathbf{D}_i\dot{\mathbf{q}}_i + \mathbf{K}_i\mathbf{q}_i &= \mathbf{g}_{q_i} + \mathbf{f}_{q_i}, \qquad i = 1, 2, \ldots, n \\ \mathbf{C}(\overline{\mathbf{q}}, t) &= \mathbf{0}. \end{aligned} \tag{5.17}$$

The system (5.17) may be solved using the method of Lagrange multipliers:

$$\begin{aligned} \mathbf{M}_i\ddot{\mathbf{q}}_i + \mathbf{D}_i\dot{\mathbf{q}}_i + \mathbf{K}_i\mathbf{q}_i &= \mathbf{g}_{q_i} + \mathbf{f}_{q_i} + \mathbf{C}_{\mathbf{q}_i}^\top\boldsymbol{\lambda}_i, \qquad i = 1, 2, \ldots, n \\ \mathbf{C}(\overline{\mathbf{q}}, t) &= \mathbf{0}, \end{aligned} \tag{5.18}$$

where $\mathbf{C}_{\mathbf{q}_i}^\top$ is the transpose of the derivative of $\mathbf{C}$ with respect to the parameters of part i of the object and $\boldsymbol{\lambda}_i$ is the vector of Lagrange multipliers for part i. The term $\mathbf{C}_{\mathbf{q}_i}^\top\boldsymbol{\lambda}_i$ represents the unknown generalized constraint forces for part i which are introduced into its system of equations as a result of the constraints. Given initial conditions $\overline{\mathbf{q}}(0)$ and $\dot{\overline{\mathbf{q}}}(0)$ that satisfy $\mathbf{C}(\overline{\mathbf{q}}(0), 0) = \mathbf{0}$ and $\dot{\mathbf{C}}(\overline{\mathbf{q}}(0), \dot{\overline{\mathbf{q}}}(0), 0) = \mathbf{0}$, equations (5.18) can be solved, in principle, for $\ddot{\overline{\mathbf{q}}}$ and $\boldsymbol{\lambda} = (\boldsymbol{\lambda}_1^\top, \ldots, \boldsymbol{\lambda}_n^\top)^\top$.

There are two practical problems with (5.18) in vision applications. The first is that the constraints must be satisfied initially; however, the available data may not allow us to determine the exact location of an object's part. Secondly the numerical solution of (5.18) is problematic because although the constraints may be satisfied at a given time step (i.e., $\mathbf{C}(\overline{\mathbf{q}}, t) = \mathbf{0}$), they may not be satisfied at the next time step ($\mathbf{C}(\overline{\mathbf{q}}, t + \Delta t) \neq \mathbf{0}$).

Baumgarte (1972) proposed a method that remedies the above two problems by applying linear feedback control to stabilize the constraint equations in the sense of Ljapunov. Equation (5.16) is replaced in (5.18) by a damped second-order differential equation in $\mathbf{C}(\overline{\mathbf{q}}, t)$:

$$\ddot{\mathbf{C}} + 2a\dot{\mathbf{C}} + b^2\mathbf{C} = \mathbf{0}, \tag{5.19}$$

where a and b are stabilization factors. Fast stabilization suggests critical damping of $\mathbf{C}(\overline{\mathbf{q}}, t)$. We choose $a = b$ so that the differential equation has a solution of the nonoscillatory form $\mathbf{C}(\overline{\mathbf{q}}, 0)e^{-ta}$ with the quickest asymptotic decay to constraint satisfaction $\mathbf{C} = \mathbf{0}$ for fixed a, regardless of the initial value of $\mathbf{C}$. A potential problem with the constraint stabilization method is that it introduces additional eigenfrequencies into the dynamical system. Setting a in an attempt to achieve too rapid a constraint satisfaction rate can result in numerically stiff equations and instability.

In (Metaxas & Terzopoulos, 1991a) we solve for the unknown constraint forces for the case of point-to-point constraints using a method that involves the solution of a linear system whose size is of the order of the number of constraints, which usually is small. Thus we avoid the use of the potentially expensive Lagrange multiplier method. The Lagrange method is more general, however.

5.4 Force-based Tracking

In (Terzopoulos & Metaxas, 1991) we developed a tracking scheme which applies forces to the model that enable it to track dynamic data. Using (5.11), we can relate time varying measurements $\mathbf{z}(t)$ to the model's state vector $\mathbf{q}(t)$ as follows:

$$\mathbf{z} = \mathbf{h}(\mathbf{q}) + \mathbf{v}, \tag{5.20}$$

where $\mathbf{v}(t)$ represents uncorrelated measurement errors as a zero mean white noise process with known covariance $\mathbf{V}(t)$, i.e., $\mathbf{v}(t) \sim \mathbf{N}(\mathbf{0}, \mathbf{V}(t))$.

In the case of a first order system, we estimate the time derivative of the parameter vector $\mathbf{q}$ using (5.15)

$$\dot{\mathbf{q}} = -\mathbf{D}^{-1}\mathbf{K}\hat{\mathbf{q}} + \mathbf{D}^{-1}(\mathbf{f}_q + \mathbf{f}_{g_c}), \tag{5.21}$$

where (from (5.10), (5.11), (5.20); see also (Terzopoulos & Metaxas, 1991))

$$\mathbf{f}_q = \mathbf{H}^{\top}\mathbf{V}^{-1}(\mathbf{z} - \mathbf{h}(\hat{\mathbf{q}})), \tag{5.22}$$

$$\mathbf{H} = \left.\frac{\partial \mathbf{h}(\mathbf{q})}{\partial \mathbf{q}}\right|_{\mathbf{q}=\hat{\mathbf{q}}} = \mathbf{L}|_{\mathbf{q}=\hat{\mathbf{q}}}. \tag{5.23}$$

Matrix $\mathbf{H}$ maps 3-space forces $(\mathbf{z} - \mathbf{h}(\hat{\mathbf{q}}))$ scaled by $\mathbf{V}^{-1}$, to q-space generalized forces $\mathbf{f}_q$. If the data are very noisy, the entries of $\mathbf{V}$ have large values, yielding small generalized forces and changes in $\mathbf{q}$. If the data are accurate, $\mathbf{V}$ will have small entries and the generalized forces will be large.

We also decouple the equations by assuming that $\mathbf{D}$ is diagonal and constant over time. For fast interactive response, we employ a first-order Euler method to integrate (5.21). The Euler procedure updates the degrees of freedom $\mathbf{q}$ of the model at time $t + \Delta t$ according to the formula

$$q^{(t+\Delta t)} = q^{(t)} + \Delta t\, D^{-1} \left(f_q^{(t)} + f_{g_c}^{(t)} - Kq^{(t)} \right), \tag{5.24}$$

where Δt is the time step size.

For a second-order model we calculate the second derivative of q using (5.14)

$$\ddot{q} = M^{-1}(g_q + f_q + f_{g_c} - Kq - D\dot{q}). \tag{5.25}$$

For efficiency, based on the lumped masses theory, we assume that M is diagonal (see (Terzopoulos & Metaxas, 1991) for its computation) and assuming proportional damping, i.e. $D = \alpha M$ (α is the damping coefficient), we also employ a first order Euler method to integrate (5.25). The Euler procedure updates the degrees of freedom q of the model at time $t + \Delta t$ according to the formulas

$$\begin{aligned}
\ddot{q}^{(t+\Delta t)} &= \ddot{q}^{(t)} + \Delta t\, M^{-1} \left(g_q^{(t)} + f_q^{(t)} + f_{g_c}^{(t)} - Kq^{(t)} - D\dot{q}^{(t)} \right) \\
\dot{q}^{(t+\Delta t)} &= \dot{q}^{(t)} + \Delta t\, \ddot{q}^{(t+\Delta t)} \\
q^{(t+\Delta t)} &= q^{(t)} + \Delta t\, \dot{q}^{(t+\Delta t)},
\end{aligned} \tag{5.26}$$

where Δt is the time step size.

In both of the above cases taking time steps in q is straightforward; however, note that we represent the rotation component q_θ as a quaternion and that we never assemble a finite element stiffness matrix, but compute Kq in an element-by-element fashion for the local deformation degrees of freedom (Terzopoulos & Metaxas, 1991).

The above computation of generalized data forces makes use of current measurements only and does not take into account the history of prior observations and system dynamics. Shortly, we will present a Kalman filter tracker that transforms the data forces one more time before applying them as generalized forces to the model. The transformation is made in accordance with a history dependent measure of the estimation uncertainty.

5.5   Recursive Shape and Motion Estimation

We can employ the differential equations of motion of our deformable models to formulate a sequential estimator for the generalized coordinates u using continuous Kalman filtering concepts (Gelb, 1974). To this end, we rewrite the motion equations in standard first-order dynamical system form

$$\dot{u} = Fu + g, \tag{5.27}$$

where for (5.14)

$$u = \begin{bmatrix} \dot{q} \\ q \end{bmatrix}, \quad F = \begin{bmatrix} -M^{-1}D & -M^{-1}K \\ I & 0 \end{bmatrix}, \tag{5.28}$$

$$g = \begin{bmatrix} M^{-1}(g_q + f_q + f_{g_c}) \\ 0 \end{bmatrix}, \tag{5.29}$$

and for (5.15)

$$\mathbf{u} = \mathbf{q}, \quad \mathbf{F} = -\mathbf{D}^{-1}\mathbf{K}, \quad \mathbf{g} = \mathbf{D}^{-1}(\mathbf{f_q} + \mathbf{f_{g_c}}). \tag{5.30}$$

From (5.11), there exists a known vector function $\mathbf{h}(t)$ which nonlinearly relates some time-varying measurements $\mathbf{z}(t)$ to the model's state vector $\mathbf{u}(t)$. Assume also that vectors $\mathbf{w}(t)$ and $\mathbf{v}(t)$ represent uncorrelated modeling and measurement errors, respectively, as zero mean white noise processes with known covariances, i.e., $\mathbf{w}(t) \sim \mathbf{N}(\mathbf{0}, \mathbf{Q}(t))$ and $\mathbf{v}(t) \sim \mathbf{N}(\mathbf{0}, \mathbf{V}(t))$.[1]

In view of (5.27) and (5.11) the nonlinear Kalman filter equations for our dynamic model take the form

$$\begin{aligned} \dot{\mathbf{u}} &= \mathbf{Fu} + \mathbf{g}_1 + \mathbf{w} \\ \mathbf{z} &= \mathbf{h}(\mathbf{u}) + \mathbf{v}, \end{aligned} \tag{5.31}$$

where for a second order model

$$\mathbf{g}_1 = \begin{bmatrix} \mathbf{M}^{-1}(\mathbf{g_q} + \mathbf{f_{g_c}}) \\ \mathbf{0} \end{bmatrix}, \tag{5.32}$$

and for a first order model

$$\mathbf{g}_1 = \mathbf{D}^{-1}\mathbf{f}_{g_c}. \tag{5.33}$$

The vector $\mathbf{g}_1$ plays the role of deterministic disturbances and it is computed by the constraint algorithm. The state estimation equation for uncorrelated process and measurement noises (i.e., $E[\mathbf{w}(t)\mathbf{v}^\top(\tau)] = 0$) is

$$\dot{\hat{\mathbf{u}}} = \mathbf{F}\hat{\mathbf{u}} + \mathbf{g}_1 + \mathbf{P}\mathbf{H}^\top\mathbf{V}^{-1}(\mathbf{z} - \mathbf{h}(\hat{\mathbf{u}})), \tag{5.34}$$

where $\mathbf{H}$ is computed using (5.23) and the symmetric error covariance matrix $\mathbf{P}(t)$ is the solution of the matrix Riccati equation

$$\dot{\mathbf{P}} = \mathbf{F}\mathbf{P} + \mathbf{P}\mathbf{F}^\top + \mathbf{Q} - \mathbf{P}\mathbf{H}^\top\mathbf{V}^{-1}\mathbf{H}\mathbf{P}. \tag{5.35}$$

This equation can be integrated in various ways; the simplest is to use Euler's method. The term $\mathbf{G}(t) = \mathbf{P}\mathbf{H}^\top\mathbf{V}^{-1}$ is known as the Kalman gain matrix.

Note that the term $\mathbf{P}\mathbf{H}^\top\mathbf{V}^{-1}(\mathbf{z} - \mathbf{h}(\hat{\mathbf{u}}))$ of (5.34) is a generalized force resulting from the instantaneous discrepancy between the measurements $\mathbf{z}$ and the estimated state of the model $\hat{\mathbf{u}}$. This term is equivalent to the external data forces applied to the dynamic models in (Terzopoulos et al., 1988; Terzopoulos & Metaxas, 1991; Metaxas & Terzopoulos, 1991a), which enables them to track dynamic data. However, we employed a unit covariance matrix $\mathbf{P}(t) = \mathbf{I}$.

---

[1] Kalman filtering is optimal for linear system and measurement models, assuming the associated noise processes are Gaussian (Gelb, 1974). The Gaussian noise assumption may not be realistic in many applications. Often in practice, however, all we can economically measure about the characteristics of a noise process is its autocorrelation function; hence, a Gaussian model is the natural and most convenient choice.

The improvement offered by the Kalman filter can be explained intuitively by realizing that the covariance matrix $\mathbf{P}(t)$ is no longer merely a unit matrix, but comprises a time-varying measure of the uncertainty in the estimate $\hat{\mathbf{u}}$ (Gelb, 1974). The measure depends on current and prior observations, system dynamics, and modeling errors. Consequently, the Kalman gain matrix $\mathbf{G}$ becomes "proportional" to the uncertainty in the estimate and "inversely proportional" to the measurement noise. If, on the one hand, measurement noise is large and state estimate errors are small, the term in parentheses in (5.34) is due mainly to noise and only small changes in the state estimates should be made. On the other hand, small measurement noise and large uncertainty in the state estimates suggest that the term contains significant information about errors in the estimates. Therefore, the difference between the actual and the predicted measurement will be used as a basis for strong corrections to the estimates.

5.5.1   Implementation Issues

If we were to use the full Kalman filter equations (5.31) in applying deformable models to real-world motion tracking situations, the cost of computing (5.34) would be high because the size of the error covariance matrix depends on the size of $\mathbf{u}$ which can be large. An important consideration for active vision applications, however, is real-time performance, preferably on general purpose computers. This suggests taking a well-known approach to implementing efficient Kalman filters: suboptimal filter design (Gelb, 1974). There are many ways to simplify the Kalman filter equations, such as decoupling states, deleting states, choosing simplified filter gains, etc. Appropriate simplifications are often based on an understanding of the particular dynamical system used in the Kalman filter equations, and may lead to a significantly reduced computer burden with little reduction in estimation accuracy.

We can simplify the Kalman filter equations (5.31) through state decoupling. This solution is dictated by the decoupled form of the linear dynamic system of differential equations (5.27) that govern the motion of our deformable models. In this system of equations, the computation of the translation, rotation and deformation degrees of freedom is done in parallel. This is achieved by diagonalizing the part of the $\mathbf{P}$ matrix that corresponds to the translation, rotation and global deformation degrees of freedom respectively. The remainder of $\mathbf{P}$ corresponds to the local deformations and has the same form as the stiffness matrix $\mathbf{K}$ (Terzopoulos & Metaxas, 1991); i.e., it is a sparse nondiagonal matrix and its time derivative (5.35) may be computed on a per-element basis. Each symmetric elemental error covariance matrix is a full matrix, since the stiffness matrix of an element is also a full symmetric matrix (Terzopoulos & Metaxas, 1991), i.e., its nodal displacements are interdependent. Therefore, it is never necessary to compute the time derivative of the large part of $\mathbf{P}$ associated with the local deformation parameters

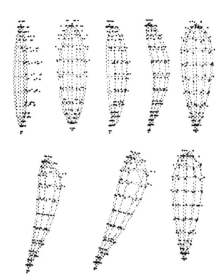

Figure 5.3
Tracking a fully deformable squash shaped object using noisy data (black dots).

(nodal variables) of the deformable model.

5.5.2   Examples

As a demonstration of some of our algorithms, we present two examples of nonrigid tracking and time-varying shape estimation from 3D data. We couple the models to the data through virtual spring forces calculated through exhaustive search for the nearest node of the model to each datapoint. This method is simple and robust, though inefficient for large models compared to the other methods proposed in (Terzopoulos & Metaxas, 1991).

Figure 5.3 shows a nonrigid motion estimation example using 20 frames of 3D datapoints (black dots) which were synthesized by periodically sampling the surface of a dynamic squash-shaped model undergoing both global and local deformations in response to a force applied near its top. To introduce noise, we corrupted the sampled data by perturbing them by ±5% with the sign chosen randomly. Figures 5.3(a) and (b) show two views of the data and the initial ellipsoidal shape which is not at the center of gravity of the data. Figure 5.3(c) shows an intermediate step of the fitting process, driven by data forces from the first frame of the motion sequence. Figures 5.3(d) and (e) show the model fitted to the initial data. Figure 5.3(f) shows an intermediate frame of the model tracking the nonrigid motion of the squash, while Figure 5.3(g) shows the final state of the model with readily apparent local deformations.

Figure 5.4 demonstrates a Kalman filter tracker whose system model consists of five deformable superquadric parts constrained together to model the torso and arms. The tracker is applied to 120 frames of 3D datapoints

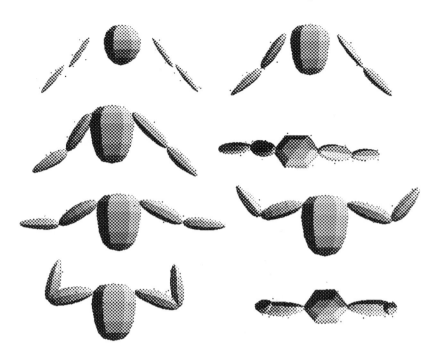

Figure 5.4
Tracking of raising and flexing human arm motion from sparse 3D data (black dots).

acquired by monitoring a person raising and flexing his arms. The data were acquired using WATSMART, a non-contact, three-dimensional motion digitizing and analysis system. It can track as many as 64 individual marker points attached to the subject to be monitored and can produce three dimensional coordinates at a rate ranging between 19–400 Hz. Active infrared light emitting diodes serve as markers and they are independently detected by optoelectric measurement cameras. At least two cameras must see a marker before its three dimensional coordinates can be calculated using a direct linear transformation technique. Our data were collected using 4 cameras and 32 markers at a sampling rate of 50 Hz.

The models were automatically initialized to the center of mass of the relevant data and their initial orientations were computed using the matrix of central moments of the data. The initial size along the longest axis (we did not initialize the model along the other two axes) was set by simply calculating the distance between the furthermost data points along the initial model centered coordinate system (Solina & Bajcsy, 1990). The initial Kalman filter covariance matrix was $\mathbf{P}(0) = \mathbf{I}$, and we used $\mathbf{Q} = 0.1\,\mathbf{I}$ and $\mathbf{V} = 4.0\,\mathbf{I}$. Local deformations were not permitted in this experiment, since the available data were very sparse, i.e., about 6 to 13 points per deformable superquadric part.

Figure 5.4(a) shows a view of the range data and the initial models. Figure 5.4(b) shows an intermediate step of the fitting process driven by data forces from the first frame of the motion sequence, while Figures 5.4(c) and (d) show the models fitted to the initial frame of data. Figures 5.4(e) and (f) show intermediate frames of the models tracking the nonrigid motion of the arms, while Figures 5.4(g) and (h) show two views of the final position of the models.

There are tradeoffs between local and global deformations. Global deformations require relatively few datapoints to abstract the gross shapes of objects. By contrast, local deformations can provide a more accurate approximation to the exact shape of a complex object, but their recovery generally requires more data. The symbiosis of local and global deformations within deformable superquadrics offers the best of both worlds.

5.6   Conclusion

We have presented an approach to tracking nonrigid 3D objects that makes use of dynamic deformable models. The modeling primitives that we have described are able to deform both globally and locally and they may be connected together through hard constraints to create articulated models. The models are governed by mechanical principles, expressed in the form of Lagrangian equations of nonrigid motion. Our approach features a recursive estimation technique, a Kalman filter that employs the Lagrange equations as a system model in order to robustly estimate rotation, translation, and deformation parameters as it tracks sparse, noisy 3D data.

6   Data Association Methods for Tracking Systems

Bobby Rao

Tracking is the problem of estimation of a time-variant metric parameter (the kinematic state of the target[1]) from uncertain observations of the parameter. This problem divides in two equally important parts:

1. Optimal estimation of the state of the target.

2. Data association to link the sensing process to the estimation mechanism.

Optimal state estimation involves deducing the "best possible" (in some predefined sense) estimate of the state from a sequence of measurements. Data association is concerned with ensuring that only the appropriate measurements are considered by the estimator. Whilst it is commonly perceived that a solution to the first part of the problem is the goal of any tracking system design, in reality it is the second part of the problem that carries the key to satisfactory performance of any tracking system.

In this chapter we will highlight the issues which influence the development of data association policies and describe the most commonly used solutions to the problem. It should be noted that although some of these solutions were developed initially within the framework of a Kalman Filtering estimation mechanism, all the data association methods described below are *independent* of the estimation mechanism employed.

6.1   Optimal Estimation of the State

Given a temporal sequence of noisy measurements of the state, all of which are known to have arisen from the target in question, an estimate can be derived in several ways. Linear regression (Curwen *et al.*, 1991), linear recursion (Rao, 1991) and non-linear filtering approaches (Bar-Shalom & Fortmann, 1988) have all been employed with success but the single most popular estimation technique is the recursive linear estimator: the Kalman Filter (figure 6.1). Its applications in visual tracking have been extensively discussed already in chapters 1, 3 and 4; see also chapters 16 and 18.

Among the reasons for the popularity of this technique in tracking systems are the following:

1. The recursive loop structure of the algorithm allows the estimate of the state to be adjusted incrementally with each new set of measurements.

2. The prediction stage forms a link between the current estimate and the next estimate to create a notional "track".

3. Evaluation of the variance of the estimate occurs as part of the loop.

---
[1]The *target* is the artefact that is to be tracked.

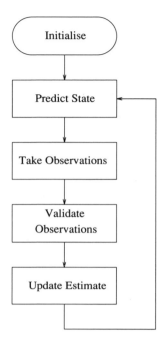

Figure 6.1
The structure of the Kalman filtering algorithm

4.   The estimator is optimal in a Bayesian (minimum variance) sense if all
the state and observation noises are Gaussian, otherwise it is the optimal
linear estimator.

In order that any estimation method can produce an estimate of the state
that is as accurate as possible it is essential that only measurements arising
from the target in question are employed. The process of removing falsely
generated observations is known as *validation* and the process of deciding
which of the validated measurements the estimator should use is known as
data association.

6.2   Observation and Validation

The observation process is affected by two forms of uncertainty: uncertainty
in each measurement due to sensors' inherent inaccuracy, and uncertainty in
the number of measurements produced during each sensing step. Uncertainty
in the observation process due to sensor inaccuracy may be modeled by an
additive noise term $\mathbf{v}(t)$. It is unlikely that a sensor will produce exactly one
observation per sensing step because there is always a chance that several
measurements are taken simultaneously or that the detection process will fail
to detect the target at all. Additional unwanted measurements are known as

clutter. This uncertainty in the number of observations may be represented as follows:

$$\mathbf{z}_\ell(t) = \mathbf{h}(\mathbf{x}, t) + \mathbf{v}(t) \quad \ell = 0, \cdots, a_t \tag{6.1}$$

where $\mathbf{z}_\ell(t)$ is one of the a_t observations taken by the sensor at time t, related to the state $\mathbf{x}$ through some function $\mathbf{h}(\mathbf{x}, t)$. Since some of these observations may be due to clutter it is necessary to check each observation to ensure that unwanted observations are removed. This process is known as validation and should occur before an update can take place. In the Kalman Filter validation can be achieved by comparing a sensor's observations at time t with the observation $\hat{\mathbf{z}}(t \mid \tau)$ predicted from the time of the previous update, τ, and accepting only those which lie within a certain predetermined error bound. The validation test is given by

$$\boldsymbol{\nu}_\ell^\top(t)\mathbf{S}_\ell^{-1}(t)\boldsymbol{\nu}_\ell(t) \le \gamma \tag{6.2}$$

where

$$\boldsymbol{\nu}_\ell(t) = \mathbf{z}_\ell(t) - \hat{\mathbf{z}}(t \mid \tau)$$

is the innovation and $\mathbf{S}(t)$ is the covariance of the innovation. Equation 6.2 is a χ^2 test on the statistical significance that $\mathbf{z}_\ell(t) = \hat{\mathbf{z}}(t \mid \tau)$, but it is often interpreted as defining a "validation region" centred on the state prediction $\hat{\mathbf{x}}(t \mid \tau)$ in observation space since any observations which lie "within" the region are accepted as valid (see Figure 6.2). The power of the significance test (the size of the validation region) is determined by γ and drawn from χ^2 tables once a value for the confidence bounds of significance have been chosen. The confidence bounds are usually chosen empirically.

The observations used to update the filter are then drawn from the set of *validated* measurements, $\{\mathbf{Z}(t)\}$, which is defined as

$$\{\mathbf{Z}(t)\} = \begin{cases} \{\mathbf{z}_\ell(t)\}_{\ell=1}^{b_t} & b_t \ge 1 \\ \emptyset & b_t = 0 \end{cases} \tag{6.3}$$

where $\emptyset$ is the empty set and b_t is the number of observation taken at time t. In the Kalman Filter, if no valid observations ($b_t = 0$) are taken at time step t, the state and variance predictions are used to update the filter. If $b_t > 1$ we require a method to choose the correct measurement from all the validated possibilities. This is the problem of *data association*.

6.3   The Data Association Problem

Data association is concerned with choosing which elements of a set of measurements to use to update a state estimate. In the single target case where a solitary object is being tracked by a single filter, the data association problem reduces to: *which of the b_t validated measurements should be used to*

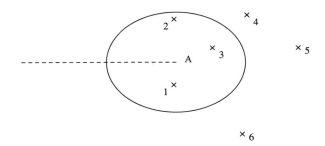

Figure 6.2
The dotted line shows track A's trajectory and the ellipse is the current validation region, centred on the prediction of the target's position. The sensing process has yielded six measurements at this time step, three of which have been validated. Which of the data points $1 - 6$ should be used to update the track A?

update the filter. Since only one target is to be tracked we can regard all data outside the validation region as being due to clutter and discard it.

In the more general multi-target case data association becomes more complicated (see Figure 6.3). Given that there are number of targets to be tracked concurrently, each by a separate filter, the data association problem is: *which of the observed data points should be associated with which track?* This is a relatively simple problem if the tracks are spaced widely apart and the clutter density is low, but becomes non-trivial when the clutter density increases or tracks pass close to each other or cross paths

Also, in the most general case, the number of targets may vary so data points outside filters' validation regions cannot be discarded as noise because they may be due to new targets. We therefore require a reliable method of initiating tracks for new targets and removing tracks for targets thought to have left.

Consider the cases in Figure 6.4. In each case we have two tracks, 1 and 2, whose validation regions are centred on their predictions $\hat{x}_1(.)$ and $\hat{x}_2(.)$ respectively. The observations taken by this node are labelled z. For case A, where the tracks are non-interfering, data association is unambiguous: z_1 to track 1 and z_2 to track 2. In a single target tracking scenario the point z_3, which falls outside all current validation regions, would be discarded as clutter. In a multi-target scenario the data point could well be due to a new target that has just entered the environment or simply be clutter.

In case B where the validation regions overlap we can see how it is possible for an observation to lie within more than one track's validation region at the same time. In situations such as this data association is not so simple, but in a crowded environment this type of data association problem is likely to be encountered. Therefore when a tracking system is faced with several observed data points it must

1.   Associate to each track the "best possible" data point.

2.   Avoid assigning the wrong data points to the wrong tracks, especially

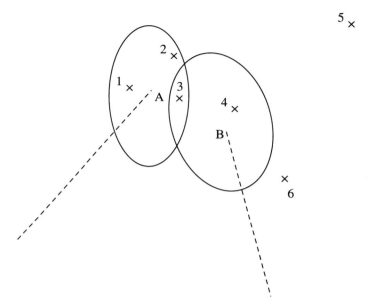

Figure 6.3
An example of potential problems in multi-target data association. Given two tracks
A and B with overlapping validation regions, and observations 1–6, which data points
should be associated with which track? With which track should point 3 be associated?
Are points 5 and 6 due to noise or due to new tracks?

when objects pass close to each other.

3.   Initiate new tracks for data points thought to have arisen from new
objects in the environment.

4.   Discard all the remaining points as clutter.

6.4   Data Association Techniques

There are two approaches to data association

1.   Assume a target generates only *one data point* per observation step
(most commonly used).

2.   Assume a target generates *several data points* per observation step
(model based methods).

We propose to concentrate on the first approach. Within the first approach
there are two classes of data association algorithm: optimal (in a Bayesian
sense) and suboptimal. The optimal approach is known as Multiple Hypothesis Data Association. Of suboptimal approaches, two are popular: Nearest
Neighbour Data Association and All Neighbour Data Association. Most

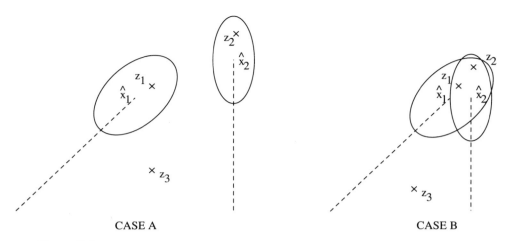

Figure 6.4
Two tracks 1 and 2 with their associated validation regions centred on their predictions $\hat{x}_1$ and $\hat{x}_2$, together with observations $\mathbf{z}$ taken at that time. Case A is simple for a data association algorithm but case B shows how difficulties can arise.

tracking systems employ data association algorithms that are derivatives of these three data association methods.

6.4.1 The Multiple Hypothesis Data Association Algorithm

The data association problem can be solved in manner that is optimal in a Bayesian sense (i.e. the correct points are always assigned to the correct filters) if a multiple hypothesis method is used (Reid, 1979; Bar-Shalom & Fortmann, 1988). In a multiple hypothesis data association algorithm the probabilities of all possible combinations of matches between current observations and previous observations are evaluated at each time step.

A hypothesis tree is "grown" from time step to time step, with each branch representing a particular match combination. The algorithm is optimal in a Bayesian sense because no irreversible (and possibly incorrect) decisions about matching observations to tracks are made. The expectation is that, after a number of time steps, the probabilities of the more likely match combinations grow at the expense of the less likely combinations.

The algorithm is virtually impossible to implement in strict form because the complexity of the hypothesis tree grows exponentially with the number of observation points. However, it is usually found that many branches of the tree have associated probabilities which reduce to nearly zero very quickly and most implementations of the algorithm concentrate on developing efficient pruning mechanisms to remove these branches at each time step (Kurien, 1990; Cox & Leonard, 1991). Further approaches to limiting the growth-rate of the hypothesis tree include considering only validated data points per track and combining all sequences which are identical for the last n steps. These processes render the algorithm suboptimal but the art is to prune the tree such that in practice the overall result remains practically optimal in a Bayesian sense.

The growth of the tree can be curtailed most drastically if, as opposed to evaluating and retaining all possible matches combinations between current and all past observations, only matches between current observations and current tracks are considered. This approach has yielded the two popular data association methods given below.

6.4.2 The Nearest Neighbour Data Association Algorithm

In the nearest neighbour method it is assumed that only one data point can be associated to a track, and in multi-target cases, that a data point can be associated to only one track. The approach is a likelihood method in which the likelihood $\Lambda(\mathbf{z}^\ell)$ of a data point being the correct match for a filter is usually equated to the minimum normalized innovation:

$$\arg\max_\ell \left[\Lambda\{\mathbf{z}_\ell(t)\}\right] = \arg\min_\ell \left[\boldsymbol{\nu}_\ell^\top(t)\mathbf{S}_\ell^{-1}(t)\boldsymbol{\nu}_\ell(t)\right]. \tag{6.4}$$

There are two main problems with the nearest neighbour method.

1.   With some probability, the nearest data point is not always the most appropriate one to use and the result of Equation 6.4 is false. This problem has been addressed in (Fitzgerald, 1990), by employing a more sophisticated statistical approach to calculating match likelihoods.

2.   In multi-target cases where the targets' validation regions intersect the method is order dependent. An illustration of this problem is shown in Figure 6.5. The closest match to both tracks A and B is point 1. If track A is considered first and point 1 associated to it there is no match available for track B. In this case a better matching policy is to match point 2 to track A and point 1 to track B.

The nearest neighbour data association problem can be solved optimally if formulated as a linear programming task in which the aim is to find the particular combination of data points to filters which minimizes some overall function of match-to-track innovations. However with high clutter density this is usually too computationally intensive to be practical and with a low probability of detection several equally likely solutions can be the result.

Despite these drawbacks the nearest neighbour policy remains popular because it is computationally very cheap. Track management is also relatively simple. New tracks may be initiated for data points left unvalidated, and tracks which have not been able to validate data for a predefined number of observation steps may be considered redundant and deleted (Rao, 1991). This data association policy is most effective for single target tracking in low clutter density, or for tracking multiple non-interfering targets in low clutter density.

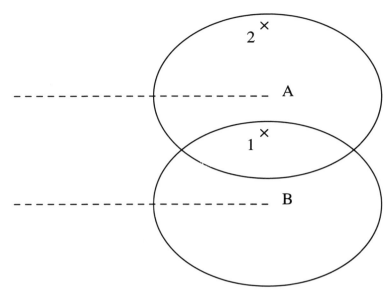

Figure 6.5
The basic nearest neighbour algorithm will associate point 1 to track A leaving track B
without a match. In fact point 2 should be associated to track A and point 1 to B.

6.4.3   All Neighbours Data Association Algorithms

In an all neighbours approach, many data points can be associated with a
track, and in multi-target cases, a data point can be associated with more
than one track. Whilst this removes the problem of order dependency, it is
at the expense of a computationally far more expensive algorithm than in a
nearest neighbour approach. The most well known implementation of this
type data association method is, in the single target case, the Probabilistic
Data Association Filter (PDAF) (Bar-Shalom & Fortmann, 1988), and in the
multi-target case, the Joint Probabilistic Data Association Filter (JPDAF)
(Fortmann *et al.*, 1983).

In the PDAF, the update $\hat{\mathbf{z}}(t)$ used for the filter takes into account all
validated data points[2]. We define

$$\hat{\mathbf{z}}(t) = \sum_{\mathbf{z}_\ell \in \mathbf{Z}(t)} w_\ell(t)\mathbf{z}_\ell(t) \tag{6.5}$$

where the weight $w_\ell(t)$ associated with a point is the probability that the
point ℓ is the correct one to associate with the target. The weights arise
from probabilistic modeling of the observation process and the environment.
Typically it is assumed that noise in the observation process is a Gaussian

---

[2]In fact *all* the observed points should be considered by a filter but those outside the
validation region are considered unlikely to affect $\hat{\mathbf{z}}(t)$ significantly and so are ignored for
computational ease.

additive, and that the spatial occurrence of clutter is drawn from a Poisson distribution and this leads to the following expressions (Bar-Shalom & Fortmann, 1988) for $w_\ell(t)$ and $w_0(t)$ (the probability that none of the observations in $\mathbf{Z}(t)$ is actually due to the target)

$$w_\ell(t) = e_\ell(t)\left[b(t) + \sum_{\mathbf{z}_\ell \in \mathbf{Z}(t)} e_\ell(t)\right]^{-1} \quad \forall \ell \; \mathbf{z}_\ell \in \mathbf{Z}(t) \tag{6.6}$$

$$w_0(t) = b(t)\left[b(t) + \sum_{\mathbf{z}_\ell \in \mathbf{Z}(t)} e_\ell(t)\right]^{-1} \tag{6.7}$$

$$e_\ell(t) \; \stackrel{\triangle}{=} \; (P_G)^{-1}\mathcal{N}[\boldsymbol{\nu}; 0, \mathbf{S}(t)] \tag{6.8}$$

$$b(t) \; \stackrel{\triangle}{=} \; m(t)(1 - P_D P_G)[P_D P_G V(t)]^{-1} \tag{6.9}$$

$$V(t) = g^2 \pi |\mathbf{S}(t)|^{1/2} \tag{6.10}$$

where P_D is the probability of detection of the target, P_G is the probability that the measurement falls within the validation region which, if two dimensional and defined in terms of "number (g) of sigmas", has a volume $V(t)$, and $m(t)$ is the number of elements in set $Z(t)$. The term $\mathcal{N}[.]$ is a zero mean normal probability density function of argument $\boldsymbol{\nu}$ and with a variance $\mathbf{S}(k)$.

In the JPDAF the update $\hat{\mathbf{z}}^i(t)$ for a track i is given by

$$\hat{\mathbf{z}}^i(t) = \sum_{\mathbf{z}_\ell \in \mathbf{Z}(t)} w_\ell^i(t)\mathbf{z}_\ell(t). \tag{6.11}$$

The probabilities, $w_\ell^i(t)$, that observation ℓ has arisen from target i are evaluated *jointly* across all tracks (Bar-Shalom & Fortmann, 1988), but to reduce computation the validation regions of each track are used to evaluate which observation points could, with some significant probability, be due to more than one target. A further simplification is to consider the volume of every track's validation region to be equal to the volume of the entire surveillance region. Therefore, whilst the validation regions help to exclude statistically insignificant joint association possibilities, they have negligible effect on the *evaluation* of the probabilities of joint events.

$$w_\ell^i(t) = c\lambda^\phi \prod_{\mathbf{z}_\ell \in \mathbf{Z}(t)} \left[\mathcal{N}_\ell^i[\mathbf{z}_\ell(t)]\right]^{a_\ell} \prod_{i=1}^N (P_D)^{\delta_i}(1 - P_D)^{1-\delta_i}, \quad \ell = 1, \ldots, b_t \tag{6.12}$$

where

$$\mathcal{N}_\ell^i[\mathbf{z}_\ell(t)] \; \stackrel{\triangle}{=} \; \mathcal{N}[\mathbf{z}_\ell(t); \hat{\mathbf{z}}_\ell^i(t \mid \tau), \mathbf{S}_\ell^i(t)]$$

and c is a normalizing constant, a_ℓ is a binary indicator that is set to one only if observation point ℓ lies within a track's validation region, $\phi = \sum_{i=1}^{b_t}(1 - a_\ell)$, is the total number of false measurements at time t, λ is the spatial density of clutter (i.e. λV should equal ϕ, where V is the volume of the surveillance region), P_D is the probability of detection, N is the number of targets and δ_i is a binary term that is set to one only if any measurements fall within the validation region of track i.

There are several problems with an all neighbours approach:

1.   Since it is assumed that each target generates only one valid datum and all clutter is drawn independently from a statistical (usually Poisson) distribution, any clutter which is correlated with the target will not be recognized as such and will be incorporated via Equation (6.5). Persistent interference such as a shadow or a wake will not be filtered out by the JPDAF whereas a nearest neighbour method would probably ignore it (see Figure 6.6).

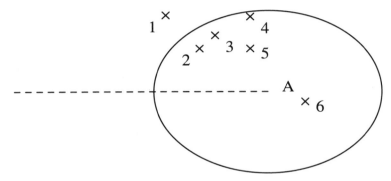

Figure 6.6
In the PDAF all the validated data points will influence the final value of the observation update used, in this case to detrimental effect. Only data point 6 is due to the target of interest. Data points 1–5 are due to its shadow but validated data points 2–5 will bias the update.

2.   The initial PDAF and JPDAF presented in (Fortmann *et al.*, 1983; Bar-Shalom & Fortmann, 1988) have no provision for initiation or removal of tracks. The number of targets is assumed to be fixed and known in order that the weights $w_\ell(t)$ can be evaluated. With the use of multiple model filters it has become possible to incorporate track initiation into the PDAF (Bar-Shalom, 1990) but no such advance has been forthcoming in the JPDAF and it is unclear whether the multiple model approach used in (Bar-Shalom, 1990) is extendable to the multi-target case.

3.   An all neighbours approach is prone to producing coalesced state estimates when validation regions overlap significantly and many data points are shared. This problem is particularly bad when many validation regions are bunched together or when validation regions grow large.

4.   The computation required to evaluate the weights $w_\ell(t)$ is not trivial and in the JPDAF can be expensive. Various "short-cut" approaches to evalua-

tion of these weights have been proposed (Fitzgerald, 1990) but computation is still more intensive than a nearest neighbour approach.

All neighbours approaches are popular because they are free of the hazard of order dependency and in cases that suffer from dense clutter they are able to track interfering targets more reliably than nearest neighbour methods.

6.5 A Vision Based Tracking System

As an illustration of some of the concepts described above we now briefly describe the design of a vision based tracking system[3].

The task is to track targets such as people and mobile robots as they move around a factory assembly room, 10m×10m in size. The sensing system consists of four CCD cameras situated at the four upper corners of the room and Figure 6.7 shows the output of each of the cameras during a typical scene in which a person is traversing the room. Since people and robots may enter and leave the room at will it is evident that the number of targets is neither constant nor predictable.

6.5.1 Data Preprocessing

All targets in the room are "terrestrial" (i.e. they have a point of contact with the floor) and so targets may be tracked according to their (x, y) position on the floor. We define the x and y axes of the coordinate frame using the (perpendicular) walls of the room and one of the corners of the room is chosen as the origin. All of the sensors have their raw observation data preprocessed to conform to this coordinate frame.

Since speed is of the essence, only crude image processing techniques are employed. Each image from each camera is differenced with a reference image of the empty room to reveal "event" pixels. These events are grouped together and then boxes drawn around distinct pixel groups (see Figure 6.8). Knowing the orientation of each camera and assuming that the base of each box is coincident with the floor, the (x, y) coordinates of the centre of the base of each box is used as input to the data association algorithm.

6.5.2 Data Association

Optimal data association can be achieved through implementation of a multiple hypothesis policy but as real-time performance is a prerequisite, this approach is not viable. In this case a computationally cheaper sub-optimal solution is preferable and we have to choose between an all neighbours or nearest neighbour policy. This choice depends crucially on the type of data that the sensing system is likely to provide.

---

[3]This work was the result of a collaboration between Oxford University Robotics Research Group and British Aerospace Sowerby Research Centre, Bristol.

Examination of the data provided by the sensing system reveals that persistent clutter is likely to be encountered when tracking people. Swinging arms and people's heads frequently become "detached" from the main body (as shown in Figure 6.8) resulting in false data points that are correlated with true data.

This fact, combined with the requirement for a data association policy that can support on-line track initiation and removal implies that an all neighbours (JPDAF) approach is inappropriate. Therefore, in this case, the best data association policy is nearest neighbour (Rao, 1991).

6.5.3   Estimation

Finally it remains to choose the estimation mechanism. Note that the choice of estimator is entirely independent of choice of data association policy. For this application a Kalman Filter using a first order model of target dynamics gives sufficiently adequate accuracy and typical output of the tracker is shown in Figure 6.9.

Figure 6.7
Four contemporaneous views of the environment, one from each camera, showing a typical target: a person walking around the room.

Camera no. : 2

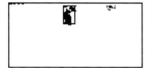

Camera no. : 1

Camera no. : 3

Camera no. : 4

Figure 6.8

An event (the person in the room) has been detected by differencing images from the cameras with their respective reference images. The event points are deghosted and a "four-connected pixels" algorithm produces connected shapes around which a box is drawn. The base of the boxes are projected on to the floor to give (x, y) coordinate data for the tracker. In camera 1 we can see how a person's head can become detached from the body to generate another (unwanted) event. The output from camera 4 shows two large events but only the one in the top right-hand corner corresponds to the person.

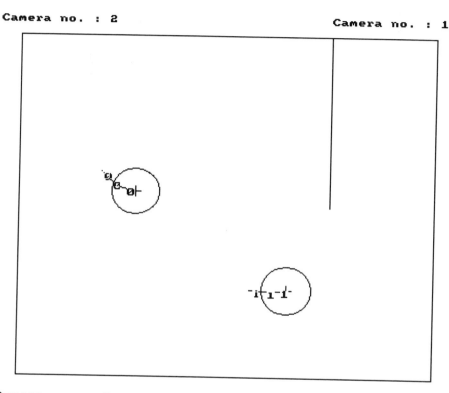

Figure 6.9
The output of the tracking system showing an outline of the room, camera locations and the positions of two targets labeled 0 and 1. The last three positions of the targets are shown for track clarity and the validation regions associated with each track's predictions are depicted as circles. Note the small dots which are the measurement points produced by all cameras. Target 0 is turning a corner so some camera's data points fall outside its validation region.

6.6 Conclusions

In this chapter we have outlined the issues that affect data association policy design. Ultimately the data association mechanism that is employed is determined by the application. However, in general it can be stated that if clutter is very low, or real-time performance is not a priority, and the computational and memory requirements are met, then a multiple hypothesis approach should be used. If clutter is low and targets are not expected to pass close to each other very frequently then a nearest neighbour policy can suffice. In cases of dense clutter or where frequent target interaction is expected, an all neighbours policy is advisable.

Counter-examples to all the above statements can be found and it is unlikely that a standard data association policy will perform exactly as required for any tracking system. The development of the right data association and track management policies is usually a heuristic process based on experimentation using the specific sensing system that will be employed, within the particular environment to be monitored.

7   Color Region Tracking for Vehicle Guidance

Jill D. Crisman

Combining perception with behavior is a central concept of active vision, and is essential to achieve robust, real-time interaction of a robot with a complex, dynamic world. These visual behaviors often do not require accurate reconstruction of the three-dimensional world, which are extremely expensive to compute. In this chapter, we explore a road detection system, SCARF (Supervised Classification Applied to Road Following), which actively tracks the road location in a sequence of color images. SCARF does not accurately reconstruct a three-dimensional road model, yet it still achieves robust continuous motion steering of a mobile robot on roads.

In a navigation system, SCARF identifies the center line of the road in the image. An approximate linear calibration back-projects the center line of the road to a ground plane in front of the vehicle. A pure pursuit path planning algorithm steers the vehicle to a point on the line a fixed distance from the vehicle. Since the motion of the vehicle is approximately known, we can predict the location of SCARF's previously detected road in the next image frame. However, since we sample the scene close in space, we use the previously detected location of the road in the image as a prediction for the next road location. The navigation system would also use a map knowledge-base and possibly other sensors for obstacle detection and landmark recognition.

SCARF is unique among road detection systems in that it detects unstructured roads and intersections without *a priori* shape knowledge. Unstructured roads are especially difficult since these roads have no lane or road edge markings, may have degraded road surfaces with potholes and broken road edges, may not be well cleaned from leaves or snow, may have strong shadows from neighboring trees, and may not be mapped so that *a priori* intersection shapes are unknown. These roads are typical in rural areas.

For each pixel in the image, the likelihood that the pixel belongs to the road surface (Section 7.1) is computed. This process produces a road surface likelihood image which is used by a model matching algorithm (Section 7.2) to select the road or intersection model that best matches the road surface likelihood image. The model is then back-projected to the ground plane and a steering angle is generated for the vehicle (Section 7.3). Results of processing are shown in Section 7.4.

7.1   Road Surface Identification Using Color

The goal of the road surface identification is to determine the likelihood of each individual pixel being part of the road surface. This occurs in three stages: pre-processing, color-model formulation, and classification. The pre-processing stage filters the input image to reduce its size and the noise content. The color model formulation determines a set of Gaussian models for both the road and nonroad colors. The classification step then compares each pixel in the reduced size image with the road and nonroad color models to determine the pixel's likelihood of being part of the road surface, thus forming a road surface likelihood image. These steps will now be described in more detail.

Pre-processing

This module takes the full resolution input color image and produces a low resolution color image. This reduces the amount of data for faster processing of the input image. We want to maintain information about the original colors of the image while eliminating some of the noise inherent in the imaging process. The reduction replaces a block of pixels in the original image with one pixel in the reduced image. There are several methods for using the multiple pixel values in the high resolution image to determine the low resolution pixel value. Sub-sampling, averaging, and median filtering have all been tried in SCARF and all techniques have worked to some extent. We have empirically found that the best results are obtained when the image reduction is done by a combination of sub-sampling and averaging. The original image is sub-sampled, but the average over a smaller neighborhood around the high resolution pixel is used to reduce the effect of noise. This provides a good trade-off between noise reduction and speed, without excessively blurring the input data. We typically reduce 240×256 color images to be 64×64 pixels.

Color-Model Formulation

This module derives several Gaussian color models for both road and nonroad colors. This allows several colors to represent the road surface and several colors to represent nonroad objects. These models are formed by first determining sample sets in the image. Using the pixels from the road and nonroad sample sets, samples are clustered into classes of similarly colored pixels. Then a Gaussian model is fit to each set of road and nonroad sample classes.

To form the Gaussian models, regions of road and nonroad sample pixels are selected in the reduced resolution image. Only pixels lying on the ground plane (i.e. below the horizon) are considering during our region formation. The sample region of road pixels is selected to lie well within the predicted location of the previously detected road. The pixels in this region form a set of road sample pixels $\{x\}_{road}$. The pixels lying well outside the predicted road location are used to form nonroad sample set $\{x\}_{nonroad}$. Selecting pixels that lie away from the predicted road edges provides a margin for error for inaccurate knowledge of vehicle motion and inexact fitting of shape models.

Pixels in the road and nonroad sample sets are separated into subsets or classes having similar colors using a standard nearest mean clustering

method (Duda & Hart, 1973). All sample road region pixels are first arbitrarily assigned to one of the four road color classes, i.e. $\{\omega_r; 0 \leq r \leq 3\}$.
The mean value of each class is then computed. Next, each sample pixel is
re-classified into the class whose mean is closest to the sample pixel value.
The process of computing means and re-classifying is repeated until none of
the pixels change their class. Typically this iteration converges rapidly in
a few steps, so we compute a fixed number of iterations (typically 4). An
identical procedure is performed on the nonroad samples to obtain nonroad
sample sets $\{\omega_n; 4 \leq n \leq 7\}$.

The road and nonroad sample class are then used to compute a Gaussian
color model. Each class is modeled by the mean color $\mathbf{m}_i$ of a sample subset,
a covariance matrix $\mathbf{C}_i$ representing how the individual colors elements are
interrelated, and the number of samples in the class N_i. The models are
computed using standard statistical equations on the sample sets:

$$\mathbf{m}_i = \frac{1}{N_i} \sum_{\mathbf{x} \in \omega_i} \mathbf{x}_i$$

$$\mathbf{C}_i = \frac{1}{N_i} \sum_{\mathbf{x} \in \omega_i} \mathbf{x}_i \mathbf{x}_i^\top - \mathbf{m}_i \mathbf{m}_i^\top. \tag{7.1}$$

Classification

This module takes the reduced color images and the color models and computes the probability that each pixel $\mathbf{x}$ in the image is part of the road
surface based on how well the color of the pixel matches the color model.
Each pixel is assigned the value $p(\text{road} \mid \mathbf{x})$, the probability of road for the
pixel value $\mathbf{x}$.

For each pixel $\mathbf{x} = [R \; G \; B]^\top$ in the reduced color image, we compute
$p(\text{road} \mid \mathbf{x})$ using Bayes Rule:

$$p(\text{road} \mid \mathbf{x}) = \frac{p(\mathbf{x} \mid \text{road})p(\text{road})}{p(\mathbf{x})}, \tag{7.2}$$

where $p(\mathbf{x})$ is calculated by

$$p(\mathbf{x}) = p(\mathbf{x} \mid \text{road})p(\text{road}) + p(\mathbf{x} \mid \text{nonroad})p(\text{nonroad}). \tag{7.3}$$

The *a priori* probabilities $p(\text{road})$ and $p(\text{nonroad})$ are computed as the percentage of samples used to form the road and nonroad color models, respectively. These are effectively the expected area of the road and nonroad
regions. Because of the clustering formation of the classes, the road classes
ω_r are assumed to be nearly disjoint. Therefore the likelihoods $p(\mathbf{x} \mid \text{road})$
and $p(\mathbf{x} \mid \text{nonroad})$ are found as the maximum of each of the road's or
nonroad's color class probabilities:

$$p(\mathbf{x} \mid \text{road}) = \max_{\omega_r}\{p(\mathbf{x} \mid \omega_r)p(\omega_r)\}$$

$$p(\mathbf{x} \mid \text{nonroad}) = \max_{\omega_n}\{p(\mathbf{x} \mid \omega_n p(\omega_n))\} \tag{7.4}$$

where $p(\omega_r)$ is the percentage of road sample pixels used to compute the color model for ω_r and $p(\omega_n)$ is the percentage of nonroad sample pixels used to compute the color model for ω_n. From our statistical color models, we know that

$$p(\mathbf{x} \mid \omega_i) = (2\pi)^{-3/2} |\mathbf{C}_r|^{-1/2} \exp\left\{-\tfrac{1}{2}(\mathbf{x} - \mathbf{m}_i)^\top \mathbf{C}_i^{-1}(\mathbf{x} - \mathbf{m}_i)\right\}. \tag{7.5}$$

We can find the maximum of the above probability functions by computing the maximum of its natural logarithm, which saves the computation of the exponential function for each class. Therefore,

$$\ln\big[p(\mathbf{x} \mid \text{road})\big] = \max_{\omega_r}\left(L_r - \tfrac{1}{2}(\mathbf{x} - \mathbf{m}_r)^\top \mathbf{C}_r^{-1}(\mathbf{x} - \mathbf{m}_r)\right) \tag{7.6}$$

$$\ln\big[p(\mathbf{x} \mid \text{nonroad})\big] = \max_{\omega_n}\left(L_n - \tfrac{1}{2}(\mathbf{x} - \mathbf{m}_n)^\top \mathbf{C}_n^{-1}(\mathbf{x} - \mathbf{m}_n)\right)$$

where $L_i = -\tfrac{1}{2}\ln[(2\pi)^3|\mathbf{C}_i|]$ is a constant that is calculated only once per image for each class.

Using this procedure, we label each pixel $\mathbf{x}$ with the likelihood that it is a road pixel based on how well it matches a multi-class Gaussian model for road and nonroad colors. These pixel values form a road surface likelihood image.

7.2   Road Model Matching

This module selects, from a candidate set of road and intersection interpretations, the one that best matches the road surface likelihood image. This is done using a matched filtering technique (Kastleman, 1979). A binary image (or mask) is created for each candidate road and intersection that models how the candidate interpretation would ideally appear in the image. The candidate whose mask best matches the likelihood image is selected as the interpretation.

The following paragraphs describe the components of this module. We first describe our parameterized the road and intersection model and the assumptions that we make about the shapes of the intersections. Next we present our search strategy that selects possible parameter combinations that will be tested. To test the models, we generate an ideal road surface likelihood image for each possible interpretation. Finally, we describe the candidate matching algorithm which compares the ideal with the current road surface likelihood image and generates a confidence of each interpretation. The candidate with the highest confidence is selected as the interpretation.

Road and Intersection Modeling

The intersection model contains the values $\{B, k_r, k_c, \{\theta_b\}, w, v_r\}$. There are B branches in the intersection which all meet at the common point, or kernel location, (k_r, k_c) in the image. The center lines of the branches are represented by the kernel row and the angle at which the branch leaves the intersection with respect the a vertical line, $\{\theta_b\}$ (one for each adjoining road). A width parameter w is used to describe the constant horizontal road width in the image at the last row b_r of the image, and the v_r parameter specifies a constant vanishing row in the image.

We assume that the roads are straight and lying on a ground plane. This assumption fixes the vertical location of the vanishing point v_r in the image. We also assume that the width of the road w is constant in the image. Although these assumptions limit the number of road possibilities that we model, we have found that by sampling the road frequently these approximations can still identify roads in the image well enough to navigate the robot through hills, valleys, and winding curved roads. These assumptions limit the dimensionality of the model and therefore provide a better match than higher-order models in noisy images.

Search Strategy

An exhaustive search of all road and intersection candidates specified by our model, even with the ground plane and constant width assumptions, is computationally very expensive. Just allowing the system to locate roads and up to four-branch intersections, we would need to test more than k^6 possible interpretations, where k is the number of possible values for each parameter. For example, if we only test the 10 row and column positions around (k_r, k_c), and we search 10 possible angles around the previous intersection location, we would still need to test 10^6 road and intersection possibilities.

To limit the number of candidates, road and intersection candidates are evaluated in a sequence. First the best single road is found in the road surface likelihood image. This search only requires two parameters, k_c and θ_1. We assume that the kernel location is at the horizon row so that $k_r = v_r$ (which is constant) leaving k_c and θ_1 as the only remaining variable parameters of the model. By evaluating these interpretations (described in the following sections), we select the main road with highest confidence ρ_1. If the confidence falls below a threshold T, no main road is found.

If a main road is found, a search begins for an intersection branch that, when added to the main road, forms the best y-shaped or λ-shaped intersection. Since we have already found the main road, we know that the kernel location (k_r, k_c) must lie somewhere on the center line of the main road. Therefore we allow as we allow k_r to vary a unique k_c can be computed. The only remaining variable is the angle of the branch θ_2. The confidence ρ_2 of the best combined main road and branch is compared with the confidence of the single road interpretation ρ_1. If the confidence of the single road is larger, the process exits with a straight road interpretation of the image.

If ρ_2 is larger than ρ_1, the intersection of the center lines of the main road and the main branch determine the kernel location (k_r, k_c) of the intersection in the image. In the branch matching, an interpretation space for all

possible branches extending from the kernel location is computed. The intersection construction then finds the best possible set of branches to form the
intersection interpretation and the confidence ρ of the intersection reported
by the system. Each matching phase of the interpretation generation module evaluates possible intersection interpretations using the same evaluation
procedure.

Using this search procedure, we perform two two-dimensional search problems and a single-dimensional search. Assuming that each parameter is allowed to have k different values, we now need to compare only $2k^2 + k$
possible interpretations.

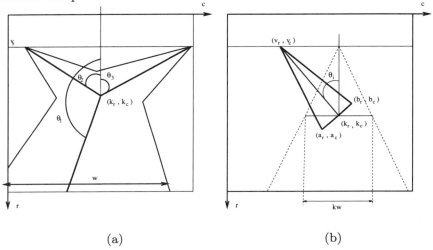

(a)   (b)

Figure 7.1
Intersection modeling. (a) shows the parameters $\{B, k_r, k_c, \{\theta_b\}, w, v_r\}$ of a three branch
intersection. (b) shows the parameters necessary to detect the first main road and the
parameters for identifying a branch extending from this road.

Candidate Generation

The candidate interpretation masks are idealized binary road images containing 1 if the pixel lies on the road surface of the candidate and 0 otherwise.
The masks are the same size as the reduced image, typically we use mask of
size 60×64. This mask is matched against the surface information generated
by SCARF, as described in the next section.

To start the mask generation, the candidate interpretation mask is filled
with 0, then for each branch of the input intersection model, the branch
road edges and a cross-section of the branch are computed. The pixels lying
within the branch road edges and the branch cross-section are then given the
value 1 in the candidate interpretation mask. After all the branches have
been filled, the resulting mask will have a 1 at every pixel location on the
road of the interpretation, otherwise the locations will have the value 0.

The end points (a_r, a_c) and (b_r, b_c) of the cross-section of a branch are given by the following equations:

if $0 \leq \theta_i \leq 180°$

$$a_r = k_r + \beta w_k \sin \theta_i \qquad a_c = k_c - w_k \cos \theta_i$$
$$b_r = k_r - \alpha w_k \sin \theta_i \qquad b_c = k_c + w_k \cos \theta_i$$

otherwise

$$a_r = k_r + \alpha w_k \sin \theta_i \qquad a_c = k_c - w_k \cos \theta_i$$
$$b_r = k_r - \beta w_k \sin \theta_i \qquad b_c = k_c + w_k \cos \theta_i$$

where w_k is the horizontal width of a vertical road at the kernel location and is computed by:

$$w_k = \frac{(k_r - v_r)}{(b_r - v_r)} w. \tag{7.7}$$

The parameters α and β are used to approximate the perspective projection of distances in the image plane. These parameters scale the horizontal width of the road to approximate the vertical road widths in the image. This approximation was chosen since the calibration of many test sequences were unknown. This approximation has been successful at representing intersections in the test sequences as well as intersections on vehicle tests. These scalings are assumed to be constants for every row.

The orientations of the branch road edges are determined by the vanishing point of the center line of the branch. Since all lines parallel to the center line in the ground plane will intersect at the vanishing point (due to perspective projection), the branch edge lines will intersect at the vanishing point. The vanishing point (v_r, v_c) is determined from the branch center line. The branch edges are determined from the vanishing point and the cross-section end points.

Candidate Evaluation

Candidate interpretations are evaluated by comparing the idealized candidates computed in the previous section with the road surface likelihood image. If the candidate interpretation mask is $q(r, c)$ and the likelihood image from the classification is $p(r, c)$, then the correlation value is computed by the equation

$$\lambda = \frac{1}{RC} \sum_{r=1}^{R} \sum_{c=1}^{C} p(r, c) - q(r, c). \tag{7.8}$$

This measures the difference between the candidate interpretation mask and the likelihood image. Since the maximum difference between the images is equal to the number of pixels in the image, and the correlation value is normalized by the number of pixels in the image, a confidence value ρ can be computed from $\rho = 1 - \lambda$. The confidence ρ is a value between 0 and 1.

7.3   Steering Angle Generation

So far we have described how roads and intersections are detected in images. Now we describe how these interpretations translate into steering commands for the vehicle. First the center lines of roads are back-projected onto to a ground plane. Then a pure-pursuit algorithm is applied to track the center line of the road.

Calibration

The ground plane coordinate frame (x, y) is defined with respect to the robot vehicle where x is to the right of the vehicle and y is straight ahead of the vehicle. The image is defined by row and column parameters (r, c). This calibration assumes that the camera is not rolled, therefore every row location in the image maps to a unique y location on the ground. Specifically, only two rows of the image are calibrated, r_1 and r_2. These rows correspond to y_1 and y_2 on the ground plane. Also for these rows in the image, we measure the number of horizontal pixels p_1 and p_2 in the image corresponding to a meter on the ground plane. The column locations, c_1 and c_2 corresponding to $y = 0$ are measured. Therefore, using this model, pixels lying in the two calibrated rows, having position (r_i, c) can be back-projected to the ground plane by $x = (c - c_i)/p_i$ and $y = y_i$. Similarly, positions lying on the calibrated y locations y_1 and y_2 can be projected into the image using $r = r_i$ and $c = xp_i + c_i$.

To back-project a line from the image to the ground plane, the line is intersected with the calibrated row locations in the image to have a two-point description of the line. Then the positions are back-projected as described above. Similarly to project a line from the ground plane to the image, the line is intersected with the calibrated y locations in the ground to have a two point description of the line, and positions are projected as described above.

To back-project an arbitrary point, for example the kernel location of an intersection, from the image to the ground plane, we first define two different lines in the image that pass through the point and intersect with the calibrated row locations. We back-project the two lines and then compute their intersection on the ground plane. Similarly, to project an arbitrary point from the ground plane to the image, we first define two different lines on the ground that pass through the point and intersect with the calibrated y locations. We then project the two lines and then compute their intersection in the image.

This calibration uses a simple linear camera model with some camera position assumptions (i.e., the camera is not rolled with respect to the ground plane). This calibration does not account for lens distortion. However, it is good enough to map the ground plane to the image for our experimental navigation systems that typically run at slow speeds. For faster navigation systems, a more accurate transformation between what is seen in the image and what is represented on the ground plane may be necessary. However, for our current systems, this simple calibration seems sufficient.

Path Planning

Now we have the center lines of the road and branches represented on the ground plane and need to compute a steering angle for the vehicle. We currently assume that the vehicle runs at a constant speed. Our strategy is to servo the vehicle toward the center of the road on which we want to drive. If an intersection is detected, a map based navigation system should select the branch on which the vehicle should travel.

We can intersect the center line of the desired road with line at a fixed y distance in front of the vehicle. Using the x position of the center line of the road at that fixed distance, we compute the rate of turn of the vehicle as

$$\frac{d\tau}{dt} = \gamma x \tag{7.9}$$

where γ is a gain constant related to the vehicle speed. For more details see (Wallace *et al.*, 1985).

7.4 Results

SCARF has been successful at detecting a variety of road in varying conditions. It has been tested extensively on the Navlab, a test vehicle designed and constructed at Carnegie Mellon University. Figure 7.2 shows processing in difficult shadows. The road is located successfully in this and similar sequences and has been used to navigate the Navlab through these conditions. Figure 7.3 shows the results at an unstructured intersection. In the first few frames of the sequence, the intersection branch is selected that actually corresponds to a curving road. If this were only a curving road, SCARF would have stopped selecting a branch as it grew closer to the curve. In this sequence, as the intersection grows closer it is correctly identified and tracked as it moves off the image.

The intersection shown in Figure 7.3 is interesting since the main road has a width of 3.1 meters while the branch has only a width of 1.7 meters. While this intersection violates the assumption that the road must be the same width, SCARF can still detect it. This shows the robustness of the intersection models — even though the models appear limited in their representation, they capture the general shape of the intersection well enough for navigation. In this example, we show only the first branch of the detected intersection. Often we used only the initial branch since this was sufficient to navigate the Navlab through the test site. By not detecting the location of all branches, we saved computation time and could therefore process images faster. Detection of straight roads takes 6 seconds running on a Sun 4. To detect intersections requires 12 seconds on the average. We have run extensive tests on the Navlab over a winding bicycle path, at speeds up to $\frac{1}{2}$m.s^{-1}. This has been done in all seasons, under all types of weather conditions. It has successfully navigated during rainy weather, when the images appear grey and colorless; on the brightest sunny days, when the nearby trees cast extremely dark shadows across the road; and in the fall, when leaves cover the nonroad areas and sparsely cover the road. More extensive results are shown in (Crisman, 1990) Recently, SCARF has been reimplemented on a Masspar machine and can now process 10 frames/second (Thorpe, 1991) — 60 times faster than the Sun4 version.

7.5   Related Work

There are many different single road detection algorithms which do not detect intersections. Many road detection methods (Kenue, 1989; Wallace et al., 1986; Waxman et al., 1987; Liou & Jain, 1986; Tsugawa et al., 1979) use gradient based techniques to find specific structured features of roads such as road edge lines, lane markings, or intact road edges. Gradient methods are typically very sensitive to noise. To overcome the difficulties often associated with edge-based edge tracking, (Dickmanns et al., 1990) (see also chapter 18) and (Kluge & Thorpe, 1988) use explicit shape knowledge to constrain the search for road edges or lane markings. These systems usually have very fast processing speeds and are very well suited for navigation on structured roads, but only a few of these techniques have shown any success on unstructured roads. SCARF does not rely on the explicit shape knowledge that these other systems require.

Other systems identify road surfaces using a histogram and threshold approach (Wallace et al., 1986; Goto et al., 1986; Kuan et al., 1987; Turk et al., 1988). These systems are robust on certain unstructured roads, but can run into difficulty in shadows or degraded road surface conditions. The Shadow Boxing System (Turk et al., 1988) is much more successful at handling shadow conditions, but would experience difficulties if the road surface is degraded or partially covered by leaves.

In Figure 7.4, we show the road surface likelihood image and compare it with other commonly used road features. The top row illustrates the three road scenes. Immediately underneath the road scenes we show the magnitude of the Sobel edge operator to illustrate the gradient information that is available in the image. In the corresponding third row, we show a histogram and threshold result where we hand selected the threshold value to give the best possible results. For this image, the black regions represent the detected road surface. In the final row of the figure is the road surface likelihood image. In these images, the brighter the pixel in the image, the more likely it is to belong on the road surface.

In the highway scene shown in the first column, all features can success-

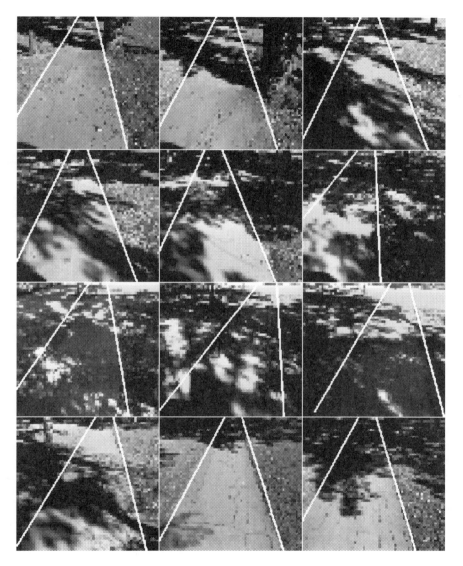

Figure 7.2
Detection of unstructured roads in dark shadows. SCARF can detect road in widely fluctuating illumination. The lines drawn on the image show the location of the detected road.

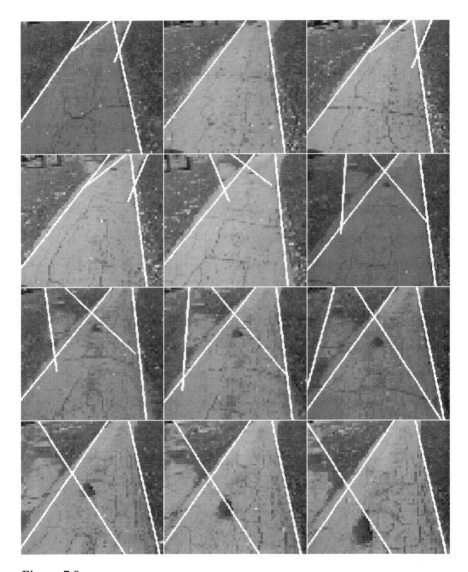

Figure 7.3
Results on a 'y' Shaped Intersection. SCARF detects roads and intersections on a sequence
of images. The lines drawn over the image show the locations of the detected road and
intersection.

fully mark out the road location. In the second column, the features of a degraded road surface speckled with leaves is shown. The road edge location is obscured by the random placement of the leaves. The histogram and threshold approach detects the intact road, misses the degraded road, and has a random response from the leaves. In the final column, the image showing dark shadow conditions, the edge detection has no response to the road edge in the darkest shadows as shown in the the bottom left of the image. The histogram and threshold method easily distinguishes shadow from nonshadow, but cannot distinguish road from nonroad. SCARF detects the road surface. Notice that in the darkest shadow at the bottom left of the image, the intermediate brightness in the image depicts an uncertain probability. These pixels will be weighed less in the matching of the road surface.

We found three other documented road detection systems (Wallace *et al.*, 1986; Kuan *et al.*, 1987; Kushner & Puri, 1987) that could detect intersections when this work was completed in 1990. These three systems rely on clean intersection images and a good prediction of the intersection shape. The intersection predictions often come from a map stored inside the navigation system. SCARF still has an advantage since it does not require this *a priori* shape knowledge.

7.6   Conclusions

This chapter describes the SCARF road and intersection detection system. This system specializes in detecting unstructured roads, the most difficult road following scenario. This is the first road detection system that can detect intersections without map shape and location information. It determines the branch angles strictly by the color data in the input image. It has successfully driven the Navlab mobile robot on numerous occasions, in a variety of weather conditions. The success of this system can be attributed to (1) a likelihood measure associated with classification, (2) an area-based matching technique, (3) the straight road model, and (4) sampling and adjusting the color models of road and nonroad in each image.

The likelihood measure from the classification causes shadowed pixels (whose color matches pretty well with both shadowed road and shadowed nonroad colors) to be weighted less in determining the road location than those pixels having distinctive road or nonroad colors. The area-based matching does not depend on the roads having clean road edges. Also since more data points are used for locating the road, the area-based technique is less sensitive to noise. The straight road models are also less sensitive when matching noisy data since there are fewer parameters to the model. A curved road, if sampled often, can be represented by a piecewise straight road model. Since the color model is adjusted at each step of the processing, it can adjust to changing illumination and current road and nonroad surface appearances.

Figure 7.4
Comparison of SCARF's road surface detection with other commonly used road features.
The top row of this figure shows three road scenes. Under each road scene is 1) edge
extraction (magnitude of a Sobel edge detector), 2) histogram and threshold (hand selected
threshold for optimum results, and 3) the road surface likelihood image.

II Control of Vision Heads

A key goal of active vision is to enable vision systems to investigate, and respond to, the environment. One of the most direct ways of achieving this goal is by building vision heads which can alter their directions of gaze in response to external stimuli. The following three chapters describe systems of this type.

Chapter 8 describes how to use visual feedback to hold the observer's gaze on a object while both the observer and target are moving. Such gaze holding is necessary to stabilize the image, thereby removing motion blur. Two specific mechanisms are investigated: (i) vergence control to fixate a pair of cameras at a moving object thus enabling the system to estimate the depth of the object, and (ii) smooth pursuit to keep the target centered in the retinas of the cameras. In both situations an error criterion is defined and a feedback loop is set up to control the degrees of freedom of the cameras so as to reduce the error.

Chapter 9 motivates the need for vision systems to alter their gaze in order to attend to different parts of their environment, depending on the task being performed. One of the earliest illustrations of this task dependence are the classic experiments of Yarbus (1967) who showed that the pattern of eye movements made by observers viewing a picture were strongly influenced by questions that they had been asked about the picture. Clark and Ferrier use control theory to enable the camera to attend to salient points in the image and to track these points as they move. Their system is influenced by models of the human oculomotor system and uses DC motors to drive the pan, tilt and vergence angles corresponding to the degrees of freedom of the camera. It has an inner control loop, to control vergence, saccade and smooth pursuit, and an outer loop which implements attentional shifts.

Chapter 10 provides an analysis of the design considerations for building head-eye systems. What tasks should the head-eye system perform and what degrees of freedom does it need to perform these tasks? What accelerations and deccelerations are necessary and can the actuators be found to produce them? How can delays in the feedback loops be best dealt with? What types of computer architectures are good for implementing such systems?

Computer heads can be used for many purposes, such as surveillance systems, or as adjuncts to mobile robots. The chapters have been chosen to emphasize their fundamental ingredients; (i) tracking, (ii) attentional shifts, and (iii) design principles.

8 Real-time Smooth Pursuit Tracking

Christopher Brown, David Coombs and John Soong

8.1 Binocular Gaze Holding

Multiple visuomotor controls can cooperate in the task of holding gaze on a moving target. We discuss two such controls, binocular vergence and smooth pursuit, and their cooperative use (Coombs, 1991). We describe a non-visual control for stabilizing gaze against egomotion (Soong & Brown, 1991). The hardware we use has two cameras sharing a common tilt platform but with independent pan controls. However, this independence is not used until Section 8.6: until then the algorithms apply equally to a system with symmetric (perhaps hardware-mediated) vergence.

There is an increasing amount of work on binocular gaze control, and we only mention a few examples here (see also chapter 10) Clark and Ferrier (1988) (see chapter 9) built a gaze control system based on the model described in (Robinson, 1987). The system acquires and tracks white and black blobs using the first few moments and intensity value of each object. Vergence has been used cooperatively with focus and stereopsis for surface reconstruction (Abbott & Ahuja, 1988) and active exploration of the environment (Krotkov, 1989). This work combines stereo, vergence and focus to build precise range maps; vergence enables the systems to "foveate" areas of interest to obtain higher precision and confidence in their range estimates.

8.2 Vergence

This section describes the vergence system. *Vergence* of eyes or cameras that share a common tilt plane results in the optic axes intersecting at some point in the tilt plane. The vergence angle of a binocular system is the angle between the optic axes of its cameras. By analogy with primate visual systems having a central high-resolution fovea, we say a camera foveates a target if the target is at the center of the visual field.

The vergence system can be thought to control the distance from the cameras to the fixation point along some specified gaze direction. The vergence problem can be defined as that of controlling the vergence angle to keep the fixation distance appropriate for the current gaze target. Since the desired vergence angle is directly related to target distance, any sensory cue to depth or depth changes may be useful to the vergence system. In humans, there is a strong link between the accommodation (focussing) and vergence systems. The most obvious direct cue is binocular disparity, but other depth cues (such as motion, texture, and shading) can also be used, as can information about depth changes (*e.g.* measured or predicted self motions, dilations or contractions of the visual field).

In systems with foveas, vergence can emerge from binocular target foveation. Currently most robot vision systems do not have foveas, but this is changing. Vergence has many advantages nevertheless. Fixating an object of interest puts points on the object near the optic axis in both cameras. In some cases this permits the use of simplifying assumptions (*e.g.* replacing perspective projection with orthography) that make analysis significantly easier. By definition, the fixation point has a stereoscopic disparity of zero, and points nearby tend to have small disparities. This makes it possible to use stereo algorithms that accept only a limited range of disparities. Disparity filtering is a context-limiting technique discussed below.

Vergence Error

We use a simple feedback control model for vergence control. The vergence system must measure the current vergence error. The most important source of this information is the visual system, but other sources may also be useful. For instance, one can predict the error that will result from a gaze shift to a target of known depth. Vergence changes due to self motion can also be taken into account (see Section 8.6).

The most useful visual cue to vergence error is binocular disparity, and the mapping from disparity to vergence error is simple. Disparity measurement has been studied extensively in the context of stereo depth reconstruction. Unfortunately most of the disparity estimators used for stereopsis are too powerful and slow for use in real-time vergence application. We use a simple phase correlation-like measure between sub-sampled left and right images, or "foveal" windows of such images.

The *power cepstrum* of a signal is the Fourier transform of the logarithm of its power spectrum. It was introduced in (Bogert *et al.*, 1963) as a tool for analyzing signals containing echoes, and has been investigated as a stereo fusion mechanism possibly implemented in the columnar architecture of the primate brain (Yeshurun & Schwartz, 1989a). Without the nonlinear logarithm step, the cepstrum is simply the autocorrelation. The nonlinear logarithm operation is a compressive one that attenuates narrow-band signals and emphasizes broad-band ones. Thus the cepstral filter acts like a combination of "interest operator" and matched filter correlator (for details, see the appendix of (Olson & Coombs, 1991)). In our application the right and left images are concatenated into a single rectangular image and the power cepstrum is computed using integer FFT on a digital signal processing chip. The filter yields a disparity histogram, and the vergence error is measured as the (x, y) location of the highest peak in disparity space – it should be brought to $(0, 0)$.

Since this error measure is based on *what* disparities are present but not *where* they are, the target should dominate the scene (be associated with the most common disparity). This in turn can be accomplished by spatial windowing and pursuit

in dynamic scenes with many distractors (we describe this approach in Section 8.4). However, another more general approach is to track the disparity peak of interest regardless of its size, keeping it at zero disparity.

The vergence error-computation system is implemented on MaxVideo digitizers, convolvers, frame stores (one each per camera), and the EUCLID signal processing board. Stereo images are digitized from synchronized cameras, and the images are blurred by convolution with a Gaussian kernel ($\sigma = 2.5$ pixels). Foveation (windowing) is accomplished by "zooming" and subsampling the images. This much work takes between one and two RS-170 frame times (33 to 67 milliseconds). For 32×32 windows, the cepstral step takes 51 milliseconds, not including the 8 ms required to acquire the VME bus and read the sample arrays from the frame buffer (Olson & Coombs, 1991).

Vergence Control

The host computer (SUN Sparc) finds the maximum peak in the cepstral filter output, converts the pixel disparity to angular coordinates, and applies the control law to issue identical and opposite (symmetric) vergence velocity commands to the camera motors. Symmetric vergence allows us to decouple the vergence and tracking controls for simplicity, but is not necessary. The Sparc issues the motor commands *after* initiating the next digitization in order to allow digitization to proceed concurrently with motor control. This causes a slight delay in issuing the motor commands, but permits a substantially higher overall sampling rate. The loop consistently takes three frame times to complete. Thus, the system achieves a servo rate of 10 Hz. Attempts to attain the theoretically possible 15 Hz rate have been thwarted by technical difficulties with capturing images and issuing motor commands concurrently with estimating disparity.

We use a proportional integral derivative (PID) controller (*e.g.* see (Dorf, 1980)) in cascade with the camera motor to generate oculomotor responses to reduce the estimated disparity (Fig. 8.1). The controller gains were chosen empirically to obtain slightly underdamped response, resulting in a small overshoot in the step response. The demonstration system's responses to a step input is shown in Fig. 8.2. The system's response to sinusoidal stimuli of frequencies up to 2 Hz suggests that the system has second order characteristics and that its constant time delay produces the expected linear phase shift.

8.3   Zero Disparity Filtering

Features that have no stereo disparity can be detected in real time using a disparity filter. The region of space that contains objects that project onto the retinas with no stereo disparity is called the *horopter*. Ideally, disparity filtering can thus be used to isolate a target at a given range from its foreground and background. Our nonlinear zero-disparity filter (ZDF) has vertical edges for features, since they are identifiable features that can

PID Controlling an Integrator
in a Negative Feedback Loop

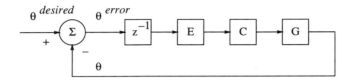

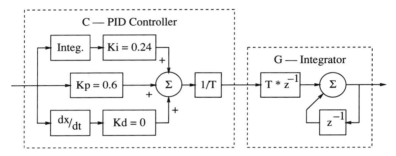

Figure 8.1
Gaze Holding Control System: The vergence and smooth pursuit pan and tilt controllers
are independent PID controllers like that shown here.

give useful information about horizontal disparity (Fig. 8.3). The first step
is to construct a vertical edge image of each image in the stereo pair. Then
these images are compared in corresponding locations. If an edge is present
in both images, then a feature appears in the resulting zero-disparity image.
The edges must be of like phase (*i.e.* light to dark, or dark to light). The
windowed output of the ZDF is input to the smooth pursuit system.

8.4   Smooth Pursuit Control

The goal of *smooth pursuit* is to keep the target centered in the retinas of
actively controlled cameras. We have implemented a smooth pursuit system
that uses precategorical visual cues (*i.e.* cues available prior to object recognition). Specifically, the smooth pursuit system simply tracks the centroid of
the contents of the windowed ("foveated") ZDF output. The pursuit system
rotates the cameras in tandem (the same signal is sent to each pan motor)
to keep gaze directed toward the target.

There are two natural measures of target following performance: position error and velocity mismatch. The goals of image-centering and slip-

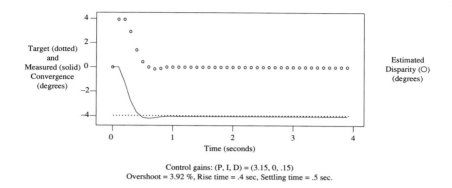

Control gains: (P, I, D) = (3.15, 0, .15)
Overshoot = 3.92 %, Rise time = .4 sec, Settling time = .5 sec.

Figure 8.2
Response to a step in disparity: *Rise time* is the earliest time the response reaches 90% of its final (steady-state) value, and *settling time* is the earliest time the response stays within 5% of its final value. The sample interval is 0.1 seconds.

(a)   (b)   (c)

Figure 8.3
Zero disparity filtering of the scene shown in stereo images (a) and (b) yields output shown in (c).

minimizing can conflict (in fact they do in linear control). Smooth camera movements can only improve one of these measures at the expense of the other. A nonlinear scheme could use intermittent saccadic (fast) movements to reduce positional error, while a continuously running smooth pursuit control component tries to minimize target slip. A simpler approach is to give precedence to one of the goals. In this implementation, cameras smoothly pursue the target simply by servoing on its position error (the (x, y) image position of the centroid of the contents of the foveal window).

Pursuit uses independent PID controls for pan and tilt (Fig. 8.1), and we have experimented with $\alpha - \beta - \gamma$ prediction to overcome delays in the system (Bar-Shalom & Fortmann, 1988). An $\alpha - \beta - \gamma$ filter is a steady-state

Kalman filter (one with constant coefficients in the state and measurement equations). It is much simpler to compute than a full Kalman filter, and in effect it combines measurements and the predicted state of the target in fixed proportions to produce an optimal estimate of target state (under correct modeling and noise assumptions). An $\alpha - \beta$ filter assumes constant velocity, but we use the $\alpha - \beta - \gamma$ filter, which is based on a constant acceleration model (in laboratory, not image, coordinates) and which predicts sinusoidal signals more effectively. If the error signal can be successfully predicted, the latency of processing can be mitigated by controlling the system with predicted error signals and comparing the observed error with the predicted error once the visual signal is processed. The predictive filter is also useful to cope with signal dropout: the target dynamics can be run forward and the predicted position of the target can be tracked until the system decides to give up.

Using the $\alpha - \beta - \gamma$ predictor in the loop to predict the delayed signal can lead to more accurate tracking. Figure 8.4(a) shows the camera movement and tracking error as the camera tracks the image of a dark object in approximate harmonic motion with a period of about five seconds. The object is rotating in a plane and thus its distance from the camera varies and its velocity is not purely sinusoidal. The error is measured as the off-axis angle of the centroid of the object's image. There is approximately 80 ms delay in the system. The small phase difference between the sinusoidal waveforms of the target and camera motion induces a surprisingly large error. In Figure 8.4(a) an $\alpha - \beta - \gamma$ filter is used ($\lambda = 1$) with no predictive advance, so the tracking signal is smoothed somewhat. In Figure 8.4(b) the filter extrapolates the signal 50 ms into the future. The result is livelier tracking (in fact more advance destabilizes tracking) but error is reduced.

8.5   Combining Pursuit and Vergence Controls

Fig. 8.5 shows how vergence, zero disparity filtering, and tracking work together. Vergence and tracking use foveally-processed visual signals.

The gaze parameter angles for pan (θ_{pan}), verge (θ_{verge}) and tilt (θ_{tilt}) map fairly directly, though not identically, onto the Rochester head's mechanical degrees of freedom, ($\phi_{left}, \phi_{right}, \phi_{tilt}$). There is a single tilt motor, so

$$\theta_{tilt} = \phi_{tilt}.$$

The pan and verge angles are related to the left and right pan camera angles by

$$\theta_{pan} = \tfrac{1}{2}(\phi_{right} + \phi_{left})$$
$$\theta_{verge} = \phi_{right} - \phi_{left}.$$

These equations relate the static angles. However, the motor controller must convert the pan and verge velocity commands to left and right pan

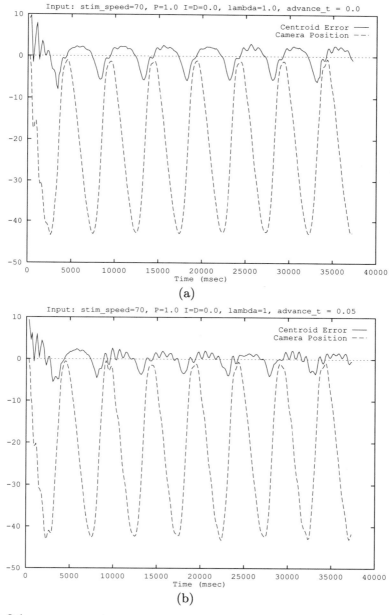

Figure 8.4
Camera motion and error when tracking an object in approximate harmonic motion. (a)
Delay of approximately 0.08s induces small phase lag but large tracking errors. (b) Camera
motion and error using $\alpha - \beta - \gamma$ predictor to advance the signal by 0.050s.

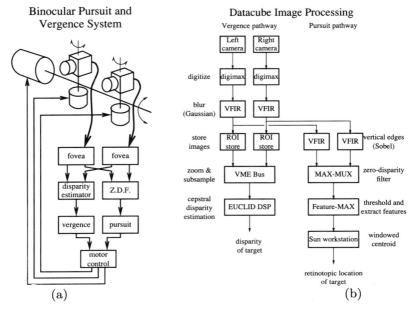

Figure 8.5
(a) Binocular Vergence and Pursuit system. (b) Datacube Image Processing: Nearly all
of the visual processing is carried out on a Datacube MaxVideo image processing system.

motor velocities. Differentiating with respect to time, we obtain the motor
velocities:

$$\dot{\phi}_r = \dot{\theta}_p + \tfrac{1}{2}\dot{\theta}_v$$
$$\dot{\phi}_l = \dot{\phi}_r - \dot{\theta}_v$$
$$= \dot{\theta}_p - \tfrac{1}{2}\dot{\theta}_v.$$

Thus the pan velocity is transmitted to both camera pans, and the vergence
is split evenly between them.

Each of the three gaze control systems operates independently, with no
explicit cooperation. This simplifies the control laws (but see (Brown, 1990b;
Coombs & Brown, 1991)). In this experiment no predictive filtering was
used.

Figure 8.6 shows a stereo robot's-eye view of a typical setup and the
measured camera pan, tilt and convergence angles and visual error signals
for a target object moving in a horizontal circle through a field of distractors.
These measurements were recorded from a run with the target rotating at
0.1 Hz, and the pan angle trace reveals rotational camera velocities as high
as 13 deg/s, with the cameras lagging behind the apparent target velocity,
as indicated by the non-zero observed retinal error.

In order to illustrate the function of each component of the gaze holding
system, selected control components were removed from the system, and the

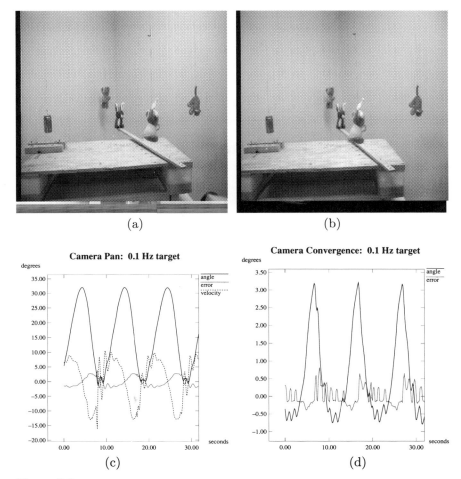

Figure 8.6
Gaze holding camera traces for PID control with no prediction. (a,b) show the robot's-eye stereo view of a typical setup. Measured traces of the pan (c) and vergence changes (d) show the performance of the gaze holding system in following the target.

resulting behaviors are compared with the behavior of the complete system. (Fig. 8.7). The first trace in (e) shows the behavior of the unimpaired system for comparison. The second trace illustrates the loss of track on the target object that results from the removal of foveal processing (or peripheral suppression). The third trace demonstrates the system's inability to track the target if the vergence angle is held constant. The final trace shows how the system is distracted by objects at all distances when zero-disparity filtering is eliminated. For stability reasons, foveal reduction was also eliminated for this experiment. Including extra-foveal edges in the "target" centroid calculation dilutes the effect of features entering and leaving the "foveal" area that caused the instability. These ablation experiments show that each piece of the system contributes to the performance, and it is the combination of the simple components that allows each part to be simple.

Results of Ablation on Camera Pan Angle

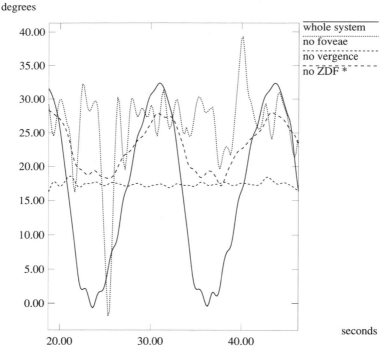

Figure 8.7
Results of "ablation" experiences (see text).

In other experiments the Puma arm moved the robot head during the pursuit task. Since gaze-holding is is purely driven by visual feedback we would expect the system to be robust against head motion, and indeed it proved to be. We would expect to be able to use information about self-motion to make tracking more robust. The following section addresses this idea in a preliminary fashion.

8.6   Nonvisual Gaze Holding

We have seen that cooperation between vergence and pursuit controls can hold the gaze from a moving platform on an object moving in a cluttered scene. If the control system were also to have direct input as to the platform motion, motion compensation could relieve the tracking system and improve performance.

Here we describe nonvisual gaze stabilization that compensates with camera pan and tilt motions for head motions in translation and rotation, so as to foveate a point fixed in space. In many practical cases the resulting tilt commands are identical and both cameras can be centered on the target despite the shared tilt degree of freedom. The technique extends easily to stabilize a moving target if its 3-D trajectory is known or can be estimated (as by a predictive filter). We have implemented such a non-visual trajectory follower, but at this writing we have not integrated non-visual control with vergence and pursuit control.

Data on robot position is obtained from its controller: Robot head location is reported as (x, y, z, O, A, T), the 3-D location of the origin of head coordinates and the Euler angles that determine its orientation (Brown & Rimey, 1988). This information, along with the known (x, y, z) position of the target, can be converted into pan and tilt motions that will bring the object to the center of the field of the camera. Differencing these pans and tilts gives velocities, which are used to control the camera angles using the "velocity-streaming" mode of the Compumoter camera motor controllers. Alternatively, differencing the sequence of output location sextuples yields a sequence of velocity signals in robot location parameters. Inverse jacobian calculations translate these velocities into error signals in pan and tilt angle velocities. In either case, the resulting pan and tilt angle velocity errors are input to a PID motor controller with the following equation:

$$m_n = K_g \left(K_p e_n + K_i \sum_{k=0}^{n} c^{n-k} e_k + K_d \frac{e_n - e_{n-1}}{\Delta t} \right)$$

where m_n is the control output, K_g is the global gain, K_p is the proportional gain, K_i is the integral gain, K_d is the differential gain, c is the integral decay constant, e_n is the error at the nth iteration, and Δt is the sampling interval (Fig. 8.8).

In a test experiment, the robot control software (VAL-II) commands the robot head to follow a circular path in the (vertical) zy-plane. A process-control program under VAL reads back robot (x, y, z, O, A, T) positions to the host computer, which runs either the position differencing or the Jacobian method. The head trajectory has 150mm radius (completed in about

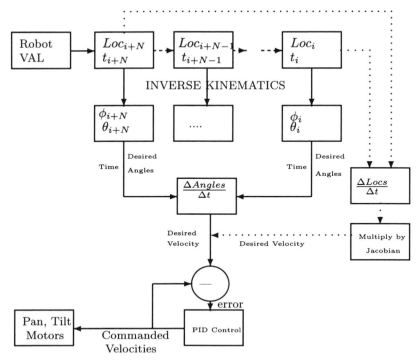

Figure 8.8
The control diagram for the process. Dotted lines show the Jacobian data path.

10.9 seconds, so the linear speed of the robot is about 8.6526 cm/sec), with the target is 84cm from the center of revolution, perpendicular to the plane of the trajectory. The target is of size 5.34×3.8 cm. In both cases the excursion of the gaze center from the center of the target measured at the target varies from 0 to about 3 cm throughout the trajectory. Computing the error (the image coordinates of the centroid of the target, which should stay at $(0,0)$) would involve visual processing that would in turn slow down the controls.

One drawback to the Jacobian approach to stabilization is that the program only tries to set the current eye velocities such that they offset the current head velocities. As positional error accumulates from delay in the system, noise in the position readings, problems with the robot head velocity computation, and any other source, the fixation location on wanders away from the original target. The I(ntegral error) term in the controller should be taking care of this problem to some extent but it is only as good as the input data, which is actually differentiated position. This points to a need to combine positional and velocity control in the stabilization controller. It would be best if position and velocity were measured by independent mechanisms (say target centroid for position, retinal slip (optic flow or motion blur) for velocity). We found the Jacobian version drifted in pan angle at the rate of 0.00023 radians/sec (i.e. about one centimeter at the 84cm range after 50 seconds). In contrast, the position differencing approach did not drift.

For the tilt motor, (P gain, I gain, D gain, integral decay, global gain) = $(1.5, 0.1, 0.5, 0.46, 0.58)$. The substantial differential gain is explained below. For the pan motors, (P gain, I gain, D gain, integral decay, global gain) = $(1.0, 0.1, 0.5, 0.46, 0.58)$.

The head was not designed for easy kinematics calculations: While the inverse kinematics are rather simple, the Jacobian equations are quite impressive (Soong & Brown, 1991). Although the computation of the Jacobian is much more computationally intense, both algorithms run at about 13 Hz. By themselves, the Jacobian and differencing methods take 1.251 ms (800 Hz) and 0.312 ms (3205 Hz), respectively. The lower frequency of the actual system is caused by communication delays between the host computer and VAL, and the host computer and the motor controllers.

Our PID gains were chosen empirically to reduce the stabilization error. The high differential component is unusual. First, this high differential gain makes the control loop sensitive to acceleration and helps the motors to catch up the motion of the robot. Differencing is dangerous but the data is relatively noiseless. The second reason for the particular choice of gains is somewhat obscure. In fact, with the almost-sinusoidal nature of the signal, the PID controller is implementing a form of prediction. The integral and derivative of a sine is a cosine, and addition of sinusoids can produce a phase shift:

$$\sin(x + y) = \sin x \cos y + \cos x \sin y.$$

When we plot the behaviour of the controller it turns out to lead the signal by an amount that cancels out some internal delays (Brown & Coombs, 1991; Brown, 1990b). This is amusing, but we would not expect to realize this predictive benefit on general target trajectories.

8.7 Conclusion

Gaze holding is one functional half of the general gaze control problem — the other half is gaze shifting. Gaze holding with moving cameras stabilizes images on the retina, thus minimizing motion blur and in turn making it easier to hold gaze on a target. During active following, motion blur also de-emphasizes the background, which makes low-level vision even easier. In a binocular system the vergence that is part of gaze holding has other beneficial effects for low level vision, such as limiting disparities for stereo matching, or the zero disparity filter we use in this work.

We have shown a visual-feedback solution to the gaze-holding problem while observer and target are moving. Robust gaze holding can be implemented with cooperating simple mechanisms. In the cooperative verging and tracking reported here, the pursuit system is driven by the centroid of intensity in the windowed output of a filter that passes features with zero stereo disparity. The vergence system uses a global disparity measure applied to the same window to keep the foveated object at zero disparity. This symbiotic cooperation of the pursuit and vergence system enables precategorical visual processing to suffice to support gaze holding. Feedforward and other compensatory techniques can be applied if the observer's self-motion is known, and we describe a non-visual, proprioceptive approach to gaze holding using explicit kinematic information.

9   Attentive Visual Servoing

James J. Clark and Nicola J. Ferrier

In this chapter we will concern ourselves with two aspects of the active vision paradigm. First, we will motivate the desirability of directed, or attentive, trajectory control of camera position. Second, we will describe details of how such control can be implemented in an actual robotic system. In particular, we detail the implementation of a visual servo control system which implements attentive control of a binocular vision system through specification of gains in parallel feedback loops. The servo type of control that we propose is based on models of mammalian oculomotor control systems (Collewijn & Tamminga, 1984; Kandel and Schwartz, 1981; Robinson, 1968). For alternative possibilities see chapters 8 and 10.

9.1   Camera Motions for Directed Vision

The camera motions in a system using *directed* vision follow a definite trajectory specified by the vision subsystem. Depending on the type of robotic system the camera is attached to, this motion can be carried out in a number of ways. The most common situations are:

• Camera rigidly fixed to a mobile platform. In this situation, the vision system will have control over the motion, typically left-right-forward-backward in a plane, of the mobile platform.

• Camera rigidly attached to a robot arm, which can itself either be fixed to a base (such as a typical industrial robot), or to a mobile platform. In this case the vision system will have control over the motion of the robot arm, and perhaps control over the base if it is mobile. If the vision system does not have any control over the motion of the base then there may be information directly transmitted to the arm controller from the base controller to permit any motion of the base to be compensated for by the arm, without needing any additional visual processing.

• Camera attached to a *head*, which is attached to a (mobile or fixed) base. This arrangement has less flexibility and more restricted range of motion than where the camera is attached to a six degree of freedom arm, but will typically be faster and more precise. In this case the vision system will have control over the relative position of the camera with respect to the *neck* of the head. This approach has the advantage that the motion of the arm and base are free for manipulation activities.

The form of the control that we have over camera position is clearly application dependent and will vary with the particular directed vision process that is needed. For gross exploration, where the camera needs to peer behind objects or look into rooms, clearly the use of a mobile base is indicated. For situations where the exploration is only needed in a limited region, such as the workspace of a fixed industrial region, mounting a camera on a dextrous robot arm may be sufficient. This type of system could be used in the active object mapping approach of Ferrier (1992) as that method requires that the camera be moved about an object, but does not require motion over large distances. In cases where directed exploration is not required, a head type of camera motion may be all that is required. A head system may be used, for example in the optimal active shape from shading technique described in (Ferrier & Clark, 1990) or the incremental stereo technique of Geiger and Yuille (1987). In both of these examples the small precise motions available in a head camera system are all that are required.

An important class of directed vision processes, and ones that are appropriate for head camera systems, are those involving *attentive* vision. Recall by attentive vision we mean visual processes in which the computational resources available to the vision system are focussed on different parts of the scene. This focussing can operate either by moving the camera so that different parts of the scene become visible, or by changing which parts of the image are being processed at any given time. This mode of attention forms the basis for Ullman's visual routine paradigm (Ullman, 1984), in which sequences of elementary image analysis operations are performed to obtain properties of, and relations between objects, in a scene. Focus of attention may also refer to the selection of a given set of image processing operations that are to be used to extract information from the scene. For example, a given visual task may require that corners of objects be detected, while another visual task may require that the color of objects be determined. In each of these two cases different features would be attended on.

As we are concerned here with active vision, where camera motions are paramount, we will only talk about the type of attentive vision in which shifts in the focus of attention are created through camera motions. Furthermore, since most of the attentive vision algorithms are those that are suitable for head camera systems we will for the rest of the paper concern ourselves only with head camera systems, although much of what we say will be applicable to arm and base mounted camera systems as well.

9.2   Saliency Based Feedback Control of Camera Motion

In all of the proposed directed and attentive active vision algorithms there are two common tasks to be performed. One is to figure out where to direct the camera gaze next (the *next look* problem (Swain & Stricker, 1991)), and the other is to then carry out the motion that will let one look there.

In directed vision applications there are two different forms that the camera motion can take. The first is a *saccadic* motion which brings the camera to view on a particular part of the scene. An exploratory algorithm will typically generate a sequence of such camera motions. The second form of camera motion is a *pursuit* motion where the desired motion is a non-constant smooth trajectory. Examples of algorithms which generated this type of motion include those which track moving objects, the optimal shape from shading technique of Ferrier and Clark (1990) as well as their active object mapping algorithm (Ferrier, 1992).

One can think of an approach for deciding what camera motion to carry out that bases the decision on a measure of the saliency of a given point in the camera's positional configuration space. That is, based on the visual data coming from the camera, and depending on the particular directed vision algorithm being performed, a saliency value is computed for each possible position (or perhaps each increment in position) that the camera can achieve. The camera is then moved to the configuration of maximum saliency. At this point a region of interest (ROI) processor may perform more complicated visual tasks. A pursuit motion or other trajectory can be obtained by constantly changing the saliency map so as to shift the point of maximum saliency over time in the required direction.

Assuming that one adopts such a saliency based camera motion control scheme, one must answer the question of how to determine what is the saliency measure to be used, and how is it to be computed? In the context of human visual search, or exploration, Treisman and Gelade (1980) identified a "preattentive" stage wherein certain features, primitives, are detected in parallel across the visual field. Possible primitives include colour, line ends (terminators), spatial frequency, motion, line orientation, binocular disparity, and texture (Beck & Ambler, 1973; Burr & Ross, 1986; Hurlbert & Poggio, 1986; Frisby & Mayhew, 1980; Marr & Ullman, 1981; Treisman & Gelade, 1980; Wilson & Bergen, 1979). These features could then be combined to produce a saliency map by forming a weighted combination of the feature values. Depending on the precise weights, the point of maximum saliency will appear at different points. Changing these weights corresponds to shifting the point of maximum saliency, and hence, in our view, changing the focus of attention.

Servo model of attention

One can describe the control of a mechanical system through a differential equation relating the effect of control inputs to the state of the system as follows:

$$\dot{x}(t) = f(x(t)) + G(x(t))v(t) \; ; \; y(t) = h(x(t)) \tag{9.1}$$

where $x(t)$ is an n-dimensional state vector, $v(t)$ is a m-dimensional vector of controls and $y(t)$ is a p-dimensional vector of sensor signals (which depends on the system state x). The system state usually includes the positions of the various mechanical degrees of freedom of the structure. The function $G(\cdot)$ relates the effect of the control vector $v(t)$ on the system state. The control vector can be independent of the sensor variables $y(t)$ in which case we have *open loop* control, or it can depend on the sensor variables in which case we have *closed loop* control (assuming, of course, that the sensor variables are functions of the system state).

To make the open loop/closed loop distinction more explicit one can write the control vector as the sum of an open loop component and a closed loop component as follows:

$$v(t) = u(t) + k(y(t)) \qquad (9.2)$$

The term $u(t)$ represents a vector of open loop control inputs, or setpoints, that we wish the system to follow. The function $k(\cdot)$ operates on the sensor variables $y(t)$ to provide the state feedback required for closed loop control.

The above formalism captures both the physical nature of the system (through the G and f functions) and the activities the system is to undertake (through the u, k, and y functions). One can absorb the definition of the $y(t)$ functions into the k function by assuming that all possible observations are available and that the k *selects* the observations that are used in any given control scheme. The k function is of critical importance in our saliency based scheme. Let us assume that k is a linear operator, i.e.

$$v(t) = u(t) + K(t)y(t) \qquad (9.3)$$

where $K(t)$ is a time varying matrix of feedback gains. Let us further interpret the vector $y(t)$ as a feature vector, derived from the camera image. It is clear that by altering the elements of $K(t)$ we alter the relative effect that the various features have on the control signal $v(t)$ and hence on the position of the camera.

In the remainder of the chapter we present details of an attentive vision system that we have implemented that is based on this servo model of attention. This system is a dual level system. The first, or inner, level performs automatic vergence and pursuit operations based on set points and mode controls supplied by the outer level. The outer level sends setpoints and feedback gains to the inner level which are themselves based on a set of setpoints and feedback gains provided by the user as input to the outer level. Hence the user controls the outer level which then controls the inner level. In this case the outer level gains k's describe what visual routines, or modes, are to be applied to the binocular visual input (the $y(t)$'s) to generate the control signals (the $v(t)$'s). Changes in attention are implemented by supplying the outer level motion control component with a new set of feedback gains. Visual routines which involve many shifts in attention are implemented by sending the controller a mode containing a sequence of feedback gains and setpoints.

9.3   The Harvard Head Oculomotor Control System

In this section we describe the physical configuration of our robotic "head" and describe the implementation of the low level oculomotor control system for our attentive binocular vision system. This control system is based on models of mammalian oculomotor control systems.

The mechanical structure of our binocular image acquisition system is shown in figure 9.1. This mechanism can be attached to a mobile platform or it may be rigidly fixed to a worktable overlooking the workspace of a robot for assembly or inspection tasks. The "head", shown in figure 9.2, has seven degrees of freedom that must be controlled. Three of these degrees of freedom are associated with the orientation of the cameras, while the other four have to do with the state of the cameras' aperture and lens focus. The three mechanical degrees of freedom are: 1) Pan, which is a rotation of the inter-camera baseline about a vertical axis, 2) Tilt, which is a rotation of the inter-camera baseline about a horizontal axis, and 3) Vergence, which is an antisymmetric rotation of each camera about a vertical axis. With these three degrees of freedom one can theoretically place the intersection of the optical axes of the two cameras (what we will refer to as the fixation point) anywhere in the three dimensional volume about the head. In practice, the volume of accessible fixation points will be restricted due to the limited range of motions of the degrees of freedom.

The distance to the surface of exact focus can be controlled with the electronic focus on the lens. This distance ranges from a near distance of about 30 cm to essentially an infinite distance away. The focus control is an integral part of any attentive vision system as it allows us to focus on the point of fixation. With no focus control, the features that we are fixating on may be out of focus. The ability to control lens focus also allows us to obtain depth information monocularly through focusing (Krotkov, 1987), or through defocus measurements (Hwang *et al.*, 1989; Pentland, 1987). Our system also allows control over the lens aperture, which affects the amount of light received by the image sensor, and the depth of focus (not to be confused with the depth of the surface of exact focus). It is important to be able to adjust the aperture to maintain sufficient light levels for the image sensor. The aperture control in our system is automatic, and responds to changing light levels, and is not dependent on any attentive inputs. DC motors are used to drive the pan, tilt, and vergence axes. The pan axis is driven directly, while the tilt axis is belt driven, mainly due to space considerations. The vergence motor drives a lead screw, which then causes the camera rotations through a kinematic chain. The relationship between the vergence motor rotation (or the lead screw displacement) and the camera vergence angle is approximately linear (within 1 percent over the range of travel) which makes the programming of the vergence control simple. The focus motion is generated via a motor encased in the lens housing. Control signals to this motor are generated by an integrated circuit also located in the lens housing. A digital data stream, suitably encoded, must be sent to the focus motor driver I.C., to command a change in focus. The manufacturer of the lens, Canon, would not release details on the specifications of the required command data streams, so we determined the proper data sequences

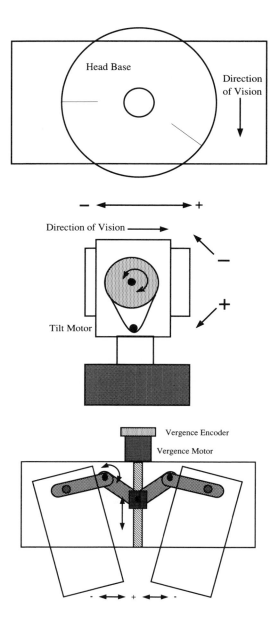

Figure 9.1
A schematic view of the Harvard head showing the sign conventions for the pan, tilt, and vergence angles.

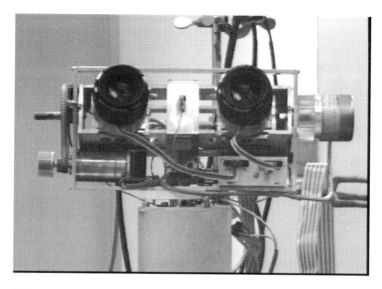

Figure 9.2
A frontal view of the Harvard head.

ourselves. These details are available from the authors, subject to certain disclosure conditions.

One can partition the control of the pan, tilt, and vergence axes of the head mechanism into three descriptive regimes. These are, *saccades*, *pursuit*, and *vergence*. Taken together, these three modes of operation allow control over shift in attention, and maintenance of attention. A saccade is a rapid motion of the pan and tilt axes which causes a coupled motion of the optical axes of the two cameras, resulting in a change in the direction of gaze of the cameras. In a saccade, both cameras move in the same direction. This motion is not enough to allow independent control of the gaze direction of each camera. To obtain this one uses a vergence movement. A vergence movement is a coupled motion of the two cameras wherein the the two cameras rotate in opposite directions. Taken together, the saccadic and vergence systems allow the fixation point of the binocular camera system to be arbitrarily controlled. Once the saccadic and vergence systems have fixated the cameras on a feature in the scene, the pursuit system is then used to track the feature. The pursuit system adjusts the velocity of the pan and tilt axes so as to minimize the retinal velocity (the velocity as measured in the camera images) of the fixated feature. This will keep the feature fixated as long as it does not move in depth. If it moves in depth the vergence system will adjust the vergence angle (the relative angle between the two cameras) to maintain fixation.

The human oculomotor system is very complex and it is not yet fully understood. It contains many interacting functional modules, such as (Kandel and Schwartz, 1981) the Frontal Cortex (for making plans and intentions), the Occipital Cortex (for visual reflexes and smooth pursuit tracking movements), the Pontine Reticular Formation (for both saccadic and pursuit movements), the Cerebellum (for coordinate transformations), the Superior Colliculus (for relating visual input to oculomotor commands), and the Vestibular System (for allowing the eyes to compensate for body motions). The control system that we have described in this chapter takes on the functionality of many of these modules, and we do not claim our system as a model for any particular part of the human oculomotor control system. We have, however, used some models of the human oculomotor system in developing our system.

In humans, the physiological evidence indicates that saccades are controlled with a sampled data system, while pursuit motions are continuously controlled (Robinson, 1968; Robinson, 1987). The latency, or reaction time of the human saccadic system has been determined to be about 200 milliseconds (Robinson, 1968), although it has been observed that anticipatory behaviour can reduce this latency time (Dallos & Jones, 1963). This latency is the time it takes from the moment of change in retinal position of an attended feature to the moment that a motor command is given to generate the saccade. Presumably the bulk of this time is taken up in processing the retinal image to determine the position of the feature. During this period the oculomotor system is insensitive to further changes in the retinal position of the feature, and the saccade that is generated is that appropriate to the retinal position of the feature as it was 200 milliseconds prior to the generation of the saccade. If the feature moves during this refractory period the saccade will result in a position error. From this observation came the sampled data model of the oculomotor control system, originally proposed by Young and Stark (1963).

Young and Stark treated the pursuit system as a sampled data system as well. Upon further psychophysical examination this assumption turned out to be incorrect, and the pursuit system is now thought to use a continuous time data system, or at least a sampled data system in which the sampling rate is much higher than the sampling rate for the saccadic system (Robinson, 1965). It has been observed (Collewijn & Tamminga, 1984) that pursuit movements are not always smooth, but will include saccadic components if the visual feature being pursued has a large retinal velocity. Presumably these saccades are necessary if the pursuit system can not keep up with the moving object. In this case a cumulative position error builds up, and when this error reaches a certain threshold a saccade is generated in order to reduce the position error.

The control scheme that we use to control the pan, tilt, and vergence degrees of freedom of our head system is based on the model of human oculomotor control described by Robinson (1968). This model postulates separate subsystems for pursuit and saccadic motion. These subsystems are depicted in figure 9.3 (adapted from (Robinson, 1968)). Time delays are denoted by square boxes with the delay time (in milliseconds) within the box. Transfer functions are denoted within the boxes for the filters. The target position is denoted by T and the eye position by E.

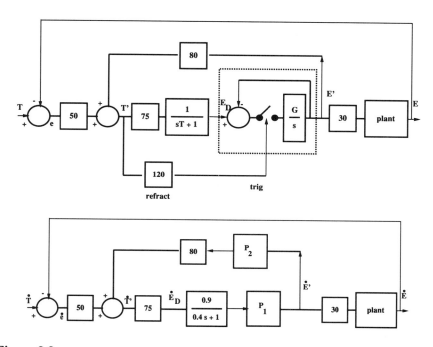

Figure 9.3
Robinson's model for the human oculomotor control system. TOP: Saccades, BOTTOM: Pursuit.

There are two interesting features of Robinson's model. The first is that the sampled data nature of the saccadic system. The desired retinal position, E_D, is sampled (with a pulse sampler), and held by a first order hold (an integrator). The output of this sample/hold is then used as a setpoint to the plant (in this case the local motor controller). The actuator will then try to move the camera to the desired position. During the period between sampling pulses, the output of the sample/hold is being held constant, and hence the desired eye position is being held constant, even though the image of the feature to be attended to may be moving. A sample/hold does not appear to be present in the pursuit system.

The second feature of Robinson's model to be noted is that there is internal positive feedback in the control loop. This positive feedback is necessary in the case of the pursuit system (figure 9.3b) to prevent oscillations due to delays in the negative feedback loop. The negative feedback is provided by the vision system which, in the case of the pursuit system, detects the velocity of a feature, computes the retinal velocity error (which is equal to the retinal velocity since the desired retinal velocity is zero for tracking purposes), and causes the eye to move in a manner to reduce this error. However, these computations can not be done instantaneously, so there is a delay between the time at which an visual observation is made and the time at which the control command based on this observation is available. To eliminate the oscillations that can occur with this feedback, a compensatory internal positive feedback is inserted into the loop. This is done by adding a delayed "efference copy" of the current eye velocity to the computed retinal velocity error. The delay is such that the efference copy that is added to the velocity error is that measured at the same time that the visual observation (that the retinal velocity error is based on) is made. The sum of the retinal velocity error and the delayed efference copy gives a new desired eye velocity which is input to the plant (eye muscles or motor driver). The effect of this positive feedback path is to essentially eliminate the negative visual feedback. The saccadic system is modeled in the same way, except that position control is being done instead of velocity control. In the saccadic system, however, the internal positive feedback is not really needed to ensure stability, as stability is gained through the use of the sample/hold. Nonetheless, the available evidence indicates that the human saccadic system does use internal positive feedback to compensate for delays.

Note that the internal positive feedback scheme implies that the saccadic system directs the eye to move to an absolute position, in head coordinates, rather than to move by a certain displacement in a given direction. The issue of whether saccadic control of eye movements is head coordinate based or retinotopic coordinate has been long a subject of discussion among neurophysiologists. The current evidence, according to Robinson (1968) and others, suggests that head based coordinates are used.

Details on a model for the vergence system are sketchy, but Robinson (1968) indicates that the vergence system is continuous (no sample/hold is used) and uses internal positive feedback (although this is by no means certain). This is similar to the pursuit system save that position control is being done instead of velocity control and that the vergence system responds more slowly than the pursuit system.

Based on Robinson model as described above we have implemented the control scheme that is depicted schematically in figure 9.4 for the Harvard head. The pan, tilt, and vergence motors are driven by a pulse width modulated MOSFET amplifier. The input to this amplifier is derived from the output of a Dynamation motor controller board. The Dynamation board is indicated in figure 9.4 by the box taking in the shaft encoder position from the motor and which outputs a drive signal to the motor amplifier. The Dynamation board takes set point inputs over a VME bus connection to a SUN computer. These setpoints can either be position setpoints (in the case of vergence or a saccade) or velocity setpoints (in the case of pursuit). The Dynamation can output to the VME bus (and then on to the SUN computer) an efference copy of the current motor position. This efference copy is delayed, in the SUN computer, by a time equal to the time taken to perform visual

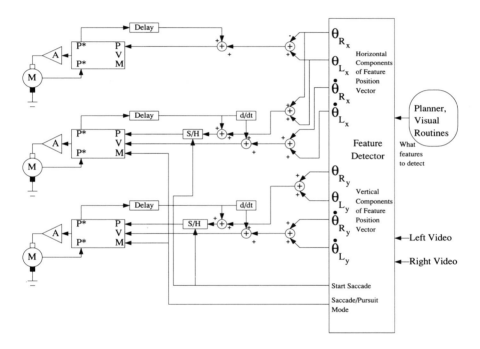

Figure 9.4
The control system used for the Harvard head.

feature localization, and added to the current position errors, determined by the visual feature localization process. The Dynamation board does not have a tachometer, so that an velocity efference copy is not available. Thus we generate one by differentiating the position efference copy. The sampling rate of the Dynamation board is very high (more than 1000 samples per second), however, so that this estimate of velocity should be accurate.

The feature detection and localization is performed in a special purpose image processing system, manufactured by Datacube . This system can do image processing operations such as 8×8 convolution, histogramming, and logical neighborhood operations on a 512×512 pixel image at video rates (30 frames per second). Thus the latency per operation is 33 milliseconds. Most feature detection operations require more that one frame time however. In our initial experiments we implemented a feature detector that could detect black blobs or white blobs, in about 3 frame times. Therefore the latency of our feature detector was about 100 milliseconds. The Datacube system, after it detected the presence of a feature, would output the position and velocity of the feature over the VME bus to the SUN workstation. The SUN workstation then computes the quantities $\theta_{R_x} + \theta_{L_x}$, $\dot{\theta}_{R_x} + \dot{\theta}_{L_x}$, $\theta_{R_y} + \theta_{L_y}$, $\dot{\theta}_{R_y} + \dot{\theta}_{L_y}$, and $\theta_{R_x} - \theta_{L_x}$, where θ_{R_x} is the x component of the retinal disparity in the right camera, θ_{R_y} is the y component of the retinal disparity in the right camera, θ_{L_x} is the x component of the retinal disparity in the left camera, θ_{L_y} is the y component of the retinal disparity in the left camera, and $\dot{\theta}$ indicates a retinal velocity. The difference in the left and right x components of the retinal position is added to the delayed position efference copy of the vergence motor. Thus this difference will be driven to zero. The sum of the left and right retinal position errors in both the x and y directions are added to the delayed position efference copies of the pan and tilt motors respectively. This will, during a saccade, drive these sums to zero. Combined with the driving of the difference of the x retinal position errors to zero by the vergence, the result will be that the x and y retinal position errors in both cameras will be driven to zero, as desired. A saccade trigger signal (that opens up the sample/hold) is generated by the feature detection system when the retinal position error is greater than threshold value. During the saccade, visual processing is turned off to prevent saccades being generated while the saccadic motion is being performed.

During pursuit the sum over the two cameras in each of the x and y retinal velocity errors will be driven to zero. If the system has the correct vergence, then the x and y component of the retinal velocity error will be driven to zero in each eye, and not just the sum of the errors in the two eyes.

We have performed simple blob tracking experiments which show that the system operates as desired, in that the vergence and saccadic modes result in fixation of the feature as we move it about in space.

9.4   Modal Control of Attention

The inner level control loop described in the previous section is controlled by an outer loop which implements attentional shifts in camera positions.

The first stage in our visual attention model acquires the images and extracts "primitives" in parallel across the visual field. The results from this stage are a set of feature maps $y_i(x, y, t)$ which indicate the presence or absence of a feature at each location in the image. Simple feature maps may indicate the presence of a specific color or line orientation. Complex feature maps may perform texture and figure-ground segmentation or more complex feature maps may implement inhibition from neighboring regions to compute which regions are different from their surroundings.

The next stage of the model combines the results from the feature maps. The output from the feature maps are "amplified" with different "gains", $k_i(t)$ for each map y_i and then these amplified values are summed to form the saliency map, $S(x, y, t)$. The value of the map at each location is a numeric indicator of how "salient" is the information at that location. Hence finding the location with the maximum value will give the most salient location with respect to the given amplifier gains, $k_i(t)$. As the notation indicates, these gains may vary over time, thus changing the location of the most salient feature. If more than one location shares the same maximum value, one location must be chosen (it does not make sense to attend to a location in the middle of two salient features, one or the other location must be picked). Figure 9.5 shows this attention model.

It can be seen that this model incorporates many of the psychophysical results observed earlier. Adjusting the gains of a particular feature map will direct attentional resources to occurrences of that feature. A decaying gain function, $k(t)$, will decrease the saliency of a location over time and hence another location will become more salient and attention will change to a new location. For example, consider the detection of a red T in a field of green L's. Suppose attention is first be directed at the red T. As the gain in the feedback path corresponding to the color red decreases and the gain corresponding to the color green increases, the focus of attention will change locale, to attend to the nearest green L. Another psychophysical result which is captured in our model is that higher cognitive levels can actively select which features to attend to by adjusting $k_i(t)$. Human attention can be consciously applied to a visual task so humans must be able to consciously select the more salient features.

Koch and Ullman (1984) describe the Winner-Take-All (WTA) network which will locate the most conspicuous location (one whose properties differs most from the properties of its neighbors). The locations which differ significantly from their neighbors are singled out and a numeric value representing the "conspicuousness" is assigned. The results from each primitive detector are combined into a global saliency map which combines the value

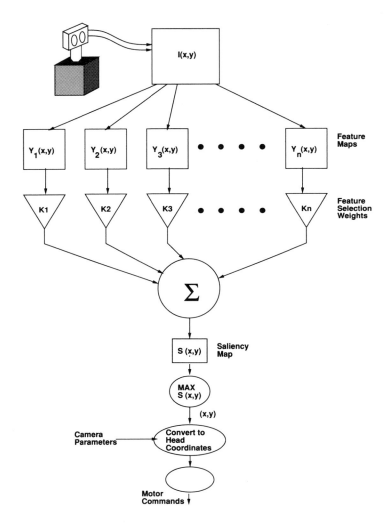

Figure 9.5
Saliency based attentive feedback control of camera position.

from each feature map and assigns a global measure of conspicuity. The WTA network finds the maximum value of "conspicuity" and locates that maximum. Attention can be allocated to the position which gave the highest value for further processing.

It can be seen that the WTA scheme uses the same models of attention. The values assigned in the global saliency map of Koch and Ullman corresponds to the saliency map of this model when using an appropriate set of gains. The WTA scheme is an *implementation* which deals with the problem of finding the maximum of the saliency map and localizing it. The notion of winner-take-all is appropriate since only one location can be attended to at one time. Koch and Ullman actually suggest the idea of a higher cognitive process adjusting the "conspicuousness" of a feature to selectively inhibit or attend on a specific feature, which corresponds to changing $k(t)$ in this model.

We implement our modal attention scheme with two nested feedback loops. The gains of the inner feedback loop which is concerned with setpoint control of the head positioning motors remains constant, as the load on the head motors remain roughly constant. One need only determine the position feedback gains k once, such that the step response of the motor to the inner level setpoints is critically damped. These gains are set in the Dynamation controller board, which handles the inner level control loop. The sensory input to the inner level is the motor shaft position, measured with the shaft encoders. The velocity of the motor shafts are not measured directly but are computed from the position measurements through differentiation as described in the previous section. The inner control loop is switched between position control and velocity control by the outer control level. This is done, in effect by sending a (u, k, T) triple (following Brockett (1988), we refer to this triple as a *mode*, where T is a time interval, u is a setpoint or trajectory during this time interval, and k are the feedback gains to be used in this interval) in which the k's decide which measurement (position or velocity) will be used to control the motor. The setpoints u that are input to the inner level control loop also come from the outer control loop in these (u, k, T) triples.

The k's in the (u, k, T) motion control system definitions concerned with the outer, visual, feedback loop will change due to changes in the focus of attention. The feedback selection process at this level is much more complicated than the inner level feedback selection in which only direct position or velocity feedback was being selected for. In the outer level, one still selects for position or velocity feedback but, in addition, one must select the feature(s) to be used to detect the scene element whose position or velocity is fed back. This feature selection is performed by adjusting the weight we apply to a given feature in the control feedback loop.

The outer control level accepts *modes* as input which allocate attention to specific features and produces different modes for the inner loop. The output modes consist of position and velocity setpoints and a time interval in which to apply these setpoints. The modes accepted by this outer level are again of the form (u, k, T) where u is the desired position (always 0 for foveation – to center target on visual field), k is a vector which represents which features to detect (the amplifier gains) and T is the time period in which the mode is to be applied.

In the language given earlier, $y(t)$ is the feedback vector. In this case, $y(x, y, t)$ is a pair of images (left and right "eyes"). Referring to the model given earlier, $K(t) = (k_1(t), k_2(t), ..., k_n(t))$ is a vector containing the "weights" to be applied to the results from the primitive operations (feature maps). With these gains, the saliency map can be computed and the maximum found. The location of the maximum must then undergo a coordinate transform in order to obtain the setpoints in head coordinates. This transformation will depend on the camera parameters and the particular configuration of the "head" and hence can be absorbed in the $G(\cdot)$ term in equation (1). The idea that alteration of the gains of visual feedback paths result in shifts in attention, (or vice versa) has some support from physiological studies (Haenny *et al.*, 1985; Moran & Desimone, 1985; Petersen *et al.*, 1985; Wurtz *et al.*, 1980; Wurtz *et al.*, 1984) which indicate that the responses of neurons involved in visual perception are modulated by changes in the focus of attention.

Figure 9.6 shows the lowest two stages of the modal control. A mode, (u, k, T), which was generated at a higher level, is input into the intermediate level (denoted M2). Over a time period, $0 \leq t \leq T$ the weights associated with the feature maps will be $K(t) = (k_1(t), k_2(t), ..., k_n(t))$. At each instant of time, t, the controller, C_2 determines a location as the "most salient feature" of the image. This location undergoes a coordinate transform (denoted by G) to convert the location to a desired head position. These positions (at each time, t) are output to the inner loop (denoted M1). In the inner loop, M_1, the controller C_1 drives the head motors based on positional errors generated as the difference between the actual head position and the desired head position input from the outer level, M_2.

9.5   Summary

In this chapter we have provided a brief explanation of the desirability of active vision. We gave a number of typical applications of active vision. We described a control system for a binocular camera mechanism which allows shifts in focus of attention to be made in a natural, device independent manner. Shifts in focus of attention are accomplished via altering of feedback gains applied to the visual feedback paths in the position and velocity control loops of the binocular camera system. By altering these gains we can perform a feature selection operation, by which the *saliency*, in the sense of Koch and Ullman (1984), of a given feature is enhanced, while the saliency of other features are reduced.

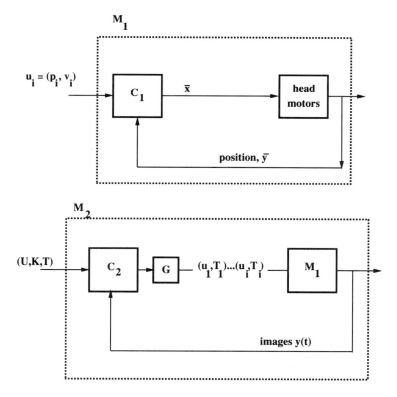

Figure 9.6
The two lowest stages of the modal control system.

The control system that we have described in this system is a two level one. The first, or inner, level performs the direct control over the position and velocity of the motors attached to the cameras. This level is based on models of the human oculomotor control system. The outer level controls the focus of attention, in that it determines what features are going to be used in determining where to look next.

10 Design of Stereo Heads

David W. Murray, Fenglei Du, Philip F. McLauchlan, Ian D. Reid, Paul M. Sharkey and Michael Brady

Purposive and active vision promises to open up exciting new avenues of experiment, in which the researcher has to relinquish precise control over scene conditions and the behaviour of the vision system. But to reach this experimental Elysium, the vision researcher needs apparatus; not only an accurate mechanical device to steer the cameras, but also a high bandwidth closed-loop vision sensor and controller. He immediately encounters other significant problems more familiar to control engineers: What is an appropriate mechanism? How can the time/speed requirements of the task be met? What is the control state, and observer and control law? And so on.

In this paper we outline the design considerations behind our construction of a steerable stereo head/eye platform, the mechanical design and that of the gaze controller and vision systems. We show how the kinematics of the platform can be used to relate image measurements with the scene motion in a static frame.

10.1 The way of the flesh

The starting point for much work in stereo head design has been the human oculomotor control system, which is indeed remarkable for its agility, stability, and range of operation. Many computer vision researchers (Ballard & Ozcandarli, 1988; Brown, 1990b; Pahlavan & Eklundh, 1991) have based their work on studies of human oculomotor physiology which identify competences (Carpenter, 1988) such as saccadic shifts of eye direction, pursuit that tracks a point of interest, the optokinetic reflex (OKR) in which optic flow is used to stabilize images, vergence to shift the stereo fixation point, accommodation, and the vestibulo-ocular reflex (VOR) that stabilizes the image when the head is moving (though this last seems to be driven primarily from proprioceptive rather than visual information). This has typically led to control architectures with separate loops for each of these competences.

Unfortunately, it is all too easy to overlook the exquisite mechanism and control of the human eye — on the mechanical side it has low inertia and can rely on muscles for its actuation, muscles which have properties unmatched by commercially available motors, particularly with regard to low friction, high efficiency, high power/size ratio, co-actuation to control stiffness, and rapid acceleration. On the control side, the physiological behaviours themselves are not fully understood, are probably nonlinear, and are therefore difficult to simulate. Also, for vision, the eye can rely on a processor of phenomenal power honed by an evolution motivated by the species' needs and activities.

Thus although animate vision in general and the human visual system in particular may inspire, it is the specific tasks to be carried out by the machine vision system that we must analyze to establish the engineering performance requirements for our stereo head.

But what visual tasks? In the reconstructionist approach the emphasis is on scene recovery for navigation and object recognition. In active vision, we suggest that the most important goal is *looking* — that is, allocating and later reallocating computational resources or attention over time with little high level input. Compared with the 3D reconstructionist approach, this relies considerably more on robust 2D vision processes, and most crucially, competent real-time motion processing.

Looking is exercised to an extent that exceeds current competence in the following scenario. Suppose the head system is gazing idly in a room where there is no activity. A person now enters the room. How is the system first attracted to the moving person and how does it shift its gaze to initiate tracking of the person as he crosses the room? While the system is tracking, someone else enters the room. Is the system distracted by the second person? Suppose it is, but the first person then throws an object at the cameras, "threatening" the system. How should it react, and what should it do once the threat has passed?

10.2   Mechanical devices

To perform the above surveillance task, the sensor platform must first transfer the sensor's gaze as quickly and accurately as possible to a new position and velocity provided by the vision system; this requires the controller to generate the appropriate sensor trajectory from old to new positions. Secondly it must be able to stabilize the sensor on the target, matching position and/or velocity; images become hopelessly blurred if there is too much relative motion lateral to the optic axis between camera and observed object. Thirdly, it must provide proprioceptive data on positions and velocities. Minimally, this includes angular position and velocity of each moving axis, and may require 3D velocity and acceleration data, eg from gyros and accelerometers.

To redirect gaze quickly and accurately there is a need to build special hardware. Bandwidth considerations for active gaze control rule out mounting a camera on a commercial robot arm or vehicle. Bandwidth and accuracy considerations rule out relatively cheap commercially available surveillance platforms, whilst cost rules out systems designed for military applications. (Military weapons/sensor platforms have been developed for vehicles such as tanks that are stiffly coupled to the environment and that are subject to enormous accelerations because of undulating terrain. In many cases they appear significantly over-designed for robotics applications.)

Degrees of freedom

When transferring its gaze from one point in the scene to another, the single human eye possesses three degrees of freedom, all rotational. However, observations made around the middle of the last century by Donders indicated that the eye exploits only two of these degrees of freedom. Listing's Law (Listing, 1855) provides a more precise account of the movements of the human eye when moving the point of fixation, stating that rotation of the eye occurs about an axis perpendicular to the primary or resting forward direction.

Would-be constructors of mechanical moving head/eye systems are faced with similar choices of whether, and then how, to restrict the rotational degrees of freedom of their mechanisms. A mechanism based on Listing's Law is difficult to realize, but two more practicable designs are available. The first is the common-elevation (or Helmholtz) configuration in which both cameras tilt up and down about a common elevation platform and verge independently about axes perpendicular to the elevation plane, as shown in Figure 10.1a. In the other configuration, the independent gun-turret (or Fick) model, each camera verges around an axis which remains vertical, and elevates about an independent horizontal axis (Figure 10.1b).

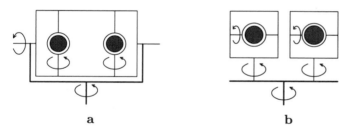

a   **b**

Figure 10.1
Two platform models, the common elevation model (a) and the independent gun-turret model (b). The addition of the azimuthal pan axis, shown thicker, results in four and five degrees of freedom for these configurations.

The imaging conditions are different in the two cases (and indeed different again from Listing's Law). In the independent gun-turret configuration each camera "maintains the vertical", having zero rotation or cyclotorsion about the optic axis. The cameras in the common-elevation configuration exhibit in general finite and different cyclotorsions. We have been unable to find overriding benefits for one or other configuration in terms of machine vision (Murray, 1992) (indeed at small convergence angles the models are identical to first order), but the need to couple the two elevation axes by control in the gun-turret configuration, so that the optic axes remain coplanar, is a distinct disadvantage, and therefore in our work we have adopted the common-elevation platform.

The neck has a further three degrees of freedom, giving to the human extra ranges of elevation and pan, and a roll axis. For the mechanical common elevation platform, camera tilt is not restricted, and for surveillance there is no particular requirement for stabilization along the roll axis (though there certainly is for vehicle mounted platforms). There is an advantage however in a further azimuthal pan axis, as it increases the field of view and enables symmetry to be maintained in stereo viewing in the steady state.

The addition of this pan axis makes a total of four degrees of freedom (pan, elevation and two vergence axes) for the common elevation platform which may in turn be augmented with focus, zoom and iris for each camera. With well matched cameras and lenses, zoom and iris can be coupled between cameras, though there are dangers of, say, a specular reflection in one camera "blinding" both. For most working distances, focus may also be coupled between cameras, and may be coupled to the vergence axes, though obtaining depth from focus information within the working stereo volume would require decoupling. Zoom, though useful, causes difficulties for gaze control. First it requires high level intervention to cause it happen, and secondly it causes potentially misleading image responses — for example, it can generate image divergence without motion.

The common elevation design has been adopted for the European Esprit Project "Real Time Control of Gaze" involving SAGEM, GEC Research, INRIA, and our laboratory in Oxford. The platform, whose detailed mechanical design and construction has been carried out at GEC Research's Marconi Research Centre (Edge, 1991), is shown in Figure 10.2.

Figure 10.2
The stereo platform built by GEC Research in the Esprit Project "Real Time Control of Gaze". The cameras are fitted with a motorized focus, zoom and iris lens, a substantial payload. (The right camera is removed in this view). The platform is able to accept other sensors or light sources.

Speed and accuracy

To establish lower bound performance specifications we return to the surveillance scenario. Suppose that the surveillance target is rotating about the

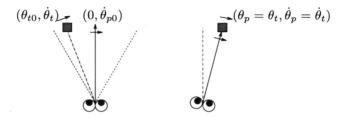

Figure 10.3
The target enters the field of view but because of delays in the vision system the head initiates a response some time later. The $\theta = 0$ direction is defined as the gaze direction at the start of response $t = 0$, and relative to this fixed frame the position and velocity of the target at $t = 0$ are $(\theta_{t0}, \dot{\theta}_{t0})$, and those of the head are $(0, \dot{\theta}_{p0})$. The head is driven in a bang-coast-bang fashion to track the target.

vertical pan axis on which the camera platform is mounted, and let the axis be driven in a bang-(coast)-bang manner — starting from position $\theta_{po} = 0$ and velocity $\dot{\theta}_{po}$, a period T_u at maximum acceleration $S|\ddot{\theta}_{pmax}|$ in one direction (where $S = \pm 1$), a (possible) period T_c at maximum speed $S|\dot{\theta}_{pmax}|$, followed by a period T_d of maximum acceleration $-S|\ddot{\theta}_{pmax}|$ in the reverse direction — until the velocity and position of the camera match those of the target (Figure 10.3). The vision system will insert some (known) delay T_v from receipt of images to delivery to the controller of the target's angular position and velocity, so that, assuming some model for target velocity (here that it is constant), it is possible to derive the target velocity $\dot{\theta}_t$ and position θ_{to} relative to a fixed axis in the gaze direction just as the head begins to move. A straightforward but tedious analysis shows that the sign S of the initial acceleration is determined from

$$S = \begin{cases} +1 & \text{if } (\dot{\theta}_t - \dot{\theta}_{po})^2 + 2|\ddot{\theta}_{pmax}|\theta_{to} \geq 0 \\ -1 & \text{otherwise.} \end{cases} \tag{10.1}$$

If the motion is not velocity limited one finds that

$$T_u = \frac{1}{|\ddot{\theta}_{pmax}|}\left[\frac{\dot{\theta}_t - \dot{\theta}_{po}}{S} + \sqrt[+]{\tfrac{1}{2}(\dot{\theta}_t - \dot{\theta}_{po})^2 + S|\ddot{\theta}_{pmax}|\theta_{to}}\right] \tag{10.2}$$

$$T_d = \frac{1}{|\ddot{\theta}_{pmax}|}\sqrt[+]{\tfrac{1}{2}(\dot{\theta}_t - \dot{\theta}_{po})^2 + S|\ddot{\theta}_{pmax}|\theta_{to}}$$

$$T_c = 0.$$

However if it is found that $\left|\dot{\theta}_{po} + T_u S|\ddot{\theta}_{pmax}|\right| > |\dot{\theta}_{pmax}|$ using the above expression for T_u then the motion is velocity limited and the periods must be replaced by

$$T_u = \frac{S|\dot{\theta}_{pmax}| - \dot{\theta}_{po}}{S|\ddot{\theta}_{pmax}|}, \tag{10.3}$$

$$T_d = \frac{S|\dot{\theta}_{pmax}| - \dot{\theta}_t}{S|\ddot{\theta}_{pmax}|},$$

$$T_c = \frac{1}{S|\dot{\theta}_{pmax}| - \dot{\theta}_t} \left[\dot{\theta}_t(T_u + T_d) + \tfrac{1}{2} S|\ddot{\theta}_{pmax}|(T_d{}^2 - T_u{}^2) \right.$$

$$\left. - S|\dot{\theta}_{pmax}|T_d - \dot{\theta}_{po}T_u + \theta_{to} \right].$$

As a concrete example, suppose that the camera's field of view is 60° and that the target's angular velocity is 60°s^{-1} (a person walking briskly 3m from the camera), and that the vision system's latency, the delay between image capture and delivery of position and motion information, is 0.1s. Let the head be initially at rest, $\theta_{po} = 0$, and let its maximum speed be considerably greater than the maximum expected tracking speed, say $|\dot{\theta}_{pmax}| = 120°\text{s}^{-1}$. Figure 10.4 shows the angle θ_p turned through by the head until tracking is achieved as a function of maximum acceleration. Note that there is a

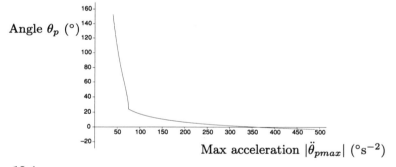

Figure 10.4
Angle turned by azimuthal axis until tracking is achieved as a function of maximum acceleration $|\ddot{\theta}_{pmax}|$.

critical value below which capture becomes slow. This occurs when the target overtakes the accelerating head before capture, which occurs if $|\ddot{\theta}_{pmax}| < (\dot{\theta}_t - \dot{\theta}_{po})^2/2\theta_{to}$, 75°s^{-2} in our example. A trajectory below this value is shown in Figure 10.5a. Above this value it becomes progressively harder to reduce the capture angle, and the final design figure for acceleration is limited by motor size and cost. The RTCG platform shown earlier has the rather high maximum acceleration about the neck axis of 400°s^{-2}, which in our example enables the axis to achieve tracking by the time the target crosses the original static gaze direction. The trajectory for this value is shown in Figure 10.5b; note that, in contrast to the less agile axis, the initial movement is towards the target.

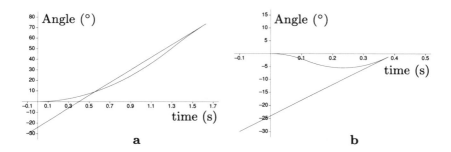

Figure 10.5
Trajectories of azimuthal rotation versus time for maximum head pan accelerations of (a)
$60°\text{s}^{-2}$ and (b) $400°\text{s}^{-2}$.

There are advantages for control in making the accelerations available
from the vergence axes considerably higher than that from the pan axis. At
first sight this should be easy as their inertial load is much less (though given
the 2kg mass of typical zoom lenses, not insignificant). However, the mass of
the vergence motors may not be too large, as they contribute to the inertial
load on the pan motor. We find that accelerations of around $500°\text{s}^{-2}$ are
possible at reasonable cost.

The minimum tracking speed required depends on the resolution of the
feature tracker (say $0.01°$) and the repetition rate (10Hz) of the tracker, ie,
around $0.1°\text{s}^{-1}$.

Motors

We have seen that one key design requirement in developing a stereo platform is high acceleration and deceleration. A second is close controllability.
The former argues for hydraulic or pneumatic actuation (see, for example,
the MIT-Utah hand design (Jacobsen *et al.*, 1989)), the latter for electrical
motors. The complexity of the poorly-understood behaviours (saccade, pursuit, vergence, OKR, VOR) that need to be achieved and controlled argues
persuasively for electric drives. Rapid accelerations imply that inertial mass
and stiction should be reduced as much as possible, and hence that backlash
must be minimized. At this stage of our understanding this also implies
that one should aim to maximize mechanical stiffness and hence reduce the
degrees of freedom, and that the speed of joint local controllers should be
maximized.

Several recent experimental stereo platforms have used stepper motors
simply because they are easy to interface, but their sluggish acceleration
and poor stiction characteristics lead to difficulties later. A better solution
is to use DC servo motors.

The platform shown in Figure 10.2 has direct drive DC servo motors for
elevation and vergence axes, and a geared DC motor for the pan axis. A

second device, nearing completion in our laboratory (Sharkey & Murray, 1992), has similar dynamic performance, but uses geared DC motors with negligible backlash from the gearbox. The design of this second platform is modular, so that a single camera, vergence and elevation axes form a monocular head, and the addition of a second monocular head and central pan axis forms a complete four degree of freedom platform, the two elevation axes being reduced to one by rigid mechanical coupling.

10.3   The head controller

In this section we outline briefly the principles behind our design for the head controller. It is convenient to subdivide the controller into two parts, a low-level motor controller, and a higher-level gaze controller.

The low-level motor controller is not concerned with visual input. Rather it takes inputs specifying the desired position and velocities of the head joints, and outputs current to the motors. In our work, each of the four motors is driven by a local PID controller, using feedback of velocity and position derived from shaft encoders. The feedback information, supplied at 500Hz, is also required by the vision modules, and is stored in a FIFO buffer large enough to cope with the latency of the vision processors.

The inputs to the low-level controllers are supplied by the higher level gaze controller. The rôle of this unit is to accept rather high level commands, such as "pursue the fastest object", and to output the joint position and velocity commands to the low-level controller. This controller uses feedback from the vision system.

The control of gaze is the subject of study by several groups (Brown, 1990b; Clark & Ferrier, 1988; Pahlavan & Eklundh, 1991; Viéville & Faugeras, 1991) (chapters 8 and 9), and the principal issues are ones of interactions between control modes and delay. The importance of these two has been highlighted particularly by the work of Brown (1989, 1990a, 1990b) at the University of Rochester. He discusses the use of the Smith predictor (Smith, 1957; Smith, 1958) to overcome delay, which exploits the fact that the desired transfer function of a system with a real controller $C^*(z)$ with a delay k between it and the plant $P(z)$ is the same as the delayed output from a system with an ideal controller $C(z)$ and no delay between it and the plant. Equivalence between the loops shown in Figures 10.6(a) and (b) requires

$$\frac{O(z)}{I(z)} = \frac{C^*(z)P(z)z^{-k}}{1 + C^*(z)P(z)z^{-k}} = \frac{C(z)P(z)}{1 + C(z)P(z)}z^{-k} \qquad (10.4)$$

whence

$$C^*(z) = \frac{C(z)}{1 + C(z)P(z)(1 - z^{-k})} \qquad (10.5)$$

as shown in Figure 10.6(c). For the gaze control subfunctions (saccade, pursuit etc), Brown and co-workers proposed separate parallel subcontrollers (where possible PIDs), whose output is combined and cascaded into the local motor PID controller.

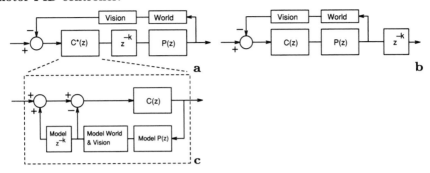

Figure 10.6
The Smith predictor. The transfer functions of (a) and (b) are equivalent, enabling the actual controller $C^*(z)$ with inherent delay z^{-k} to be derived in terms of the ideal controller $C(z)$ as at (c). Note that the plant, world and vision have to be modelled and that the predictor takes no account of delay in the feedback loop.

We contend that there are several difficulties with these approaches to delay and interactions.

Concerning the parallel subcontrollers, we note that interactions between the subfunctions are frequent, requiring equally frequent switching between *subcontrollers*, which is hard to achieve smoothly. Furthermore, cascading a PID subcontroller into a further PID controller forms a high order control system for which the selection of the parameters is typically complicated.

Concerning the elimination of controller delays, we suggest that the Smith predictor may not be optimal. First, modelling the plant in the face of the nonlinearities of the local controllers is hard, as is modelling the vision processes. Secondly, for a "sluggish" system with a small time delay (and the joint control of heads is in this regime) the conventional PID controller is a better controller (Marshall, 1979). Finally, the most significant and variable delays in a gaze control system occur not in the controller-plant cascade, but in visual sensing, *which lies in the feedback loop*. The Smith predictor is unable to account for delays outside the controller/plant cascade, and any attempt to incorporate the feedback delay into the controller delay leads to control of the output of the vision system, and not the desired control of the head!

Thus in our system we are incorporating a prediction section in the feedback loop. Using the kinematical results presented in the next section we transform the visual information into a static system frame and use it and delayed head joint angle and velocity information to update a temporal model using a Kalman Filter. A prediction over the delay period is made to provide prompt visual feedback to the gaze controller.

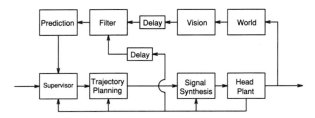

Figure 10.7
The gaze control loop used in our work. Filtering and prediction are used to overcome
the delay in the visual feedback.

The gaze controller is described in detail in (Du & Brady, 1991; Du *et al.*,
1991), and here we only give an overview of its components, sketched in
Figure 10.7. The supervisor uses a rule base to determine what action to
take on the basis of the visual input, the state of the head, and the overall
user requirements. For example, if the overall requirement is to track the
fastest object and the required gaze direction is, say, $> 5°$ away from the
current direction then the head will saccade. The trajectory planner again
uses a rule base to transform the desired action to the trajectories of the
joints according to the state and characteristics of the head. In order to
handle the cooperations and interactions in gaze control and to increase the
performance of the gaze controller, a signal synthesis and adaptation stage
is inserted between the planner and the gaze controller. Instead of adjusting
the control parameters of local controllers to deal with the nonlinearities
and disturbance in the plant, the signal synthesis and adaptation mechanism
tries to synthesize the best instruction to the local controller according to
the desired motion, the state of the local controller and the plant dynamics.

10.4   The vision system

The physiological oculomotor control responses indicate that the primary
inputs to control of gaze from vision are overall image motion to drive OKR,
windowed image motion to drive pursuit of an object of interest, and disparity to drive vergence. Earlier we suggested that the most crucial for an
ongoing active system are the motion processes.

It becomes obvious when considering the visual tasks engendered by the
surveillance scenario, that a single motion process is insufficient. A glance at
the gradients of the target and camera trajectories in Figure 10.5 shows that
the range of motion expected is $\sim 60°\text{s}^{-1}$ when not tracking down to $\sim 0°\text{s}^{-1}$
— equivalent to 20 pixel/frame down to 0 pixel/frame. Furthermore, the
image motion must alert the system, for instance, to something new moving
in the visual field or some object about to strike the head. The system
must also use motion to indicate exactly which objects are of interest. In
other words, if it is to survive, an active head requires a motion system

able to provide (at frame rates and with low latency) alarms, segmentation and visual stabilization — indeed the full range of 2D abilities for which motion is deemed useful in the literature. On top of this we must allow for different appearance in the objects to be pursued; one may exhibit strong edges, another strong corners, another strong texture.

To deal with the rich variety of world tasks that demand motion understanding, a similarly rich variety of motion sensors is required. Such sensors range from the crude, fast and robust to the more refined and stately, and must span more than one representation of image motion. The cruder processes must run autonomously, and supply bootstrap information for the more sophisticated ones and, as knowledge sources, report not only their motion information, but also the reliability of that information. Before discussing the algorithms we are implementing, it is worth considering how the position and motion of objects in the scene are related via the head mechanism to the position and motion of objects in the image.

Imaging and kinematics

The controllable head platform enables the gazing cyclopean frame to be directed anywhere within the sphere of gaze, but the specific way that the cameras' rotational degrees of freedom are restricted will affect where scene points are imaged, and what image motion is induced in response to scene and head motion. Because of the unmechanical flexible properties of the eye, and the approximate nature of Listing's Law, the physiological literature (Carpenter, 1988; Westheimer, 1957) tends to consider redirection of gaze in terms of rotations about fixed axes in a static frame, followed by a rotation about the gaze direction through the angle of cyclotorsion. The inexactness of Listing's Law is accounted for by allowing slop in the cyclotorsion angle. For an engineered device, there is neither scope nor need for this flexible description, and the imaging geometry and motion are completely specified in terms of the head's kinematics.

Consider the transformations linking the camera frames (l, r) and the system frame (s). To fixate on a particular point $\mathbf{G}^s$ referred to the system frame, the head first rotates about the pan axis through some angle θ_p, the common platform elevates through θ_e to bring the fixation point into the plane of the cameras' optic axes, and then the left and right cameras rotate by angles θ_l and θ_r about vergence axes perpendicular to the platform to align both optic axes onto the point. The three stages are illustrated in Figure 10.8. Using homogeneous coordinates, a general point $\mathbf{R}^s = (R_x^s, R_y^s, R_z^s, 1)^\top$ in the system frame is at

$$\mathbf{R}^l = [M^{le}][M^{ep}][M^{ps}]\mathbf{R}^s \tag{10.6}$$

$$\mathbf{R}^r = [M^{re}][M^{ep}][M^{ps}]\mathbf{R}^s \tag{10.7}$$

in the left and right cameras, where the matrices are

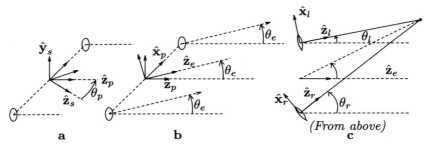

Figure 10.8
A rotation of θ_p about $\hat{\mathbf{y}}_s$ transforms the system into the pan frame (a). The head elevates by θ_e about $\hat{\mathbf{x}}_p$ to bring the gaze point within the elevated frame (b). The cameras rotate by θ_l and θ_r about axes perpendicular to the elevation platform to achieve fixation (c).

$$[M^{ps}] = \begin{pmatrix} C_p & 0 & -S_p & 0 \\ 0 & 1 & 0 & 0 \\ S_p & 0 & C_p & 0 \\ 0 & 0 & 0 & 1 \end{pmatrix} \qquad [M^{le}] = \begin{pmatrix} C_l & 0 & -S_l & -IC_l/2 \\ 0 & 1 & 0 & 0 \\ S_l & 0 & C_l & -IS_l/2 \\ 0 & 0 & 0 & 1 \end{pmatrix}$$

$$[M^{ep}] = \begin{pmatrix} 1 & 0 & 0 & 0 \\ 0 & C_e & -S_e & 0 \\ 0 & S_e & C_e & 0 \\ 0 & 0 & 0 & 1 \end{pmatrix} \qquad [M^{re}] = \begin{pmatrix} C_r & 0 & -S_r & IC_r/2 \\ 0 & 1 & 0 & 0 \\ S_r & 0 & C_r & IS_r/2 \\ 0 & 0 & 0 & 1 \end{pmatrix}$$

where I is the interocular separation and $C_p = \cos\theta_p$, $S_p = \sin\theta_p$, and so on. Under perspective projection, the general point is imaged at

$$\mathbf{r}^l = -\frac{f}{R_z^l}\begin{pmatrix} 1 & 0 & 0 & 0 \\ 0 & 1 & 0 & 0 \end{pmatrix}\mathbf{R}^l \; ; \quad \mathbf{r}^r = -\frac{f}{R_z^r}\begin{pmatrix} 1 & 0 & 0 & 0 \\ 0 & 1 & 0 & 0 \end{pmatrix}\mathbf{R}^r \, , \qquad (10.8)$$

where f is the focal length.

From the forward kinematics of the head we can derive the location of the gaze point given the vector of joint angles $\boldsymbol{\theta} = (\theta_p, \theta_e, \theta_l, \theta_r)^\top$. Considering only the 3-space coordinates, the relationships are nonlinear, of the form $\mathbf{G}^s = \mathbf{g}(\boldsymbol{\theta})$, and explicitly for the device described

$$\mathbf{G}^s = \frac{I}{\tan\theta_r - \tan\theta_l}\begin{pmatrix} \sin\theta_p\cos\theta_e + \frac{1}{2}\cos\theta_p(\tan\theta_r + \tan\theta_l) \\ \sin\theta_e \\ \cos\theta_p\cos\theta_e - \frac{1}{2}\sin\theta_p(\tan\theta_r + \tan\theta_l) \end{pmatrix}. \qquad (10.9)$$

Differentiating with respect to time gives the motion of the gaze point in terms of the joint angular velocities

$$\dot{\mathbf{G}}^s = [G]\dot{\boldsymbol{\theta}} \, , \qquad (10.10)$$

where $[G]$ is the Jacobian matrix, $[G] = \partial\mathbf{g}/\partial\boldsymbol{\theta}$. Thus, provided the vision system can maintain fixation on a single scene point, given the joint angles and velocities it is possible to build a model of the motion of the fixation point $(\mathbf{G}^s, \dot{\mathbf{G}}^s)$ in the system frame. However, it is important to note that because of delay in the vision system, this model itself must be computed using time-delayed joint information (see Figure 10.7), and prediction is required to produce a current tracking error signal. Simulations of such a system using point tracking have been reported in (Du & Brady, 1991; Du et al., 1991).

It is also important to consider the motion of scene and image points which are not fixated, as the system may wish to fixate on these next. The expressions for the fixation point did not involve the image positions and velocities because these are zero by definition, but to recover 3D information for other points it is necessary to establish correspondence between left and right images. Without going into detail, given the image positions $(\mathbf{r}^l, \mathbf{r}^r)$ of a scene point and the joint angles $\boldsymbol{\theta}$ the scene point in the system frame is $\mathbf{R}^s = \mathbf{f}(\mathbf{r}^l, \mathbf{r}^r, \boldsymbol{\theta})$, where $\mathbf{f}$ is a vector of nonlinear functions. Again by differentiating one can relate the scene motion to the measured visual motion and joint motion via a Jacobian matrix $[F]$: $\dot{\mathbf{R}}^s = [F](\dot{\mathbf{r}}^l, \dot{\mathbf{r}}^r, \dot{\boldsymbol{\theta}})^\top$.

The inverse kinematics, the retrieval of joint angles and velocities from gaze position and motion, are not so straightforward because given the three coordinates of the gaze point in the system frame it is not possible to derive all four joint angles $\boldsymbol{\theta} = (\theta_p, \theta_e, \theta_l, \theta_r)^\top$ — an extra constraint is required. Two constraint regimes are used in our design. The first requires that in steady state the trajectory planner uses $\theta_l = -\theta_r$, requiring the pan frame to be looking in the direction of the gaze point. Then $\tan \theta_l = -\tan \theta_r$ and

$$\mathbf{G}^s = \mathbf{g}^*(\theta_p, \theta_e, \theta_r) = \begin{pmatrix} \sin \theta_p \frac{I \cos \theta_e}{2 \tan \theta_r} \\ \frac{I \sin \theta_e}{2 \tan \theta_r} \\ \cos \theta_p \frac{I \cos \theta_e}{2 \tan \theta_r} \end{pmatrix}, \tag{10.11}$$

whence the reduced vector $\boldsymbol{\theta}^* = (\theta_p, \theta_e, \theta_r)^\top$ is

$$\boldsymbol{\theta}^* = \begin{pmatrix} \arctan G_x^s / G_z^s \\ \arctan \frac{G_y^s}{\sin \theta_p G_x^s + \cos \theta_p G_z^s} \\ \arctan \frac{I}{2 \sqrt[+]{(G_x^s)^2 + (G_z^s)^2}} \end{pmatrix}. \tag{10.12}$$

Differentiating the expression for $\mathbf{G}^s$ and inverting the 3×3 Jacobian $[G^*] = \partial \mathbf{g}^* / \partial \boldsymbol{\theta}^*$ we find that if the target is being tracked in the steady state regime the joint angular velocities are given by $\dot{\boldsymbol{\theta}}^* = [G^*]^{-1} \dot{\mathbf{G}}^s$. The second constraint regime demands that during transitions trajectories are built using a constrained trajectory for the least agile axis, here the pan axis θ_p. New reduced vectors of joint angles $\boldsymbol{\theta}^\dagger = (\theta_e, \theta_l, \theta_r)^\top$ and velocities can then be derived using the technique outlined above.

The above gives an account of how 3D vision and head motions are related. In the human system, much of the input to control is derived directly from 2D vision using a single eye without explicit reference to the 3D scene, and the vision system we are building places a similar emphasis on 2D vision competences, particularly motion processing. With a single camera and without depth, we have only gaze *directions*. A moment's thought shows that it is impossible to transform the gaze direction between frames which are separated by a translation, and so it is not possible to transform the gaze direction from the camera's local frame to the system frame, or between the local frames if the head is rotating about the pan axis. In this case, we use the approximation that the interocular spacing I is zero, or equivalently that the camera is fixated at infinite depth. Consider a feature imaged at $\mathbf{r}^r$ in the right camera's image plane. With $I = 0$, this defines a direction parameterized by two angles $(\phi^s, \rho^s)^\top$ (elevation and azimuth) in the static system frame. Using the coordinate transformations it is easy to find $(\phi^s, \rho^s)^\top = \mathbf{h}(\mathbf{r}^r, \boldsymbol{\theta}^*)$ and hence $(\dot{\phi}^s, \dot{\rho}^s)^\top = [H](\dot{\mathbf{r}}^r, \dot{\boldsymbol{\theta}}^*)^\top$, where $[H] = \partial \mathbf{h}/\partial \boldsymbol{\theta}^*$. Thus measurements of image position and motion in just one camera can be related to angles and angular motions in the static frame and vice versa, allowing a Kalman filter to be constructed for the directions of moving objects on the gaze sphere.

The separate use of 3D models with fixation and correspondence and 2D models without correspondence is repeated in the vision system. The vision processes are divided into coarse "peripheral" processes which run continually on the entire image but in one camera without correspondence, and more acute processes which run in "foveal" windows in both cameras with correspondence. The rôle of the coarse processes is more in acquiring new objects of interest, whereas the acute processes are concerned with fixation and tracking.

Vision processes

The key coarse vision process carried out over the entire image is the detection of objects moving independently of the background, and the reporting of their image position and velocity. To derive coarse, but robust, measures of image motion having constant latency and at frame rate, we apply the motion constraint equation $\boldsymbol{\nabla} I \cdot \dot{\mathbf{r}} + \partial I/\partial t = 0$ (Horn & Schunck, 1981; Schunck, 1986) to each smoothed and eightfold subsampled image field. At each pixel this yields values of $\mathbf{v}$, the component of image motion $\dot{\mathbf{r}}$ along the spatial gradient direction, as

$$\mathbf{v} = -\left(\frac{\partial I}{\partial t}\right)\frac{1}{|\boldsymbol{\nabla} I|^2}\boldsymbol{\nabla} I. \tag{10.13}$$

Components whose magnitudes are below threshold are removed.

To segment the motion we first subtract the image motion due to the known motion of the head. For surveillance of objects at large depths, so that the interocular distance is negligible, the head motion will, to a good approximation, be entirely rotational, which in turn induces image motion which is independent of depth and given by (Murray & Buxton, 1991)

$$\dot{\mathbf{r}}_{rot} = -\Omega \wedge \mathbf{r} - (\Omega \wedge \mathbf{r} \cdot \hat{\mathbf{z}})\mathbf{r}/f \tag{10.14}$$

where all quantities are referred to a camera frame. It is straightforward to show that in the left camera, for example,

$$\Omega^l = \begin{pmatrix} \dot{\theta}_p \sin\theta_e \sin\theta_l + \dot{\theta}_e \cos\theta_l \\ \dot{\theta}_p \cos\theta_e + \dot{\theta}_l \\ \dot{\theta}_p \sin\theta_e \cos\theta_l - \dot{\theta}_e \sin\theta_l \end{pmatrix} . \tag{10.15}$$

The actual value subtracted is of course the component of $\dot{\mathbf{r}}_{rot}$ in the direction of $\mathbf{v}$, that is $\dot{\mathbf{r}}_{rot} \cdot \mathbf{v}/v$.

After subtraction, the residual background motion is close to zero and a search is made for spatially and temporally connected regions where the motion is well above the background level, labelling such regions with a simple measure of significance. The motion vectors within the segmented region are fitted using least squares to either a constant or affine field.

The algorithm is more fully discussed in (McLauchlan & Murray, 1991), and here we give just a brief example. Figure 10.9(a) shows one image field from a sequence where an independently moving mannequin's head is viewed by a camera which is rotating. Figure 10.9(b) shows the edge-normal components of flow computed from the subsampled image. After subtracting the background and segmenting, the region of independent motion found is shown in Figure 10.9(c). For a constant motion field approximation, each flow vector inside the segmented region provides a constraint line $\dot{\mathbf{r}} \cdot \mathbf{v} = v^2$ for the full flow $\dot{\mathbf{r}}$ (Schunck, 1989), and the resulting least squares fit in velocity space is illustrated in Figure 10.9(d). The ellipse, magnified 8-fold for clarity, gives estimates of the velocity errors in orthogonal directions. The recovered velocities and positions of the segmented regions are passed to a multiple Kalman Filter, which arbitrates as to what is old and what is new.

If the controller triggers a saccade to a new region of interest, it initiates higher acuity motion processes inside a foveal window. At the start of the slow down phase from saccade to pursuit the motion can still be large (eg Figure 10.5(b)), and is best measured again using a spatio-temporal process, the motion signal output being used as an error signal for minimization. Once the motion is sufficiently small, a feature detector is used to provide more high acuity tracking. Two such processes have been implemented, a corner detector (Wang & Brady, 1991) and a snake tracker (see chapter 3).

An example (Torr *et al.*, 1991) of the cooperation between prompt, coarse and robust processes and slower, higher acuity processes is shown in Figure 10.10. The mannequin's head in front of the camera (a) is detected by the coarse motion detector (b), which initiates an elliptical snake tracker

Figure 10.9
One frame from a sequence where a moving mannequin is viewed by a rotating camera (a) and the smoothed and subsampled image with motion vectors (b). The segmented region is shown in (c), and (d) shows the least squares fit to the constraint lines in velocity space.

within the motion region (c). The camera is rotated suddenly (here by a robot arm) to centre the ellipse on the image (d) and, as the target is moved (e, f), the camera rotates to keep the ellipse in the image centre. Both camera and ellipse motions are updated using Kalman filters, providing some robustness to occlusion for short periods.

10.5   The physical architecture for vision and control

The initial exploration of the vision processes has been carried out on a mixture of pipelined processors, workstations and small numbers of parallel processors. We are now developing a larger hybrid parallel processor, consisting of pipelined processors for early image-wide operations, such as convolution and image subtraction, and a configurable network of MIMD processors for 2D and 3D vision processes and for gaze control (Figure 10.11).

   Image capture and early operations over the whole image are achieved using Datacube's range of pipelined processors. The basic system comprises

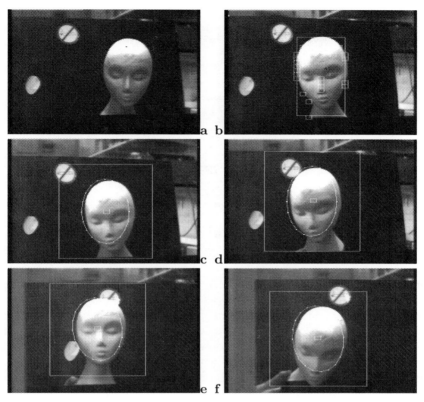

Figure 10.10
Coarse motion used to demarcate a region of interest followed by tracking using an elliptical snake.

two stereo video channels, each consisting of an image capture board, and an 8×8 convolver to provide smoothing. A framestore provides optional deinterlacing, though to reduce motion blur we typically operate on individual fields. The Datacube boards are controlled over VMEbus by a Motorola 68030 cpu running OS-9.

The MIMD network consists of some thirty INMOS Transputer modules (TRAMs). Each TRAM contains a 25Mips/3.5Mflop T805 processor with 1MB DRAM and four $1.4MBs^{-1}$ communication links which are either hardwired to neighbouring TRAMs or connected via programmable crossbar switches which allow the network topology to be altered. A SUN Sparc2 workstation provides the user interface and code development platform. The Transputers are programmed using INMOS Parallel C.

Video data are transferred from the video bus to several VRAMs each readable by a Transputer. One interface delivers subsampled image data to the cluster of TRAMs dedicated to recovering coarse motion estimates across

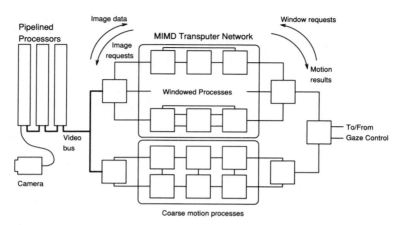

Figure 10.11
An outline of one channel of the vision machine. Data from the pipelined processors performing early vision are transmitted to a MIMD Transputer Network, part of which performs coarse operations on the entire image, and part which performs higher acuity operations on small image windows. Output from this network is sent to further Transputers which run the high level gaze controller.

the entire image and to deriving the segmentation and triggering alarms. Two more interface Transputers act as window servers, one each for left and right channels, delivering foveal windows (typically 64×64 pixels) via a link to clusters of worker TRAMs. When the gaze controller finds a region of interest from the segmentation of the coarse data, it sends a message to a cluster, giving details of the region's position and velocity and requesting that it perform a windowed operation (eg corner detection). The head of a cluster of worker TRAMs is responsible for requesting windowed image data from the window server TRAM and its tail responsible for delivering results onwards to gaze controller.

III Geometric and Task Planning

The previous two sections dealt with technical issues — tracking and control — which form part of the essential technology of Active Vision. In contrast, this section deals with experimental systems performing specified tasks. They are decidedly experimental, in contrast with the more mature systems of the following section. But they are somewhat adventurous in putting to the test new ideas from Active Vision and from Artificial Intelligence.

The first two chapters of the section, 11 and 12, are decidedly geometric in flavour. In chapter 11 some of the tracking technology of the first section is applied to a hand-eye robot. This robot has to retrieve a known object, in a known position amidst unmodelled obstacles. Robot motion has the dual function of reaching towards the goal and also exploring freespace visually by manipulating the vantage point. It is an active system both in the sense that it uses real-time structure from motion to elicit surface shape and in the sense of focussing attention. The motion planning system of chapter 12 is active in a similar sense, but here the coupling between perception and action is potentially tighter. The tracked deformation of a contour is shown to be capable of giving continuous "readings" of various *differential invariant* measures of the image-motion field. These in turn can be regarded as a position and attitude sensor that can be fed back into a real-time navigation or manipulation control system. Three-dimensional theory is used to validate the principles of the system. However the system itself takes the form of a direct *two-dimensional* coupling between the image-motion field and the controlled action.

The notion of direct coupling of perception and action, without an explicit 3D intermediary, is very appealing. For the problem of chapter 12 such a coupling can be designed by appealing to geometric arguments. However, rational design may not always be achievable and, even when it is, adaptation in the light of online experience is most desirable. Chapter 13 develops and demonstrates such adaptation using learning techniques from Artificial Intelligence (AI) and Neural Networks. In order to facilitate the study, a simple creature with rudimentary sensors is allowed to roam a simulated world. Punishment and reward are applied in a preset formula taking into account speed and mean free path. Direct mappings between sensory input and motor output evolve as experience accumulates. It is shown most elegantly how the learned motor response embodies intuitive actions such as backing off and swerving, triggered by appropriate configurations of proximate obstacles.

The last chapter of this section of the book, chapter 14, is an exploration of a planning problem of a very different kind. The problem retains a geometrical element but deals primarily with eliciting the descriptive structure of a visual scene. The scene is drawn from a known class for which some background knowledge is available (the particular example used is a table set for a meal). At first this seems like a Marrian problem in exhaustive description of a visual scene. In fact the visual process is highly directed and focussed, in the manner of Active Vision. Visual exploration is entirely driven by the specific question asked (e.g. "is the table laid for breakfast?"). Visual exploration is regarded as a sequence of actions, each of which is chosen for its "information-gathering" value in relation to the specific question. Technically, the system is driven by Bayesian methods developed in AI. As such, this chapter is a piece of pioneering work in an area that cries out for development: the harnessing of AI knowledge representation and reasoning in real-world seeing robots.

11 Visual Exploration of Free-space

Andrew Blake, Andrew Zisserman and Roberto Cipolla

11.1 Introduction

Over the last few years, significant advances have been made in estimation of surface shape from visual motion, that is from image sequences obtained from a moving camera. By combining differential geometry (DoCarmo, 1976) with spatio-temporal analysis of visual motion (Longuet-Higgins & Pradzny, 1980; Maybank, 1985; Faugeras, 1990) it has been shown that local surface curvature can be computed from moving images (Giblin & Weiss, 1987; Blake & Cipolla, 1990; Cipolla & Blake, 1990; Vaillant, 1990; Arbogast & Mohr, 1990). The computation is robust with respect to surface shape, configuration of the surface relative to the camera and the nature of the camera motion. For example the ability to discriminate qualitatively between rigid features and silhouettes on smooth surfaces has been demonstrated (Cipolla & Blake, 1990). Particularly important for collision-free motion, the "sidedness" of silhouettes is computed, that is, which side is solid surface and which is free space. Furthermore quantitative analysis of silhouettes is possible and this is useful for motion planning, to produce economical and smooth paths. In fact image motion measurements can be used directly to approximate minimal length paths based on geodesics (Blake *et al.*, 1991).

This paper reports on progress in building a robot with active vision that can manipulate objects in the presence of obstacles (figure 11.1). Our Adept

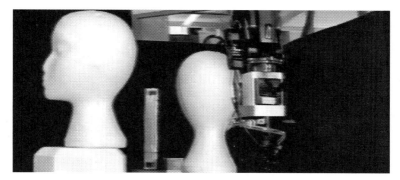

Figure 11.1
The robot directs the camera's gaze towards one of two obstacles, attempting to plan a path between them. The goal object is marked by the vertical white column in the distance.

robot has a camera and gripper on board and is able to make exploratory movements around its workspace. As it moves, it monitors the image motion and deformation of contours, using the dynamic contours described in chapter 3.

As in earlier versions of our system (Blake & Cipolla, 1990; Cipolla & Blake, 1990), contour motion is used to interpret occlusion and surface cur-

vature. More recently we have built on further features: incremental building of a free-space model, incremental planning of robot motion and search
strategies for navigation. Currently we use a suction gripper for object manipulation but plan to replace this with a parallel jaw gripper for greater
versatility. Initial experiments show the feasibility of using the splines obtained from dynamic contours to plan grasps for a parallel jaw gripper.

11.2   Visual analysis of curved surfaces

Recent work in our laboratory has shown that, by combining differential
geometry (DoCarmo, 1976) and static contour analysis (Koenderink, 1984)
with analysis of visual motion (Longuet-Higgins & Pradzny, 1980; Maybank,
1985) local surface curvature can be computed from moving images (Blake &
Cipolla, 1990; Cipolla & Blake, 1990). The apparent contour is the boundary of the image of a smooth surface. It is the perspective projection of
a smooth curve — an "extremal boundary" — onto the image plane (figure 11.2). Figure 11.3 demonstrates the ability to discriminate qualitatively

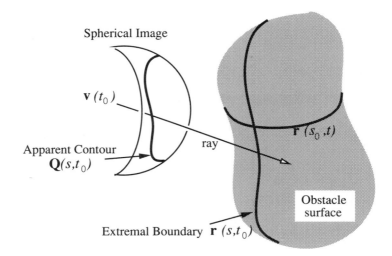

Figure 11.2
For a given vantage point, $\mathbf{v}(t_0)$, the family of rays emanating from the viewer's optical
centre that touch the surface defines an s-parameter curve $\mathbf{r}(s, t_0)$ which is the extremal
boundary from vantage point t_0. The spherical perspective projection of this extremal
boundary — the apparent contour, $\mathbf{Q}(s, t_0)$ — determines the direction of rays which
graze the surface. The distance along the ray is $\lambda(s, t_0)$. A typical t-line of our "epipolar"
parameterisation is shown as the curve $\mathbf{r}(s_0, t)$.

between rigid features and extremal boundaries on smooth surfaces. Despite
much effort, attempts over the last two decades to make this distinction by
photometric analysis have been relatively unsuccessful. However, by allowing

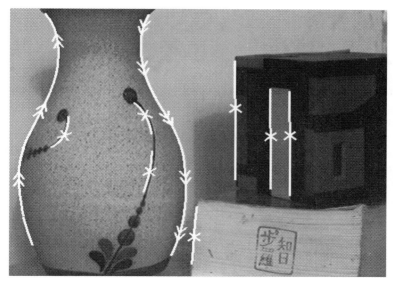

Figure 11.3
Vase and block, one frame from an image sequence with a moving camera. Labels on contours display results of qualitative curvature analysis. A cross denotes a rigid feature, a surface crease or marking. A double arrow indicates an "apparent contour" or silhouette. The obscuring surface is to the right of the arrowed direction. (After (Cipolla & Blake, 1990).)

small camera motions and observing the resulting contour deformations the distinction can be made reliably. Particularly important for collision-free motion, the "sidedness" of apparent contours is computed, that is, which side is solid surface and which is free space. Useful quantitative analysis of apparent contours is also possible, yielding full information about local surface curvature.

11.2.1   Apparent contours and surface shape

Figure 11.2 illustrates the notation for surface geometry and image measurements. Using the convention of Maybank (1985) that the image is projected onto a unit sphere through its centre, a point $\mathbf{r}(s,t)$ on a visible surface projects to a vector $\mathbf{T}(s,t)$ on the image sphere:

$$\mathbf{r}(s,t) = \mathbf{v}(t) + \lambda(s,t)\mathbf{T}(s,t),$$

where, at time t, $\mathbf{v}(t)$ is the position of the viewer and $\lambda(s,t)$ is the distance from the viewer to the point $\mathbf{r}(s,t)$. The direction of the light ray from viewer to surface point $\mathbf{r}(s,t)$, in the *world* frame, is

$$\mathbf{T}(s,t) = R(t)\mathbf{Q}(s,t) \tag{11.1}$$

where $R(t)$ is a rotation operator describing the orientation of the camera frame relative to the world frame and $\mathbf{Q}$ is an image point in the *camera* frame. The parameterisation s, t is not uniquely determined (the "aperture problem"). We fix it to be the "epipolar parameterisation" (Blake & Cipolla, 1990; Bolles *et al.*, 1987) defined by $\mathbf{r}_t \times \mathbf{T} = 0$ (where $\mathbf{r}_t \equiv \partial\mathbf{r}/\partial t$).

The motion is assumed to be known and to be rigid, that is, only the camera is moving. Translational motion $\mathbf{U}$ and rotational motion $\mathbf{\Omega}$ are defined by: $\mathbf{U} = \mathbf{v}_t$ and $(\mathbf{\Omega}\times) = R_t$ where $\times$ denotes vector product.

Image measurables are apparent contour points $\mathbf{Q}(s, t)$ in the camera frame which can be converted via (11.1) into world frame points $\mathbf{T}(s, t)$. From first and second spatial and temporal derivatives of an apparent contour point $\mathbf{T}$ we can compute distance and surface shape. The surface normal is given by

$$\mathbf{n} = \frac{\mathbf{T} \times \mathbf{T}_s}{|\mathbf{T} \times \mathbf{T}_s|} \tag{11.2}$$

and the distance λ to the extremal boundary point $\mathbf{r}$ (see also (Bolles *et al.*, 1987)):

$$\lambda = -\frac{\mathbf{U} \cdot \mathbf{n}}{\mathbf{T}_t \cdot \mathbf{n}}. \tag{11.3}$$

For navigation purposes we will also be interested in the following two quantities. The *normal curvature*, the curvature of a section-curve through the surface in the $\mathbf{T}, \mathbf{n}$ plane, is

$$\kappa_n = \frac{\mathbf{T} \cdot \mathbf{N}_t}{|\mathbf{r}_t|} \tag{11.4}$$

where the curve normal $\mathbf{N} = -\mathbf{n}$, equal and opposite to the surface normal and

$$\mathbf{r}_t = (\lambda_t + \mathbf{T} \cdot \mathbf{v}_t)\mathbf{T} \tag{11.5}$$

which is a function of image measurables. The *geodesic torsion* (DoCarmo, 1976)

$$\tau_g = \frac{\mathbf{B} \cdot \mathbf{N}_t}{|\mathbf{r}_t|} \tag{11.6}$$

where the "binormal" vector $\mathbf{B} = \mathbf{T} \times \mathbf{N}$. Both normal curvature κ_n and geodesic torsion τ_g can clearly be computed from absolute image motion.

11.2.2   Surface sensor

We can regard the vision sensor as a surface sensor, therefore, as if the computations of the previous section were packaged with the sensor. The sensor computes range, curvature and geodesic torsion, together with appropriate, statistically derived error bounds. It functions by making exploratory motions transversely to the line of sight. The clearance needed for these exploratory motions must be allowed for in path-planning.

Given the practicalities of camera optics, the sensor has no *upper* limit of range but does have a *lower* limit, the near point of focus, typically 50mm in our system. This is exactly opposite to the Lumelsky and Skewis model of a range sensor for path-planning purposes (Lumelsky & Skewis, 1990) which has an upper limit but no lower limit. Consequently the sensor cannot operate continuously during path-execution to monitor current clearance. Instead it must look ahead, estimate the next path segment, and then travel blind until the next obstacle comes into view.

11.3   Extrapolating geodesic paths

Assuming surface shape is not known *a priori*, the only information is the position $\mathbf{g}$ of the goal and what is visible to the surface sensor at the start position $\mathbf{v}(0)$, namely the extremal boundary (figure 11.4). One might ex-

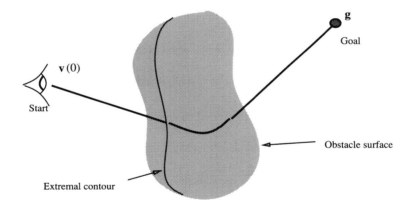

Figure 11.4
An arm-mounted camera is initially at $\mathbf{v}(0)$ and is to move to a goal point $\mathbf{g}$, avoiding a single obstacle surface. We consider only the case where the minimal path has a single contact with the surface although clearly, for a non-convex obstacle, the path could leave the obstacle and subsequently hit it again. The path consists of three parts, the straight segment from $\mathbf{v}(0)$ to the extremal boundary, followed by a helical geodesic approximation, followed by another straight section to $\mathbf{g}$.

trapolate the surface in some way, then grow a geodesic on the extrapolated surface but that would be a computationally expensive procedure. It is far more efficient to extrapolate the geodesic itself. The following argument (first described in (Blake *et al.*, 1991)) shows that the surface sensor provides exactly the necessary initial conditions to initiate an approximated geodesic.

The apparent contour $\mathbf{T}(s, 0)$, as seen from the initial position $\mathbf{v}(0)$ at time

$t = 0$, is the projection of the extremal boundary $\mathbf{r}(s,0)$ onto the surface. Normal curvature $\kappa_n(s,0)$ and geodesic torsion $\tau_g(s,0)$ can be computed along the contour, via equations (11.4) and (11.6). The following theorem states that this is sufficient to specify uniquely a helical approximation $\mathbf{R}(u)$ to the geodesic.

THEOREM 11.1 (GEODESIC INITIAL CONDITIONS) Given $\mathbf{r}$ on the surface, $\mathbf{T}$, $\mathbf{N}$, κ_n and τ_g: (a) There is a unique helix $\mathbf{R}(u)$ passing through $\mathbf{r}$ with tangent $\mathbf{R}_u = \mathbf{T}$, normal $\mathbf{R}_{uu}/|\mathbf{R}_{uu}| = \mathbf{N}$, curvature $\kappa = \kappa_n$ and torsion $\tau = \tau_g$. (b) The helix $\mathbf{R}(u)$ agrees up to 3rd order with the unique geodesic of the surface that joins smoothly onto the straight line from $\mathbf{v}(0)$ to $\mathbf{r}$. (c) In the case that the obstacle is either cylindrical or spherical, the helix is exactly a geodesic of the surface.

The proof of (a) follows from the fact that helices are the family of curves with constant curvature and torsion (DoCarmo, 1976). Hence κ_n and τ_g specify the member of the family of helices up to isometry (i.e. the shape of the helix) and $\mathbf{r}$, $\mathbf{T}$ and $\mathbf{N}$ specify a rigid transformation. (b) follows from the facts that $\kappa = \kappa_n$ so that (DoCarmo, 1976) the geodesic curvature κ_g of the helix is zero, establishing agreement up to second order, and that $\tau = \tau_g$, agreement to 3rd order. (c) holds because the geodesics of cylinder and spheres are all helices (in fact, for spheres, they are circles which are a special case of helices).

The helical approximation to the geodesic can be written in terms of its Frenet-Serret frame (DoCarmo, 1976) which is $\mathbf{T}, \mathbf{N}, \mathbf{B}$. Note that the binormal $\mathbf{B}$, by equation (11.2), must be parallel to the image contour $\mathbf{T}_s$. The helix is conveniently parameterised by the winding angle θ:

$$
\mathbf{R}(\theta) = \left[(1 - \cos\theta)\mathbf{N} + \sin\theta(\mathbf{T}\cos\alpha - \mathbf{B}\sin\alpha) \right.
$$
$$
\left. + \theta\tan\alpha(\mathbf{T}\sin\alpha + \mathbf{B}\cos\alpha) \right] \frac{\cos^2\alpha}{\kappa_n} + \mathbf{r}, \tag{11.7}
$$

where

$$
\tan\alpha = \frac{\tau_g}{\kappa_n} \tag{11.8}
$$

— the pitch of the helix is just the ratio of geodesic torsion to normal curvature. It can also be shown, using the *conjugacy* of $\mathbf{T}$ and $\mathbf{r}_s$ (Koenderink, 1990), that the pitch angle α is simply the angle between the binormal $\mathbf{B}$ and the extremal boundary direction $\mathbf{r}_s$. The axis of the helix is parallel to $\mathbf{r}_s$.

Finally, at every point $\mathbf{r}$, the approximated geodesic should be continued, in order to test whether it can form part of a smooth path to $\mathbf{g}$. This can be done by looking for a solution to two simultaneous equations for the point $\mathbf{R}$ at which the approximated geodesic joins the straight line from $\mathbf{R}$ to the goal. The first equation is the helix equation (11.7) and the second is the smoothness condition that the tangent direction $\mathbf{R}_\theta$ of the helix at the join is parallel to the vector from $\mathbf{R}$ to the goal $\mathbf{g}$. Differentiating equation (11.7) with respect to θ this condition can be expressed in terms of θ:

$$K(\mathbf{R}(\theta) - \mathbf{g}) = \cos\theta(\mathbf{T}\cos\alpha - \mathbf{B}\sin\alpha) \qquad (11.9)$$
$$+ \tan\alpha(\mathbf{T}\sin\alpha + \mathbf{B}\cos\alpha) + \mathbf{N}\sin\theta$$

where K is a constant. Now the test for the existence of an (approximately) extremal path through $\mathbf{r}$ is simply to test whether (11.7) and (11.9) have a simultaneous solution for θ, K.

The test for optimality of path can be approximated by a closed form expression in the limit of large curvature κ. As might be expected, it reduces to simple force-balance along the extremal boundary which can now be regarded as a wire. The geodesic consists, in this limit, simply of two straight lines from start and goal respectively, meeting on the wire. The angles between each straight line and the wire must be equal and opposite for static equilibrium.

11.4   Circumnavigation of single obstacles

Practical navigation is somewhat flexible to the positioning of an obstacle, using the convergence of the dynamic contour tracker, run at coarse scale for target-acquisition, to lock onto the apparent contour. Then the camera scans horizontally with the contour tracking at fine-scale. Resulting motion is analysed and used in several ways. First the *sign* of the estimated normal curvature κ_n determines the *sidedness* of the apparent contour — which side is free-space and hence navigable. Second, the magnitude of κ_n is used to extrapolate a smooth path around the object. Third, error in $1/\kappa_n$ from the regression analysis is "added on" to the path to ensure safe clearances. Uncertainty is simply incorporated into the procedure of the previous section by using a value for the radius of curvature which exceeds $1/\kappa_n$ by the appropriate tolerance. This results in a motion along a *parallel surface* (DoCarmo, 1976) to the true obstacle surface.

Performance is limited, currently, by vibration of the robot (of approximate amplitude 0.1mm). This means that the movement of the robot necessary for visual computation of curvature is somewhat extended, lasting for about 5 seconds at a visual sampling rate of 25Hz. Recursive least squares analysis of the image motion limits the effects of vibration somewhat. The result is that distance λ to the apparent contour can be computed quite accurately from visual motion, typically 200 ± 0.5mm. Curvature, as expected from theory, is less accurate. Radius of curvature $1/\kappa_n$ is typically measured to within ± 10mm. The accuracies quoted above are quite sufficient to assist path-planning. Figure 11.5 shows the arm with camera moving from start to goal, along a horizontal planar path, around a curved obstacle. A sec-

Front view	Side view

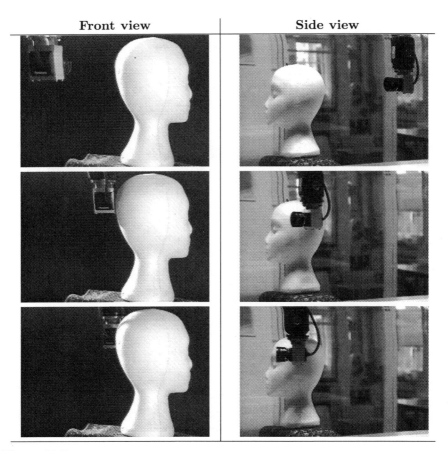

Figure 11.5
Three frames from a sequence shows the arm-mounted camera following a planar path
around a curved obstacle.

ond example shows navigation along a geodesic path using the pitch angle
α obtained from normal curvature and geodesic torsion, as in (11.8).

11.5   Active exploration of free-space

Following the first version of our manipulation system (Blake *et al.*, 1991),
we have investigated a more complex version of the manipulation problem in
which the workspace is cluttered with *several* obstacles. In addition to visual
and spatial geometry, we now need to add A^* search to guide incremental
path-planning. Path-planning consists of repeating a cycle of exploratory
motion, clearing a swathe of freespace (figure 11.8), and viewpoint prediction. After several of these cycles, over which the robot "jostles" for the best
view of the goal (box lid), it may find itself jammed between obstacles and

Figure 11.6
An approximated geodesic path. This sequence shows the robot driving the camera over the central helical section of an approximated geodesic path, touching the obstacle surface.

the edge of its workspace. In that case it backtracks to an earlier point in its search of freespace and investigates a new path. So far we have demonstrated these techniques with up to three different, unmodelled obstacles in the workspace.

11.5.1   Obstacle detection

It is an assumption of the system that a particular object, in a known location, is to be grasped and brought back to the robot's starting point. The robot learns the location of the object by looking at it across a clear workspace before the task begins. An edge feature on the object is tracked with a dynamic contour and its 3D location is computed by structure from motion using the "Epipolar Plane Image" (EPI) (Bolles *et al.*, 1987). This is a graph of image feature position versus robot position for a motion transverse to the camera's optic axis, as in figure 11.7. Recursive quadratic regression is used to compute the gradient of the graph which is proportional to inverse distance. A major extension of the original EPI idea is that the second derivative of the graph is used to compute surface curvature. This is simply an application of equations (11.3) and (11.4) for the case of transverse motion. Note however that although the analysis of the EPI by linear regression has been regarded as restricted to robot motion transverse to the line of sight (Bolles *et al.*, 1987) this is not the case. *Rectification* (Wolf, 1983) of image measurements onto a plane parallel to the motion is sufficient. This allows us to fixate a particular image feature, for which the camera must of course be panned, without giving up the EPI and consequent convenience for statistical filtering.

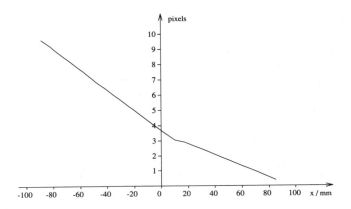

Figure 11.7
Epipolar Plane Image for occluding feature. The image position of a tracked feature is plotted as a function of the position of the moving camera. The change of gradient occurs here as an occlusion event occurs. This can be used as a trigger to switch the tracker from one object to another.

The benefit of using a recursive filter is that visual tracking is truly active, continually adapting in response to the changing cumulative estimate of scene geometry. Active control thus determines the *duration* of exploratory motions; motion continues until the covariance of the recovered depth and curvature fall within acceptable limits. Furthermore, tracking itself is adaptive. The current estimate of 3D object position is used to predict the position of the next image observation. As motion proceeds, positional covariance is reduced and prediction becomes more accurate. Consequently the speed of the robot can increase as its tracking motion progresses. Furthermore, immunity to losing the tracked contour is built up.

The recursive filter is also self-validating. It rapidly signals the change of gradient that occurs when some feature moves to occlude the feature being tracked (figure 11.7). This occurs, for instance, as the robot moves across the scene in figure 11.1. If it moves towards the left, tracking the left-hand boundary of the more distant obstacle, the boundary of the nearer obstacle will occlude and tracking will switch to that boundary. The occlusion event is detected by a "validation gate", a standard mechanism of Kalman filtering (see chapter 6 and (Bar-Shalom & Fortmann, 1988)), which is triggered when the square of the innovation[1] exceeds the innovation variance sufficiently to cause a χ^2 hypothesis test to fail.

---

[1]Innovation is the difference between an actual measurement and its predicted value, at a particular time-step in a Kalman filter.

11.5.2 Freespace representation

Freespace is explored visually. Since the portion of our SCARA robot that penetrates the working volume is approximately a vertical cylinder it is reasonably efficient to project 3D freespace onto a horizontal plane. Path-planning is guaranteed safe but not necessarily optimal, in common with well-known heuristic approaches such as Brooks' freeway method (Brooks, 1983). Within the plane, freespace is represented as a union of triangles (figure 11.8). The robot then translates on one horizontal plane (Lumelsky's assumption for a cartesian arm (Lumelsky, 1986)).

Visual exploration however must involve vertical scanning (using camera tilt) as well as horizontal. Thus the robot is frequently seen eyeing a particular visual feature up and down. Clearance at all heights within the workspace can be determined by projecting the ray at each point of the obstacle's silhouette onto the freespace plane, as a line. Making use of the visually inferred sidedness of the silhouette (see earlier), the line becomes the boundary of a free half-plane. The intersection of such half-planes sweeps out an area that is guaranteed free for robot-motion. (Note that the sweeping process need not actually be performed point by point but can be computed analytically for each span of the dynamic contour.)

11.5.3 Active exploration

Initially, the robot camera/gripper is positioned in a region that is guaranteed to be free (see bottom of figure 11.8). Robot motion is planned incrementally within the freespace plane. From a vantage point that has already been guaranteed free, the visual tracker is directed to make a further survey.

The robot begins by looking in the direction of the known object location. If the dynamic contour does lock, an EPI computation determines whether it is the goal object that is being tracked or some other obscuring feature which happened to lie along the same line of sight. If the dynamic contour fails to lock onto a feature, there must be an obstacle in the way so the robot pans the camera until the dynamic contour, which is just dangling in the image plane, locks onto a new feature. Panning for features continues until curvature analysis of the EPI can identify an extremal boundary and determine the sidedness of occlusion. A path can then be planned on the appropriate side of the boundary. Surface curvature, estimated from the EPI, is used to judge how far the robot should move before it might get a clear sight of the goal object (assuming no further obstacles). However, motion will not proceed until a sufficiently large chunk of freespace has been cleared by panning the line of sight. This is to ensure that the bulk of the camera/gripper head can move without collision *and* make the necessary exploratory motions at its new destination.

The sequence of exploratory motion, path-planning and change of vantage-point continues until the goal is reached. Progress may be monotonic as in

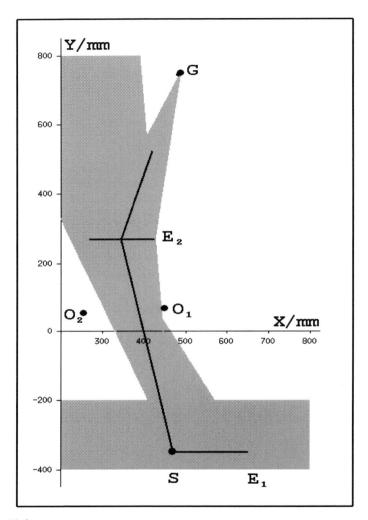

Figure 11.8
This freespace map is built incrementally by the active robot as it explores its environment, in search of the goal G. Initially the robot is at S, in an area of guaranteed freespace (the rectangle at the bottom). The robot directs its gaze toward the goal and, fails to find it. It then pans until it finds an image feature. It moves along the line E_1 to recover the distance to the obstacle feature O_1, identify it as an extremal boundary and compute surface curvature. It then pans towards obstacle O_2, clearing an area of freespace sufficient to move through. Then it plans a new vantage point (where there should be a clear view of the goal if there are no further obstacles) including a free line E_2 for exploratory motion. From there it looks towards the goal, finds a feature, makes an exploratory motion to compute distance and hence verifies that the goal has been sighted. There is a clear path to pick up the object.

figure 11.8. Often, though, exploration encounters a dead end, forcing back-tracking to occur (figure 11.9).

11.5.4   Extended performance

As it stands, the system is able to explore freespace effectively but quite slowly. The robot "contemplates" a gap between obstacles for 10 or 20 seconds, changing viewpoint and scanning the line of sight, before finally building up sufficient confidence to go through. This is largely because exploratory motions must be relatively long to defeat noise when computing surface curvature. Another limitation is that both background and foreground cannot be densely textured since image contours are explored serially in the quest for an occluding contour. How can these limitations be overcome?

One possibility is to use parallax which is well known to be a robust indicator of relative depth (Koenderink & Van Doorn, 1975; Longuet-Higgins & Pradzny, 1980). On specular surfaces parallax is also a robust cue for curvature, one that is used in human vision (Blake & Bulthoff, 1991). In the current context, the spatial derivative of parallax — "rate of parallax" (Blake & Cipolla, 1990; Cipolla & Blake, 1990) — is important because it gives a relative measure of curvature at an extremal boundary. The enhanced robustness of parallax-based measures appears mathematically as a reduced dependence on knowing the viewer's motion. For the robot, this means that the effects of vibration during motion are attenuated. Shorter exploratory motions are then sufficient to compute depth and curvature to given tolerances. The drawback of this method however is the necessity to capture and track simultaneously *pairs* of adjacent contours.

In the case of densely textured foreground and background it is attractive to use raw parallax rather than rate of parallax. In dense texture, parallax and occlusion of contours are direct cues to surface occlusion. Raw parallax can be computed robustly with very short exploratory motions. It becomes highly desirable to track several contours at once, for efficiency, and this can be achieved using the kind of parallel architecture that was described in chapter 3.

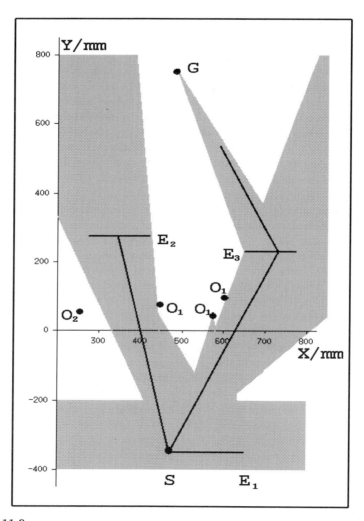

Figure 11.9
Now an extra obstacle has been inserted in the workspace, between E_2 and the goal G.
The final verification of the goal in figure 11.8 encounters the new obstacle and therefore
fails. The robot backtracks to the previous point at which it had a choice, S in this
case. Now it pans to the right looking for an alternative feature. The active visual search
process is now repeated on the right and, via exploratory search along E_3, finally succeeds
in sighting and verifying the goal.

12 Motion Planning Using Image Divergence and Deformation

Roberto Cipolla and Andrew Blake

12.1 Introduction

Relative motion between an observer and a scene induces deformation in image detail and shape. If these changes are smooth they can be described locally by the first order differential invariants of the image velocity field (Koenderink & van Doorn, 1975) – the curl, divergence, and shear (deformation) components. These invariants have simple geometrical meanings which do not depend on the particular choice of co-ordinate system. Moreover they are related to the three dimensional structure of the scene and the viewer's motion – in particular the surface orientation and the time to contact[1] – in a simple geometrically intuitive way. Better still, the divergence and deformation components of the image velocity field are unaffected by arbitrary viewer rotations about the viewer centre. They therefore provide an efficient, reliable way of recovering surface orientation and time to contact.

Although the analysis of the differential invariants of the image velocity field has attracted considerable attention (Koenderink & van Doorn, 1975; Kanatani, 1986) their application to real tasks requiring visual inferences has been limited (Nelson & Aloimonos, 1988; Francois & Bouthemy, 1990). This is because existing methods have failed to deliver reliable estimates of the differential invariants when applied to real images. They have attempted the recovery of dense image velocity fields (Campani & Verri, 1990) or the accurate extraction of points or corner features (Kanatani, 1986). Both methods have attendant problems concerning accuracy and numerical stability. An additional problem concerns the domain of applications to which estimates of differential invariants can be usefully applied. First order invariants of the image velocity field at a single point in the image cannot be used to provide a *complete* description of shape and motion as attempted in numerous structure from motion algorithms (Ullman, 1979). This in fact requires second order spatial derivatives of the image velocity field (Longuet-Higgins & Pradzny, 1980; Waxman & Ullman, 1985). Their power lies in their ability efficiently to recover reliable but incomplete solutions to the structure from motion problem which can be augmented with other information to accomplish useful visual tasks.

In this chapter we describe the reliable, real-time extraction of these invariants from image data and their application to visual tasks. First we present a novel method to measure the differential invariants of the image velocity field robustly by computing average values from the integral of simple functions of the normal image velocities around image contours. This is equivalent to measuring the temporal changes in the area of a closed contour

---

[1]The time duration before the observer and object collide if they continue with the same relative translational motion (Gibson, 1979; Lee, 1980).

and avoids having to recover a dense image velocity field and taking partial
derivatives. It also does not require point or line correspondences. Moreover
integration provides some immunity to image measurement noise.

Second we show that the 3D interpretation of the differential invariants of
the image velocity field is especially suited to the domain of *active vision* in
which the viewer makes deliberate (although sometimes imprecise) motions,
or in stereo vision, where the relative positions of the two cameras (eyes) are
constrained while the cameras (eyes) are free to make arbitrary rotations
(eye movements). Estimates of the divergence and deformation of the image
velocity field, augmented with constraints on the direction of translation,
are then sufficient to efficiently determine the object surface orientation and
time to contact.

The results of preliminary experiments in which arbitrary image shapes are
tracked snakes (see chapter 1) are presented. This uses a real-time B-spline
snake tracker developed for visual guidance of a robot arm (Blake *et al.*,
1991) and subsequently extended to the "Dynamic Contour" described in
chapter 3. The invariants are computed as closed-form functions of the
B-spline snake control points. This information is used to guide a robot
manipulator in obstacle collision avoidance, object manipulation and navigation.

12.2   Differential Invariants of the Image Velocity Field

Review

For a sufficiently small field of view (Thompson & Mundy, 1987; Cipolla,
1991) and smooth change in viewpoint the image velocity field and the
change in apparent image shape is well approximated by a linear (*affine*)
transformation (Koenderink & van Doorn, 1975). The latter can be decomposed into independent components which have simple geometric interpretations. These are an image translation (specifying the change in image
position of the centroid of the shape); a 2D rigid rotation (vorticity), specifying the change in orientation, (curl $\mathbf{v}$); an isotropic expansion (divergence)
specifying a change in scale, (div $\mathbf{v}$); and a pure shear or deformation which
describes the distortion of the image shape (expansion in a specified direction with contraction in a perpendicular direction in such a way that area
is unchanged) described by a magnitude, (def $\mathbf{v}$), and the orientation of the
axis of expansion (maximum extension), μ. These quantities can be defined as combinations of the partial derivatives of the image velocity field,
$\mathbf{v}$ (Koenderink & van Doorn, 1975; Cipolla, 1991). The curl, divergence
and the magnitude of the deformation are scalar invariants and so do not
depend on the particular choice of image co-ordinate system (Koenderink
& van Doorn, 1975; Kanatani, 1986). The axes of maximum extension and
contraction change with rotations of the image plane axes.

Relation to 3D shape and viewer motion

The differential invariants depend on the viewer motion (translational velocity, $\mathbf{U}$, and rotational velocity, $\boldsymbol{\Omega}$), depth, λ and the relation between the viewing direction (ray direction $\mathbf{Q}$) and the surface orientation in a simple and geometrically intuitive way (Koenderink, 1986):

$$|\operatorname{curl} \mathbf{v}| \;=\; -2\boldsymbol{\Omega} \cdot \mathbf{Q} + |\mathbf{F} \times \mathbf{A}| \tag{12.1}$$

$$\operatorname{div} \mathbf{v} \;=\; \frac{2\mathbf{U} \cdot \mathbf{Q}}{\lambda} + \mathbf{F} \cdot \mathbf{A} \tag{12.2}$$

$$\operatorname{def} \mathbf{v} \;=\; |\mathbf{F}|\,|\mathbf{A}| \tag{12.3}$$

where μ (which specifies the axis of maximum extension) bisects the 2D vectors $\mathbf{A}$ and $\mathbf{F}$:

$$\mu = \frac{\angle \mathbf{A} + \angle \mathbf{F}}{2} \tag{12.4}$$

and where $\mathbf{A}$ is the component of viewer translation perpendicular to the visual ray and scaled by depth, λ, and where $\mathbf{F}$ represents the surface orientation as a *depth gradient* scaled by depth[2]:

$$\mathbf{F} = \frac{\operatorname{grad}\lambda}{\lambda} \; . \tag{12.5}$$

The magnitude of the depth gradient, $|\mathbf{F}|$, determines the tangent of the *slant* of the surface (angle between the surface normal and the visual direction). It vanishes for a frontal view and is infinite when the viewer is in the tangent plane of the surface. Its direction, $\angle \mathbf{F}$, specifies the direction in the image of increasing distance. This is equal to the *tilt* of the surface tangent plane. The exact relationship between the magnitude and direction of $\mathbf{F}$ and the slant and tilt of the surface (σ, τ) is given by:

$$|\mathbf{F}| \;=\; \tan \sigma \tag{12.6}$$

$$\angle \mathbf{F} \;=\; \tau \; . \tag{12.7}$$

The geometric significance of these equations is easily seen with a few examples. For example, a translation towards the surface patch leads to a uniform expansion in the image, i.e. positive divergence. This encodes the distance to the object which due to the speed–scale ambiguity[3] is more conveniently expressed as a time to contact, t_c:

$$t_c = \frac{\lambda}{\mathbf{U} \cdot \mathbf{Q}} \; . \tag{12.8}$$

---

[2]Koenderink (1986) defines $\mathbf{F}$ as a "nearness gradient", $\operatorname{grad}(\log(1/\lambda))$. In this paper $\mathbf{F}$ is defined as a scaled depth gradient. These two quantities differ by a sign.

[3]Translational velocities appear scaled by depth making it impossible to determine whether the effects are due to a nearby object moving slowly or a far-away object moving quickly.

Translational motion perpendicular to the visual direction results in image deformation with a magnitude which is determined by the slant of the surface, σ and with an axis depending on the tilt of the surface, τ and the direction of the viewer translation. Divergence (due to foreshortening) and curl components may also be present. This formulation clearly exposes both the speed–scale ambiguity and the *bas–relief* ambiguity (Harris, 1990). The latter manifests itself in the appearance of surface orientation, $\mathbf{F}$, with viewer translation (object rotation), $\mathbf{A}$, and means that from two weak perspective views it is impossible to determine whether the deformations in the image are due to a nearby *shallow* surface or a far away *deep* structure.

Note that divergence and deformation are unaffected by (and hence insensitive to errors in) viewer rotations such as panning or tilting of the camera whereas these lead to considerable changes in point image velocities or disparities. (This is similar to the use of motion parallax (Longuet-Higgins & Pradzny, 1980; Cipolla & Blake, 1990; Cipolla, 1991) where the relative image velocities of nearby points are used to recover relative depth without knowledge of viewer rotations.) As a consequence, the deformation component efficiently encodes the orientation of the surface while the divergence component can be used to provide an estimate of the time to contact or collision.

12.3   Recovery of Differential Invariants From Area Moments of Closed Curves

The differential invariants of the image velocity field conveniently characterise the changes in apparent shape due to relative motion between the viewer and scene. They can in principle be recovered from a dense image velocity field (Nelson & Aloimonos, 1988) or from point (Kanatani, 1986) and line correspondences (Koenderink, 1986) in a small neighbourhood. In practice accurate point and line correspondences are not always available. Often we can only reliably extract portions of curves (although we can not usually rely on the accuracy of the end-points) or closed contours. Contours in the image sample the image velocity field. It is usually only possible, however, to recover the normal image velocity component from local measurements at a curve (Ullman, 1979; Hildreth, 1984). This information is usually sufficient to estimate the differential invariants within closed curves.

Our approach is based on relating the temporal derivative of the area of a closed contour and its moments to the invariants of the image velocity field. This is a generalisation of the result derived by Maybank (1987) in which the rate of change of area scaled by area is used to estimate the divergence of the image velocity field. The advantage is that point or line correspondences are not used. Only the correspondence between shapes is required. The computationally difficult, ill-conditioned and poorly defined process of making explicit the full image velocity field (Hildreth, 1984) is avoided. Moreover, since taking temporal derivatives of area (and its moments) is equivalent to the integration of normal image velocities (scaled by simple functions) around closed contours our approach is effectively computing average values of the differential invariants (not point properties) and has better immunity to image noise leading to reliable estimates. Areas can also be estimated accurately, even when the full set of first order derivatives can not be obtained.

The moments of area of a contour, I_f, are defined in terms of an area integral with boundaries defined by the contour in the image plane:

$$I_f = \int_{a(t)} f \, \mathrm{d}x \mathrm{d}y \tag{12.9}$$

where $a(t)$ is the area of a contour of interest, $c(t)$, at time t and f is a scalar function of image position (x, y) that defines the moment of interest. For instance setting $f = 1$ gives us area. Setting $f = x$ or $f = y$ gives the first-order moments about the image x and y axes respectively.

The moments of area can be measured directly from the image (see below for a novel method involving the control points of a B-spline snake). Better still, their temporal derivatives can also be measured. Differentiating (12.9) with respect to time and using a result from calculus[4] we can relate the temporal derivative of the moment of area to an integral of the normal component of image velocities at an image contour, $\mathbf{v}.\mathbf{n}$, weighted by a scalar $f(x, y)$. By Green's theorem, this integral around the contour $c(t)$, can be re-expressed as an integral over the area enclosed by the contour, $a(t)$:

$$\frac{d}{dt}(I_f) = \oint_{c(t)} [f\mathbf{v}.\mathbf{n}] \mathrm{d}s \tag{12.10}$$

$$= \int_{a(t)} [\mathrm{div}(f\mathbf{v})] \mathrm{d}x \mathrm{d}y \tag{12.11}$$

By simple vector algebra:

$$\mathrm{div}(f\mathbf{v}) = f \, \mathrm{div} \, \mathbf{v} + (\mathbf{v}.\mathbf{grad} f) \ . \tag{12.12}$$

Making the approximation that the partial derivatives of $\mathbf{v}$ are constant in the area of interest, it can be shown (Cipolla, 1991) that substituting (12.12) into (12.11) gives a linear relation between the temporal derivative of a moment of area I_f, and the velocity field together with its partial derivatives. The coefficients of such a relationship are also moments of area. The various moments of area are directly measurable from the image (see below) so a given relation (for a particular f) can be solved to obtain a certain weighted sum of the velocity field and its partial derivatives. In this way, it is possible

---

[4]This equation can be derived by considering the *flux* linking the area of the contour. This changes with time since the contour is carried by the velocity field. The *flux* field, f, in our example does not change with time. Similar integrals appear in fluid mechanics, e.g. the *flux transport theorem* (Davis & Snider, 1979).

to obtain various components of the affine approximation to the velocity field.

Consider the case in which $f = 1$. The relation (12.11) becomes simply the very useful result that the divergence of the image velocity field can be estimated as the derivative of area scaled by area:

$$\frac{d}{dt} a(t) = a(t) \operatorname{div} \mathbf{v} \ . \tag{12.13}$$

Increasing the order of the moments, i.e. different values of $f(x, y)$, generates new equations and additional constraints. In principle, if it is possible to find six linearly independent equations, we can solve for the affine transformation parameters and combine the co-efficients to recover the differential invariants. The validity of the affine approximation can be checked by looking at the error between the transformed and observed image contours. The choice of which moments to use is a subject for further work. In practice certain contours may lead to equations which are not independent and their solution is ill-conditioned. The interpretation of this is that the normal components of image velocity are insufficient to recover the true image velocity field globally, e.g. a fronto-parallel circle rotating about the optical axis. This was termed the "aperture problem in the large" by Waxman and Wohn (Waxman & Wohn, 1985; Bergholm, 1989). Note however, that it is always possible to recover the divergence from a closed contour.

12.4   Surface Orientation and Time to Contact

It has already been noted that measurement of the differential invariants in a single neighbourhood is insufficient to solve completely for the structure and motion since (12.1), (12.2), (12.3) and (12.4) are four equations in the six unknowns of scene structure and motion. In a single neighbourhood a complete solution would require the computation of second order derivatives (Longuet-Higgins & Pradzny, 1980; Waxman & Ullman, 1985) to generate sufficient equations to solve for the unknowns. Even then the solution of the resulting set of non-linear equations is non-trivial.

In the following, the information available from the first-order differential invariants alone is investigated. It will be seen that the differential invariants are sufficient to constrain surface position (expressed as a time to contact) and orientation and that this partial solution can be used to perform useful visual tasks when augmented with additional information.

With knowledge of translation but arbitrary rotation

An estimate of the direction of translation is usually available when the viewer is making deliberate movements (in the case of active vision) or in the case of binocular vision (where the camera or eye positions are constrained). It can also be estimated from image measurements by motion parallax (Longuet-Higgins & Pradzny, 1980).

If the viewer translation is known, (12.2), (12.3) and (12.4) are sufficient unambiguously to recover the surface orientation and the distance to the object in temporal units. Due to the speed–scale ambiguity the latter is expressed as a time to contact. A solution can be obtained in the following way.

1.   The axis of expansion (μ) of the deformation component and the projection in the image of the direction of translation ($\angle\mathbf{A}$) allow the recovery of the tilt of the surface from (12.4).

2.   We can then subtract the contribution due to the surface orientation and viewer translation parallel to the image axis from the image divergence (12.2). This is equal to $|\operatorname{def} v|\cos(\tau - \angle\mathbf{A})$. The remaining component of divergence is due to movement towards or away from the object. This can be used to recover the time to contact, t_c. This can be recovered despite the fact that the viewer translation may not be parallel to the visual direction.

3.   The time to contact fixes the viewer translation in temporal units. It allows the specification of the magnitude of the translation parallel to the image plane (up to the same speed–scale ambiguity), $\mathbf{A}$. The magnitude of the deformation can then be used to recover the slant, σ, of the surface from (12.3).

The advantage of this formulation is that camera rotations do not affect the estimation of shape and distance. The effects of errors in the magnitude and direction of translation are clearly evident as scalings in depth or by a 3D affine transformation (Koenderink, 1986).

With fixation

If the cameras or eyes rotate to keep the object of interest in the middle of the image (nulling the effect of image translation) the magnitude of the rotations needed to bring the object back to the centre of the image determines $\mathbf{A}$ and hence allows us to solve for surface orientation, as above. Again the major effect of any error in the estimate of rotation is to scale depth and orientations.

With no additional information – constraints on motion

Even without any additional assumptions it is still possible to obtain useful information from the first-order differential invariants. The information obtained is best expressed as bounds. For example inspection of (12.2) and (12.3) shows that the time to contact must lie in an interval given by:

$$\frac{1}{t_c} = \frac{\operatorname{div}\mathbf{v}}{2} \pm \frac{\operatorname{def}\mathbf{v}}{2} \ . \tag{12.14}$$

The upper bound on time to contact occurs when the component of viewer translation parallel to the image plane is in the opposite direction to the depth gradient. The lower bound occurs when the translation is parallel to the depth gradient. The upper and lower estimates of time to contact are equal when their is no deformation component. This is the case in which the viewer translation is along the ray or when viewing a fronto-parallel surface (zero depth gradient locally). The estimate of time to contact is then exact. A similar equation was recently described by Subbarao (1990).

The solutions presented above use knowledge of a single viewer translation and measurement of the divergence and deformation of the image velocity field. An alternative solution exists if the observer is free to translate along the ray and also in two orthogonal directions parallel to the image plane. In this case measurement of divergence alone is sufficient to recover the surface orientation and the time to contact (12.2).

12.5   Implementation and Experimental Results

Tracking closed loop contours

Multi-span closed loop B-spline snakes (see chapter 3) are used to localise and track closed image contours. The snakes are initialised as points in the centre of the image and are forced to expand radially outwards until they were in the vicinity of an edge where image "forces" make the snake stabilise close to a high contrast closed contour. Subsequent image motion is automatically tracked by the snake.

B-spline snakes have useful properties such as local control and continuity. They also compactly represent image curves. In our applications they have the additional advantage that the area enclosed is a simple function of the control points.

From Green's theorem in the plane it is easy to show that the area enclosed by a curve with parameterisation $x(s)$ and $y(s)$ is given by:

$$a = \int_{s_0}^{s_N} x(s)y'(s)\mathrm{d}s \qquad (12.15)$$

where $x(s)$ and $y(s)$ are the two components of the image curve and $y'(s)$ is the derivative with respect to the curve parameter s. For a B-spline:

$$\mathbf{x}(s) = \sum_i f_i(s)\mathbf{q}_i \qquad (12.16)$$

(where f_i are the spline basis functions with coefficients $\mathbf{q}_i$ (control points of the curve) (Bartels *et al.*, 1987)) the area is given by:

$$a(t) \quad = \quad \int_{s_0}^{s_N} \sum_i \sum_j (q_{x_i} q_{y_j}) f_i f_j' ds \tag{12.17}$$

$$= \quad \sum_i \sum_j (q_{x_i} q_{y_j}) \int_{s_0}^{s_N} f_i f_j' ds. \tag{12.18}$$

Note that for each span of the B-spline and at each time instant the basis functions remain unchanged. The integrals are thus computed off-line in closed form. (At most 16 coefficients need be stored. In fact due to symmetry there are only 10 possible values for a cubic B-spline). At each time instant multiplication with the control point positions gives the area enclosed by the contour. This is extremely efficient, giving the exact area enclosed by the contour. The same method can be used for higher moments of area as well. The temporal derivatives of the area and its moments is then used to estimate image divergence and deformation.

Applications

Estimates of divergence and deformation can be used in the visual guidance of a robot manipulator in tasks including collision avoidance, landing reactions, object manipulation and navigation (Cipolla, 1991).

Braking

Figure 12.1 shows four samples from a sequence of images taken by a moving observer approaching the rear windscreen of a stationary car in front. In the first frame (time $t = 0$) the relative distance between the two cars is approximately 7m. The velocity of approach is uniform and approximately 1m/time unit.

A B-spline snake is initialised in the centre of the windscreen, and expands out until it localises the closed contour of the edge of the windscreen. The snake can then automatically track the windscreen over the sequence and measure the apparent area, $a(t)$, shown in Fig. 12.2a (relative to the initial area, $a(0)$) as a function of time, t. For uniform translation along the optical axis image divergence (estimated as the rate of change of the area enclosed scaled by area) can be used to compute the time to contact. Figure 12.2b plots the variation of the time to contact with time. For uniform motion this should decrease linearly. The experimental results are plotted in Fig. 12.2b. The variation is linear, as predicted. These results are of useful accuracy, predicting the collision time to the nearest half time unit (corresponding to 50cm in this example).

Collision avoidance and object manipulation

It is well known that image divergence can be used in obstacle collision avoidance. Nelson and Aloimonos (1988) demonstrated a robotics system which computed divergence by spatio–temporal techniques applied to the images of highly textured visible surfaces. We describe a real-time implementation based on image contours and "act" on the visually derived information.

Figure 12.3 shows the results of a camera mounted on an Adept robot manipulator and pointing in the direction of a target contour. The closed contour is localised automatically by initialising a closed loop B-spline snake in the centre of the image. The snake "explodes" outwards and deforms under the influence of image forces which cause it to be attracted to high contrast edges.

The robot manipulator then makes a deliberate motion towards the target. Tracking the area of the contour and computing its rate of change allows us to estimate the divergence. For motion along the visual ray this is sufficient information to estimate the time to contact or impact. The estimate of time to contact – decreased by the uncertainty in the measurement and any image deformation (12.14) – can be used to guide the manipulator so that it stops just before collision (Fig. 12.3d). The manipulator in fact, travels "blindly" after its sensing actions (above) and at a uniform speed for the time remaining until contact.

If the translational motion has a component parallel to the image plane, the image divergence is composed of two components. The first is the component which determines immediacy or time to contact. The other term is due to image foreshortening when the surface has a non-zero slant. The two effects can be computed separately by measuring the deformation. The deformation also allows us to recover the surface orientation.

Note that unlike stereo vision, the magnitude of the translation is not needed. Nor are the camera parameters (focal length and aspect ratio is not needed for divergence) known or calibrated. Nor are the magnitudes and directions of the camera rotations needed to keep the target in the field of view. Simple measurements of area and its moments – obtained in closed form as a function of the B-spline snake control points – were used to estimate divergence and deformation. The only assumption was of uniform motion and known direction of translation.

Figure 12.3 shows an example in which a robot manipulator uses these estimates of time to contact and surface orientation to approach the object surface perpendicularly so as to position a suction gripper for manipulation. The image contours are shown in Fig. 12.3a and 12.3b highlighting the effect of deformation due to the sideways component of translation. The successful execution is shown in Fig. 12.3c and 12.3d.

12.6 Conclusions

We have presented a simple and efficient method for estimating image divergence and deformation by tracking closed image contours with B-spline snakes. This information has been successfully used to estimate surface orientation and time to contact.

Figure 12.1
Using image divergence to estimate time to contact. Four samples of a video sequence taken from a moving observer approaching a stationary car at a uniform velocity (approximately 1m per time unit). A B-spline snake automatically tracks the area of the rear windscreen. The image divergence is used to estimate the time to contact (see below). The next image in the sequence corresponds to collision!

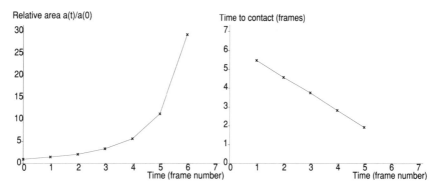

Figure 12.2
Apparent area of windscreen and estimated time to contact.

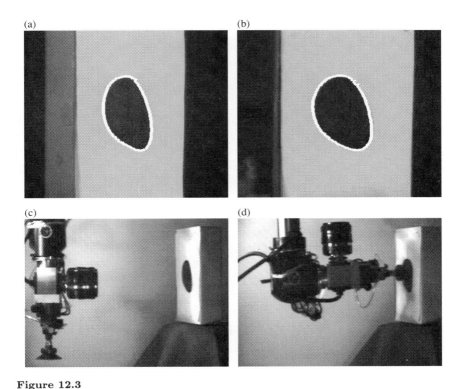

Figure 12.3
Visually guided object manipulation using image divergence and deformation. (a) The image of a planar contour (zero tilt and positive slant, i.e. the direction of increasing depth, **F**, is horizontal and from left to right). The image contour is localised automatically by a B-spline snake initialised in the centre of the field of view. (b) The effect on apparent shape when the viewer translates to the right while fixating on the target (i.e. **A** is horizontal, left to right). The apparent shape undergoes an isotropic expansion (positive divergence which increases the area) and a deformation in which the axis of expansion is horizontal. Measurement of the divergence and deformation can used to estimate the time to contact and surface orientation. This is used to guide the manipulator so that it comes to rest perpendicular to the surface with a pre-determined clearance. Estimates of divergence and deformation made approximately 1m away were sufficient to estimate the target object position and orientation to the nearest 2cm in position and 1° in orientation. This information is used to position a suction gripper in the vicinity of the surface. A contact sensor and small probing motions could then be used to refine the estimate of position and guide the suction gripper before manipulation (d).

13 Adaptive Local Navigation

Tony Prescott and John Mayhew

13.1 Introduction

An effective link between perception and action is achieved by mapping the temporal flow of sensory data into a stream of actions that achieves desired goals. For a mobile robot, however, the limitations of real-time activity and finite computational resources restrict the extent to which optimal actions can be chosen through forward search using accurate world models. For tasks in which success depends on sequences of appropriate behaviour, problems such as noisy sensors, uncertainty about the world, and the combinatorial explosion of possible futures combine to ensure that some assumptions must be made and short-cuts in the decision process found. It has been argued that fast and robust behaviour might be better achieved through task-dedicated modules that use direct sensor data, little internal state, and relatively simple decision mechanisms to choose between alternative actions. But to do without plans and models means that actions are selected only in the context of a narrow time window. Behaviour cannot then be organised efficiently with respect to long-term goals which will only be achieved in an opportunistic manner. Fast reactions are gained through compromising the effectiveness of action.

One answer to this dilemma lies in the development of adaptive modules that can monitor their performance with regard to their goals and improve their choice of control behaviour accordingly. By appropriate use of past experience a robot can circumvent forward planning by selecting behaviours that have been successful in similar situations in the past. However, if a system is to learn directly from the achievement of rewards it must be able to make do with delayed and uninformative training data. Knowing that a desired result has been obtained leaves the learning system to solve the difficult "credit assignment" problem of deciding how each action in the sequence leading up to the goal contributed to the final outcome. Fortunately, algorithms have been developed that make this form of learning possible. Specifically, Barto, Sutton and Anderson (Barto *et al.*, 1983; Sutton, 1988) have formulated methods of "reinforcement" learning that allow a system to explore the space of alternative perception–action mappings adapting its behaviour so as to improve its ability to reach rewarded states. Recent work by Watkins (1989) has shown that such reinforcement learning algorithms are implementing an on-line, incremental approximation to the dynamic programming (DP) (Ross, 1983) method for determining optimal control. Here we adopt the term "heuristic" dynamic programming (HDP) used by Werbos (1990) to describe learning algorithms of this type.

Classical dynamic programming is a search method for determining optimal control over a finite state-space where, in each discrete cell, there is a limited number of possible actions. Control behaviour (the *policy*) is defined as optimal if the action chosen in every state maximises the *return* (the sum of future rewards) that is achieved. To compute this optimal control requires accurate models of both the transition function, which maps every state/action pair to a new state, and the reward function, which gives the value of the expected pay-off to be received in any state. Given these prerequisites dynamic programming proceeds through an iterative search to calculate the maximum expected return, or *evaluation*, for each cell. Once this evaluation function is known the optimal policy is easily found by selecting in each cell the action that leads (on average) to the highest predicted return in the next state. "Heuristic" methods, on the other hand, do not require knowledge of state transitions or of the distribution of available rewards. Instead, the learning system uses its ongoing experience of transitions and pay-offs as a substitute for accurate models of the environment. While actively exploring the state-space HDP estimates a mapping from input states to predictions of return and uses this approximate evaluation function to provide error signals for modifying control actions.

Where time and resources allow, it is possible to combine on-line HDP learning through with off-line search of acquired models (approximating true dynamic programming) to make the most efficient use of real experience. Architectures of this type have been proposed by Sutton (1990) and Moore (1991).

If control is required in a continuous multi-dimensional space an important research issue concerns how that space should be quantised into discrete cells, for dynamic programming. A related issue is the problem of search. For large state spaces or problems in which the action-space is itself continuous, exhaustive search of all possible combinations of states and actions is not a feasible option. The likelihood of attaining good solutions depends in these circumstances on having effective strategies for exploration.

In this chapter we describe the design of a HDP module for the problem of robot local navigation. Our aim is to develop a system that will allow a mobile robot with minimal sensory apparatus (sparse range or optic flow data) to move at speed around an indoor environment avoiding collisions with stationary or slow-moving obstacles. Here we demonstrate the potential of the HDP approach to this problem using results from simulations of such a robot operating in a two-dimensional world. These results show that it is possible for a robot that is purely "reactive" (responding only to the immediate sensor input) to produce trajectories through the environment that have the appearance of planned behaviour in that they successfully anticipate long-term outcomes.

13.2   Review of heuristic dynamic programming

Barto, Sutton and Watkins (1990) provide a full account of "reinforcement" learning methods and their relationship to dynamic programming, here we give only a brief summary of the principles involved while describing the specific HDP algorithm that we employ.

The design of a control module that uses HDP is illustrated in figure 13.1. The module learns an evaluation function (V) and a policy (action) function

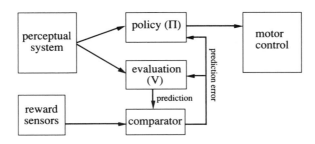

Figure 13.1
Architecture of the HDP navigation module.

(Π) for the state-space of possible input patterns. If x_t is the input state at time t this is mapped to the action $a_t = \Pi(x_t)$ and the evaluation $V(x_t)$. After performing this action the perceptual system obtains the new input x_{t+1}, the reward sensors detect any immediate payoff r_{t+1}, and an evaluation of the new state $V(x_{t+1})$ is obtained. The comparator then calculates the error ε_{t+1} in the original prediction by

$$\varepsilon_{t+1} = [r_{t+1} + \gamma V_t(x_{t+1})] - V_t(x_t). \tag{13.1}$$

We can understand this error signal in the following way. The evaluation of state x_t is an attempt to estimate the total reward that the system will receive from time t onwards, if it follows the current policy Π. One commonly used method of calculating this cumulative reward is the *expected discounted return* given by

$$R_t = r_{t+1} + \gamma r_{t+2} + \gamma^2 r_{t+3} + \gamma^3 r_{t+4} + \cdots \tag{13.2}$$

where r_{t+k} is the immediate reward at time $t + k$ and γ is the discount factor $(0 < \gamma < 1)$ indicating the extent to which rewards are valued less the further they lie ahead in time. To obtain the error in the prediction $V(x_t)$ the system obviously cannot afford to wait indefinitely before it calculates a target value. Instead, the basic idea of HDP is to wait for only a small number of time-steps (n) for which the payoffs are obtained and then use the prediction for the nth state reached as an estimate of all further rewards. This is what Watkins has called the *n-step-corrected-return*

$$R_t^{(n)} = r_{t+1} + \gamma r_{t+2} + \cdots + \gamma^{n-1} r_{t+n} + \gamma^n V(x_{t+n}). \tag{13.3}$$

For $n = 1$ this gives the prediction error shown above (equation 13.1). Watkins has shown (Watkins, 1989) that if the evaluation function is trained using the gradient descent rule

$$V_{t+1}(x_t) = V_t(x_t) + \alpha\varepsilon_{t+1} \tag{13.4}$$

(where α is a learning rate) then over sufficient trials the prediction will converge to give an accurate estimate of the expected return under the current policy. However, he also shows that it is not necessary to restrict the use of $R_t^{(n)}$ to a single value of n as a weighted average of different $R_t^{(n)}$ will also give convergence. The significance of this is that a gradient descent rule can be defined so that a weighted average of corrected returns can be computed incrementally[1]. This is achieved by storing an eligibility trace $m(x)$ for each input state x that is visited such that

$$m_{t+1}(x) = \begin{cases} 1 & \text{iff } x \text{ is the input pattern at time } t \\ \lambda m_t(x) & \text{otherwise} \end{cases} \tag{13.5}$$

where λ is a constant $(0 < \lambda < 1)$ indicating the rate at which the trace decays. Using this eligibility trace[2] the update rule for the evaluation function becomes

$$V_{t+1}(x) = V_t(x) + \alpha \, \varepsilon_{t+1} \, m_{t+1}(x). \tag{13.6}$$

The advantage of such a scheme is that it allows a much faster rate of learning since the evaluation of several states is adjusted at each time-step.

13.2.1   Improving the policy

The prediction error can also be used to improve the policy at the same time as learning the evaluation function. Exactly how this is done varies for different versions of HDP. Here we describe a method that is applicable to problems for which the possible actions at each state form a vector space. If the action a_t performed in state x is varied from the stored action $\Pi(x)$ (by adding some random noise) then the policy can be adjusted by the gradient descent rule

$$\Pi_{t+1}(x_t) = \Pi_t(x_t) + \beta\varepsilon_{t+1}\big(a_t - \Pi(x_t)\big) \tag{13.7}$$

where β is a learning rate. The effect of this learning rule is that if the prediction error is positive (i.e. a_t was better than expected) then the policy for x_t is moved towards a_t, if the error was negative then a_t gave an outcome that was worse than was anticipated so the policy is moved in the opposite direction. This learning rule which was proposed by Watkins (1989) can be extended by using a policy eligibility trace $n(x)$ such that

$$n_{t+1}(x) = \begin{cases} \Delta a_t = (a_t - \Pi(x_t)) & \text{iff } x \text{ is the input at time } t \\ \lambda n_t(x) & \text{otherwise.} \end{cases} \tag{13.8}$$

---

[1] for proof see Watkins (1989).
[2] Using the decay rate of 0.7 the eligibility trace for any input becomes negligible within a short time, so in practice it is only necessary to store a trace for the most recent input patterns.

There is no guarantee, however, that this method will lead to optimal control for problems in which locally optimal policies are possible. The ability of such algorithms to find good solutions therefore depends both on the initial policy and (crucially) the method for generating exploratory actions. One possibility is to apply a global annealing process such that the amount of additive noise starts high but diminishes as learning proceeds. A better alternative is to allow the exploratory component of each action to be determined by a further adjustable parameter thus allowing the degree of noise to be adjusted locally depending on how well the system is performing in each region of the input space. Williams (1988) has proposed a method of achieving this by representing actions in terms of random variables specified by gaussian probability distributions. In what follows we describe a gradient descent method for learning policy components $\Pi^\mu(x)$ and $\Pi^\sigma(x)$ that specify this gaussian distribution for any state x.

The action for the current time-step y_t is sampled from the distribution $N(\mu, \sigma)$ where

$$\mu = \Pi_t^\mu(x_t) \quad \text{and} \quad \sigma = \Pi_t^\sigma(x_t).$$

Estimates of the mean and standard deviation are obtained by gradient descent on the log likelihood of the gaussian distribution of y

$$g(y, \mu, \sigma) = \frac{1}{\sqrt{2\pi}\,\sigma} e^{-\frac{(y-\mu)^2}{2\sigma^2}}. \tag{13.9}$$

The local gradients $\Delta\mu$ and $\Delta(\ln \sigma)$ are given by the partial derivatives

$$\Delta\mu = \frac{\partial \ln g}{\partial \mu} \quad = \quad \frac{y - \mu}{\sigma^2}$$

$$\Delta(\ln \sigma) = \frac{\partial \ln g}{\partial \ln \sigma} \quad = \quad \frac{[(y-\mu)^2 - \sigma^2]}{\sigma^2}. \tag{13.10}$$

(Here $\ln \sigma$ is used as the adjustable parameter for the standard deviation since if σ itself were used it could acquire a negative value.) These update gradients can be used with eligibility traces n_t^μ and n_t^σ defined by

$$n_{t+1}^\mu(x) = \begin{cases} \Delta\mu_t & \text{iff } x \text{ is the input at time } t \\ \lambda n_t^\mu(x) & \text{otherwise,} \end{cases} \tag{13.11}$$

and

$$n_{t+1}^\sigma(x) = \begin{cases} \Delta(\ln \sigma)_t & \text{iff } x \text{ is the input at time } t \\ \lambda n_t^\sigma(x) & \text{otherwise.} \end{cases} \tag{13.12}$$

Learning rules for the policy components are then given by

$$\Pi_{t+1}^\mu(x) = \Pi_t^\mu(x) + \beta^\mu \varepsilon_{t+1} n_{t+1}^\mu$$
$$\Pi_{t+1}^\sigma(x) = \Pi_t^\sigma(x) + \beta^\sigma \varepsilon_{t+1} n_{t+1}^\sigma \tag{13.13}$$

where β^μ and β^σ are learning rates. This learning method is similar in spirit to a recursive version of maximum likelihood estimation for μ and σ based on all experience to date.

13.3   Storage and generalisation

So far we have assumed that the input to the learning system consists of
series of discrete states taken from a finite set such that learning individual
state-action pairs is possible. However, for problems such as navigating using
a depth map we wish to learn actions over a continuous multi-dimensional
input-space. The straight-forward approach of simply dividing up the eu-
clidean space using a single hyper-cuboid grid will fail here due to "the curse
of dimensionality": not only would a large amount of space be required to
store the adjustable parameters (much of it possibly unused) but learning
would occur extremely slowly as each cell would be visited very infrequently.
To overcome this problem our learning architecture uses an artificial neural
net to provide a coarse-coded quantisation of the input that requires only
a finite number of parameters to represent a possibly infinite space. The
neural net used is the CMAC ("Cerebellar Model Articulation Computer")
originally proposed by Albus (1971) as a model of information processing in
the mammalian cerebellum. The use of CMACs to recode the input to HDP
systems has also been described by Watkins (1989).

The CMAC technique divides the input space into a set of overlapping but
offset tilings. Each tiling consists of regular regions of pre-defined size such
that all points within each region are mapped to a single stored parameter.
The tilings are virtual in that it is not necessary to store a pointer for each
tile but merely to have a hashing function which can generate the memory
address of the parameter for a given tile as and when it is needed. The value
of the stored function at any point is calculated by averaging the parameters
stored for the corresponding regions in all of the tilings. By averaging over
relatively large overlapping regions the CMAC provides local generalisation
allowing an approximation to a continuous function to be learned rapidly.

A function $f(x)$ stored in a CMAC of T tilings is computed using the
following algorithm:

$$\text{For } i = 1 \text{ to } T \text{ do } k_i = hash(t_i) \tag{13.14}$$

where t_i is the tile in tiling i containing the point x and $hash$ is a function
that maps a given tile into an element of a finite array of vector or scalar
parameters $w = w[1], w[2], \ldots, w[n]$. The value of the function is then given
by

$$f(x) = 1/T\big(w[k_1] + w[k_2] + \cdots + w[k_T]\big). \tag{13.15}$$

13.4   The robot simulation

Our simulation models a three-wheeled mobile vehicle, called the "sprite",
operating in a simple two-dimensional world (500×500 cm) consisting of
walls and obstacles in which the sprite is represented by a square box (30×30

cm). The perceptual system simulates a laser range-finder giving the logarithmically scaled distance to the nearest obstacle at set angles from its current orientation. An important feature of the research has been to explore the extent to which spatially sparse but frequent data can support complex behaviour. We show below results from simulations using only three rays emitted at angles $-60°$, $0°$, and $+60°$. The controller operates directly on this unprocessed sensory input. Figure 13.2 shows the simulated robot in a sample environment.

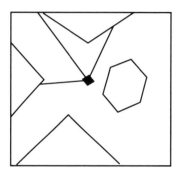

Figure 13.2
The sprite casting three depth rays in a two-dimensional world.

In the experiments described below each sensory dimension was quantised into five discrete bins to form $5\times5\times5$ cuboid tilings of the three-dimensional space of depth vector patterns. Five such tilings were overlaid to form each CMAC, each tile being mapped to a separate adjustable parameter[3].

The policy acquired by the learning system has two elements (f and θ) (each specified by gaussian pdfs) corresponding to the desired forward and angular velocities of the vehicle. These are converted by simple inverse kinematics into desired left and right wheel-speeds (the third wheel acts merely as a castor to give stability) which the motor system then attempts to match. Restrictions on acceleration and braking enforce a degree of realism in the model's ability to initiate fast avoidance behaviour.

To store the functions learned by the sprite requires five CMACs in all, four to store the policy functions $\Pi = (f_\mu, f_\sigma, \theta_\mu, \theta_\sigma)$, and the fifth to record the evaluation. Figure 13.3 illustrates the architecture for accessing the function storage.

The continuous trajectory of the vehicle is approximated by a sequence of discrete time steps. In each interval the sprite acquires new perceptual data then performs the associated response generating either a change in position or a feedback signal indicating that a collision has occurred preventing the move. After a collision the sprite reverses slightly then attempts to rotate

---

[3] For larger input spaces (formed by adding additional sensors) a hashing function has be used to effectively reduce the number of stored parameters.

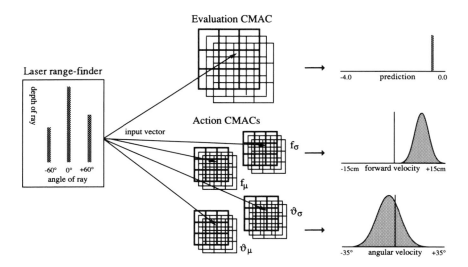

Figure 13.3
Function approximation for actions and predictions using CMACs.
(CMACs of 3×3×3 tilings are shown here in place of the 3-dimensional 5×5×5×5 CMACs used in the simulation.)

and move off at a random angle (90–180° from its original heading), if this is not possible it is relocated to a random starting position.

13.5   Reinforcement and exploration

In order for the sprite to learn useful local navigation behaviour it has to move around and explore its environment. If the sprite is rewarded solely for avoiding collisions an optimal strategy would be to remain still or to stay within a small, safe, circular orbit. To generate more interesting behaviour some additional "drive" signal is required to encourage exploration. There are therefore two sources of reward in the simulation. To promote obstacle avoidance the sprite carries a set of external touch sensors (one for each corner of the vehicle) which are combined to deliver the reward signal

$$r_t^o = \sum_{i=1}^{4} o_i \quad \text{where} \quad o_i = \begin{cases} -1.0 & \text{if sensor } i \text{ touches an obstacle} \\ 0 & \text{otherwise.} \end{cases} \tag{13.16}$$

To encourage movement the sprite also has an internal source of reward r_t^s which is a function of the vehicle's current absolute forward velocity and is maximal when it is travelling at just below its top speed[4]. The total reward at any time is therefore given by

[4]In these simulations we use a gaussian function which has a maximum of zero when the absolute forward speed is 4/5ths of the vehicle's top speed.

$$r_t = r_t^o + r_t^s. \tag{13.17}$$

To further promote adventurous behaviour the initial policy over the whole state-space is for the sprite to have a positive forward velocity and zero angular velocity.

It can be shown that a system which has a high initial expectation of future rewards will settle less rapidly for a locally optimal solution than one with a low expectation. Therefore the evaluation function is set initially to the maximum reward attainable by the sprite[5].

Improved policies are found by deviating from the currently preferred set of actions. However, there is a trade-off to be made between exploiting the existing policy to maximise the short term reward and experimenting with untried actions that have potentially negative consequences but may eventually lead to a better policy. The algorithm described above results in an automatic annealing process (Williams, 1988) as the variance of each gaussian element decreases as the mean behaviour converges to a local maximum. However, the width of each gaussian can also increase if the mean is locally sub-optimal allowing for more exploratory behaviour. The final width of the gaussian depends on whether the local peak in the action function is narrow or flat on top. The behaviour acquired by the system is therefore more than a set of simple reflexes. Rather, for each circumstance, there is a range of acceptable actions which is narrow if the robot is in a tight corner, where its behaviour is severely constrained, but wider in more open spaces.

13.6   Results

To test the effectiveness of the learning algorithm we compared the performance of the sprite before and after fifty-thousand training steps on a number of simple environments. Over 10 independent runs in the environment shown in figure 13.4 the average distance travelled between collisions rose from approximately 0.9m before learning to 47.4m after training, at the same time the average velocity more than doubled to just below the optimal speed. The requirement to maintain an optimum speed encourages the sprite to follow trajectories that avoid slowing down, stopping or reversing. However, if the sprite is placed too close to an obstacle to turn away safely, it can perform an n-point-turn manoeuvre requiring it to stop, back-off, turn and then move forward. It is thus capable of generating quite complex sequences of actions. Furthermore, although the sprite has no perceptual inputs near its rear corners its behaviour is adapted so that turning movements implicitly take account of its body shape.

We have found some differences in the sprite's ability to negotiate different environments with the effectiveness of the avoidance learning system varying for different configurations of obstacles. However, only limited performance

---

[5]since all rewards are negative the maximum attainable is zero.

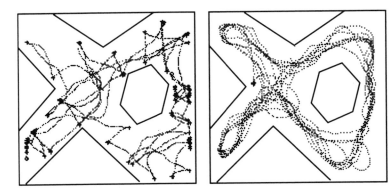

Figure 13.4
Sprite paths before and after training for 50,000 simulation steps.
(The trajectories shown were recorded over two-thousand time-steps: crosses show colli-
sions, circles new starting positions.)

loss has been observed in transferring from a learned environment to an
unseen one (figure 13.5) which is quickly made up if the sprite is allowed to
adapt its policies to suit the new circumstances. Hence we are encouraged
to think that the learning system is capturing some fairly general strategies
for obstacle avoidance.

Most of the avoidance learning occurs during the first 20,000 steps of the
simulation; thereafter the sprite optimises its speed with little change in
the number of collisions. The learning process is therefore quite rapid, we
estimate that if a mobile robot with a sample rate of 5Hz could be trained in
this manner it would begin to move around competently after roughly one
hour of training.

To illustrate the annealing process we show below (figure 13.6) a record of
the size of the σ components of the action elements f and θ over a training
run. For both elements we see the expected fall in the variance as the
learning converges. The increase in variance following transfer to the new
environment may indicate the ability of the algorithm to expand the width
of the local gaussians in order to increase exploration.

Finally, we illustrate the different kinds of tactical behaviour acquired by
the sprite using three dimensional slices through the two policy functions
(desired forward and angular velocities). Figure 13.7 shows samples of these
functions recorded after fifty thousand training steps in an environment containing two slow moving rectangular obstacles. Each graph is a function of
the three rays cast out by the sprite: the x and y axes show the depths of
the left and right rays and the vertical slices correspond to different critical
depths of the central ray (9, 35 and 74cm). The graphs show clearly several
features that we might expect of effective avoidance behaviour.

Most notably, there is a transition occurring over the three slices during

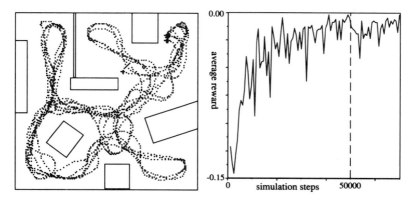

Figure 13.5
Sprite behaviour in a novel environment. The trajectories on the left show behaviour (without learning) after transfer from the training environment. The graph on the right records the change in the reward received over a training run in which the sprite was transferred to the new situation after 50,000 simulation steps and allowed to adapt its policies to suit the new circumstances.

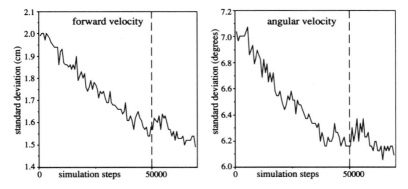

Figure 13.6
Change in policy exploration over training.

which the policy changes from one of braking then reversing (graph a) to one of turning sharply (d) whilst maintaining speed or accelerating (e). This transition clearly corresponds to the threshold below which a collision cannot be avoided by swerving but requires backing-off instead.

There is a considerable degree of left–right symmetry in most of the graphs. This agrees with the observation that obstacle avoidance is by and large a symmetric problem. However some asymmetric behaviour is acquired in order to break the deadlock that arises when the sprite is faced with obstacles that are equidistant on both sides. As an alternative to learning asymmetric behaviour the system could be trained to acquire a symmetric policy for all

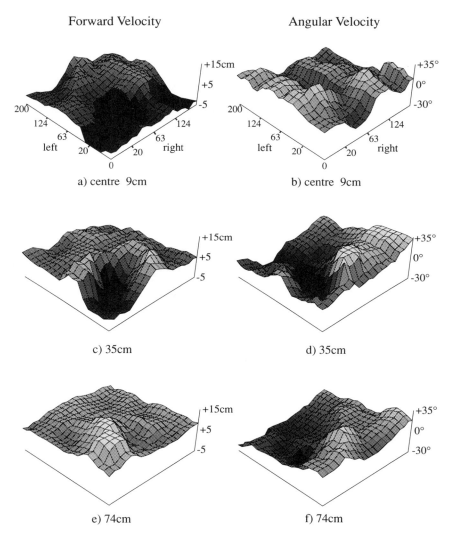

Figure 13.7
Surfaces showing the values of the action functions f and θ for different input depth
patterns. The left and right axis show the depths of the left and right rays respectively.
The vertical slices correspond to depths of the central ray of 9, 35 and 74 cm.

imbalanced input patterns. Inputs in which the left and right sides are equal could then be passed to a separate decision module which would bias the robot's movement towards one side or the other according to its own designs.

13.7 Conclusion

We have demonstrated that successful local navigation behaviour can arise from sequences of learned reactions to raw perceptual data. The trajectories generated often have the appearance of planned activity since individual actions are only appropriate as part of extended patterns of movement. However, planning only occurs as an implicit part of the HDP learning process that allows experience of rewarding outcomes to be propagated backwards to influence future actions taken in similar contexts. This learning process is effective because it is able to exploit the underlying regularities in the robot's interaction with its world to find an effective mapping from sensor data to motor actions.

14 Task-oriented Vision with Multiple Bayes Nets

Raymond Rimey and Christopher Brown

14.1 Task-oriented Vision

This chapter defines a task-oriented system as one that performs the minimum effort necessary to solve a specified task from a variety of possible ones. We consider a visual question-answering system to illustrate techniques, but a system for navigation or manipulation could be based on the same principles. Depending on the task, the system decides which information to gather, which operators to use at which resolution, and where to apply them. Table 14.1 summarizes the key differences between the standard passive, reconstructionist (or Marrian) vision paradigm and the task-oriented approach.

In what follows we present the basic framework of a task-oriented computer vision system, called TEA, that uses Bayes nets and a maximum expected utility decision rule.

Our approach has as background a large amount of research into visual attention, *e.g.* (Humphreys & Bruce, 1989), classical work in eye movements, *e.g.* (Yarbus, 1967), and recent advances in active vision, *e.g.* (Burt, 1988; Ballard, 1991), including camera movements and foveal–peripheral sensors, *e.g.* (Yeshurun & Schwartz, 1989b; Bolle *et al.*, 1990). Specifically, our tools are decision theory, utility theory, and Bayesian probabilistic models (Garvey, 1976; Bolles, 1977; Feldman & Sproull, 1977; Durrant-Whyte, 1988; Chou & Brown, 1990; Shafer & Pearl, 1990). Two recent key developments are Bayes nets (Pearl, 1988), and influence diagrams (Shachter, 1986). Applications using these new techniques are beginning to appear. The first large experimental system that applied Bayes nets to computer vision is by Levitt (Levitt *et al.*, 1989). The formulation of that system using influence diagram techniques is discussed in (Agosta, 1990). A sensor and control problem involving a real milling machine is solved using influence diagram techniques in (Agogino & Ramamurthi, 1990). A special kind of influence diagram, called a temporal belief network, is discussed in (Dean *et al.*, 1990; Dean & Wellman, 1991), and is being studied for an application in sensor based mobile robot control.

Table 14.1
Key differences between passive vision and task-oriented vision.

Passive vision	Task-oriented vision
use all vision modules	use only some vision modules
process entire image	process areas of the image
maximal detail	sufficient detail
extract representation first	ask question first
answer question from representation data	answer question from scene data
unlimited resources	resource limitations

14.2   Preliminaries

Figure 14.1
An example scene in the application domain.

We present experimental results from the TEA-1 system, our second implementation of the general TEA framework. Figure 14.1 shows a typical scene from TEA's domain. Our goal is to support many different visual tasks efficiently. In TEA, a task is to answer a question about the scene: Where is the butter? Is this breakfast, lunch, dinner, or dessert? We are particularly interested in more qualitative tasks: Is this an informal or fancy meal? How far has the eating progressed? Is this table messy?

The TEA system gathers evidence visually and incorporates it into a Bayes net until the question can be answered to a desired degree of confidence. The TEA system runs by iteratively selecting the evidence gathering action that maximizes an expected utility criterion involving the cost of the action and its benefits of increased certainties in the net:

1. List all the executable actions.

2. Select the action with highest expected utility.

3.   Execute that action.

4.   Attach the resulting evidence to the Bayes net and propagate its influence.

5.   Repeat, until the task is solved.

We assume a spatially-varying sensor that can be pointed in space. In the TEA system the peripheral image is a low-resolution image of the entire field of view from one camera angle, and the fovea is a small high-resolution image (*i.e.* window) that can be selectively moved within the field of view. We assume the system can not view the entire scene at once.

14.3   A Composite Bayes Net

A Bayes net is a way of representing the joint probability distribution of a set of variables in a way that is especially useful for knowledge representation. Nodes in the net represent variables with (usually) a discrete set of labels (*e.g.* a *utensil* node could have labels (*knife, fork, spoon*)). Links in the net represent (via tables) conditional probabilities that a node has a particular label given that an adjacent node has a particular label (Pearl, 1988; Henrion, 1990; Neapolitan, 1990; Shafer & Pearl, 1990; Dean & Wellman, 1991; Peot & Shachter, 1991).

The Bayes net formalism also includes a form of inference. Belief in the values for node X is defined as $BEL(x) = P(x \mid e)$, where e is the combination of all evidence present in the net. The evidence consists of "evidence reports", which are produced by evidence gathering actions that directly support (affect) the possible values of a particular node (*i.e.* variable) in the net. The inference mechanism can propagate the effect of an evidence report and recompute belief values for all other nodes. An elegant propagation solution exists when the network is a tree (Pearl, 1988). Variations on this solution have been used for polytrees and for general networks (Pearl, 1988). Other methods for general trees also exist (Lauritzen & Spiegelhalter, 1988; Jensen *et al.*, 1990). A new result, the revised polytree algorithm (Peot & Shachter, 1991), generally subsumes all the above results. Stochastic simulation approaches are also being developed (see (Henrion, 1990; Peot & Shachter, 1991)).

Our first demonstration system, TEA-0 (Rimey, 1992), had a single net to encode task and domain knowledge. The problem with using a single net for many complex tasks is that the necessary domain knowledge is of different sorts. TEA-1, described here, uses four kinds of knowledge structured into separate networks. As in previous vision systems, TEA has a PART-OF net (Levitt *et al.*, 1989) and an IS-A tree (Levitt *et al.*, 1989; Chou & Brown, 1990). The *expected area* net and *task* net presented here are new, as is the composite net that results from linking the four.

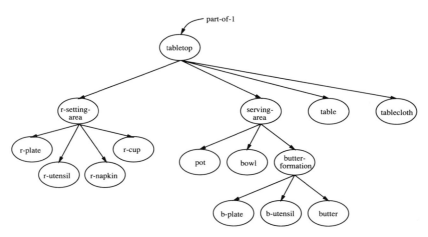

Figure 14.2
A PART-OF Bayes net.

A PART-OF Net

A PART-OF net (Fig. 14.2) models the physical structure of the scene. All nodes in this net have the same set of possible values: *present* and *notPresent*. The conditional probability on each network link indicates the likelihood that a subpart exists.

An Expected Area (Object Location) Net

Geometric relations between objects are modeled by the *expected area* net, used in combination with the PART-OF net. The two networks have the same structure: A node in the PART-OF net identifies a particular object within the sub-part structure of the scene, and the corresponding node in the *expected area* net identifies the area in the scene in which that object is expected to be located. In TEA-1 we assume a fixed camera origin, and the location of an object in the scene is specified by the two camera angles (pan and tilt) that will cause the object to be centered in the visual field.

Thus each node in the expected area net represents a 2D discrete random variable. The root node of a tree has only an *a priori* probability, which we assume is given. The *BEL* of this variable is a function on a discrete 2-D grid, with a high value corresponding to a scene location for which the object is expected with high probability. Figure 14.3 shows two examples of expected areas. Each link in the *expected area* net has an associated conditional probability, $P(location \mid parentLocation)$. It is unrealistic to enumerate this conditional probability, but specific values of the conditional probability (as required by the belief propagation algorithms) can be reasonably computed with a function, which in TEA-1 is the same for all the links.

A *relation map* gives the area in which an object, say A, is expected to be located, given the location of another object, say B. Currently, the values in our maps are either zero or a constant, but a map generally may contain a distribution of values. The maps are scaled according to the dimensions of object B, which are known if the object has previously been detected by a visual action. Otherwise the expected dimensions of object B must be used. Once a relation map has been scaled it is convolved with the expected area of object B, thus producing the new expected area of object A.

The expected area for node A is actually calculated not from a single node like node B, but by combining "messages" about expected areas sent to it from its parent and all its children. This combination is performed within the calculation of $BEL(A)$. Generally, it is useful to characterize relations as "must-be", "must-not-be" and "could-be". Combination of two "must-be" maps would then be by intersection, and in general map combination would proceed by the obvious set-theoretic operations corresponding to the inclusive or exclusive semantics of the relation. In TEA-1, however, all the relations are "could-be", and the maps are essentially unioned by the belief calculation.

The cost of a visual operation is often proportional to the area over which it must be applied. The expected area of a node X can be used to scale the cost of visual operators by the ratio r_X^ℓ of expected to scene areas. Let $\ell \in (0,1)$ be a confidence level, which usually will be chosen close to 1 (typically 0.9). Let G_X^ℓ be the smallest subset of all the grid points G_X for node X, such that their probabilities add up to ℓ. The value of r_X^ℓ is the size of the subset G_X^ℓ divided by the size of the set G_X. $r_X^\ell = 1$ means that node X's object could be located anywhere in the entire scene. Over time, as other objects in the scene are located and as more and tighter relations are established, the value of r_X^ℓ approaches zero.

An IS-A Tree

A taxonomic hierarchy models *one* random variable that can have many mutually exclusive values, where the possible values can be organized into subsets forming a tree hierarchy. The full hierarchy of subsets can be represented as a tree structured graph.

A special version of a Bayes net has been developed to incorporate the mutual-exclusivity constraint (Pearl, 1988; Chou & Brown, 1990). Each leaf node h_i in the tree has a belief $BEL(h_i)$. Since an intermediate node represents the disjunction of all its children, its BEL value is the sum of its children's BEL values. Evidence e that supports a subset S of the leaf nodes is added to the network by weighting the leaves' BEL values by a likelihood ratio. The new BEL values of the leaves are computed as $BEL'(h_i) = KW_i BEL(h_i)$, where K is a normalizing factor so the new BEL's sum to one, and W_i is a weight $W_i = \begin{cases} \lambda & h_i \in S \\ 1 & \text{otherwise} \end{cases}$ that is based on the likelihood ratio of the evidence $\lambda = \frac{P(e|S)}{P(e|\neg S)}$. Evidence that supports the set

S will have λ greater than 1 and thus will increase BEL for the members of S proportional to the strength of the evidence. The updated BEL values can be calculated using a global algorithm, as the above equations suggest, or using a propagation-based algorithm (Pearl, 1988).

The Task Net

Task specific knowledge is contained in a *task* Bayes net (for example, Figure 14.4). One feature of task knowledge is that subtask nodes can be shared by several tasks. Questions such as "Is this a fancy meal?" may be answered using a range of image clues. Some simple tasks, such as "Where is the butter?" do not require a task net since they only involve one particular node in a net.

Calculating BEL through a Composite Network

The organization of the composite network for TEA-1 is shown in Figure 14.5. It consists of four separate net structures: a PART-OF net, an *expected area* net, IS-A trees, and a *task* net. An IS-A tree is associated with each node in the PART-OF net that corresponds with an object.

The *task* net serves to combine the BEL values contained in all the other networks, in a manner that reflects the knowledge and information needed to solve the specific task for which the *task* net was created. Here we describe how information can be transferred from the other nets into the task net, so that BEL values can be calculated in the *task* net. This calculation will be used in a later section to calculate a utility for an evidence gathering action in one of the other networks — it is these task-specific utilities that guide the operation of the system.

BEL values are calculated in the composite net as follows: (1) Propagate belief in each of the networks, except the *task* net. That is, TEA-1 makes the assumption that each of the separate networks in the composite net, except the *task* net, maintains its BEL values independently of the other networks. (2) Construct *packages* of BEL values from the other networks for transfer to the *task* net. A package is treated as an evidence report that is attached to a node in the *task* net. A package serves to transfer belief from one knowledge domain to another. (3) Propagate belief in the task network.

The construction of a package for transporting BEL values is somewhat domain specific, in particular it depends on the values of the node in the task net that the package is attached to. We use one general kind of package that combines belief about the presence of an object in the scene with belief about the detailed classification of the object. Let the object's node in the PART-OF net have the following belief values: $BEL(present) = \alpha$ and $BEL(notPresent) = 1 - \alpha$. And, in the object's IS-A tree, let the subset of desired classifications for the object have the following belief values: $BEL(\omega_i) = \beta_i$, for each class ω_i in the subset. Assuming that a node in the task net needs information about this object, the package contains the following values: $(\alpha\beta_1, \alpha\beta_2, \ldots, \alpha\beta_d, 1 - \alpha\sum_d \beta_i)$. This package is attached as an evidence report to the corresponding node in the task net, whose variable in this case would have the following possible values: ω_1, ω_2, ..., ω_d, and *notPresentOrOther*.

For example, if the object was that corresponding to the **r-utensil** node in the PART-OF net, the subset of desired classifications for that object is $\{fork, knife, spoon\}$, and the package is:

$$(\alpha\beta_{fork}, \alpha\beta_{knife}, \alpha\beta_{spoon}, 1 - \alpha(\beta_{fork} + \beta_{knife} + \beta_{spoon})).$$

This package is attached to the **utensil-type** node in the *task* net. The possible values of that node are: *fork*, *knife*, *spoon*, and *notPresentOrOther*.

14.4   Actions in a Bayes Net

All actions in the TEA system are visual, and are constructed from one or more low-level *vision modules*. In TEA, each module can operate on either a foveal image or a peripheral image. At this stage, we are not developing special-purpose visual modules that are guaranteed to perform well in a specific application: rather our primary goal is to develop a framework in which any module with quantifiable performance can be incorporated.

Examples of some low-level vision modules are: 1) histogram matching to locate and identify objects by color, 2) grayscale template matching using Sobel edge information to find instances of known objects by correlation detection, 3) Hough transform for circle detection, 4) matching object representations built of straight lines by geometric hashing or relational structure matching.

Table 14.2
Summary of actions for plates.

Tree node	Action name	Vision module	Possible outputs
plate	per-detect-template-plate	grayscale template	*present*
	per-detect-hough-plate	circle hough	*present*, *notPresent*
	per-classify-plate	color histogram	*paper*, *ceramic*
	fov-classify-plate	color histogram	*paper*, *ceramic*

One or more vision modules may be used in a *visual action*. Each kind of object usually has several actions associated with it. TEA-0 had 11 visual actions related to 5 objects. TEA-1 currently has 20 actions. Some examples of visual actions are summarized in Table 14.2. Per-detect-template-plate uses a model grayscale template to detect the presence of a plate in the peripheral image and save its location. Per-detect-hough-plate uses a Hough transform for plate-sized circles for the same purpose. For per-classify-plate, a precondition is that the plate location must have been

determined previously. A color histogram is used to classify the plate as
paper (blue) or ceramic (green), using a window centered on the plate in the
peripheral image. `Fov-classify-plate` moves the fovea to the plate and
proceeds as for `per-classify-plate` but with foveal data. Similar actions
exist for other kinds of objects. TEA-1 also contains a special table finding
action, since knowing the exact location and extent of the table is very useful. The `table` action assumes that the camera initially views some portion
of the table top. It then scans the camera to the left until a large vertical
line, the edge of the table, is located. The process is repeated for the other
edges of the table.

Some actions (like `per-classify-plate` above) have *preconditions* that
must be satisfied before they can be executed. TEA-1 currently uses four
types of precondition: that a particular node in the expected area network be
instantiated, that it not be instantiated, that it be instantiated and within
the field of view for the current camera position, and of course the empty
precondition.

Using Actions with a Composite Net

An action node that is connected to a Bayes net node X represents a random variable that is a visual action's "evidence report". Before the action
is executed, an action node is a "chance" node like most of the nodes in
the net, and the node contains the *BEL* of the evidence report. After an
action is (successfully) executed its action nodes are changed to be "instantiated" nodes (see (Pearl, 1988)) and set to the values of the evidence
reports. For example, the `per-classify-utensil` action might generate
the evidence report $(4.9, 1.4, 2.7)$, which contains the scores for each of the
objects (*fork, knife, spoon*). The impact of this evidence on the other nodes
in the net is determined as usual by the conditional probability table on its
link to its parent.

An action in a system that uses a composite net generally can post evidence reports to several different nets. For the `PART-OF` net, evidence is
handled as above. All evidence reports are of the same form, containing
scores for the possible values: *notPresent* and *present*. The *expected area*
net also handles evidence as above. The conditional probability of an action
node may be specified using a parameterized 2D distribution, such as a bi-
variate Gaussian distribution. Action nodes can not be used in an `IS-A` tree.
Instead, evidence is injected into the tree via the weight W_i associated with
each leaf node h_i. If it is necessary to estimate the expected impact of an
evidence report, it is always possible to use some kind of expected value for
the λ values used to compute W_i. The *task* net handles evidence as above,
but actions generally should not post evidence directly to the *task* tree, since
such actions would be task-specific, something we want to avoid.

For example, the `per-detect-utensil` action posts evidence both to
the **r-utensil** node in the `PART-OF` net and to the object's corresponding

IS-A net, supporting equally the nodes in the subset named *utensil*. The
`per-classify-utensil` action posts evidence only to the object's corresponding IS-A net, supporting the nodes under *utensil* to varying degrees.
The `fov-classify-utensil` action is similar to `per-classify-utensil` but
presumably gives better evidence, reflected by the likelihood ratios.

14.5   Calculating an Action's Utility

The utility $U(\alpha)$ of an action α is of the form

$$U(\alpha) = \frac{V(\alpha)}{C(\alpha)}.$$

$C(\alpha) = r_A^\ell C_0(\alpha)$ is the cost of executing the action. $C_0(\alpha)$ is the execution
time of action α on the entire peripheral image (or the foveal image, if α is a
foveal action). r_A^ℓ is the fraction of the image covered by the expected area
of the object A associated with the action, when a confidence level of ℓ is
used (recall Section 14.3). We currently use $\ell = 0.9$. Before any actions have
been executed, no objects have been located, and so all r_A^ℓ values are close
to 1.0. Over time, as other objects in the scene are located and as more and
tighter relations are established, the value of r_A^ℓ will approach zero.

All actions in TEA are *information gathering* actions. Hence $V(\alpha)$ above
is meant to represent the value of the action, — how useful it is for achieving
the task's goal. Therefore TEA uses a fundamental measure of information,
Shannon's measure of average mutual information (see, *e.g.* (Proakis, 1983;
Pearl, 1988)): $I(x,y) = \log_2 \frac{P(x|y)}{P(x)}$. I describes the information content
about the event x that is provided by the occurrence of the event y (and
vice versa).

The average mutual information between two random variables is

$$I(X,Y) = \sum_x \sum_y P(x,y) I(x,y) = \sum_x \sum_y P(x,y) \log \frac{P(x,y)}{P(x)P(y)}.$$

When X and Y are nodes in a (single) Bayes net, the probabilities can be
replaced by belief:

$$I(X,Y) = \sum_x \sum_y BEL(x,y) \log \frac{BEL(x,y)}{BEL(x)BEL(y)} \tag{14.1}$$

where $BEL(x,y) = BEL(x \mid y)BEL(y)$. The values of $BEL(x)$ and $BEL(y)$
are respectively available at nodes X and Y in the Bayes net. The values of
$BEL(x \mid y)$ can be calculated by temporarily instantiating node Y to each
of its values, propagating beliefs, and taking the resulting value of $BEL(x)$
as $BEL(x \mid y)$ (Pearl, 1988).

In a single Bayes net, the value of an action α is: $V(\alpha) = I(target, \alpha)$,
where α refers to the action node for action α, and the task's goal is represented by the node *target*.

Calculating an Action's Value Using a Composite Net

When a composite net is used there are two differences in how a quantity like $I(target, \alpha)$ is calculated. First, the action α may post several evidence reports, one to each net. Second, the *target* node and the action's evidence reports are normally in different Bayes nets. The calculation is similar to that above.

Let action α produce several pieces of evidence $\alpha_1, \alpha_2, \ldots, \alpha_g$, which are combined to form the evidence reports that are added to the component networks. Let $\hat{\alpha}$ be the cross product of all the possible combinations of the separate pieces of evidence. The value of action α is calculated as $V(\alpha) = I(target, \hat{\alpha})$, which is calculated like equation (14.1), but with $\hat{y}$ substituted for y, and where $BEL(x, \hat{y}) = BEL(x \mid \hat{y})BEL(\hat{y})$. The values of $BEL(x \mid \hat{y})$ can be calculated by temporarily instantiating the evidence reports to the values in each possible cross product $\hat{y}$, propagating beliefs, and taking the resulting value of $BEL(x)$ as $BEL(x \mid \hat{y})$. Note that beliefs are transferred from the other nets to the *task* net via evidence packages.

The value of $BEL(x)$ is available at node X in the Bayes net, but calculating a value for $BEL(\hat{y})$ poses a problem. If the components of the $\hat{y}$ cross product are assumed independent, $BEL(\hat{y})$ can be calculated as $BEL(\hat{y}) = \prod_y BEL(y)$. While convenient, this conflicts with the assumption, in the calculation of $BEL(x \mid \hat{y})$, that the components of $\hat{y}$ are partially dependent. Alternatively, a consistent independence assumption about the components of the cross product can be maintained by computing $I(X, Y)$ independently for each component of the cross product, and summing the results, $I(X, \hat{Y}) = \sum_Y I(X, Y)$. We currently use the former method.

Accounting for Future Value

It is important to "look ahead" at the future impact of executing an action. TEA-1 uses the following "lookahead" utility function for action α.

$$U(\alpha) = \frac{V(\alpha) + V(\beta)}{C(\alpha) + C(\beta)} + H \sum_{X \in Net} \Delta U(X) \qquad (14.2)$$

where

$$\beta = \arg \max_{\gamma \in LocPre(\alpha)} \frac{V(\gamma)}{C(\gamma)}.$$

The first term in equation (14.2) accounts for the future value of establishing the location of an object. $LocPre(\alpha)$ is the set of actions that have a precondition satisfied by executing action α. Let β be the "best" of the actions in that set. The new utility of action α is an average over both α and β, more specifically an average of the value and cost of the two actions α and β.

The second term in equation (14.2) accounts for the future impact of making expected areas smaller. Each node in the expected area network contributes a term $\Delta U(X)$ to the utility:

$$
\begin{aligned}
\Delta U(X) &= \max_{\gamma \in Actions(X)} \left[\frac{V(\gamma)}{s_X^\ell C_0(\gamma)} - \frac{V(\gamma)}{r_X^\ell C_0(\gamma)} \right] \\
&= \left[\frac{r_X^\ell}{s_X^\ell} - 1 \right] \max_{\gamma \in Actions(X)} U(\gamma).
\end{aligned}
$$

This term is the increase in utility of the best action that affects X. Recall that r_X^ℓ is the fraction of the entire scene covered by the expected area at node X, when a confidence level of ℓ is used. s_X^ℓ is like r_X^ℓ except it assumes that the location of action α's associated object is known. It is computed in a manner similar to $BEL(x \mid y)$ above: The expected area node corresponding to α's associated object node is temporarily instantiated as a point at the center of its expected area mass, beliefs are propagated in the *expected area* net, and the resulting value of r_X^ℓ is taken as s_X^ℓ. $H \in (0,1)$ is a gain factor that specifies how much to weigh the second term in equation (14.2) relative to the first term.

Equation (14.2), where the action values are calculated using a composite net, is the utility function actually used in the TEA-1 system.

14.6   Experimental Results

This section presents experimental results using the TEA-1 system described above[1] to decide whether a table is set for either a fancy meal or an informal meal. The scene in Figure 14.1 was used. This scene shows a "fancy" meal.

The sequence of actions executed by TEA-1 is summarized in Table 14.3. The *a priori* belief of the table setting being fancy is 0.590, compared with 0.410 that it is informal. As the system executed actions to gather specific information about the scene, the belief that the setting is a fancy one approaches 0.974. The following text discussed a few important points in the sequence of executed actions.

The system begins at time step 0 with the *a priori* belief values mentioned above (*i.e.* for informal and fancy). Figure 14.6(a) shows the camera's initial viewpoint. Note how little of the entire table scene is visible.

One line in Table 14.3 represents one cycle in the decision loop of the system. For example, at time step 1 the cycle consists of the following: 1) The utility of each executable action is computed, as shown in Table 14.4. 10 of the 20 available actions are executable now, the other 10 have unsatisfied

---

[1]There is one exception. The second term in equation 14.2, which accounts for the future impact of making expected areas smaller, has not been implemented yet.

Table 14.3
The sequence of actions selected and executed by TEA-1. The belief values shown are
those after incorporating the results from each action.

time	$U(\alpha)$	α, an action	$BEL(informal)$	$BEL(fancy)$
0		a priori	0.410	0.590
1	10.000	table	0.400	0.600
2	10.505	per-detect-hough-cup	0.263	0.737
3	42.839	per-classify-cup	0.343	0.657
4	11.374	per-detect-hough-plate	0.340	0.660
5	11.917	per-classify-plate	0.041	0.959
6	20.982	per-detect-utensil	0.041	0.959
7	58.810	per-classify-utensil	0.033	0.967
8	4.320	per-detect-napkin	0.026	0.974
9	3.342	fov-classify-cup	0.026	0.974
10	2.405	fov-classify-plate	0.026	0.974
11	1.759	per-detect-hough-bowl	0.026	0.974
12	0.687	per-detect-butter	0.026	0.974
13	0.486	fov-verify-butter	0.026	0.974

preconditions. 2) The `table` action has highest utility and is selected[2]. 3)
That action is executed. 4) The results obtained by the action are added to
the composite network and the belief values are updated. As a result the
value of $BEL(fancy)$ increases to 0.600. (The increase is small since knowing
that the table exists has little impact on the goal.) 5) Finally, the decision
cycle repeats.

Table 14.4
Action utilities at time step 1.

$U(\alpha)$	α, an action
10.000	table
2.545	per-detect-hough-cup
1.357	per-detect-template-cup
1.103	per-detect-utensil
1.064	per-detect-hough-plate
0.554	per-detect-napkin
0.343	per-detect-template-plate
0.049	per-detect-hough-bowl
0.029	per-detect-butter
0.013	per-detect-template-bowl

At time step 2 the `per-detect-hough-cup` action is executed. This action
moves the camera to the center of the cup's expected area and then tries
(successfully) to detect a cup. Figure 14.7(b) illustrates the execution of

---

[2]Because the second term in the utility equation 14.2 is not implemented yet, and determining the table location is important since it makes the expected areas of other objects
much smaller, we artificially set $U(\text{table})$ to a large value. All other utilities are calculated
using the real equation.

this action. The `per-detect-hough-plate` action executed at time step 4, as shown in Figure 14.6(b), is similar. In both cases the action processes only the portion of the image data that is within the expected area when thresholded by a 0.9 confidence level.

The `per-detect-napkin` action uses a color histogram to detect a (red) napkin. When the action is executed at time step 8, shown in Figure 14.6(c), the expected area of the napkin is small enough that it doesn't cover the pink creamer container located just above the napkin, thus avoiding falsely detecting the creamer as the napkin.

Foveal actions are another way to limit processing to smaller contextual areas in the scene. For example, Figure 14.6(d) shows the execution of the `fov-classify-plate` action at time step 10. The figure shows a zoomed display of the fovea, centered on the plate, and the results of matching one model color histogram (for a ceramic color) against the image data.

Camera/fovea movements and expected areas are very useful for limiting the portion of a scene or image that an action processes. As more objects are located via actions, the expected areas for the remaining objects (not yet located by actions) get narrower. We demonstrate this via a separate experiment, illustrated in Figures 14.7 and 14.8. Assume that TEA-1 has located (in this order) the table, then the plate, and finally the napkin. Figure 14.8 shows how the cup's expected area gets narrower as each of these other objects is located in turn, and Figure 14.7 shows how the `per-detect-hough-cup` action would *hypothetically* perform after each object is located in turn. Part (a) shows the situation before any other objects have been located. The expected area is rather large, much larger than the field of view. The camera movement, made to the center of the cup's expected area, is much higher than the true location of the cup, and the action mistakenly detects the creamer container as the cup. The situation improves once the table is located, as shown in part (b). The expected area is small enough to fit in the field of view and its center corresponds better with the cup's actual location. A small portion of the image is masked out by the expected area, and the cup is correctly detected, but this is just lucky since the creamer and many other objects are still in the unmasked area. Part (c) shows the situation after the plate has been located. The cup's expected area is much smaller. Finally, in part (d), once the napkin has been located, the cup's expected area is small enough that the action is very likely to detect the cup correctly.

In summary, the points of camera fixation that occur through the thirteen steps of Table 14.3 are shown in Fig. 14.9.

14.7   Extensions

TEA-0 and TEA-1 are "myopic", making decisions by only looking one step ahead. The anticipatory utility function is an improvement, trying to pack look-ahead into the utility of a single action. Ultimately our problem involves full-scale planning, in which sequences of actions are evaluated as to their expected utility. We intend to develop a simple planning system (TEA-2) using Bayes nets. The idea is to substitute a search in action space rather than to try to pack all the intelligence into a (quasi-static) utility function.

One claim of this work is that vision algorithms can be more robust and reliable if they are known to work in a limited context. For example, TEA can use simple color histograms for object identification only because it has foveated a small area of the image previously. We want to explore limited context effects that arise naturally in task-oriented vision when the vision problem is known to be simplified (by camera actions, foveal processing, and generally by satisfaction of preconditions).

We want to investigate vision modules that can run for different periods of time, improving their results the longer they run (*e.g.* some scale space algorithms, multi-feature classifiers, and anytime algorithms (Dean & Wellman, 1991)). Such vision actions are generalizations of TEA's peripheral–foveal actions which produce a peripheral result at one cost and follow it up with a foveal action for a further cost. An evidence/time function can quantify the incremental benefit of such an action. New control strategies should then emerge, such as running a set of incremental actions cyclically to attain the maximum evidence per unit time from the set.

We plan to solve multiple tasks in multiple domains using the same set of visual actions. This exercise will test the generality of our knowledge representations and visual actions and probably encourage us to extend and modify both. Also we expect to encounter interesting new problems for visual actions used in answering qualitative questions such as "Is this desk messy?". New domains may necessitate the use of more complex knowledge representations, in particular non-tree Bayes nets.

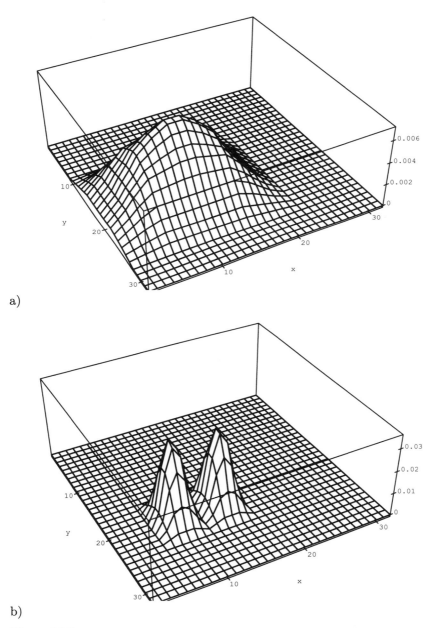

a)

b)

Figure 14.3
The expected area (a) for **r-setting-area** (a place setting area) before the location of any
other object is determined, and (b) for *napkin* after the location of the table and plate
have been determined.

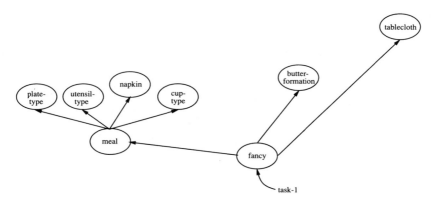

Figure 14.4
A *task* Bayes net.

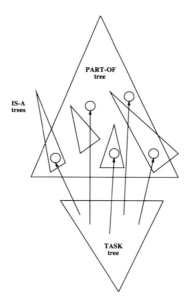

Figure 14.5
The organization of the composite net used by TEA-1.

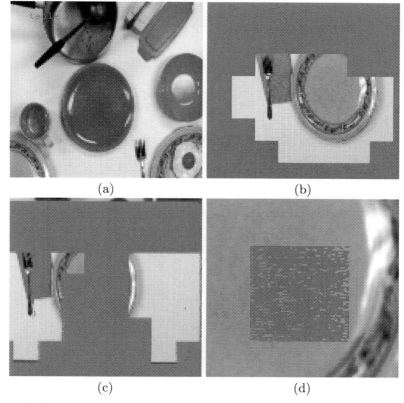

(a)   (b)

(c)   (d)

Figure 14.6
Processing performed by individual actions. (a) The camera's initial viewpoint. (b)
Results from the `per-detect-hough-plate` action executed at time step 4. (c) Results
from the `per-detect-napkin` action executed at time step 8. (d) Results from the `fov-classify-plate` action executed at time step 10.

(a)   (b)

(c)   (d)

Figure 14.7
Performance of a cup detection action as the cup's expected area narrows over time. (a)
Before any objects have been located. (b) After the table has been located. (c) After
the table and plate have been located. (d) After the table, plate and napkin have been
located.

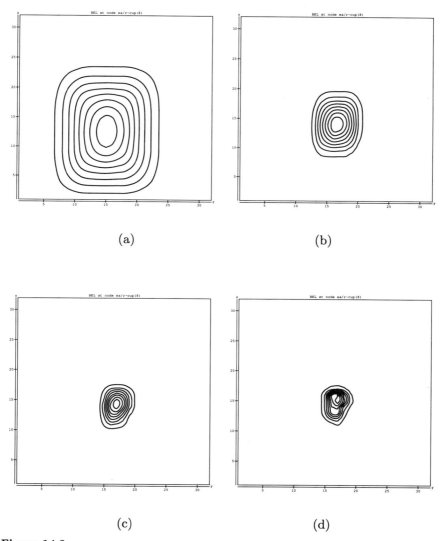

(a)

(b)

(c)

(d)

Figure 14.8
Narrowing of cup's expected area over time. (a) Before any objects have been located.
(b) After the table has been located. (c) After the table and plate have been located. (d)
After the table, plate and napkin have been located.

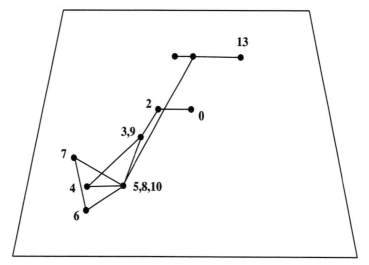

Figure 14.9
Points fixated in the scene during the action sequence of Table 14.3.

IV Architectures and Applications

One of the most exciting aspects of Active Vision is the success of the systems designed to perform useful tasks. The following section describes four state of the art systems.

Chapter 15 describes a system of transputers strung together to perform (almost) real time depth recovery and object recognition. The depth is obtained by the highly effective PMF stereo algorithm. The resulting depth map can then be used to detect, in parallel, objects in the world described by 3D models using characteristic views to obtain viewpoint independence. Currently about 10 seconds are needed to locate a number of objects. The system can also be adapted to track a number of features in parallel.

The DROID system, in Chapter 16, uses controlled egomotion to construct a 3D geometric description of the scene. It identifies and tracks feature points, such as corners, and uses triangulation with Kalman filtering to estimate depth. This results in a system that can estimate position accurately and quickly for sequences of images taken from helicopters. The depth map can also be used for obstacle avoidance and detecting navigational landmarks. Real time implementations of the system are practical.

Medical imaging is another domain where active vision can be usefully be applied. Chapter 17 describes a medical imaging system for tracking structures in, highly noisy, ultrasound images. These images are first filtered and edges are extracted. Active deformable models are then used to track the structures.

The book ends with, arguably, the most advanced existing active vision system. Chapter 18 describes Dickmann and his group's pioneering research using a 4D spatio-temporal approach to automatically control a car. Essential to this work is the idea of a sophisticated internal model of key features in the environment which can be updated by Kalman filters using visual inputs. This results in a system able to automatically drive a car at speeds of up to one hundred kilometers an hour. The system can be extended to add many extra desirable abilities, such as the detection of objects in the road. The basic principles involved are very general and can be applied to other domains, such as guiding an aircraft on its approach to landing.

All the systems described in this section are constantly evolving as the range of tasks they are desired to perform increases and as faster hardware becomes available. They rely mainly on networks of transputers joined together to form a parallel system. This enables new modules, for perfoming novel tasks, to be incorporated by linking additional transputers to the network. We expect that these systems will keep increasing in sophistication and power.

15 A Parallel 3D Vision System

Michael Rygol, Stephen Pollard, Chris Brown and John Mayhew

We describe a working multi-transputer stereo vision system which exploits various forms of parallelism in a number of visual competences. The system is implemented upon a specialised hardware architecture that provides distributed video datapaths to the processor array. We exploit stereo and spatial parallelism to recover 3D scene descriptions from passive stereo vision. To recognise and recover the positions of modelled objects, we exploit featural data parallelism at both the object and sub-object level. We also describe a real-time object tracking algorithm that exploits featural parallelism in the concurrent tracking of a set of object features.

These competences have been integrated into a general purpose architecture and we present some performance results and descriptions of the use of this vision engine in two application domains.

15.1 Introduction

Vision can provide an animal with a rich description of its environment, allowing it to perform a wide range of tasks. However, trying to provide a machine with visual ability has proved to be extremely difficult. Current techniques require enormous computing power and for the most part operate offline in a snapshot manner. To achieve real-time dynamic vision demands investigation of parallel processing techniques.

Visual processing is generally decomposed into three levels:

Iconic-to-iconic This processing forms the low-level stage of scene interpretation and generally consists of relatively simple operations upon image data to tag pixel locations with such characteristics as edge strength or topological information. Such operations are generally spatially localisable and repeated over the image array, lending themselves to implementation in pipelined hardware or parallel implementation upon SIMD machine architectures.

Iconic-to-symbolic This *medium-level* processing typically receives data from the lower level stages to extract *symbolic* descriptions such as segmentation and feature extraction. Such operations are more suited to implementation upon a general purpose computer although certain medium-level operations are amenable to implementation in hardware and upon SIMD computers.

Symbolic-to-interpretation Such processes extract *meaning* from the data produced by the earlier stages such as object recognition. The algorithmic complexity of current high-level vision algorithms generally require implementation upon general purpose computers.

The competences that we have developed are recovery of 3D scene geometry from passive stereo vision, object recognition and real-time object tracking. These competences have been combined into an integrated system.

The work described in this chapter has a number of goals:

1.   To demonstrate that it is possible to develop a large-scale parallel vision system as opposed to the parallelisation of a single image processing routine as is often presented elsewhere.

2.   To investigate the suitability of our prototype general purpose vision engine, MARVIN, for exploiting numerous forms of parallelism within a single overall application.

3.   The development of *practical* techniques to efficiently develop and execute parallel vision algorithms.

4.   The development of a "vision coprocessor" to allow high performance *parallelised* visual capabilities to be easily integrated into robotic systems.

15.2   A Brief Survey of the Field

Much of the work up to date in the field of parallel vision has been the exploitation of various flavours of fine-grained parallelism using SIMD computers to perform local pixel-based operations upon images to perform such operations as greyscale equalisation, convolution, and simple edge detection.

However, advances in microprocessor technology now allow systems to exploit MIMD architectures for medium and coarse grain parallelism. MIMD vision systems have been constructed from various general purpose microprocessors and more recently, the Inmos transputer. The current state of the art suggests that high performance vision engines should combine multiple processors, fast video datapaths and provide further support for the lower levels of processing in the form of dedicated hardware or SIMD subsystems. Examples of work in this field include HBA (Wallace & Howard, 1989), Kiwivision-2 (Valkenburg & Bowman, 1989), NETRA (Choudhary et al., 1990), the Image Understanding Architecture (Shu et al., 1990) and the Warwick Pyramid Machine (Nudd et al., 1990).

The main content of this chapter concentrates on the development of medium to high level visual competences upon the MARVIN machine architecture.

15.3   Hardware Architecture of the Vision Engine

The architectural design of MARVIN (Multiprocessor ARchitecture for VIsioN) was intended to provide what were perceived to be the main requirements of a high-performance vision engine for robotics applications:

1. Large computing power.

2. High-bandwidth datapaths for video dataflow.

3. Support for various levels of vision processing.

4. Real-time response.

The differing requirements of the computations of the three levels of vision processing are best served by a *heterogeneous* computer architecture. MARVIN provides capability for both pipelined frame-rate hardware for low-level operations and a general purpose sub-system for medium and high level scene interpretation operations.

The need to provide the vision system with sufficient general purpose computing power demands the investigation of parallel processing techniques. We chose the T800 transputer as the parallel processing element of the architecture as it provides high performance at each node, a microcoded scheduler, interprocess communications and allows the simple construction of general purpose processor arrays to perform higher level operations with a relatively coarse grain of parallelism.

MARVIN incorporates an array of 25 processors which are wired as a regular, fully-connected mesh with 3 rows, 8 columns and an extension for the *root* transputer. The selection of a mesh architecture is not formally justified but we believe it offers a flexible architecture to allow experimentation as well as ensuring that no processor is more than one hop away from the incoming video data, as shown in figure 15.1. The machine is hosted by a SUN 3/110 workstation and is further described in (Brown & Rygol, 1989). A scaled down version of the architecture (with only four columns) is illustrated in figure 15.1. Two links from the root transputer are connected to the host machine. Link 0 provides the usual boot path and I/O interface whereas link 1 provides a dedicated communications path to tditool (a multi-window tool, running in Sunview) allowing multi-processor console I/O (Brown & Rygol, 1990).

A high performance parallel vision engine requires efficient dissemination of image data from the ccd camera to the array of processing elements to reduce the message passing delays of a distributed memory machine. This is especially important for *stereo* processing as twice the amount of data needs to be transferred. Rather than provide a single transputer with access to incoming video data and dispersing it to other processors via the transputer links, our solution to this problem is to provide 4 *distributed* byte-wide, bidirectional video busses to the processor array. A locally developed transputer card, named TMAX, allows a T800 processor to *simultaneously* acquire (or transmit) up to 4 image streams (or numerous regions-of-interest). These video busses may be used together to allow fast distribution of data up to 32 bits wide. Although these video busses may be used as a fast medium for interprocessor communication, in practice we have utilised them as a means of distributing image data to the processor array from the digitiser along

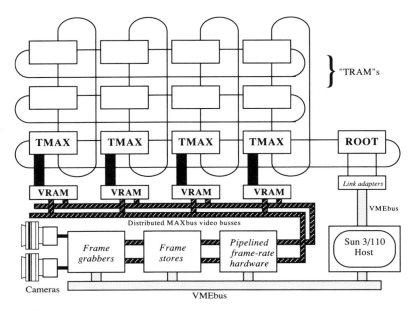

Figure 15.1
The architecture of MARVIN.

with the display of distributed output data. The TMAX offers 1Mbyte of
video memory (VRAM), allowing the storage of up to 4 512 by 512 images
and up to 4 Mbytes of DRAM.

The stereo images (512 pixels square) are simultaneously acquired from a
pair of ccd cameras via Digimax digitisers and may be stored in Framestore
image stores. We use the MAXbus [1] as the means of image distribution.
The framestores share a number of MAXbus ports with the row of TMAX
cards through which synchronised image acquisition can be achieved by using
a shared interrupt signal connected to the event requests of the TMAX
processors. The video dataflow of images from the pair of cameras to the
TMAX array is shown in figure 15.2.

The proportion of TMAX processors in the transputer array is a trade-
off between cost and performance. As such, we use 8 TMAX cards, the
remaining processors are 2Mbyte TRAMs (Transputer Modules).

The provision of the TMAX component of the transputer array provides
8 processors with *direct* access to the incoming video streams, allowing scope
for distributed real-time visual processing. All other processors are vertically
adjacent to a TMAX card.

A recent addition to the MARVIN architecture is a stereo convolver board
which allows frame-rate convolution on a pair of images. This board is
interposed between the framestores and the TMAX array. Work is in hand to

---
[1]Datacube Inc., Peabody, MA, USA.

exploit further the MAXbus facility by adding compatible cards to perform other low level image processing operations at frame rate (e.g. edge detection, corner detection).

A full description of MARVIN and its visual capabilities can be found in (Rygol, 1991).

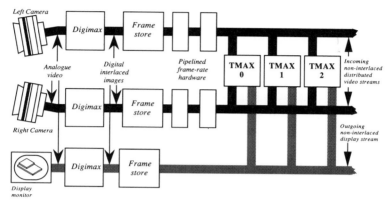

Figure 15.2
Video dataflow of MARVIN.

15.4   The Runtime Environment

All transputers are programmed in Parallel C [2] and run within a locally developed runtime environment (named MRE (Brown & Rygol, 1990)), summarised here for completeness. This environment provides the programmer with an abstraction of the machine, simplifying the expression of interprocessor parallelism and communication. As we have adopted a fixed processor configuration, we provide a message routing infrastructure to simplify interprocess communication. Each processor has a resident *router* process which is responsible for managing the dataflow between all processes executing on each transputer and data flowing through each processor. Interprocess communication is provided by exchanging addressed messages, in a method similar to *datagrams*. To inform the routers of local task names, a process may register over a number of ports to the local router with a number of task identification handles, in effect instructing the router to forward any incoming messages that are addressed to this process through the relevant ports.

In order to simplify the cross-network message addressing, the location of remote processes may be obtained by means of a *nameserver* task, allowing network-wide registration of server processes. Conversely, client processes

---

[2]3L Ltd, Livingston, Scotland.

may interrogate the nameserver to obtain the location of a specified server resource in a variety of modes, for example, to ensure single client access to a specified server process. Thus, any processes in the network may communicate in a simple manner, allowing dynamic changes of inter-process communication topologies.

To speed up network loading, new tasks are loaded into the system in a dynamic manner. When the system is booted, a dynamic loading skeleton is loaded into the network, reading a high level configuration file (the MCL language (Brown & Rygol, 1990)) for information regarding task parameters and placement. For further flexibility, tasks may also be loaded onto the network by any process at any time by means of a function call.

The MRE provides a homogeneous programming environment across the transputer array and provides each process with the following facilities:

- Transparent standard C filesystem and I/O access.

- The creation and communication with UNIX processes on the host machine.

- To communicate with extra-network UNIX processes on the local area network via UNIX sockets, simplifying communication between any transputer and any SUN-workstation on the local ethernet.

15.5   Control Architectures

The modules described in this chapter have been implemented as "vision resource servers". That is, access to the capabilities of a parallel module is simplified by providing an interface to the module via a single ("virtual") process utilising remote procedure calls within a client/server model. The system is then comprised of numerous vision building blocks which cooperate via commands from the hierarchical and distributed control architecture, as shown in figure 15.3. We have found that this method greatly simplifies the implementation and integration of individual vision modules into the system.

All of the visual competences described in this chapter have been made available to other workstations (via socket-based requests) on the local area network and allow workstation-based applications to access the functionality of MARVIN via a number of client remote procedure calls. This provision of a "vision coprocessor" has greatly simplified the integration of the visual capabilities into other applications.

15.6   Parallel Recovery of 3D Scene Descriptions

In order to obtain information about the environment, we attempt to recover the three-dimensional structure of a scene from a stereo pair of images, expressed as a set of geometrical primitives that correspond to physical features in the world.

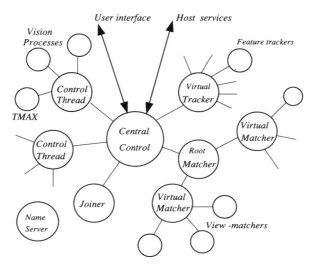

Figure 15.3
Control architecture.

This vision system is derived from the our TINA system (Porrill *et al.*, 1987a) which employs edge based stereo triangulation as a basis for three dimensional scene description.

To ease understanding we firstly describe the core of the vision algorithms, ignoring parallel implementation details.

15.6.1   The Core Vision Algorithms

The stereo camera rig comprises two Panasonic WD-CV50 ccd cameras with a focal length of approximately 14mm with an interocular separation of approximately 22cm. The cameras are calibrated (using an algorithm developed by Tsai (1986)) to recover the extrinsic and some intrinsic parameters of the stereo camera rig. The calibration information allows the (arbitrary) camera geometry to be transformed into a parallel camera geometry in order to simplify the stereo matching process described later. This calibration need only be updated if the relative camera positions are changed.

The pair of images are subsequently processed with a single scale ($\sigma = 1.0$) application of the Canny edge operator (Canny, 1986). This reduction of image information to a smaller data set consisting of pertinent edge information simplifies the extraction of higher level scene descriptions, described later. This edge operator is fairly robust and resilient to image noise, consisting of four stages:

1.   A two dimensional convolution. Although a 2D convolution is computationally expensive, it may be decomposed into 2 1D convolutions, along the rows and then along the columns. The recent introduction of pipelined

frame-rate hardware to perform the convolution has greatly reduced the computation time.

2.   The gradients for both x and y orientations of the blurred image are obtained by a simple Laplacian operator, corresponding to the first derivative of the image intensity contour at each pixel location.

3.   Edge elements (*edgels*) with a gradient (one metric of edge strength) below a specified threshold are discarded. The orientation of the potential edge element is used to ensure that the edge is a local maximum in the direction orthogonal to the orientation of the edge, allowing non-maximal edges to be discarded. Edges are obtained to sub-pixel acuity by applying a quadratic fit to the gradient profile.

4.   Each resultant edge is processed to recover further information about the connectivity of the edge with other edges. Linked edges are built into strings and isolated edges with a contrast less than an upper threshold are discarded unless they form part of an edge string.

The edgel data are maintained as interconnected lists, describing their spatial relationships. Each edgel (stored as a C structure) is then *rectified* using the calibration information to compute the edge position in the image plane of the parallel camera geometry.

Identifying the correct correspondences between the left and right edgels obtained from the same physical feature allows the depth (distance from the viewing sensor) of that particular point to be computed from simple triangulation. However, robust stereo matching is non-trivial due to problems such as occlusion, noise and the inherent difficulties in identifying the correct edgels to match. Moreover, a naive approach suggests a (restricted) 2D search space in the right image for each edgel obtained from the left.

We use a locally developed algorithm, PMF (Pollard *et al.*, 1985b), for stereo matching. In PMF, matches between edges from the left and right images are preferred if they mutually support each other through a disparity gradient constraint and if they satisfy a number of higher level grouping constraints, most notably uniqueness, ordering (along epipolars) and figural continuity. As the right edgels are stored in their *rectified* positions, the search space for a corresponding match for a left edgel is reduced to a 1D search along a single epipolar (a virtual raster equivalent to both left and right images) obtained from the rectified position of the left edge element.

As well as being matched, edge strings are processed to recover descriptions of the two dimensional geometrical elements they may represent. This representation is currently limited to straight line segments. However, work is in hand to extend this to descriptions of ellipses and planar curves.

The line-fitting algorithm applies a recursive fit and segment strategy to the 2D edgel strings. Segmentation points are included when the underlying string deviates from the current line fit. The fit is computed by orthogonal regression.

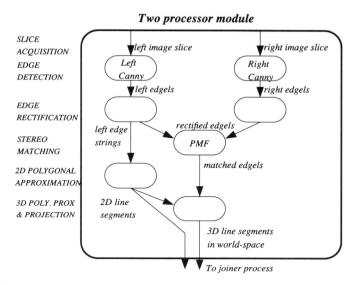

Figure 15.4
TINA processes and dataflow within a processor pair module.

Given descriptions of the two dimensional geometry (in a single view) and the results of the application of the stereo algorithm to the underlying edge strings, it is possible to recover three dimensional geometrical descriptions. Disparity values can be obtained along the 2D geometrical descriptors for each matched edge point. A second stage of 2D fitting (in length against disparity) computes the fit in disparity space. Finally, disparity data is projected into the world using transformations based upon the camera calibration.

This results in a set of geometrical descriptors pertaining to physical features in the world.

15.6.2   Parallel Implementation

As the vision modules shown in figure 15.4 exhibit a sequential dataflow from image acquisition to recovery of the scene geometry, it would seem natural to implement these modules in a pipelined structure. Figure 15.4 also shows the concurrent application of the Canny edge operator to both left and right images. Furthermore, it would seem sensible to further decompose the Canny modules into pipelined operations.

However, analysis of a pipelined implementation reveals:

1.   A pipelined implementation suffers from excessive dataflow. For example, the output of the convolution stage of a pipelined Canny implementation would result in a dataflow of 1Mbyte to the next (gradients) module. The

amount of data to be exchanged between modules higher up the processing chain is much decreased. This exacerbates the problem of maintaining optimal usage of the processors in the pipeline.

2. It is important to realise that a pipelined architecture optimises *throughput* rather than minimising *latency*. If a pipeline comprises N stages, each requiring an execution time of t (for an optimal pipeline), the temporal latency between receiving input data and producing output data is clearly Nt. When designing a reactive vision system for a moving robot we wish to minimise the *latency of response* to visual stimuli.

3. Our vision system differs from simple image processing systems in that we maintain sets of data structures at each stage of the processing. These data structures are used to express spatial and logical connectivity and simplify the representation of the data recovered. For example, the 3D data structures are obtained from 2D edge strings, stereo data and 2D primitives. Pipelining these modules would require the dismantling and rebuilding of the interconnected data structures as they are transferred from the local memory of one processor to the local memory of another.

4. The length of a pipeline is limited to the maximum number of modules in the pipeline thus limiting the number of processors available to efficiently implement the pipeline. Although certain of the processing module are amenable to spatial decomposition.

The interconnectedness of the data structures also prohibits the use of a processor farm model as recombination of data obtained from intermediate modules is non-trivial and computationally expensive.

Our analysis of the system led us to design a system with minimal dataflow whilst providing efficient usage of the processor network.

We exploit spatial parallelism by decomposing the workload into *slice-pairs*. The current implementation uses 16 of the available processors, decomposing the images into horizontal slices of approximately 64 rasters. Processing is decomposed into processor-pair modules. The 2 processors from each pair are vertically adjacent to the same TMAX. Each of these processor pairs cooperate in recovering the geometry from the allocated slice-pair and the processing for both the left and right corresponding slice is computed concurrently. Adjacent slices overlap by two rasters to overcome boundary effects.

Each of the modules are implemented as separate processes running within a multi-threaded TINA task. The control of these tasks is provided by a supervisory layer of the control architecture which allocates the regions to be processed to the TINA tasks. Upon completion of each stage in the processing a small reply packet is returned to the control architecture providing status information. This information is used to instruct the next processing modules, for example the location of the input data to the module. As these processes are implemented as a set of concurrently executing threads,

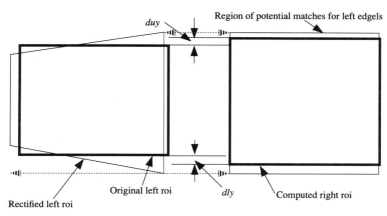

Figure 15.5
The growth of the right roi to accommodate full matching of left edgels.

their workspace is part of a contiguous address space. This allows the data
to be passed between modules by using pointers to the interconnected data
structures. The only sizable exchange of data is the transferral of edge information between the two processors prior to the stereo matching stage.
Owing to the fact that the cameras may not be parallel, the right image
slice is warped as shown in figure 15.5 so that all edges obtained from the
left slice have their counterparts available (if present) in the right slice. This
warping typically results in a slice expansion of approximately 2–5 rasters
(shown exaggerated as duy and dly) increasing vertically from the centre of
the image.

Upon commencement of the processing sequence, the image pair is acquired simultaneously into each TMAX by the control architecture with a
subsequent activation of the processing sequence. The Canny processes obtain the relevant region-of-interest (ROI) from the *tmax server* of the TMAX
processor of the local column, alleviating the need to transmit image data
across multiple processors. This server allows network wide access to the
functionality of each TMAX card and is accessible by a library of remote
procedure calls, allowing ROI acquisition, data plotting etc.

As each processor-pair provides a subset of the scene geometry (shown in
figure 15.6(a)) recombination of the distributed data is necessary. Rather
than expensively recombine the output data from each intermediate stage
of the component modules we defer data recombination until the last stage
of processing. A *Joiner* task communicates with all of the 3D geometry
tasks (figure 15.6(b)), receiving both the 2D and 3D geometrical features.
The Joiner identifies related 2D features (i.e. their endpoints are close at
the slice boundary and their directions are similar, within thresholds) and
optimally combines the component features. The features are joined by
orthogonal regression utilising the covariance information obtained from the

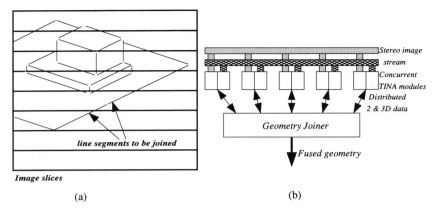

Figure 15.6
(a) Spatial distribution of the recovered geometry (b) subsequent joining.

original fit from the 2D edge strings.

The joiner subsequently returns the component line segments to the TINA tasks for the recomputation of the 3D features utilising the adjusted 2D features. The newly computed 3D data is returned to the joiner for recombination, again utilising the covariance of the fit of the component features. We adopt this strategy of utilising 2D information in the joining process as the errors in the 3D data are anisotropic; errors in depth (z) far outweigh errors in x or y.

Upon completion, the Joiner returns the integrated geometry to the client of the geometry recovery server (in this case a control task resident on the root processor). This results in a set of 3D line segments in world-space. The joining stage is relatively inexpensive, taking up to 2% of the total processing time.

The number of processor pairs required to compute the data for a single scene is allocated by the user with 8 being the number generally used.

15.6.3   Performance and Experimental Results

In order to investigate the effects of the recombination processes we compared the scene descriptions obtained from the parallel implementation with those obtained from a sequential implementation. The results of a typical test scenario are shown in table 15.1. These results were obtained from a set of objects approximately 1m from the camera rig, with an interocular separation of 20cm. The figures show the standard deviations of the differences between the two sets of recovered geometrical descriptions and describe the difference in orientation of the line segments, the difference (in world-space) of both the centroid positions and their lengths. These results show that the method of parallel decomposition and subsequent recombination results in negligible degradation of the recovered data.

Measurement	Standard Deviation (units)
Angular difference	0.036°
Centroid separation	0.65mm
Length difference	1.28mm

Table 15.1
Comparison between 3D geometry from MARVIN and the sequential vision system.

The data presented in figure 15.7 shows a graph of processing time versus number of processor pairs for a relatively complex scene. We present results for the interval 8 to 16 processors. As can be seen, we achieve an encouraging speed-up with increasing number of processors.

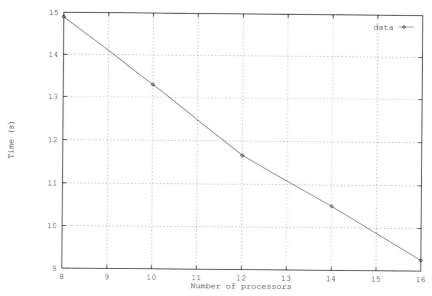

Figure 15.7
Graph of execution time *vs.* number of processors.

We present further results to give an indication of the performance of the system were we to use more processors. Although MARVIN currently has only 25 processors, we can simulate the scenario of more processors by limiting the size of the image to be processed. The graph in figure 15.8 shows a graph of processing time for an image of size 125×512. Thus, when using 16 processors the size of the slice is approximately 16 rasters, corresponding to a number of processor pairs of 512/16=32, or conversely 64 processors, giving an execution time of approximately 3.8 seconds.

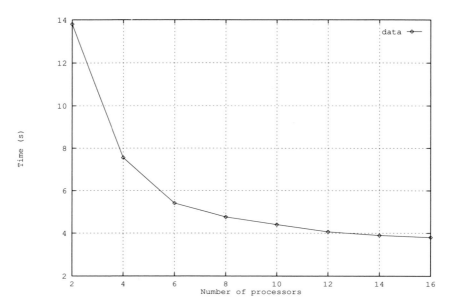

Figure 15.8
Timings for recovery of scene geometry for an image region of 125 rasters of a 512 image vs. processor count.

Although the reduction in size of the slice-pair reduces the amount of higher level support (for example, figural continuity) available to the PMF process, we have found the output data under these conditions to be satisfactory.

Table 15.2 shows the percentage of the total execution time required by the individual modules.

TINA vision module	Percentage of total processing time
Canny (left and right)	73
PMF	13
2D Polygonal approximation	2
3D Scene geometry (including joining)	4
Overheads	8

Table 15.2
Breakdown of execution time for parallel vision modules.

15.7   Concurrent Location of Modelled Objects

We now describe a parallel model matching algorithm that is able to identify and give the position and orientation of modelled objects from the recovered scene descriptions described in the previous section. The system is designed for application in industrial environments; it does not recognise "classes" of objects (for example, this is a chair) but it recognises specific descriptions of *rigid* 3D objects.

The object model is described in terms of its 3D geometrical primitives in a local coordinate frame. Currently, the model descriptions are generated manually, however, we plan to automate this process by combining the information recovered from multiple views of the object.

Our model matching algorithm attempts to identify the instance of the model description within the scene geometry. Problems of scaling are removed as all data is three-dimensional.

The model matching problem may be described as finding a mapping from a set of features in the scene to a model description. That is, recovering a list of correctly matching feature pairs and obtaining the transformation between these lists to provide the position of the object in the world.

Naive tree-searching techniques to obtain this feature mapping result in a combinatorial explosion of the search space and a corresponding computation penalty. We restrict this search space in a number of ways:

1. We exploit the parallelism inherent in a tree-searching task by distributing the search for the object over a number of processors. We partition the model description into a number of *characteristic views* (*CVs*), exploiting ideas from Chakravarti and Freeman (1980) and Mayhew (1986). Chakravarti and Freeman argue that the universe of all vantage points may be quantised into a finite set of *vantage-point domains* where each domain constitutes the range of view points that will provide features from (with no loss or gain of other features) the same CV. We define a CV as a group of features which are stable over a number of closely related viewpoints. Locating all characteristic views on one processor is computationally prohibitive.

This partitioning of the object model into localisable CVs allows a number of processors to independently locate a part of the object, rather than the whole, with a corresponding reward in computational expense.

2. The CV is represented as a *focus feature* (Pollard *et al.*, 1987; Bolles *et al.*, 1983) and a set of *support* features. Initial *cliques* of matched features are generated if other features are present in the scene that bear a similar pairwise relationship with the feature matching the focus feature and other features in the model description.

3. Following initial matching hypotheses of congruencies identified between 3D scene descriptions and the CV list, potential matches are ranked on the basis of the extent to which further support exists for the three dimensional transformation between model and scene that they implicitly represent. The specification of a minimum size of a *clique* of hypothesised matches (typically 5) prevents an unbounded search.

We exploit the partial pairwise relationships table of Grimson and Lozano-Perez (1984) to reduce the computational burden of verifying the pairwise relationships. The least squares computation of the transformation between the model description and the recovered scene description is achieved by exploiting the quaternion representation for rotations from Faugeras *et al.* (Faugeras & Hebert, 1986).

15.7.1   Architecture of the Model Matching System

We employ a three-level process hierarchy in the model matching system, as shown in figure 15.9.   Interfaces between these levels are via remote proce-

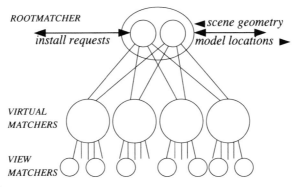

Figure 15.9
Model matching architecture.

dure calls, adopting the client/server model. The data flow between these levels is small, typically less than 12K in a contiguous packet corresponding to approximately 2 seconds of computation.

The bottom layer of the hierarchy consists of a number of so-called *view matcher* tasks, placed on every processor. The responsibility of these processes is to locate a number (typically 1) of specified CVs within the current scene geometry.

The next layer consists of a number (typically 4) of *virtual matchers*, placed upon arbitrary processors. These processes are responsible for providing a simple client interface to a model matching subsystem, concealing the internal complexities of the parallel implementation. The virtual matcher performs no model matching but manages the dataflow with its subordinate view matcher pool of processors and integrates the match information returned by the view matchers. The virtual matcher also maintains a number of server processes through which other processes in the network may access data internal to the matching process, for example, the features from the scene found to be matched with the model.

A virtual matcher is required for each object to be located, exploiting a further level of parallelism: the concurrent location of multiple objects.

Although the user may explicitly manage the matcher sub-systems directly (for example, to specify available processors) this is best managed with the

Figure 15.10
Three matched models.

aid of the *rootmatcher* task. The rootmatcher provides an interface to the entire model matching system and performs processor allocation to each virtual matcher based upon the number of processors in the system and the number of models to be located. A client of the rootmatcher may then request the location of a set of models from the current database.

This model matching system shows great potential to be distributed over a *large* parallel machine for a large database of models. Note that the name-server mechanisms provided by MRE greatly simplify the dynamic allocation of the processor resources throughout the system. Figure 15.10 shows the reprojection of the model descriptions of three located objects, located in the recovered scene geometry.

A further description of the recovery of 3D geometry and object location and how these are used to visually guide a robot in a pick-and-place task is found in (Rygol, 1991).

15.7.2 Performance and Experimental Results

The graph in figure 15.11 shows how the execution time varies with scene complexity for the location of two different models, 1 and 2. In this experiment 8 view matchers were used in the location of the object. Object 1 is a great deal more complex (with approximately 2.5 times as many features as object 2) and exhibits a lot of partial symmetries, increasing the location

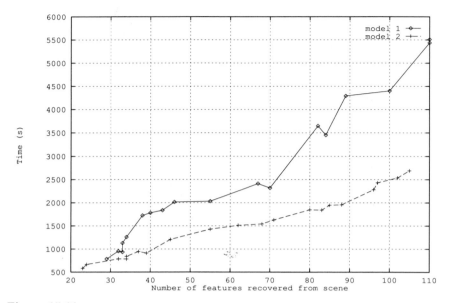

Figure 15.11
Graph of processing time *versus* scene complexity when locating two differing models.

time.

The graphs show a linear increase in execution time with "scene complexity" (randomly added clutter).

Figure 15.12 shows a graph of processor utilisation in the location of a single object for numbers of view matchers from 1 to 16 and an object comprising 16 CVs. Owing to the coarse grain of parallelism adopted, (i.e. allocating CVs to processors) we see best performances where the number of view matchers is a factor of the number of CVs describing the object, in this case 1, 2, 4, 8 and 16. A sequential implementation of these algorithms upon a SUN-2 workstation required a processing time of over one hour to locate *one* object in a scene. With MARVIN we may locate a number of objects in around 10s.

15.8   Real-time Parallel Object Tracking

In order for a machine to maintain a constant description of its environment (and the relation of the machine to the environment) the stereo images should be processed to recover pertinent information at rates exceeding those of the processes described earlier in this chapter.

We adopt an alternative approach to exploit the spatio-temporal coherence of the world. Given the predicted position of located objects, we may use this information to reduce the amount of processing involved by using

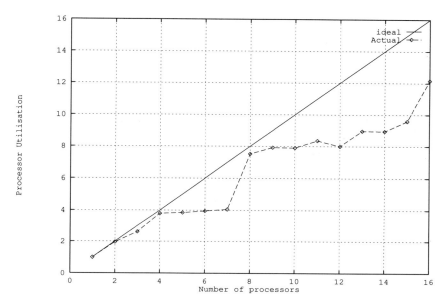

Figure 15.12
Graph of processor utilisation for the location of a single object.

predictive feed-forward techniques (Pollard *et al.*, 1990). A parallel stereo tracking algorithm has been developed which is able to return the position and orientation of a moving object in 3D every 200ms. This information may also be used to provide the position of the a robot relative to a known object, while it is moving.

We may track an object by individually tracking the set of visible *beacon* features that comprise the object. The tracking algorithm employs *featural* parallelism, in that the features are tracked concurrently. Currently, the beacon features are 3D line segments. However, the architecture will also support other primitives as they are developed. The resulting (minimised) transformation of the features of the object gives the transformation of the object as a whole. The tracker is integrated into the vision system executing on MARVIN, its architecture is shown in figure 15.13.

The tracker is structured internally as a *processor farm*. The *master* of the farm is known as the *virtual tracker* and each worker in the farm is a *feature tracker*.

Each feature tracker is resident on a TMAX to allow fast access to the stereo video stream. Image acquisition is synchronised globally such that the images remain valid in each TMAX for the duration of each track. The feature tracker receives a 3D line segment and projects this into left and right images, using the current camera calibration. Subsequently, both left and right instances of the 3D line segment are recovered. Processing is

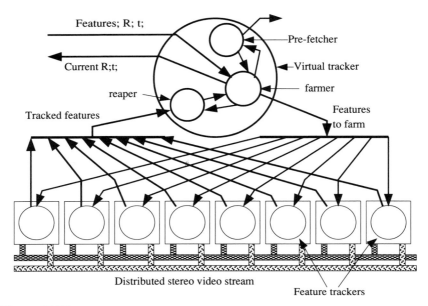

Figure 15.13
Architecture of the object tracker.

speeded up by selecting a number (typically 10) of one-pixel deep sections
of the image in a direction approximately orthogonal to the 2D orientation
of the line segment in each image and (typically) 30 pixels either side of the
expected line segment, as shown in figure 15.14 (showing a feature that has
translated up the image and to the left). A 1D implementation of the Canny
edge operator is applied to each of these sections giving the edgel closest to
the expected position. A line is fitted to these edgels and subsequently
extended (if necessary). Both the left and right projections are located in
this manner and subsequently projected into a 3D line segment. The feature
tracker returns the tracked line segment to the virtual tracker and awaits
the arrival of the next workpacket.

Referring to figure 15.13, it can be seen that the virtual tracker consists of
a number of internal parallel processes. The process labelled *farmer* receives
the following from the client of the tracker:

• A list of features to track. These are 3D line segments (obtained from
the model-matching module) and are features from the model of an object
which were successfully matched with data recovered from the scene.

• The current position and orientation of the object, defined as a rotation
R and a translation t in the camera coordinate frame.

• A control packet containing additional runtime parameters.

The farmer process subsequently sends a number of features (equal to the
number of feature trackers) into the farm. The *reaper* process is responsi-

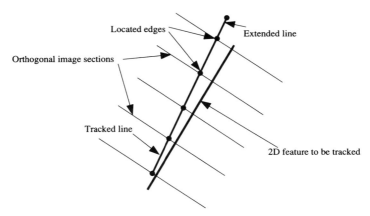

Figure 15.14
Efficient location of a 2D line segment.

ble for collecting replies from the farm and constructing the relevant data structures whilst informing the farmer process to transmit a new feature for every tracked feature returned from the farm. When data is returned from a feature tracker, the processor number is forwarded to the farmer process to initiate the transmission of a new feature to be tracked to the (now idle) processor.

When all features have been returned, tracked or otherwise, the global transformation of the object is obtained, using the quaternion representation of the rotation of the object relative to the cameras. The current position of the object is returned to the tracker client. Beacons which are *not* located are retained for future processing. Implementing a processor farm has been greatly simplified by the MRE runtime environment, using the processor id of the worker process as a destination for the next workpacket.

The transformation recovered is used to transform the previous set of beacon features to provide a more robust set of beacons for the next iteration of the tracking. This object tracker is automatically load-balanced as further features are sent into the farm, as requested.

The *pre-fetcher* process is used to initiate successive image acquisition requests while calculating the new position of the object.

15.8.1   Performance

Figure 15.15 shows a graph of the tracking cycle rates *vs.* number of feature trackers for an object with 15 beacon features.

We have found the tracking architecture able to support multiple objects with the introduction of further virtual trackers. As the feature trackers maintain no internal state, they may be utilised by a number of virtual tracker processes. We have found the tracking module able to track 2 objects at a rate of 3Hz.

Our tracking module demonstrates the need for distributed video data-

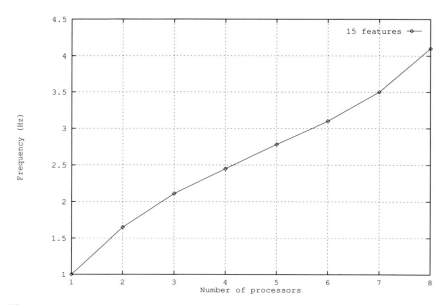

Figure 15.15
Graph of tracking cycle rate versus number of processors.

paths in a real-time vision system. Early experiments showed that the time required to transmit image data from a TMAX to a feature tracker resident on a non-TMAX processor greatly reduced (by 50%) the tracking cycle rate.

15.9   Application Demonstrations

The vision system described in this chapter has been successfully exploited in two application domains. Exploiting the parallel vision system in this way serves as a useful testbed and highlights the need for high performance and ease of system integration.

The recovery of scene descriptions and model matching modules have been used in visually guided robot "pick-and-place" demonstrations. Upon location of any objects present in the robot workcell, a precomputed "grasp position" (in the coordinate frame of the model description) is transformed into the world, using the position of the located object. The positions of the object grasp positions and their orientations are then used to visually guide the robot arm. We have found the system able to maintain a precision of <3mm at a distance of approximately 1.2m.

MARVIN has also been used to provide visual information for the navigation of an in-house autonomous guided vehicle (AGV), described further in (Rygol et al., 1991). Here we have exploited the visual capabilities of the MARVIN-based vision system to allow the vehicle to navigate about the laboratory (using the recovered scene descriptions), dock with target objects (from the positions of located objects) and follow moving objects (using the tracking module).

15.10   Conclusions

In this chapter we have described the development of a multiprocessor 3D vision system. The hardware architecture is based around the Inmos T800 transputer and provides distributed video datapaths to allow fast dissemination of image data into the processor network. In addition, MARVIN provides a hybrid processing scheme by allowing the addition of frame-rate pipelined hardware for the computation of low-level image operations.

The system exploits both stereo and spatial parallelism to recover three-dimensional scene descriptions with a processing time of 8–10 seconds.

We exploit featural parallelism in the location of modelled objects by decomposing the search for an object into a number of concurrent, separable searches for subsets (or characteristic views) of the object. The system exploits a further level of parallelism in concurrently locating numerous objects.

We again exploit featural parallelism to perform real-time object tracking by decomposing the object into a set of visible component features and tracking these concurrently, exploiting the distributed datapaths of MARVIN.

The modules comprising the system have been integrated into a general purpose environment. Access to the capabilities of the modules from client processes is made available by libraries of remote procedure calls. We have found this method to be highly successful in allowing the development of a flexible system.

Work is underway to improve both the temporal and visual performance of the vision system. We intend to design a new, larger vision engine around the new generation of transputer, the T9000, which promises to provide an order of magnitude improvement in performance, reducing the processing times to well under 1 second.

16 Geometry from Visual Motion

Chris Harris

The DROID 3D vision system uses the visual motion of image features to construct a bottom-up 3D geometric description of the viewed scene. The theoretical foundation of DROID is explained with the aid of several examples. The 3D geometry provided by DROID acts as a basis for the performance of a number of high-level tasks.

16.1   Introduction

The three dimensional (3D) geometry of a scene is generally regarded as a worthwhile intermediate representation to achieve using vision (Marr, 1982), as it can act as a starting point for the performance of a variety of high-level tasks without the computational cost of repeated recourse to the imagery. A 3D geometric representation should retain valuable structural information while discarding the large amount of redundant pixel data in an image, and so act as an information concentrator. This is important for real-time computer vision systems, because there are too many pixels in a video-rate image sequence to permit the performance of high-level or complex processing.

The utilisation of 3D geometric structures is particularly appropriate for an image sequence, in which there is much image redundancy due to continuity of motion and invariance of the 3D geometry with changing viewpoint. The images forming a sequence are assumed to exhibit a sufficient continuity, due to the smoothness or slowness of the motion of either the camera or the objects in view. The invariance of 3D geometry with changing viewpoint derives from rigidity, either globally (i.e. the entire viewed scene) or of individual objects or parts thereof. Structural rigidity allows the scene geometry to be (relatively) unambiguously extracted from visual motion in an image sequence. This should be compared to shape-from-X techniques (where X stands for shading, shadows, reflectance, texture, perspective, etc.) applied to single images, which currently seem applicable only to simple, constrained scenes.

A vision system using only geometry will have to depend on geometric accuracy – for example, the detection of an upstanding obstacle to movement will rest upon obtaining explicit height information of the obstacle in relation to the ground surface. Geometric accuracy (i.e. depth accuracy) is achieved through using a long baseline for triangulation, and so some mechanism must exist for passing image information across a large (potentially unlimited) number of images. Feature-based methods enable this to be simply performed, and do not suffer the computational expense of having to look back at past images. A disadvantage of relying solely on geometrical accuracy is that the rigorous exclusion of dubious information can lead to a relatively sparse and impoverished representation.

DROID performs a 3D interpretation of a sequence of digital images by means of automatic extraction, tracking and 3D localisation of image features (Harris & Pike, 1987). The viewed scene is assumed to be piece-wise rigid, the scenario usually being a camera moving through an otherwise static world. The DROID system is designed to operate in a structurally unconstrained environment, with no prior knowledge of scene content. Similarly, the camera(s) (one camera for monocular, two for binocular stereo, etc.) may execute arbitrary motion, excepting only that sufficient continuity exists between images. From the locations of tracked image features, DROID determines both the motion of the camera and the 3D location of the features. Reliable features are used in the construction of a dense depth map formed by a planar facet interpolation scheme. This 3D surface can form the starting point for undertaking a variety of high-level tasks, such as recognition and navigation. The functioning of DROID is summarised in figure 16.1.

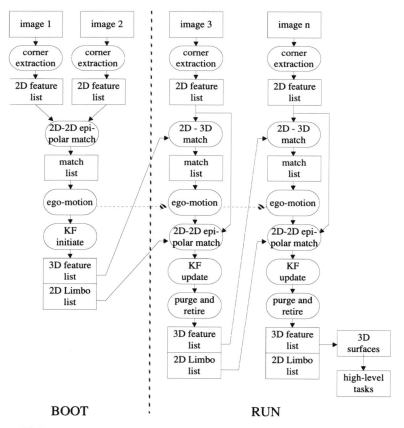

Figure 16.1
DROID process flowchart.

16.2   Feature extraction

An image contains a very large amount of data from which only a relatively small amount of salient information must be extracted if real-time processing is to be achieved. To perform this data compression, each image is analysed for discrete image tokens, or features, that are likely to correspond to objective 3D scene elements. The features should recur through the sequence of images (while still in view), and be accurately locatable. The attraction of using features, as compared to a spatially continuous method (such as the gradient optical-flow technique (Horn & Schunck, 1981)), is that appropriately chosen features encapsulate the highest quality information, forming "seeds of perception" (Brady, 1987), and processing effort is not wasted on low quality regions of the image. In addition, features can be cheap to extract, and can be developed directly into discrete high-level 3D scene descriptors.

The primary features extracted by DROID are *feature-points* or *corners*, which abound in natural and man-made scenes. Feature-points are likely to correspond to real 3D structure, such as corners of objects and surface markings, and also to texture of an appropriate scale. The spatial localisation of feature-points can give good repeatability, even for natural scenes where an image decomposition into straight-line fragments is highly erratic. The extraction of feature-points is a spatially and temporally local operation, and is both repeatable and computationally (comparatively) cheap.

On each image processed by DROID, discrete feature-points are first extracted, with feature extraction performed independently on each image. Feature-points are detected by use of a local auto-correlation operator (Harris & Stephens, 1988). Letting the image intensity (grey-level) be $I(x, y)$, at each point in the image construct the 2×2 matrix

$$\mathbf{M} = \begin{pmatrix} \langle (dI/dx)^2 \rangle & \langle (dI/dx).(dI/dy) \rangle \\ \langle (dI/dx).(dI/dy) \rangle & \langle (dI/dy)^2 \rangle \end{pmatrix} \tag{16.1}$$

where angle braces indicate local Gaussian smoothing of the arguments (a smoothing size of 1 to 2 pixels is commonly used), and the first gradients, dI/dx and dI/dy, are obtained by use of 5×5 linear masks. The eigenvalues of $\mathbf{M}$ encode the shape (the principle curvatures) of the local auto-correlation function: if both are large, the local grey-level patch cannot be moved in any direction on the image-plane without significant grey-level changes occurring, while an edge or line will have one large and one small eigenvalue. A *corner response function*, R, is formulated to respond to both eigenvalues being large, while not requiring explicit evaluation of the eigenvalues:

$$R = \frac{k}{(k+1)^2} \left(\det \mathbf{M} - \mathrm{Tr}(\mathbf{M})^2 \right). \tag{16.2}$$

The subtracted term makes the above formulation to some extent "edge-phobic", to ensure it does not respond to the stair-casing of diagonal step edges arising from the spatial under-sampling usually present in digitised images, a common failing of some corner detectors. The value of k is the maximum ratio of eigenvalues of $\mathbf{M}$ to which the response function is positive, and typically a value of 25 is used. The local 8-way maxima in the response function form candidate corners, and either the n strongest are selected, or else all those exceeding a pre-defined threshold. The convolutions used in obtaining the response function may cause a feature-point to be slightly mis-positioned, but the mis-positioning will usually be consistent over time and so be of little importance. By performing a local quadratic fit to the response function, the feature-points can be located to sub-pixel accuracy. The most important property of the feature-point extraction is its high repeatability (Kitchen & Rosenfeld, 1982), with often over 80% of the extracted points being matchable between frames, as shown in figures 16.2. To each feature-point is associated descriptive grey-level attributes, explicitly the local grey-level (as defined by a Gaussian smoothing mask), and the smoothed first spatial gradients. These attributes are assembled into an *attribute vector*, $\mathbf{a}$, which will later be used to disambiguate matches.

Figure 16.2
Extracted feature-points on two images, with matches shown as white dots.

Feature-points are attractive to work with as they are simple to track over time, and are easy to handle in 3D. Straight edge features are similarly attractive and can be handled by DROID, but they are more suited to man-made environments than natural environments, in which they are scarce (Ayache & Faugeras, 1987; Stephens, 1987). Although curving and squiggly edges are abundant in natural scenes, they can be temporally unstable, and present formidable problems in finding a suitable representation to handle the geometric information they contain.

Corner detection is currently the slowest component in DROID, taking 2 seconds on a Sparc 2 workstation for a 256×256 pixel image, while all subsequent processing takes 0·2–0·3 seconds per frame. A Transputer array can reduce this to under 1/2 second (Wang *et al.*, 1992), and dedicated video-rate hardware (25 Hz) will shortly be available from Roke Manor to process either 512×512 pixel imagery, or up to 4 camera stereo imagery at 256×256 pixels. Note that use of 512×512 pixel imagery would indicate the use of a frame-capture camera, since the two fields produced by conventional cameras are captured 1/50'th second apart, and will be irretrievably torn apart by even moderate camera motion. Since motion blur changes the appearance of image features, fast electronic shuttering of the camera is needed. Both the problems of field-tear and motion blur could be overcome by use of a mechanically tracking or foveating camera.

16.3 Camera calibration

Since DROID is based on the geometry of image features, it is essential that an accurate interpretation of the location of the features is performed. In particular, it is necessary to know the direction in space towards which each of the pixels in the image is looking; this is called the geometric calibration of the camera. By modelling the camera as a pin-hole camera with specific distortions (e.g. radial lens distortions), and using only CCD cameras whose sensing elements form a stable rectangular array, a parametric form for the geometric camera calibration can be devised. This model has been found to be good for many CCD cameras and lenses. Camera calibration is performed using two images of an accurately known planar calibration tile (Harris, 1992), resulting in accurate measurements of the focal length, aspect ratio, location of the optical centre, and up to two terms of radial distortion.

The calibration enables the extracted feature-point locations to be transformed to an "ideal" distortion-free pin-hole camera of unit focal-length (UFL), whose image-plane is positioned in front of the camera pin-hole to avoid tiresome minus signs. A Cartesian camera coordinate system is defined to have its origin at the pin-hole of the camera and Z axis aligned along the optical axis. The X and Y axes are parallel to the image plane. The image x axis is horizontal and pointing to the right, while the image y axis is vertical and pointing downwards. This gives a right-handed coordinate system, as illustrated in figure 16.3. A point positioned at $\mathbf{R} \equiv (X, Y, Z)$ in local camera coordinates will be imaged in UFL camera coordinates at

$$\mathbf{r} \equiv (x, y) = (X/Z, Y/Z). \tag{16.3}$$

This is the *perspective projection*, and henceforth all image positions will be expressed in UFL coordinates.

It will often be necessary to represent the same 3D point in two different coordinate systems, for example in camera coordinates and global coordinates. Consider a point located at $\mathbf{R}_1$ in a first coordinate system, and at $\mathbf{R}_2$ in a second coordinate system. These point locations will be related by

$$\mathbf{R}_2 = \mathbf{A}(\boldsymbol{\theta})^\top (\mathbf{R}_1 - \mathbf{t}) \tag{16.4}$$

$$\mathbf{R}_1 = \mathbf{A}(\boldsymbol{\theta})\mathbf{R}_2 + \mathbf{t} \tag{16.5}$$

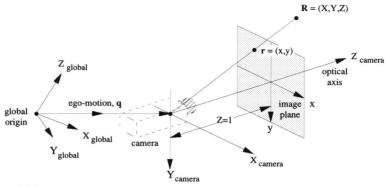

Figure 16.3
Camera coordinates and global coordinates.

where the rotation matrix, $\mathbf{A}(\boldsymbol{\theta})$, and the translation vector, $\mathbf{t}$, describe respectively the attitude and the location of the second coordinate system with respect to the first. (The superscript $^\top$ denotes matrix transpose.)

Rotations are represented by a 3-vector $\boldsymbol{\theta}$, whose direction is the axis of rotation, and whose magnitude is the (right-handed) angle of rotation in radians. The elements of the orthonormal 3×3 rotation matrix, $\mathbf{A}(\boldsymbol{\theta})$, are:

$$A_{ij} = \cos|\boldsymbol{\theta}|\,\delta_{ij} + (1 - \cos|\boldsymbol{\theta}|)\hat{\theta}_i\hat{\theta}_j - \sin|\boldsymbol{\theta}|\sum_k \epsilon_{ijk}\hat{\theta}_k, \ 1 \le i,j \le 3 \qquad (16.6)$$

where $\hat{\boldsymbol{\theta}} = \boldsymbol{\theta}/|\boldsymbol{\theta}|$, and ϵ_{ijk} is the Levi-Civita symbol. The representation is singular at $|\boldsymbol{\theta}| = 2\pi$, but this is avoided by working always with $|\boldsymbol{\theta}| \le \pi$. Note that rotation vectors are neither commutative nor associative (unless they are parallel), and that successive applications of rotations are best handled using quaternions.

The location and attitude of the camera is generally referred to as its *ego-motion*, expressed as the "6-vector", $\mathbf{q} = (\boldsymbol{\theta}, \mathbf{t})$. The ego-motion may be measured from the global origin (as illustrated in figure 16.3), or may be in some convenient local coordinates. The location and attitude of a rigid body with respect to a reference coordinate system is called its *pose*. The pose of a body is the rotation, $\boldsymbol{\theta}$, and the translation, $\mathbf{t}$, that must be applied to the body coordinate system so as to correctly position the body.

16.4   Boot-strap processing

The task of boot-strap processing is to initiate the 3D representation of the viewed scene from feature-points found in the first images, without assuming any knowledge of the scene content. The 3D representation will be in terms of Kalman Filtered points. For a monocular system, the first 2 images of the sequence are used for boot. For stereo, boot consists of a conventional stereo process performed on the 2 (or more) simultaneously captured images comprising the first frame.

16.4.1 Boot matching

The processing of a monocular image sequence is initiated with the first two images. Using a prior estimate of the camera motion, each extracted feature-point from one image generates on the other image an epipolar search line nearby which candidate matches are sought. If the prior ego-motion estimate from frame 1 to frame 2 is $\mathbf{q} = (\boldsymbol{\theta}, \mathbf{t})$, and the observed point on frame 2 is at $\mathbf{r}_2 = (x_2, y_2)$, then the epipolar line on frame 1 will pass through the image points $(t_x, t_y)/t_z$ and $(p_x, p_y)/p_z$, where $\mathbf{p} = \mathbf{A}(\boldsymbol{\theta})(x_2, y_2, 1)^\top$. The epipolar line is broadened out into a band in which match candidates are sought, and this broadening is chosen to reflect both the uncertainty in the prior estimate of the camera motion and errors in feature-point positioning. The length of the epipolar line may be truncated at some minimum and maximum depths, to reduce the number of spurious match candidates. Matching ambiguities are resolved by use of the grey-level attributes. If the attribute vectors for two points are $\mathbf{a}_1$ and $\mathbf{a}_2$, then the attribute mismatch between the points is

$$m_{1,2} = \frac{|\mathbf{a}_1 - \mathbf{a}_2|}{\sqrt{|\mathbf{a}_1|.|\mathbf{a}_2|}}. \tag{16.7}$$

For a successful match, the mismatch value must be lower than a set threshold, and if there are several candidates, the one with the lowest mismatch is chosen. Typically over 80% of the feature-points are found to be correctly matchable, and the few incorrect matches are discounted by outlier removal procedures (see below). Unmatched feature-points are kept for possible future matching; they are said to be placed in Limbo.

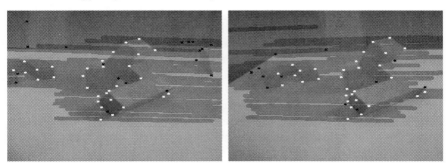

Figure 16.4
Boot search regions and feature-point matches.

16.4.2 Boot ego-motion

Using the feature-point matches, the camera ego-motion, $\mathbf{q} = (\boldsymbol{\theta}, \mathbf{t})$, is next determined. The boot-strap ego-motion is calculated by an iterative multi-dimensional Newton scheme, minimising the image-plane distances between the location of feature-points and the truncated epipolar lines of their matching features (Harris, 1987). To cope with mismatches, a robust minimisation is performed. The starting point of the iterative scheme is the prior estimate of camera motion, and good convergence is usually achieved in 4 to 6 cycles. Prior knowledge about the camera motion may be imposed by a set of soft constraints quadratically linking the 6 ego-motion parameters, $\mathbf{q}$. By varying the constraint coefficients, planar, linear, or curved motion may be imposed. It is essential that a translational constraint is imposed at boot to resolve the speed-scale ambiguity, which is otherwise left entirely unresolved by the visual data. The minimisation scheme and the form of the constraints is described below in section 16.5.2.

Once ego-motion has been determined, the 3D locations of matched points can be estimated simply by triangulation. The uncertainty in the image-plane position of a feature-point leads to uncertainty in its 3D location. This uncertainty is used to start up a Kalman Filter (KF) for each point, whose variables represent the spatial probability distribution function of the point, and consist explicitly of a 3D mean position and covariance. Strictly, it is Extended Kalman Filters that are being used, as the time evolution of the filter is only being approximated as linear. Applications of the Kalman filter in tracking were discussed earlier in chapters 1, 3, 4, 5 and 6. The KF enables subsequent observations of the point to be optimally and cheaply combined, and high spatial accuracy achieved. The initiation of the KFs is described below in section 16.5.4. For other applications of Kalman filtering in Active Vision systems see also chapter 18.

16.5   Run mode

After the 3D representation has been initiated in the boot-mode, successive frames are processed in the run-mode. The run-mode provides an evolving 3D representation, which increases in accuracy and completeness as more frames are processed. Accuracy is achieved by using Kalman Filtering to optimally combine observations of an individual feature-point seen over an extended period of time. The representation evolves by the inclusion of newly seen feature-points, and the exclusion of points that are no longer visible. In this way, an unlimited sequence of images can be processed. Much of the work of DROID is performed in so-called Disparity space, for reasons of speed and numerical stability. A point at $\mathbf{R} = (X, Y, Z)$ in Cartesian camera coordinates has coordinates $\mathbf{S} \equiv (x, y, z) \equiv (X/Z, Y/Z, 1/Z)$ in the corresponding Disparity space. Thus the first two components of $\mathbf{S}$ are the image coordinates of the perspective projection of $\mathbf{R}$, and the third component is the reciprocal depth. Note that straight lines in Cartesian space are straight in Disparity space, and similar relationships hold for both planes and conics. The KF of each feature-point is represented in Disparity space by a mean position (or centroid), $\mathbf{S}_{KF}$, and a covariance $\boldsymbol{\Sigma}_{KF}$ (a 3×3 matrix). These can be thought of as defining a Normal probability distribution function in Disparity space.

16.5.1 Run matching

In the run mode, matches are sought between extracted image feature-points and existing KFs by projecting the KFs down onto the image-plane. First of all, the KFs must be transformed from the previously used Disparity space to the Disparity space of the current estimate of camera ego-motion. This is straightforward for the centroid (by transforming to and from Cartesian space), but for the covariance, using Cartesian space is inadvisable for distant points because of poor numerical conditioning. To overcome this problem, a direct Disparity-to-Disparity transform has been devised, which uses a well-conditioned similarity transform. By these means the KFs are brought into the currently used Disparity space. The projection of the KF covariance, $\boldsymbol{\Sigma}_{KF}$, onto the image-plane is obtained by pre- and post-multiplying with the projection matrix, $\mathbf{P} = \begin{pmatrix} 1 & 0 & 0 \\ 0 & 1 & 0 \end{pmatrix}$, and its transpose, which simply serves to extract the upper 2×2 block of $\boldsymbol{\Sigma}_{KF}$. By linearly combining the projected KF covariance with the observation covariance, $\boldsymbol{\Sigma}_{obs}$, a matching covariance matrix is obtained

$$\boldsymbol{\Sigma}_{match} = k_{obs}\boldsymbol{\Sigma}_{obs} + k_{proj}\mathbf{P}\boldsymbol{\Sigma}_{KF}\mathbf{P}^{\top} \qquad (16.8)$$

where the two coefficients k govern chosen levels of statistical significance. The observation covariance, $\boldsymbol{\Sigma}_{obs}$, is usually taken to be diagonal and equivalent to, say, a few pixels. The observation covariance coefficient is chosen to be sufficiently large for it to account for uncertainty (error) in the prior estimate of camera motion. If $\mathbf{r}_{KF}$ is the perspective projection of the KF centroid,

$$\mathbf{r}_{KF} = \mathbf{P}\mathbf{S}_{KF} \qquad (16.9)$$

(trivially, the first two coordinates of $\mathbf{S}_{KF}$), and $\mathbf{r}_{obs}$ is the location of an extracted feature-point, then the feature-point is a match candidate if

$$(\mathbf{r}_{KF} - \mathbf{r}_{obs})^{\top}\boldsymbol{\Sigma}_{match}^{-1}(\mathbf{r}_{KF} - \mathbf{r}_{obs}) < 1; \qquad (16.10)$$

that is, it lies in an ellipse centred on the projected KF centroid. The searching for candidates is accelerated by using a coarse binning scheme for the feature-points, and only examining the bins which the ellipse overlays. Candidate matches are assessed using their grey-level attributes, and irresolvable contentions are discarded to ensure that no multiply-defined KFs are generated.

16.5.2   Run ego-motion

Once feature-point matches have been obtained, the ego-motion, $\mathbf{q}$, is determined by finding the camera attitude and location that brings each projected KF centroid, $\mathbf{r}(\mathbf{q})$, into best alignment with its matching observed feature-point, $\mathbf{r}_{obs}$. If $\mathbf{R}_0$ is a KF centroid location in Cartesian camera coordinates, then a relative ego-motion $\mathbf{q} = (\boldsymbol{\theta}, \mathbf{t})$ of the camera will make the centroid project onto the image at

$$\mathbf{r}(\mathbf{q}) = \big(X(\mathbf{q}), Y(\mathbf{q})\big)/Z(\mathbf{q}) \tag{16.11}$$

where

$$\mathbf{R}(\mathbf{q}) \equiv \big(X(\mathbf{q}), Y(\mathbf{q}), Z(\mathbf{q})\big) = \mathbf{A}(\boldsymbol{\theta})\mathbf{R}_0 + \mathbf{t}. \tag{16.12}$$

The measure of "best alignment" used above is given by a matching covariance, $\boldsymbol{\Sigma}_{match}$, which is, as before, an appropriate combination of the observation and projected KF covariances. The contribution of the ith matched point to an objective function to be minimised is thus

$$E_i(\mathbf{q}) = \big(\mathbf{r}(\mathbf{q}) - \mathbf{r}_{obs}\big)^\top \boldsymbol{\Sigma}_{match}^{-1} \big(\mathbf{r}(\mathbf{q}) - \mathbf{r}_{obs}\big). \tag{16.13}$$

The ego-motion determination is performed by minimising a single objective function, $E_{total}(\mathbf{q})$, which is composed of a weighted sum of contributions from each matched point, together with a prior-constraint term producing soft constraints:

$$E_{total}(\mathbf{q}) = \mathbf{q}^\top \boldsymbol{\Sigma}_{prior}^{-1} \mathbf{q} + \sum_{points,i} w_i E_i(\mathbf{q}). \tag{16.14}$$

For there to be no bias from the prior-constraint term, the ego-motion $\mathbf{q}$ is taken to be relative to the expected or anticipated camera pose. Global ego-motion is not used because rotation vectors can only be approximated as commutative near $\mathbf{q} = \mathbf{0}$. The objective function is minimised by using a multi-dimensional Newton minimisation, for which the first and second differentials of the objective function must be calculated. These are constructed analytically by using expressions for the first differentials of the projected KF centroids, $\partial \mathbf{r}(\mathbf{q})/\partial \mathbf{q}$, and by assuming that there is negligible dependence of the matching covariances on $\mathbf{q}$. Each cycle of the Newton scheme produces a new (and hopefully better) estimate of the ego-motion, $\mathbf{q}'$, from a previous estimate, $\mathbf{q}$:

$$\mathbf{q}' = \mathbf{q} - \left(\frac{\partial^2 E_{total}}{\partial \mathbf{q}^2}\right)^{-1} \frac{dE_{total}}{\partial \mathbf{q}}. \tag{16.15}$$

The starting guess of the minimisation is with the camera at its expected position (i.e. $\mathbf{q} = \mathbf{0}$), and usually 4–6 iterations gives a good convergence. The main problem with the ego-motion determination is due to incorrect matches, which, if uncorrected, significantly bias the result. This problem is overcome both by using robust minimisation techniques to de-weight the effect of the mismatches, and by performing the complete matching/ego-motion cycle twice, with tighter matching search regions on the second pass. The robust minimisation technique ascribes a weight to each point on each cycle of the Newton minimisation. The weight, w_i, of the ith point on the current cycle depends exponentially on its contribution, $E_i(\mathbf{q})$, to the objective function of the point on the previous cycle:

$$w_i = \exp\left[-c.E_i(\mathbf{q})/\bar{E}(\mathbf{q})\right]. \tag{16.16}$$

The denominator $\bar{E}(\mathbf{q})$ is the (weighted) average objective function contribution of all the points, and is used to estimate the distribution of the E_i's, and this results in outliers being continuously and strongly de-weighted.

Ego-motion determination is generally very accurate in the short to medium term, as shown in a short sequence of 10 images (numbered 0 to 81) taken from helicopter, and provided by NASA. The camera motion is primarily forwards, with a translation of about 10 feet per frame. The first frame of the sequence is shown in figure 16.10. The accuracy of the attitude component of the ego-motion, expressed as a roll-pitch-yaw decomposition, is shown in figure 16.5 by the difference between the DROID analysis and the ground truth data. The accuracy is better than 0·25 degrees, though the helicopter undergoes a yaw of 15 degrees. The accuracy of the translational components of the ego-motion is similarly shown in figure 16.6, where $-X$ is the direction of forward motion. Errors are less than 0·7 feet, which is less than 0·8% of the total flight distance.

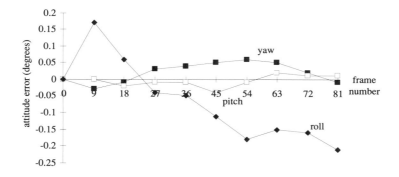

Figure 16.5
Attitude ego-motion accuracy of the NASA image sequence.

In a long image sequence, long-term drifts can occur, in which both the ego-motion and perceived structure are self-consistently in error. For example, both the camera position and the perceived structure might come to be

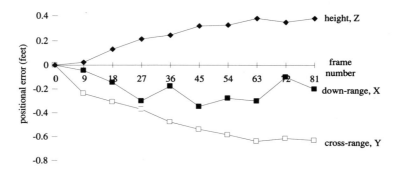

Figure 16.6
Translational ego-motion accuracy of the NASA image sequence.

displaced 1 metre to the right of their true values, and yet the visual observations will be entirely self-consistent. Although there is no feedback mechanism to correct such an error from the imagery alone, external ego-motion measurements (e.g. odometry) may be of use in resolving these ambiguities. Drifting can occur in both attitude and translation, and also in the speed-scale factor. Speed-scale drift is where both the speed of the camera and the perceived scale of the structure are in error by the same factor. The speed-scale ambiguity is resolved by using stereo, as the stereo base-line provides a yard-stick for the structure. The problem of drift is exacerbated by the camera turning by an angle greater than the width of its field-of-view, so that previously established structure is lost from sight and no longer acts as a stable reference.

In figure 16.7 is shown the recovered ego-motion from an image sequence taken from a pair of forward-looking stereo cameras mounted on a vehicle driven around a circular path of some 500 m circumference. A typical image (overlaid with later graphics) is shown in figure 16.13 lower right. In all, 1232 frames comprise a complete circuit, from frame 23 (shown as a black square), to frame 1257 (shown as a circular black dot). The plan view of the ego-motion results are shown for stereo (see section 16.7, below), and for monocular processing both with and without odometric constraints. Without the use of constraints, the speed-scale drifts severely, causing the perceived path to spiral. Applying odometry constraints (i.e. the vehicle speed) results in a nearly circular path with a start-to-finish error of 10 m (i.e. 2% of the path length), but using stereo the error reduces to 2 m (i.e. 0·4%). The poor monocular performance is suspected to be primarily due to an inaccurate camera calibration using a now superseded calibration technique.

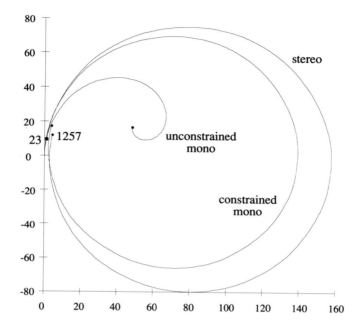

Figure 16.7
Plan view of the ego-motion.

16.5.3   Kalman filter update

Each time a point is observed and matched, a more precise estimate of its
3D position may be obtained. This is because the new observation provides
further information relating to the 3D position of the point. Kalman Filtering is a method of combining a number of noisy measurements which is, in
certain circumstances, statistically optimum. In DROID, each tracked point
has its own filter whose job is to estimate both the point's most likely 3D
location, and its positional uncertainty. An alternative approach, that of using a single high dimensionality filter containing the coupled coordinates of
all the points, permits the imposition of geometric constraints (Porrill *et al.*,
1987b), but at a high computational cost, and a danger of irrecoverably
coupling unassociated features.

To explain the use of the KF, consider just a single point, as all are treated
independently and in a similar fashion. Let the feature-point be observed in
the current image at image-plane position, r_{obs}; this is the KF measurement.
Its (estimated) positional accuracy is specified by the observation covariance
matrix, Σ_{obs}. The state space for the KF is the 3D location of the point
in Disparity space. Let the current estimate for the point's location be
S_{KF} (called the centroid), and the accompanying estimate of its positional
accuracy be given by the covariance Σ_{KF}. The covariance and centroid after

updating the KF with the current observations are given by

$$\mathbf{\Sigma}'_{KF} = \left(\mathbf{\Sigma}^{-1}_{KF} + \mathbf{P}^\top \mathbf{\Sigma}^{-1}_{obs} \mathbf{P}\right)^{-1}$$
$$\mathbf{S}'_{KF} = \mathbf{\Sigma}'_{KF} \left(\mathbf{\Sigma}^{-1}_{KF} \mathbf{S}_{KF} + \mathbf{P}^\top \mathbf{\Sigma}^{-1}_{obs} \mathbf{r}_{obs}\right) \tag{16.17}$$

where, as before, $\mathbf{P}$ is the projection matrix. The process noise term has been omitted from the KF because past observations of a point are considered to be as valid as current observations, and there is no time-evolution as the points are assumed to be stationary in Global coordinates. As DROID in fact works with the inverse covariance matrix, the former equation reduces to a matrix addition, and the latter to solving a set of 3 simultaneous linear equations. If, after update, the Disparity coordinate of the centroid is negative, it is reset to a small positive value to prevent the point subsequently flipping behind the camera.

The KFs for the points can be graphically illustrated by interpreting them as Normal probability distribution functions, and rendering the ellipsoidal surfaces of constant probability density. This is shown in figure 16.8, left, when the KFs have just been initiated at boot, but viewed from a later camera location. Note how the ellipsoidal surfaces all point towards the same point, midway between the two boot camera positions. In figure 16.8, right, are shown the ellipsoidal surfaces at a later frame in the sequence. Here some of them have been pared down to a small size by successive KF updates, while others have been seen only twice and remain elongated. A very low probability density was chosen for the rendering to make the ellipsoids large enough to see clearly.

Figure 16.8
KF ellipsoid surfaces at boot, and at a later frame.

The KF update process is illustrated in figure 16.9, in which surfaces of constant probability density are shown in Disparity space. The vertical tube represents the observed feature-point and its covariance, while the larger and smaller ellipsoids represent the KF before and after update respectively.

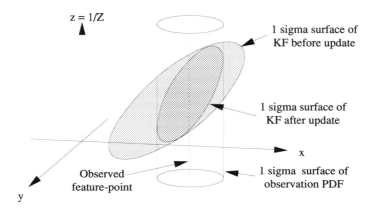

Figure 16.9
Updating of the KF in Disparity space.

16.5.4   Kalman filter creation and destruction

The feature-points on the current frame that fail to match to existing KFs, may be epipolar matched to those that remained unmatched from earlier frames and were retained in Limbo. This enables KFs for new points to be initiated. The epipolar matching is the same as in boot (section 16.4.1). The KF initiation, which is also the same as boot, simply makes use of the KF update equations applied to the pair of initial observations.

KFs which repeatedly fail to match are discarded or purged, whilst those leaving the field of view are retired (matches are no longer sought), but kept on for a while for use in the structural representation. Points that are incorrectly matched at boot will cause KFs to be initiated at locations that in general will not be supported by matches on subsequent frames, and so these erroneous KFs will be purged from the system.

The accuracy of the DROID structure is illustrated by use of the NASA helicopter sequence, the first frame of which is shown in figure 16.10. Ground truth is available for the four parked trucks. The helicopter movement is principally forwards.

DROID points which are located on the trucks are shown in plan view in figure 16.11. The ground truth points, of which there are two per truck on their left ($+$ve Y) sides, are shown as white boxes. DROID points are shown as straight line segments, whose length indicates the range variances of the KFs, the other components of the covariances being too small to plot. The camera is located off the right of the plot, and moves leftwards from $X = 594$ to $X = 487$ feet. Range estimates are good for the nearer trucks, but are worse for the distant trucks, and exacerbated by their closeness to the focus of expansion.

Figure 16.10
The first frame from the NASA helicopter sequence.

16.6 Surface interpretation

A 3D geometrical representation should ideally describe all the visible surfaces, seen in the current image or in the past, and should perhaps even infer the existence of unseen surfaces (e.g. the continuity of a wall behind a lamp-post). An ideal surface representation would use high-level components, such as planes and conics, to describe the scene, but in unconstrained environments, especially natural scenes, such components may be rare, ill-fitting or ill-conditioned. A more adaptable representation is needed, one which can cope with the inaccurate and spatially non-uniform data that is obtained from real vision systems. Since surfaces cannot be directly measured, and must be inferred from surface markings, bounding edges, etc., a flexible interpolation scheme based on the measured geometric features would be appropriate.

The maintenance of a low-level geometric representation for parts of the scene that have left the field of view for a period of time does not seem worthwhile: it is expensive to maintain (in computer time and space), and even if low-level features are seen again, they are not likely to be recognised as the same ones because of changes of appearance (scale, aspect, reflectance, etc.). Such a "forgetful" system operates both in people, as the "persistence of vision", and in DROID. Using the currently visible features to construct surfaces leads to an egocentric representation, such as a depth-map or the 2·5D sketch (Marr, 1982).

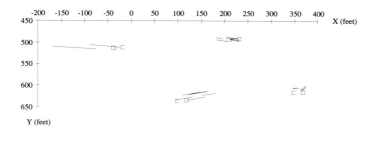

Figure 16.11
Plan view of the DROID points located on trucks in the NASA sequence.

16.6.1   Planar facet representation

The 3D points from DROID form a sparse depth map, bland regions of the image containing no points. To obtain a surface representation, an interpolation scheme based on the current image is used to construct a full depth map. As only currently visible points on the image are maintained in 3D, the single-valued (in range) surface passing through them should approximate to the depth map. The use of an egocentric (camera-based) representation avoids the danger of incorrectly associating distant points, as could occur with overhanging structure in a plan-view projection. Working with points that are sufficiently mature to be reliable, the depth map is filled-out by a piece-wise linear interpolation between the image-plane locations of the 3D points. This is performed by using the Delaunay triangulation in the image-plane: each resulting triangle is interpreted as a 3D triangular planar facet passing through three 3D points. The Delaunay triangulation (see figure 16.12) is chosen as it forms compact triangles (long thin triangles are physically implausible), and is cheap to compute (nearly linear in the number of points). The resulting surface is continuous and single-valued in range, but will not fill the entire image-plane unless supported by previously seen points now outside the image. The surface may be relatively coarse as it can be no finer than the separation of the features, and so covers over fine structure in the manner of a draped-sheet. Depth discontinuities in the surface are not currently permitted. As the surface is constructed anew at each new image, it will quickly respond to changes in the structure, but suffer from an amount of temporal instability.

The surface may be graphically illustrated by intersecting it with sets of uniformly spaced planes perpendicular to the global coordinate axes. These intersections form sets of "contour lines" on the surface, which readily reveal the 3D structure of the surface. This is illustrated in figure 16.13 for a variety of indoor and outdoor scenes.

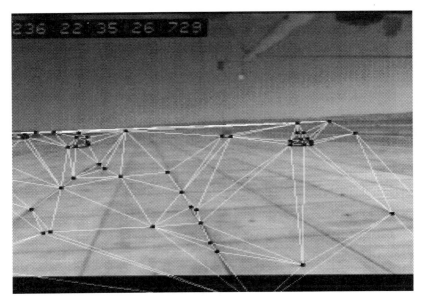

Figure 16.12
A Delaunay triangulation.

16.6.2 Using surfaces

The explicit 3D structural information made available by DROID is intended for open-ended use in a range of high-level tasks, such as obstacle detection, recognition, navigation and path-planning. Such tasks are currently being investigated in relation to performing automatic visual guidance of wheeled or tracked robot vehicles in both indoor and outdoor environments. The most immediate task is to provide safe operation (don't crash!), and this is performed by locating upstanding structural elements in the planar facet surface representation. An example of this is shown in figure 16.14, where Delaunay edges that have been classified as forming obstructions to movement and are on the vehicular path are shown in white. Obstruction detection can lead on to path-planning around such obstructions.

For movement in the vicinity of man-made structures, the location of prominent structural elements such as vertical walls and corridors, is of value. Detection of such structures can lead to their recognition on a navigational map, and so to map registration and more sophisticated navigational abilities. The detection of vertical walls is undertaken by considering the plan-view coordinates of DROID points with heights both above the floor and below that of the vehicle. A vertical wall should appear as a straight line in plan-view, and this is extracted using a Hough transform. A pair of walls forming a corridor can be similarly found, and this is illustrated in figure 16.15 by the pair of white lines located at the base of the corridor

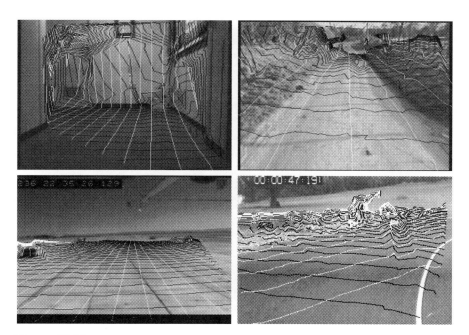

Figure 16.13
Surface contours in indoor and outdoor scenes.

walls.

16.7   Stereo

DROID may process simultaneously captured images from two or more cameras, in conventional stereo configurations or otherwise (e.g. coupled narrow and wide angle cameras, giving foveal and peripheral vision). There are several advantages to using stereo over mono: it avoids problems with speed-scale (both of resolving the ambiguity at boot, and of stopping it drifting during run mode); it doesn't suffer from a "blind-spot" centred on the focus-of-expansion; and it permits the formation of a 3D representation before camera movement has commenced.

In stereo (Sparks & Stephens, 1990), the boot-strap processing is performed on the first frame (comprising two or more stereo images), and consists only of initiating the Kalman Filters of matched points (the "ego-motion" between the stereo cameras is assumed known from a prior calibration). Subsequent frames are processed in the run mode, in which feature-points from each image are matched independently against the 3D points. The advantage of independently matching to the existing 3D points, instead of first performing stereo, is that a graceful devolution to monocular processing occurs for structure that is outside the stereo cross-over region or is

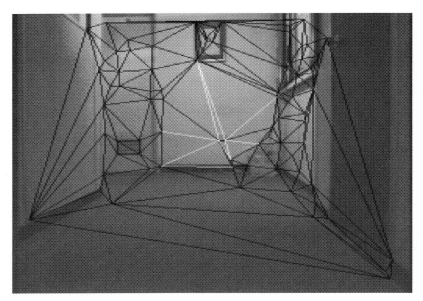

Figure 16.14
Obstacle detection by classification of Delaunay triangulation edges.

too distant to provide reliable stereo.

The main complication of stereo is in evaluating the contributions to the run-mode ego-motion objective function of feature-points seen in the second (and third ...) camera. The differentials with respect to the first camera ego-motion, $\mathbf{q}$, are needed, but it is those with respect to the second camera ego-motion, $\mathbf{q}'$, that can be calculated. Now if the stereo pose of the second camera with respect to the first is $(\boldsymbol{\phi}, \mathbf{p})$, as shown in figure 16.16, then an ego-motion $\mathbf{q}$ of the first camera will lead to an ego-motion $\mathbf{q}' = (\boldsymbol{\theta}', \mathbf{t}')$ of the second camera, where

$$
\begin{aligned}
\boldsymbol{\theta}' &= \mathbf{A}^\top(\boldsymbol{\phi})\boldsymbol{\theta} \\
\mathbf{t}' &= \mathbf{A}^\top(\boldsymbol{\phi})[\mathbf{t} - \mathbf{p} + \mathbf{A}(\boldsymbol{\theta})\mathbf{p}].
\end{aligned}
\tag{16.18}
$$

Knowing the dependence of $\mathbf{q}'$ on $\mathbf{q}$ permits the requisite differentials to be obtained using the chain rule.

16.8   Conclusions

The successful application of DROID to a wide variety of both indoor and outdoor imagery has shown that a 3D interpretation based on feature-points can be accurately and reliably performed. An accurate determination of the ego-motion may be achieved, especially using stereo or with the aid of odometry or other external measurements. The structural representation resulting

Figure 16.15
Location of detected corridor walls.

from feature-points achieves a high accuracy by the use of Kalman Filters
to coherently integrate observations over the longest possible triangulation
baseline. The 3D points can be used to construct an instantaneous depth-
map by means of the planar surface facet representation, though this may be
of low acuity. The depth-map can be used to perform a variety of high-level
tasks, such as obstacle avoidance and recognition of navigational way-points.
The completion of a real-time (5 Hz) implementation of the DROID system
is imminent, and a video-rate realisation may soon be feasible.

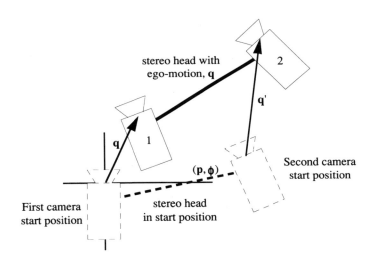

Figure 16.16
Coupled ego-motion of stereo cameras.

17 Medical Image Tracking

Nicholas Ayache, Isaac Cohen and Isabelle Herlin

17.1 The Analysis of Ultrasound Image

There is a continuously increasing demand in the automated analysis of 2D and 3D medical images at the hospital (Ayache *et al.*, 1989; Ayache *et al.*, 1990). Among these images, ultrasound images play a crucial role, because they can be produced at video-rate and therefore allow a dynamic analysis of moving structures. Moreover, the acquisition of these images is non-invasive (it does not hurt the patient!) and the cost of acquisition is relatively low compared to other medical imaging techniques.

On the other hand, the automated analysis of ultrasound images is a real challenge for active vision, because it combines most of the difficult problems encountered in computer vision in addition to some specific ones related to the acquisition mode:

- images are degraded by a very high level of corrupting noise,
- observed objects usually correspond to non-static, non-polyhedral and non-rigid structures,
- images are usually produced in polar geometry instead of cartesian geometry.

We show in the first part of this chapter how a new sonar-space filtering method combined with a snake-based tracker (see also chapters 1, 3) can be used to provide a *global* tracking of some anatomical structures in time sequences of noisy echocardiographic images.

We then show how to introduce additional shape constraints to obtain, if required, a *local* tracking of individual points along the globally tracked moving structure.

Additional details can be found by the interested readers in (Herlin & Ayache, 1992a; Herlin & Ayache, 1992b) for the first part, and in (Cohen *et al.*, 1992a; Cohen *et al.*, 1992b), for the second part. Also, this work should be compared to some previous attempts to provide an automated analysis of ultrasound images, for instance (Taxt *et al.*, 1990; Faure *et al.*, 1988; Buda *et al.*, 1983; Jenkins *et al.*, 1981; Zhang & Geiser, 1982; Unser *et al.*, 1989).

17.2 Ultrasound Image Reconstruction and Filtering

17.2.1 Geometry of Image Acquisition

The fact that ultrasound scan lines are acquired in polar coordinates creates an important anisotropy in spatial resolution. The geometric transformation which transforms the data from a polar representation to the correct cartesian representation is called scan correction.

Let us suppose that M different orientations are used to obtain an echocardiographic image, and that each return signal is digitized to L points. Fig. 17.1 shows an echographic image, with M rows and L columns, obtained using a commercial echographic machine, providing an image represented in polar coordinates. Fig. 17.2 shows the cartesian image corresponding to the same data.

Figure 17.1
Ultrasound image on raw data.

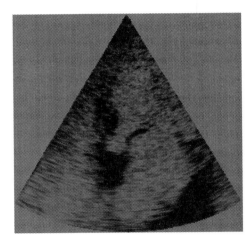

Figure 17.2
Cartesian image after conversion.

This scan conversion requires the knowledge of the following set of parameters (see Fig. 17.3):

- the angular extent of data acquisition wedge α,

- minimal distance d for data acquisition,

- total distance D for data acquisition (these distances being measured from the skin), and

- the number of rows, N, desired in the output cartesian image (The number of columns will be related to α, and we will assume square pixels).

Several methods may be used for the conversion process. Usually, the video image on the echograph is obtained by assigning to a cartesian point the grey level value of the nearest available point in polar coordinates, or the

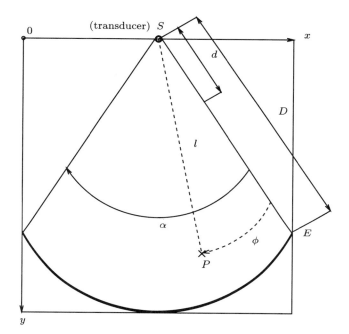

Figure 17.3
Parameters of the conversion process.

value of the bilinear interpolation of its four nearest points. An alternative method consists in using Bresenham's method, well-known in the Computer Graphics field.

In fact we found that these methods do not make optimal use of the available original data, and we introduced, a new method, sonar-space filtering, which can be used to adapt locally the computation of the convolution product in cartesian space with respect to the available resolution of the polar data. In this sense, this provides an optimal reconstruction for a chosen level of spatial filtering.

17.2.2   Sonar-Space Filtering

We assume that it is desired that the continuous input cartesian image $I(x, y)$ be filtered by the impulse response $f(x, y)$. The resulting image $R(x, y)$, in continuous space, is given by the convolution product:

$$R(x, y) = \int_{-\infty}^{\infty} \int_{-\infty}^{\infty} f(x - u, y - v) \cdot I(u, v) \, du \, dv. \tag{17.1}$$

However, the input is only available in the polar coordinate space. We thus apply the following change of variables:

$$
\begin{cases}
\theta = \left[\arctan \left(\dfrac{y}{x - x_0} \right) - \left(\dfrac{\pi - \alpha}{2} \right) \right] / \Delta_\alpha \\[2ex]
\rho = \left[\sqrt{(x - x_0)^2 + y^2} \right] e - \Delta_N
\end{cases}
$$

where

- $\Delta_N = d \frac{(L-1)}{(D-d)}$ is the distance (from the surface of the skin) where the acquisition process begins, measured in pixel units along a scan line of the raw data,

- $\Delta_\alpha = \frac{\alpha}{(M-1)}$ is the angular difference between two successive angular positions of the probe,

- $e = \frac{D}{(D-d)} \frac{(L-1)}{(N-1)}$ adjusts the pixel sampling rates along the axial direction of the beam, according to the desired height N of the cartesian image.

This yields the following:

$$
R(x, y) = \int_0^{2\pi} \int_0^\infty f \big(x - u(\rho, \theta), y - v(\rho, \theta) \big) \cdot I(\rho, \theta) \cdot |\mathbf{J}(\rho, \theta)| \, d\rho \, d\theta. \quad (17.2)
$$

Here $|\mathbf{J}(\rho, \theta)|$ is the determinant of the Jacobian matrix corresponding to the inverse transformation of variables:

$$
\begin{cases}
x = \dfrac{\rho + \Delta_N}{e} \cos \left(\theta \Delta_\alpha + \dfrac{\pi - \alpha}{2} \right) + x_0 \\[2ex]
y = \dfrac{\rho + \Delta_N}{e} \sin \left(\theta \Delta_\alpha + \dfrac{\pi - \alpha}{2} \right).
\end{cases}
$$

It is easily seen that

$$
|\mathbf{J}(\rho, \theta)| = \frac{(\rho + \Delta_N) * \Delta_\alpha}{e^2}.
$$

We have transformed the convolution in the cartesian coordinates to an infinite integral in polar coordinates, corresponding to the domain of the raw data. But the computer implementation requires a finite discrete summation.

Once the two-dimensional convolution filter f is chosen, we define its rectangle of essential support: say a rectangular window of width $2X$ and $2Y$. Outside this region of support the absolute value of the impulse response must be lower than a pre-selected threshold s, i.e.,:

$$|f(u, v)| < s \text{ if } ((|u| \geq X) \text{ OR } (|v| \geq Y)).$$

Therefore the integral is approximated by a finite integral over the domain

$$(x - X \leq u \leq x + X) \text{ AND } (y - Y \leq v \leq y + Y).$$

The filter is also sampled in this domain in order to approximate the integral by a discrete summation. Filtered numerical outputs are evaluated at original data point locations within the continuous domain.

We thus obtain the following equation:

$$R(x,y) = C \sum_k f\big(x - u(\rho_k, \theta_k), y - v(\rho_k, \theta_k)\big) \cdot I(\rho_k, \theta_k) \cdot |\mathbf{J}(\rho_k, \theta_k)|, \quad (17.3)$$

where the summation is over the discrete collection of point (ρ_k, θ_k) in polar coordinates and where C is used to normalize the data, and

$$|\mathbf{J}(\rho_k, \theta_k)| = \frac{(\rho_k + \Delta_N) * \Delta_\alpha}{e^2}.$$

We have thus transformed the computation of $R(x, y)$ into a discrete convolution on a window of size $2X$ by $2Y$, making use of image data only at points where it is defined in the polar coordinate domain. Note that for the raw data, or more generally for any sonar-like data, the sampling of the filter is not regular along the x and y axes but it rather conforms to the sampling density of raw data. In this formula, the $|\mathbf{J}(\rho_k, \theta_k)|$ value represents the surface area of the polar pixel patch in the cartesian domain. We will present in the following subsections the different values that we have chosen for the function f for different processing of the echocardiographic raw data.

17.2.3   Image Visualization

In practice, the convolution filter $f(x, y)$ is typically separable and is denoted by $f(x)g(y)$. Then, classical 1-D smoothing and derivation filters can be used.

For visualization applications of sonar-space filtering, we used the Deriche's smoothing function (Deriche, 1987), $f(x) = g(x) = L(x)$:

$$L(x) = k_2 \big(\alpha \sin(\omega |x|) + \omega \cos(\omega |x|)\big)^{-\alpha|x|} \qquad (17.4)$$

The conversion algorithm performs simultaneously a conversion to cartesian coordinates and a smoothing of the data (whose amplitude can be adjusted with α) thus producing a cartesian image with a reduced speckle. Other smoothing functions could be used instead.

17.2.4   Edge Detection

For automatic boundary tracking, we investigated the use of spatio-temporal approaches (Monga & Deriche, 1988). A time-varying edge may be represented as a surface in 3-D space, in which x and y are two spatial dimensions and t is the temporal dimension. We modify Deriche's edge detector for this goal.

We denote by α_x, α_y and α_t the filtering parameters of the Deriche filter (cf. Eq. 17.4) for the x, y and t axes respectively.

Since the 2D space is homogeneous, we can choose $\alpha_x = \alpha_y$. On the other hand, the value of α_t is independent and must be chosen according to the temporal resolution. (Another approach could be to generalize Deriche's detector with spatio-temporal functions as in (Hwang & Clark, 1990).)

We denote by G_x and G_y the two spatial components of the gradient vector and $I(x, y, t)$ the 3-D image function. Let D be the Deriche differentiation filter and L the associated smoothing filter. The two components of the gradient vector have the following expression:

- $G_x = (D_x L_y L_t) \otimes I(x, y, t)$
- $G_y = (L_x D_y L_t) \otimes I(x, y, t)$

where the subscripts are used to indicate along which axis the corresponding filter is applied and $\otimes$ denotes the convolution product.

Each component is obtained by differentiation in the associated direction and filtering in the other spatial direction and in the temporal direction. The squared norm of the gradient is defined by: $N^2(x, y, t) = G_x^2 + G_y^2$.

Finally, edges are obtained as local maxima of the gradient norm in the direction of the 2D gradient vector. The temporal dimension is only used to smooth the 3D intensity function. This produces a significant image enhancement in regions which are not moving too fast.

17.3   Global Temporal Tracking

17.3.1   Crude Initialization of Structure Edges

To obtain a crude estimation of the boundaries of anatomical structures, we use techniques from mathematical morphology. The model of a cardiac cavity is very simple. This is an ovoid region with low intensity. These regions cannot be obtained by simple thresholding because of the speckle noise. But the fine structures of the speckle may be easily suppressed by the following morphological operations (Serra, 1982):

- A first order opening eliminates the small bright structures on dark background.

- The dual operation (first order closing) suppresses the small dark structures.

After these operations, a simple thresholding gives an image C where all the cardiac cavities are represented in white. This detection can be refined by the use of higher level information. The specialist points out, using a computer mouse, the chosen cavity on the image. The whole cavity is then obtained by a conditional dilatation which begins at this point.

17.3.2   Use of an Active Deformable Model

The previous operations usually provide a gross approximation of the structure boundaries. In order to improve this crude segmentation to an accurate determination of the boundaries, we use the deformable models of (Cohen & Cohen, 1990), in the spirit of (Kass *et al.*, 1987a) (see also chapters 1 and 3).

The deformable model is initialized in the first image by the gross approximation of the structure boundaries, and evolves under the action of image forces which are counter-balanced by its own internal forces, which preserve its regularity.

Image forces are computed as the derivative of an attraction potential related to the previously computed spatio-temporal edges. Typically, the potential is inversely proportional to the distance of the nearest edge point.

Once the model has converged in the first frame, its final position is used as the initial one in the next frame, and the process is repeated. This is equivalent to a zero-mass tracking snake.

17.4   Global Tracking Results

Fig. 17.4 is a manual sketch of the image which shows where cardiac cavity is located, and can be considered the "ground-truth" of the echographic data in Fig. 17.2.

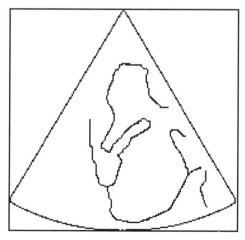

Figure 17.4
Manual sketch of the image.

Cartesian reconstruction of the polar image of Fig. 17.2 is shown in Fig. 17.5. The image has been reconstructed using direct convolution with the low-pass filter of equation 17.4 with $\alpha = 1$. Then, edges have been extracted without temporal smoothing by applying a spatial Deriche Filter (Deriche, 1987) to the cartesian image, with a resolution parameter $\alpha = 1$.

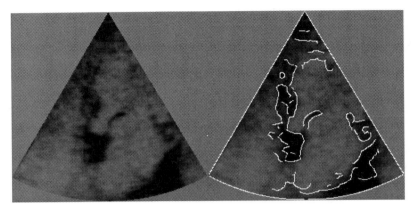

Figure 17.5
Reconstructed cartesian image and edges obtained by sonar-space filtering.

The effect of temporal smoothing can be seen on figure 17.6. There is a reduction of some local distortions on the deeper edges of the left auricle, as can been seen when comparing the bottom right cavity of figure 17.4 with figure 17.6. Simultaneously, temporal smoothing can make the mitral valve vanish (middle thin structure of the same figures), which is due to the fast motion of this structure with respect to the temporal resolution.

The chosen strategy is thus to use temporal smoothing only to study cavities (slow motion) and not when studying fast moving structures like the valves.

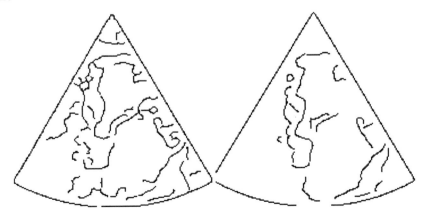

Figure 17.6
Left: no temporal smoothing of edges, right: temporal smoothing of edges.

Our methodology was applied to four different sequences obtained from two different echographs. We only present here the results obtained from a time sequence acquired in polar coordinates from a VIGMED echograph at the Hospital Henri Mondor in Creteil, France. This sequence contains 38 images from a cardiac cycle.

Fig. 17.7 shows a cartesian representation of the original data (only one image in four is displayed). Edges are shown in Fig. 17.8, and the temporal tracking of the mitral valve and the auricle are presented in Figs. 17.9 and 17.10.

17.5   Tracking Points on the Deformable Structure

The new objective is now to perform locally the tracking of each individual point on the active deformable model. The approach we developed in (Cohen *et al.*, 1992a) was an improvement of the work of (Amini *et al.*, 1991; Duncan *et al.*, 1991) to analyze the deformations of curves in sequences of 2D images.

17.5.1   Privileging High Curvature Points

This approach is based on the paradigm that high curvature points usually possess an anatomical meaning, and are therefore good landmarks to guide the matching process. This is the case for instance when deforming patients skulls (Cutting, 1989; Guéziec & Ayache, 1991; Monga *et al.*, 1992), or when matching patient faces taken at different ages, when matching multipatients faces, or when analyzing images of a beating heart. In these cases, many lines of extremal curvatures (or ridges) are stable features which can be reliably tracked between the images (on a face they will correspond to the nose, chin and eyebrows ridges for instance, on a skull to the orbital, sphenoid, falx, and temporal ridges, on a heart ventricle to the papillary muscle etc. ...).

As Duncan's team (Amini *et al.*, 1991; Duncan *et al.*, 1991), we therefore propose a method based on the minimization of an energy which tends to preserve the matching of high curvature points, while ensuring a smooth field of displacement vectors everywhere. The energy minimization is obtained through the mathematical framework of Conforming Finite Elements analysis (Ciarlet, 1987), which provides a rigorous and efficient numerical solution. Moreover we show in (Cohen *et al.*, 1992a) that the approach can be generalized in 3D to analyze the deformations of surfaces.

This approach is particularly attractive in the absence of a reliable physical or deformable geometric model of the observed structures, which is often the case when studying medical images. When such a model is available, other approaches would involve a parametrization of the observed shapes (Metaxas & Terzopoulos, 1991a) (see chapter 5), a modal analysis of the displacement field (Horowitz & Pentland, 1991), or a parametrization of a subset of deformations (Bookstein, 1989; Mishra *et al.*, 1991). In fact we believe that our approach can always be used when some sparse geometric features provide reliable landmarks, either as a preprocessing to provide an

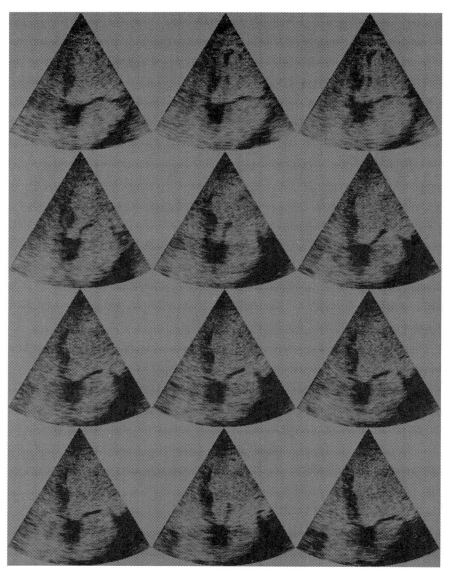

Figure 17.7
Data after scan-correction.

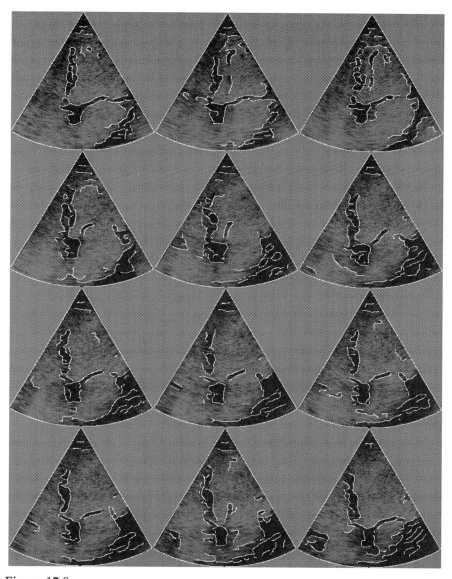

Figure 17.8
Edges.

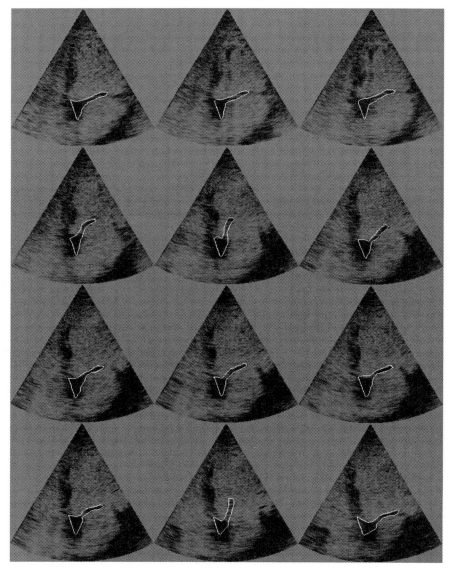

Figure 17.9
Temporal tracking of the mitral valve.

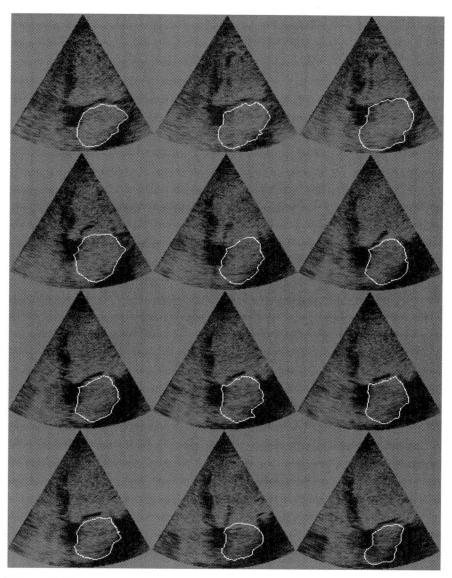

Figure 17.10
Temporal tracking of the left auricle.

initial solution to the other approaches, or as a post-processing to provide a
final smoothing which preserves the matching of reliable landmarks.

17.5.2   Modelling the Problem

Let C_P and C_Q be two boundaries of the image sequence, the contour C_Q
is obtained by a non rigid (or elastic) deformation of the contour C_P. The
curves C_P and C_Q are parameterized by $P(s)$ and $Q(s')$ respectively.

The problem is to determine for each point P on C_P a corresponding point
Q on C_Q. For doing this, we must define a similarity measure which will
compare locally the neighborhoods of P and Q.

As explained in the previous section, we assume that points of high curvature correspond to stable salient regions, and are therefore good landmarks
to guide the matching of the curves. Moreover, we can assume as a first order
approximation, that the curvature itself remains invariant in these regions.
Therefore, we can introduce an energy measure in these regions of the form:

$$E_{curve} = \frac{1}{2} \int_{\delta S} \left(K_Q(s') - K_P(s) \right)^2 ds \tag{17.5}$$

where K_P and K_Q denote the curvatures and s, s' parameterize the curves
C_P and C_Q respectively. In fact, as shown by (Duncan et $al.$, 1991; Landau
& Lifshitz, 1986), this is proportional to the energy of deformation of an
isotropic elastic planar curve.

We also wish the displacement field to vary smoothly around the curve,
in particular to insure a correspondence for points lying between two salient
regions. Consequently we consider the following functional (similar to the
one used by Hildreth to smooth a vector flow field along a contour (Hildreth,
1984)):

$$E = \int_{C_P} \left(K_Q(s') - K_P(s) \right)^2 ds + R \int_{C_P} \left\| \frac{\partial (Q(s') - P(s))}{\partial s} \right\|^2 ds \tag{17.6}$$

where

$$E_{regular} = \int_{C_P} \left\| \frac{\partial (Q(s') - P(s))}{\partial s} \right\|^2 ds$$

measures the variation of the displacement vector $\mathbf{PQ}$ along the curve C_P,
and the $\|.\|$ denotes the norm associated to the euclidean scalar product $\langle ., . \rangle$
in the space $\mathcal{R}^2$.

The weighting parameter $R(s)$ depends on the shape of the curve C_P.
Typically, $R(s)$ is inversely proportional to the curvature at P, to give a
larger weight to E_{curve} in salient regions and conversely to $E_{regular}$ to points
inbetween. This is done continuously without annihiling totally the weight
of any of these two energies (see (Cohen et $al.$, 1992a)).

17.5.3 Solving the Matching Problem

Given two curves C_P and C_Q parameterized by $s \in [0,1]$ and $s' \in [0,\alpha]$ (where α is the length of the curve C_Q), we have to determine a function f such that:

$$f : [0,1] \quad \rightarrow \quad [0,\alpha]$$
$$s \quad \rightarrow \quad s'$$

satisfying

$$f(0) = 0 \quad \text{and} \quad f(1) = \alpha \tag{17.7}$$

and

$$f = \arg\min\big(E(f)\big) \tag{17.8}$$

where

$$E(f) = \int_{C_P} \big(K_Q(f(s)) - K_P(s)\big)^2 ds + R(s) \int_{C_P} \left\| \frac{\partial\big(Q(f(s)) - P(s)\big)}{\partial s} \right\|^2 ds. \tag{17.9}$$

The condition (17.7) means that the displacement vector is known for one point of the curve. In the trivial case, where the curves C_P and C_Q are identical, solving (17.8) leads to the identity function.

In the model defined above we assumed that:

- the boundaries have already been extracted,

- the curvatures K are known on the pair of contours.

These necessary data are obtained by preprocessing the image sequence (see (Guéziec & Ayache, 1991) for instance).

17.5.4 Numerical Solution

The characterization of a function f satisfying $f = \arg\min E(f)$ and the condition (17.7) is performed by a variational method. This method characterizes a local minimum f of the functional $E(f)$ as the solution of the Euler-Lagrange equation $\nabla E(f) = 0$.

Then solving the Euler-Lagrange equation $\nabla E(f) = 0$ leads to the solution of the partial differential equation:

$$\begin{cases} f'' \|\mathbf{Q}'(\mathbf{f})\|^2 + K_P \langle \mathbf{N}_P, \mathbf{Q}'(f) \rangle + \frac{1}{R} [K_P - K_Q(f)] K_Q'(f) = 0 \\ + \text{ Boundary conditions} \end{cases} \tag{17.10}$$

where Q is a parametrization of the curve C_Q, $\mathbf{Q}'(\mathbf{f})$ the tangent vector of C_Q, K_Q' the derivative of the curvature of the curve C_Q and $\mathbf{N}_P$ is the normal vector to the curve C_P. The boundary conditions of equation (17.10) are $f(0) = 0$ and $f(1) = \alpha$ (condition (17.7)) that any solution must satisfy. In the following we consider null boundary conditions (this is done by a simple change of variables).

The equation (17.10) is solved by a finite element method. Details on the associated variational problem and the construction of the approximation space can be found in (Cohen *et al.*, 1992a) and the corresponding internal INRIA research report.

17.6   Local Tracking Results

The method was tested on a set of synthetic and real image sequences. Here, we only present the results obtained on the previously shown ultrasound images of a cardiac valve. This tracking can help the diagnosis of some heart diseases

Figure 17.11 show the tracking of each point of the valve for a selection of 8 successive pairs of contours (for other experiments, please refer to (Cohen *et al.*, 1992b). The results are given by specifying at each discretization point P_i $i = 1 \ldots N$ of the curve C_P the displacement vector $\mathbf{u}_i = \mathbf{P}_i\mathbf{Q}_i$. At each point P_i the arrow represents the displacement vector $\mathbf{u}_i$.

These results were satisfying for the all sequence of 30 images, in the sense that they met quite well the objectives of preserving the matching of high curvature points while insuring a smooth displacement field.

The method was entirely automatic, except for 4 frames (out of 30) where the user had to provide an initial estimation. This was due to excessive deformations with respect to the current temporal resolution. Anyhow, one can visualize that the results meet the objectives of preserving the matching of high curvature points while insuring a smooth displacement field.

17.7   Conclusion

We presented in this chapter an application of active vision to the tracking of points in anatomical structures in time sequences of ultrasound medical images. We presented a chain of processes, built with the following generic tools:

- sonar space filtering, to extract local edgels,
- active deformable models, to track a global structure,
- local point trackers, to follow the motion of each individual point on the global structure.

We illustrated the applicability of the whole chain by demonstrating the tracking of each point of a cardiac valve in a time sequence of ultrasound images.

Further work will go in two directions: first we shall generalize this work in 3 dimensions, following the work of (Cohen *et al.*, 1992c) and (Amini *et al.*, 1991), and second, we shall incorporate some physical model in the local tracking.

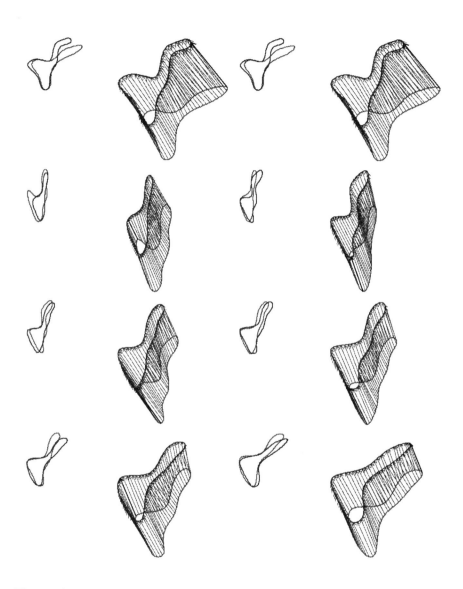

Figure 17.11
Experiments on a valve sequence (time 9–17).

18 Expectation-based Dynamic Scene Understanding

Ernst D. Dickmanns

18.1 Introduction

According to the 4D-approach to dynamic machine vision developed in our laboratory over the last decade, active vision is more than just actively controlling the viewing parameters of the camera system. The core of the method is an actively servo-maintained internal representation of the relevant spatio-temporal physical processes including objects and subjects in the visually observed scene; in the future, this will also encompass mental processes assumed to determine control decisions in subjects. Not only are spatial relationships reconstructed from image sequences but also measures of temporal coherence and causality.

A large fraction of our knowledge about the real world is concerned with the temporal domain; we learn to understand this during early life more or less subconsciously while the capability of crawling, walking and manipulating other objects under the Earth's gravity is being acquired. The temporal sequence of states of objects and their transition characteristics under certain circumstances constitute essential knowledge about the real world providing us with the capability of acting adequately, even though it does not seem to be represented explicitly. This has long been overlooked in Artificial Intelligence which concentrated its efforts on explicitly representing abstract knowledge about quasi-static relations between objects in the world.

The natural sciences and engineering technology have developed adequate methods for representing these facts about the physical world within the framework of differential equations with time as monotonically increasing independent variable. As I. Kant has elaborated in his "Critiques ..." more than two centuries ago, it has to be kept in mind that space and time are not properties of objects. We cannot help carrying them into the world by our sensing and analysis systems; we ourselves exist in these four basic dimensions. Therefore, it was decided to install the four dimensions in our machine intelligence system right from the beginning in order to be able to deal with the real world efficiently. This was the main contribution of our approach to machine vision; the rest follows almost automatically.

18.2 The sliding point "here and now"

A sensor system in the real world is always at a certain point in space at the one and only "present" time; this point in time is part of a continuous "time ray". A physical object cannot be at two different locations at the same time. In order to move from one location to another, energy is required for acceleration and deceleration, and time is required because the energy available to effect locomotion is bounded. These facts constitute constraints on the motion process which may help considerably when tracking the locomotion of objects, especially when accelerations and decelerations are very limited in magnitude as is the case in most of the occurrences in our natural and even technical environments (exceptions being bullets shot by guns for example).

Therefore, if we have a good internal representation of a situation in our environment we are in a much better position to understand the next image of a real-time sequence provided this representation allows us to predict how the process under observation is going to evolve over time taking certain control or perturbation inputs into account. If this prediction model is approximately correct one can concentrate the limited data processing capabilities on the data originating in the local environment of the predicted spot, thereby making the sensing process much more efficient; in addition, the data processing algorithms may also be adjusted to the predicted situation thereby further increasing efficiency. This positive feedback favors the evolution of powerful prediction capabilities since, in spite of additional computing resources required for prediction, the overall requirements may be decreased for the same performance level; on the other hand, completely new performance levels and a new deeper understanding of environmental processes may be achievable with this approach.

It might be argued, that human culture and its achievements are an outgrowth of nature having discovered this positive feedback during evolution.

In figure 18.1 a qualitative display is given of the internal representation density over the sliding time axis which moves from right to left. At the point "here and now" (shown stationary at the cross-section of the two orthogonal axes) sensors provide data on the actual state of the real world. These data are interpreted taking high-level spatio-temporal world models into account. These dynamical models are derived from those developed for system design and analysis in engineering. In addition, it is taken into account that the measurement data are usually superpositions of actual process states (the desired quantities to be recovered) and of measurement noise which is to be deleted. In order to be able to make this distinction, the models representing temporal behavior have to contain both the "eigen-"characteristics (meaning how states change over time when left on their own) and the response characteristics with respect to control- or perturbation inputs.

Once this is represented, predictions of the state evolution over time may be obtained at relatively low cost. Since usually neither the control nor the perturbation inputs of the future are known, prediction usually stops at one cycle (for the normal prediction-error-feedback state estimation process) or after only a few cycles in order not to incur too much uncertainty. For well known feedforward control time history inputs intended to achieve some manoeuver element (for example lane change in road vehicle guidance with a sine-like steering angle input over time using proper parameters for period T and amplitude A) reliable predictions over longer temporal ranges (seconds) are possible. Taking standard perturbation statistics into account, even longer ranges over entire maneuver sequences may be meaningful (like the

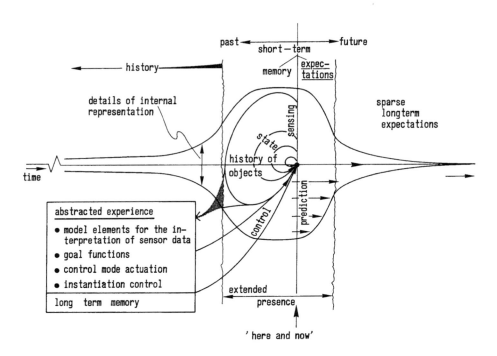

Figure 18.1
Representation density over time.

prediction of the time needed to go from point A to B). On the average, however, the number of predicted events will vanish on the future time scale to the right.

If good internal models are available for generating rich actual internal representations from the actual data measured, it will be impossible to store all these data as a "personal history of adventures"; it is not necessary, though. Since the time histories of the state variables may be regenerated from stored initial conditions, and control as well as perturbation time history inputs, once a proper model for the dynamic behavior is available, only the latter ones need be stored. For these again, instead of pointwise storing each individual time history, parameterized generic models would allow very efficient storage since a dense data input vector may be replaced by a few parameters needed to feed the proper function call. This shows that proper temporal models may be very efficient in reducing memory requirements if things are properly organized. Past process state time histories and events may then be reconstructed actively from combining only a few stored historical data with stored model knowledge. This principle is the basic advantage of the 4D approach combining space and time in an integrated manner.

This type of data compression into valid models is symbolized in figure 18.1 by the formation of a reduced tail on the past time axis (left). Quasi-static knowledge resulting from this is used later on for triggering proper control activities depending on the situation encountered. Standard perturbations are counteracted by feedback control laws which are implemented by a direct loop from the sensory data to the corresponding actuators (see center of figure 18.1) via internal state variables of recognized objects; this allows stable behavior under perturbed conditions without the explicit knowledge levels having to interact with the high frequency data stream. Only unforeseen situations and the discovery of unpredicted new features lead to an activation of the more knowledge based hypothesis generation part controlling the active set of internal dynamical models (lower left in figure 18.1).

Seen from this point of view, the entire "mental" internal world of representations has as its purpose to provide the system with capabilities of data interpretation well suited for control outputs which enable the system to achieve its goals; previous experience may be exploited for this purpose contributing to the rating of a system as being intelligent or not.

18.3   The 4D-approach as the core of expectation-driven vision

The dynamical models link time to spatial motion, in general. 3D shape models exhibit the spatial distribution of visual features which allow the system to recognize and track objects. In order to exploit both dynamical and shape models at the same time, the prediction error feedback scheme for recursive state estimation developed by Kalman and successors in the sixties has been extended to image sequence processing by our group (Wuensche, 1988). There are many publications on this approach so that only a short summary will be given here (see e.g. the survey articles (Dickmanns & Graefe, 1988b; Dickmanns & Graefe, 1988a; Dickmanns & Mysliwetz, 1992)). For other applications of the Kalman filter in Active Vision see also chapters 1, 3, 4, 5, 6 and 16.

Figure 18.2 shows the resulting overall block-diagram of the real-time core of the vision system based on these principles. To the left, the real world is shown by a block; control inputs to the vehicle carrying the camera may lead to changes in the visual appearance of the world either by changing the viewing direction or through egomotion. The continuous changes of objects and their relative position in the world over time are sensed by CCD-sensor arrays (shown as converging lines to the lower right, symbolizing the 3D to 2D data reduction). They record the incoming light intensity from a certain field of view at a fixed sampling rate. By this imaging process the information flow is discretized in several ways: There is a limited spatial resolution in the image plane and a temporal discretization of $16\frac{2}{3}$ or 20 ms, usually including some averaging over time.

Instead of trying to invert this image sequence for 3D-scene understanding, a different approach by **analysis through synthesis** has been selected.

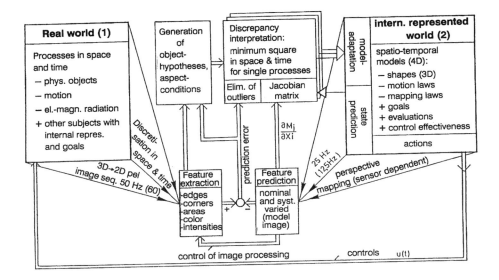

Figure 18.2
Survey block diagram of the cybernetic 4D approach to dynamic machine vision.

From previous human experience, generic models of objects in the 3D-world are assumed to be known in the interpretation process. This comprises both 3D shape, recognizable by certain feature aggregations given the aspect conditions, and motion behavior over time.

In an initialisation phase, starting from a collection of features extracted by low level pixel processing (lower center left in figure 18.2), object hypotheses including aspect conditions and motion models in space (transition matrices) have to be generated (upper center left). They are installed in an internal "mental" world representation intended to duplicate the outside real world. After the philosopher K. Popper this is sometimes called "world_2", as opposed to the real "world_1".

Once an aggregation of objects has been instantiated in the world_2, exploiting the dynamical models, the object states can be predicted for the point in time when the next measurement is going to be taken. By applying the <u>forward</u> perspective projection to those features, which will be easily visible, using the same mapping conditions as the TV-sensor, a model image can be generated which should duplicate the measured image if the situation has been understood properly. The situation is thus "imagined" (right and lower center right in figure 18.2). The big advantage of this approach is that due to the internal 4D-model not only the actual situation at the present time but also the sensitivity matrix of the feature positions with respect to state changes can be determined; the so-called Jacobian matrix (upper block in center right, lower right corner). This rich information is used for bypassing the direct perspective inversion via recursive least squares filtering through feedback of the prediction errors of the features. This means that the perspective inversion can be achieved at no extra cost once the Jacobian has been computed; the **spatial** state is estimated in a least squares error sense including its **spatial** velocity components. Note that this signal to symbol transition from picture elements (pixels) via edge features to a high-level spatio-temporal object state is achieved in just two steps; however, both data driven bottom-up and model-driven top-down components are traversed in each of the frequent (12.5 or 25 Hz) cycles in this approach as will be explicated in the next section. This approach has several very important practical advantages:

1. No previous images need be stored and retrieved for computing optical flow, or velocity components, in the image plane as an intermediate step in the interpretation process; the reference for a virtual optical flow computation may be considered to be stored in the object states; it is actively reconstructed using knowledge about perspective projection;

2. The transition from signals to symbols (spatio-temporal motion state of objects) is done in a very direct way, well based on scientific knowledge, the 4D world model integrating spatial and temporal aspects;

3. Intelligent nonuniform image analysis becomes possible, allowing one to concentrate limited computer resources to areas of interest known to carry meaningful information;

4. The position and orientation of easily visible features can be predicted and the feature extraction algorithms can be provided with information for more efficiently finding the desired ones; outliers can easily be removed thereby stabilising the interpretation process.

5. Viewing direction control can be done directly in an object-oriented manner; known egomotion can be compensated for in order to achieve better fixation performance.

Processing a variable number of features measured from frame to frame is alleviated by using the sequential filtering version. For improving the numerical performance, the UD-factorized version of the square-root-filter is used (Bierman, 1975). Details may be found in (Wuensche, 1988; Mysliwetz, 1990; Bierman, 1977; Maybeck, 1979). By exploiting the sparseness of the transition matrix in the dynamical models a speed-up can be achieved.

Special care has to be taken in the initialization phase when good object hypotheses are in demand. From feature aggregations which may have been collected in a systematic search covering extended regions of the image, the existence of objects has to be hypothesized.

18.4 The "Gestalt" idea for object recognition and tracking

Temporal invariances are captured in the dynamical models which link the changing aspect conditions over time. Spatial invariances are the 3D shapes of rigid objects or parts of articulated objects under observation. Combining both through the Gestalt idea of moving objects and via the laws of perspective projection yields the basis of dynamic scene understanding with the 4D-approach. Thus, dynamic image sequences are interpreted by exploiting a priori knowledge about objects and relevant motion processes in 3D space.

Measurable features on the surface of objects constitute the link between pixel-processing in the image plane and a symbolic reconstruction of an analog internal representation of the mapped object in the interpretation process within the computer.

Measuring and collecting all features in every image and then trying to match groups of those with all possible object interpretations in every frame would lead to a combinatorial explosion. Instead, relying on the temporal continuity conditions in finite motion processes for specific task domains, considerably reduces the number of meaningful interpretations possible. If an independent motion of the camera is superimposed on dynamic changes in the scene, an internal representation of the camera motion with respect to the other bodily motion processes is required.

For an autonomous vehicle, therefore, both egomotion and motions of other objects have to be represented separately. Both motion components may change the aspect conditions of the objects observed. Inertial measurements may give independent information on the egomotion in a fast and reliable way so that image interpretation can be alleviated by taking this information into account. Using this additional information, the corresponding effects of changing aspect conditions of other objects through egomotion may be eliminated, at least roughly. This reduces the search area for an object in the new frame. Actively predicting the remaining changes in aspect conditions and corresponding changes in feature appearance for a known 3D shape (the assumed invariant) allows us to considerably reduce the amount of image processing workload.

In natural environments when the sun is shining, shadow boundaries may yield much more pronounced intensity edges than do body boundaries; for moving objects, these shadow boundaries move over the body surface. Under these conditions the "Gestalt" idea of looking for a reasonably coordinated set of features indicative of the object searched or tracked is often the only chance for recognizing the object amongst a multitude of distracting similar features. One has to know what one is looking for in order to find it. This approach will be described later for road and road vehicle recognition in outdoor scenery. It allows us to interpret rather complex scenes with comparatively simple image processing schemes.

In (Schick & Dickmanns, 1991) this approach has been extended to generic object models with unknown parameters. The first simulation results indicate the viability of this approach for simultaneous motion and body shape recognition, at least for some restricted classes of technically fabricated objects like road vehicles.

18.5 System components

The main components of the experimental setup are a testbed vehicle for autonomous mobility and computer vision (dubbed "VaMoRs") and a special, experimental multiprocessor vision-system for real time image sequence analysis and interpretation.

VaMoRs (Figure 18.3) is a converted 5-ton van that has been equipped with all necessary actuators, interfaces and onboard power generator, etc. to be driven autonomously under computer control and to serve as a "rolling fieldlab" for computer vision research.

Figure 18.3
Testbed vehicle VaMoRs for autonomous mobility and computer vision.

An electromechanical pan-tilt platform carrying two CCD cameras mounted in the center behind the front wind-shield, hanging from the roof, provides fast 2-axis viewing direction control. Its control is part of the vision-system. Thus, the complementary vision functions of image analysis and active viewing direction control are tightly coupled. Equipped with lenses of different focal length, a scene can be analysed in the wide angle image for global features (such as the road boundaries) and with more detail in the enlarged image (e.g., for focussing on objects or obstacles ahead).

The camera pointing capability allows active search and tracking, e.g., for initial self orientation, motion blur reduction and continuous road tracking while driving. For obvious reasons it is desirable not to lose the road from the camera's field of view when the vehicle changes its heading or enters a tight curve. For obstacle recognition, especially, it is essential to have the camera actively center that part of the scene where potential obstacles are of interest.

All onboard processing for real time scene analysis and vehicle control is handled by a special, experimental multiprocessor system BVV_2 (Dickmanns & Graefe, 1988b; Dickmanns & Graefe, 1988a) and an IBM 7532 (industrial version of the IBM AT) as its host computer. The multiprocessor system of the MIMD type consists (fully configured) of 13 commercial, standard Multibus I singleboard computers spanning the performance range from 8086 to 80386. Recently, transputer components have been added.

The key feature of this multiprocessor vision-system is the physically distributed, thus truly parallel, image access capability of all CPUs directly involved in image operations. This overcomes the common I/O bottleneck of general purpose machines, in which usually only one processor has direct image access. In the BVV_2 no central frame store exits. Any processor linked to the videobus through a videobus-interface (VBI) can simultaneously access and process a subsegment (window) of the digitized 256 by 244×8 bit per pixel grayscale image. The VBI basically is a hardware-attachment to a standard singleboard computer containing a window-selection logic and two fast window-buffers storing 4k pixel each. Multiple windows can be independently positioned or changed in size, shape and sampling density under software control.

It should be noted that (except for the VBI) no custom hardware and no dedicated image processing devices are being used in this experimental system. The advantages of applying easily programmable standard microprocessors instead, proved to be significant for the system's applicability and efficiency as a research tool.

A further key point is the flexible interprocessor communication scheme based on message passing, forming a loosely coupled system requiring only modest bus bandwith. Using the communication services of the distributed operating system kernel, a desired processing structure can be defined entirely by downloadable application software. Thus, task specific cooperating processor clusters can be formed. Typically, such a CPU group consists of several "Parallel Image Processors" (PP) at a low hierarchical level that perform local feature extraction operations on their windows. The PPs of a group may be coordinated by a "General Purpose Processor" (GPP, more recently renamed 4D-object processor 4D-OP) at a higher hierarchical level, which interprets the PPs' feature-data and controls or guides the activities of its PP group (see also figure 18.4).

The host computer serves for mass storage, real-time data logging and software development.

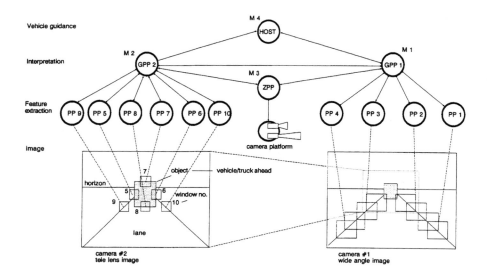

Figure 18.4
Modular processing structure for visual road vehicle guidance.

18.5.1 Processing concepts

The system contains very few hierarchical levels. The vertical processing structure can be roughly defined by four layers: L1 Feature extraction (pixel operations); L2 Single object interpretation (feature groups in time and space); L3 Situation assessment (several objects in a mission context), and L4 Vehicle guidance ("reflex"-like feedback control actions). Layers 1, 2 and 4 are reasonably well established; layer 3 is the one with the largest growth potential for more complex scenes.

The corresponding data types handled at each level are the following (at increasing levels of abstraction): T1 Raw, digitized image intensity values (signal domain); T2 Feature descriptions (2-D edges/corners in the image plane), and T3 Attributes of physical objects: 3D-shape and state vectors (position/orientation/velocity in time).

It should be noted that it takes only two processing levels to transform the raw signals first into feature descriptions and then into the problem oriented representation (object states).

There are four main functional modules structured by their subtasks: M1 Road parameter and relative lateral state estimation; M2 Obstacle detection/tracking and relative state estimation. M3 Viewing direction control, and M4 Vehicle guidance.

A tree-like communication scheme, as shown in figure 18.4, was found to best fit our algorithms and machine capabilities. The right subtree (M1) is dedicated to road boundary tracking (the "road vision module") while the left processor-group (M2) is used for obstacle detection/tracking (the "obstacle vision module"). Depending on the situation either M1 or M2 command the viewing direction of the camera. Vehicle guidance (M4) was initially handled on the host-computer, based on information from both vision modules. More recently it has been ported onto transputers.

The efficiency of this processing scheme is also reflected in the significant data rate reduction achieved in passing up through the processing levels:

Given a $256\times244\times8$ bit digitized image and taking every second frame of a 50 Hz video frame rate results in a data rate of roughly 1.6 MByte/s (per camera). Confining the attention (and processing resources) e.g., to 8 windows (sized 48×48 pixel) already reduces the actually analysed image area to less than 30% and the signal flow to about 0.5 MByte/s. If this load is shared among, for example, 4 PPs, each one has to cope with an incoming data rate of about 140 kByte/s. From this data stream, each PP extracts linearly extended features as candidates for road or lane edge elements.

A set of extracted feature descriptions to be passed up to the interpretation level is already a very compact data structure of only 30–40 bytes size per window (and interpretation cycle). Thus the road vision module has an input rate of just around 8 kByte/s. From a computing cycle period of 40 ms only a very small fraction (typically 300 μs per message and processor) is spent for communication.

Within the interpretation level (and upwards) only partial state vectors and a few global scene parameters are communicated. Messages typically contain 3 or 4 parameters and are exchanged at a 12.5 Hz rate, corresponding to the vehicle guidance module's update rate.

18.5.2   Feature extraction

The various techniques being investigated for road boundary tracking can be roughly categorized into a) edge based using intensity images b) region based using intensity images and c) region based using color images (Kuan et al., 1986; Turk et al., 1987; Wallace et al., 1986) (see also chapter 7). The approach applied here is of the first type as far as the image processing level is concerned. Though this method might be considered the most susceptible to real-world disturbances like shadows, or ill-defined ambiguous edges, it will be shown that in combination with a proper guiding and interpretation mechanism, it is efficient and robust at the same time.

On the feature extraction level, local, oriented edge operators are used both for road boundary detection and for object contour tracking. Corner finding operators can be realised by searching for adequate constellations of two edge elements. The edge operators are entirely software based, running on a standard microprocessor (8086 or 80286/8 MHz). They work directly on raw image (window) data; no prior signal conditioning or smoothing is necessary.

A severe drawback of commonly used edge finding methods (e.g., all "classical" operators) is that they are purely signal driven and lack scene-descriptive criteria; they treat "right" and "wrong" edges, due to shadows for example, equally. Poor performance will usually also result under the influence of noise or texture, both inevitable in natural scenes. But even optimized algorithms cannot resolve ambiguities at the low level, even less so if they work on local support only (such as in a window). This shows the need to include more a priori knowledge or to establish some control mechanism. In our case the guiding mechanism for real-time road boundary tracking is based on spatio-temporal scene interpretation utilizing a geometric road model, a known ego-motion model and the laws of central projection.

Even when considering the relatively simple shape of two converging road boundaries in the image, there are many sources of ambiguity and uncertainty under real world conditions: e.g. there may exist dominant edges across the road due to shadows, there may be multiple nearby parallel edges or intermittent stretches without well defined boundaries, all additionally blurred due to vehicle motion (figure 18.5).

Accepting ambiguity at the low level allows the use of simple and fast algorithms there (even more so, if only a fraction of the whole image is processed). Having to resolve ambiguity, or uncertainty, then at a higher level requires that no essential information is withheld or lost by the low level operations. This, however, will mostly occur if single, optimal results due to local criteria are extracted. So, a well balanced approach is necessary to fine tune the distribution of competence between the signal driven and the model driven processing levels.

As the proper appearance of the road boundaries in the image can be easily predicted, given the observer's relative position, local edge extraction is, in the approach used here, tightly guided and controlled by the interpretation level; i.e. the interpretation level commands the expected edge direction and location plus some optional parameters for adapting the algorithm. In return, it receives a description set of several edge candidates in the area with the orientation sought (figure 18.5), plus additional ones from potential edges with similar orientation in a limited sector around the commanded direction. These are checked against the expected edge locations, then the best candidates are selected to update the state estimates or they may be all rejected if they fall outside some allowed threshold around the reference position.

The core algorithm correlates an image subset (window) with an ideal step edge as reference pattern. A very efficient implementation of this technique on a conventional microprocessor has been originally given by (Kuhnert & Graefe, 1985), avoiding multiplications and extensively using lookup tables. Very similar directional step edge operators are described in (Canny, 1986) derived, however, under optimality assumptions with respect to shape and operator width; computational simplicity and efficiency has been less em-

Figure 18.5
Campus road scene under difficult conditions (up to three edgel candidates are shown per window.)

phasized in the latter case.

A version of Kuhnert's algorithm with a significantly improved interface to the interpretation level is being used here. It is better adapted to noisy real-world scenes and applies "bar masks" with 16 discrete orientations, yielding a directional resolution of about 11 degrees. Up to four different edge element (edgel) candidates are extracted per window, so that for the road boundaries a set of up to 32 edgels can be passed to the interpretation level for selection and further analysis.

On an Intel 80286 microprocessor (8 MHz/no waitstates) it takes less than two video cycles (40 ms) to subsequently analyse two windows (sized 48×48 pixels) at different locations for three different edge orientations and to extract a set of edge candidates for each window. Much higher performance is achievable by the transputers now being used.

18.5.3   Object-oriented recursive state estimation

The Kalman filter approach (see also chapters 1, 4, 5, 6) introduces knowledge about the dynamical behavior of a process, about the measurement relations and about the noise statistics of both process and measurements in order to obtain the best estimates of the process states in a least squares error sense recursively as new measurement data arrive. It even allows us to substitute this knowledge for missing measurements of state components; these are reconstructed in a way to best fit the overall model.

In the 4D-approach to dynamic vision, the Extended Kalman Filter (EKF) for nonlinear systems (see (Maybeck, 1979)) has been further extended to perspective mapping as the measurement process; the reconstruction capability is thereby exploited for bypassing the strongly nonlinear perspective inversion, utilizing all continuity conditions for spatio-temporally represented objects in 3D space (shape, carrying easily visible features) and time (motion constraints given by the dynamical model, the differential equations of motion).

The general form of a dynamical model for a system of order n (the number of state components necessary to uniquely specify the system state $\mathbf{x}(t)$) with r control inputs $\mathbf{u}(t)$ is, in vector notation

$$\dot{\mathbf{x}} = \mathbf{f}(\mathbf{x}, \mathbf{u}, t) + \mathbf{v}(t) \tag{18.1}$$

where $\mathbf{v}(t)$ is process noise with covariance matrix $\mathbf{Q}(t)$. The measured variables $\mathbf{y}$, an m-vector, are related to the state vector $\mathbf{x}$ through the nonlinear relation (including perspective mapping with parameters $\mathbf{p}$)

$$\mathbf{y} = \mathbf{h}(\mathbf{x}, \mathbf{p}) + \mathbf{w}, \tag{18.2}$$

where $\mathbf{w}(t)$ is a measurement noise term with covariance matrix $\mathbf{R}(t)$.

Let $\mathbf{A}(\mathbf{x}_0, \mathbf{u}_0, t_i)$ be the linearized transition matrix from $\mathbf{x}_0, \mathbf{u}_0$ at t_i to $\mathbf{x}^*$ at t_{i+1} for the deterministic part of (18.1) and $\mathbf{H}$ the Jacobian matrix of the deterministic part of (18.2)

$$\mathbf{H}(\mathbf{x}^*) = \left. \frac{\partial \mathbf{h}(\mathbf{x})}{\partial \mathbf{x}} \right|_{\mathbf{x}=\mathbf{x}^*}, \tag{18.3}$$

$\mathbf{P}$ the covariance matrix of the state variables ($n \times n$) and $\mathbf{K}$ the Kalman filter gain matrix ($n \times m$), then the EKF procedure may be summarized as follows (with $\int_{t_i}^{t_{i+1}} \mathbf{A}'\mathbf{Q}\mathbf{A}'^{\top} dt$ approximated by a constant $\bar{\mathbf{Q}}(t_i)$):

Extrapolation step (denoted by superscript $*$):

$$\mathbf{x}^*(t_{i+1}) = \hat{\mathbf{x}}(t_i) + \int_{t_i}^{t_{i+1}} \mathbf{f}\left[\mathbf{x}(t, t_i), \mathbf{u}(t)\right] dt \tag{18.4}$$

$$\mathbf{P}^*(t_{i+1}) = \mathbf{A}\hat{\mathbf{P}}(t_i)\mathbf{A}^{\top} + \bar{\mathbf{Q}}(t_i) \tag{18.5}$$

Innovation step: ($t_i \Leftarrow t_{i+1}$):

$$\mathbf{y}^* = \mathbf{h}(\mathbf{x}^*, \mathbf{p}) \tag{18.6}$$

$$\mathbf{K}(t_i) \;=\; \mathbf{P}^*(t_i)\mathbf{H}^\top \left[\mathbf{HP}^*(t_i)\mathbf{H}^\top + \mathbf{R}(t_i)\right] \qquad (18.7)$$

$$\hat{\mathbf{x}}(t_i) \;=\; \mathbf{x}^*(t_i) + \mathbf{K}(t_i)\,(\mathbf{y}-\mathbf{y}^*) \qquad (18.8)$$

$$\hat{\mathbf{P}}(t_i) \;=\; \mathbf{P}^*(t_i) + \mathbf{K}(t_i)\mathbf{HP}^*(t_i). \qquad (18.9)$$

The current best estimates are the roofed ones ($\hat{\ }$) which originate from the expected ones (eqs. 18.4, 18.5) by adding the measurement innovations with the gain matrix $\mathbf{K}$. This matrix is influenced by the covariance matrices $\bar{\mathbf{Q}}$ and $\mathbf{R}$ which give room for filter tuning in order to adjust convergence behavior (see (Maybeck, 1979; Wuensche, 1988; Mysliwetz, 1990) for details).

18.5.4 Road recognition

Figure 18.6 shows the individual influences of the lateral vehicle state and of the horizontal and vertical curvature parameters on the visual appearance of the road under standard driving conditions. The elevation of the camera

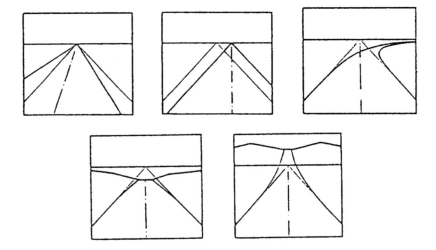

Figure 18.6
Individual influences of the lateral vehicle state and road parameters on the road image. The figures are ordered left to right and top to bottom: lateral offset, heading offset, horizontal curvature right, downward vertical curvature and upward curvature.

above the road surface h_K is the major parameter influencing these images.

18.5.5 Differential geometry representation of curves

A linear change of curvature $C = 1/R$ (R = radius of curvature) with arclength l is a good differential geometry approximation to a third order polynomial in Cartesian coordinates if the change in tangent direction χ is kept small ($|\chi| \le 10°$). The equation

$$C \;=\; C_0 + C_1 l \qquad (18.10)$$

can be integrated to give the heading direction χ from the differential geometry relation $d\chi/dl = C$. This gives

$$\chi = \chi_0 + C_0 l + C_1 \frac{l^2}{2}, \tag{18.11}$$

where χ_0 is an integration constant to be determined from the context (see
figure 18.7).

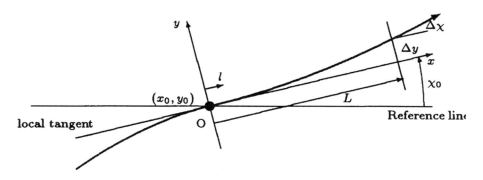

Figure 18.7
Local tangential coordinates.

Orienting a local Cartesian coordinate system in such a way that χ_0 yields
the tangent to the curve at the origin $l = 0$, results in the following relations
between the curvature parameters C and the local coordinates x and y (with
the approximations $dy = dl \sin(\chi - \chi_0) \approx dl \cdot (\chi - \chi_0)$ and $dx = dl \cos(\chi - \chi_0) \approx dl$)

$$x = x_0 + l \tag{18.12}$$

$$y = y_0 + C_0 \frac{l^2}{2} + C_1 \frac{l^3}{6}. \tag{18.13}$$

x_0 and y_0 are integration constants fixing the translational position of the
local arc; it clearly demonstrates the separation between the shape aspects
represented in C_0, C_1 and the position and orientation aspects represented
in x_0, y_0 and χ_0. In (Dickmanns, 1985) this approach has been developed for
2D shape representation including corners as curvature impulses at segment
boundaries; complex shapes may be represented efficiently in a translation-,
rotation- and size- invariant form using these *"linear curvature elements"*
integrated into the Normalized Curvature Function (NCF).

18.5.6   Recursive curvature parameter estimation

Choosing a coordinate system which is moved tangentially with the origin **0**
along the curve (see figure 18.7), and which allows at a lookahead distance
L the lateral offset y of the curve from the local tangent direction at **0**

to be measured, the following dynamical (incremental) model for recursive estimation results:

$$\frac{d}{dl}\begin{bmatrix} C \\ C_1 \end{bmatrix} = \begin{bmatrix} 0 & V \\ 0 & 0 \end{bmatrix}\begin{bmatrix} C \\ C_1 \end{bmatrix} + \begin{bmatrix} 0 \\ n(l) \end{bmatrix} \tag{18.14}$$

with the measurement equation

$$\Delta y(L) = \frac{L^2}{2}C + \frac{L^3}{6}C_1 + w(l) \tag{18.15}$$

where $n(l)$ is a driving noise term and $w(l)$ represents measurement noise. L has to be adjusted in practice according to curvature in order to be efficient and to keep $\Delta\chi$ in a range compatible with the assumptions made ($\cos \approx 1$; $\sin \approx$ argument; higher order approximation terms may easily be added); at corners (direction discontinuities) the process has to be restarted after determination of $\Delta\chi_{0corner}$.

On normal high speed roads, the radius of curvature $R = 1/C$ is usually much larger than the road width b; therefore, the curve for the skeletal line and for the left and right border lines are almost the same. Modern roads are pieced together from so called "clothoids" (characterized by constant values of C_1) and straight lines segments ($C_0 = C_1 = 0$) as well as circular arcs ($C_0 = const., C_1 = 0$).

When a vehicle drives along the road the temporal curvature change becomes

$$\frac{dC}{dt} = \frac{dC}{dl}\frac{dl}{dt} = C_1 V, \tag{18.16}$$

where V is the vehicle speed. The time derivative of eq. (18.10) yields, for a road with piecewise linearly changing curvature (see figure 18.8b), an additional term containing the time derivative of the the step function over arc length C_1, which is a sequence of Dirac impulses (see figure 18.8d).

Since the position of these impulses (corresponding to the stepwise jumps in C_1) cannot be determined reliably in noise corrupted measurements, a locally varying "averaged" clothoid model has been evaluated in (Mysliwetz, 1990). It takes into account the structure of the clothoid step function $\underline{C_{1hm}}$ in modeling the lateral offset y; however, it substitutes for the discrete step model at each measurement point in a certain look-ahead range L_L an corresponding "averaged" model (index m) for several look-ahead distances L_j according to eq. (18.15), yielding a least squares error sum for the prediction errors Δy_i.

This finally leads to the dynamical model with a noise term $n_{c1h}(t)$ driving the "constant" C_{1h} in a differential equation:

$$\dot{C}_{0hm} = C_{1hm}V$$
$$\dot{C}_{1hm} = -3\frac{V}{L}C_{1hm} + 3\frac{V}{L}C_{1h} \tag{18.17}$$
$$\dot{C}_{1h} = n_{c1h}(t),$$

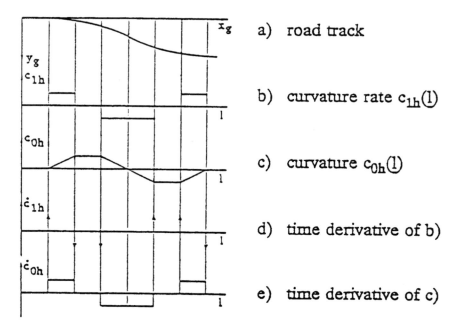

Figure 18.8
Road track and horizontal curvature terms.

which in matrix-vector notation may be written as

$$\dot{\mathbf{x}}_{ch} = \mathbf{A}_{ch}\mathbf{x}_{ch} + \mathbf{n}_{ch} = \begin{bmatrix} 0 & V & 0 \\ 0 & -3\frac{V}{L} & 3\frac{V}{L} \\ 0 & 0 & 0 \end{bmatrix} \begin{bmatrix} C_{0hm} \\ C_{1hm} \\ C_{1h} \end{bmatrix} + \begin{bmatrix} 0 \\ 0 \\ n_{c1h} \end{bmatrix} \qquad (18.18)$$

where $n_{c1h}(t)$ results from the actual measurements.

18.5.7 Horizontal measurement model

Both the lateral vehicle states and the curvature parameters enter the mapping process by the imaging sensor. Only the horizontal mapping model will be discussed here because of space limitations (for the vertical model see (Dickmanns & Mysliwetz, 1992)).

Figure 18.9 shows the horizontal road and mapping geometry. The horizontal image coordinate y_B of a road boundary edge element at the look-ahead distance L from the projection center PZ is fixed by the following road curvature parameters, mapping parameters and relative state terms:

f	focal length [mm],
ψ_V	vehicle heading angle relative to road tangent [rad],
k_y	horizontal scaling factor for the camera [pixel/mm],
y_V	lateral offset of vehicle cg from road center [m],
L	look-ahead distance [m],
b	width of road [m],
d	distance from projection center to vehicle cg [m],
C_{0hm}	average horizontal road curvature [1/m], at vehicle
ψ_K	camera heading angle relative to vehicle reference axis [rad],
C_{1hm}	average horizontal road curvature rate [$1/m^2$].

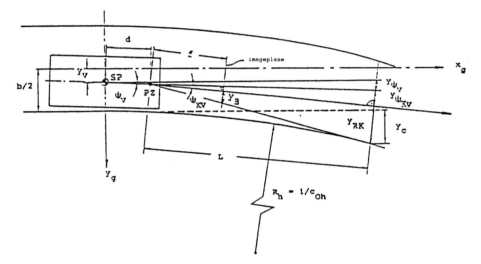

Figure 18.9
Horizontal road and mapping geometry; point SP = vehicle center of gravity, PZ – camera projection center; the following index conventions are valid: V – vehicle, K – camera, R – road, B – image coordinates, g – relative to geodetic coordinate system.

Because of the small angles involved, the sine is approximated by its argument and the cosine by 1. Since $f \ll L$, the position of the projection center and the rotation axis for the camera are assumed to have the same distance to the point at range L mapped.

It is seen from figure 18.9 that at the look-ahead distance L the following relation holds approximately:

$$y_C + \frac{b}{2} = y_{RK} + y_{\psi KV} + y_{\psi V} + y_V \tag{18.19}$$

where

$$y_C = \frac{(L+d)^2}{2} C_{0hm} + \frac{(L+d)^3}{6} C_{1hm} \tag{18.20}$$

and

$$y_{\psi KV} = L\psi_{KV}, \tag{18.21}$$

$$y_{\psi V} = (L+d)\psi_V.$$

From eq. (18.19) it follows

$$y_{RK} = \frac{b}{2} + y_C - y_V - y_\psi K_V - y_\psi V,$$

which is being mapped into y_B by the law of perspective projection as

$$y_B = \frac{(fk_y)}{L} y_{RK} \qquad (18.22)$$
[in pixel units].

In the planar case, the look-ahead distance L depends on the camera pitch angle θ_K relative to the plane and on the evaluated image line z_{Bi}; if the road is vertically curved, this curvature enters the evaluation of the look-ahead distance and the relations become more nonlinear (see (Dickmanns & Mysliwetz, 1992)).

18.5.8   Ego-motion model

The state and control variables are modified for catching the essential lateral motion constraints of a vehicle with frontwheel steering. The heading angle ψ_V describes the orientation of the longitudinal axis relative to the road tangent at the vehicle cg. The road tangent turn rate $\dot\chi$ relative to inertial space is the product: horizontal curvature times speed

$$\dot\chi = C_{0h} V. \qquad (18.23)$$

The vehicle trajectory is controlled by the steering angle λ which fixes the turn radius R of the vehicle (figure 18.10). For an infinitesimal move dl, the following approximate relationship holds for $a \gg dl$

$$dl \sin(\lambda) = a \sin[d(\psi_{Vg})]. \qquad (18.24)$$

For small angles λ and ψ the time derivative of this relation yields

$$\dot\psi_{Vg} = V \frac{\lambda}{a} \qquad (18.25)$$

where ψ_{Vg} is the heading angle with respect to inertial space. In order to obtain the heading change ψ_V relative to the road tangent at the present location of the vehicle cg along the road, the road heading turn rate has to be subtracted:

$$\dot\psi_V = V \left(\frac{\lambda}{a} - C_{0h} \right). \qquad (18.26)$$

The C_{1h} influence has been neglected due to its smallness. The vehicle heading angle ψ_V is linked to the path azimuth angle χ_V of the vehicle by the slip angle β

$$\chi_V = \psi_V + \beta. \qquad (18.27)$$

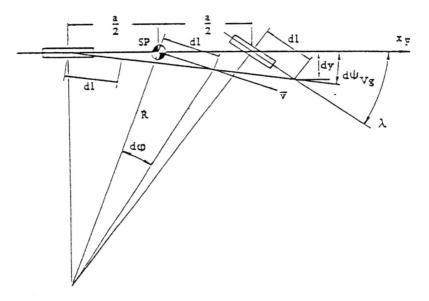

Figure 18.10
Steering kinematics.

This discrepancy between trajectory and vehicle heading occurs because of tire softness and of slipping between tire and ground. The lateral speed relative to the road then is

$$\dot{y}_V = V\sin(\chi_V) = V\chi_V. \tag{18.28}$$

The slip angle β also is constrained by a differential equation to be found in automotive dynamics literature (see (Mysliwetz, 1990))

$$\dot{\beta} = -2K\beta + \left(\frac{V}{a} - K\right)\lambda \tag{18.29}$$

with $K = k_r/(mV)$, $k_r =$ tire lateral force coefficient (150 kN/rad), $m =$ vehicle mass (4000 kg), $V =$ actual vehicle speed, $a =$ distance between front and rear axis (3.5 m) [numbers in brackets refer to our test vehicle **VaMoRs**, a Daimler-Benz van L 508 D].

The steer angle is set by a stepping motor, the dynamic behavior of which is roughly modeled as an integrator

$$\dot{\lambda} = k_\lambda U. \tag{18.30}$$

Collecting these relations a linear, velocity-dependent fourth order state model results

$$\dot{\lambda} = k_\lambda U$$

$$\dot{\beta} = -2K\beta + (\frac{V}{a} - K)\lambda$$
$$\dot{y}_V = V(\psi_V + \beta)$$
$$\dot{\psi}_V = \frac{V}{a}\lambda - VC_{0h},$$

or in matrix-vector notation

$$\dot{\mathbf{x}}_V = \mathbf{A}_V\mathbf{x}_V + \mathbf{b}_V U + \mathbf{b}_C C_{0h} \qquad (18.31)$$

where

$$\mathbf{A}_V = \begin{bmatrix} 0 & 0 & 0 & 0 \\ b_F & a_F & 0 & 0 \\ 0 & V & 0 & V \\ c_F & 0 & 0 & 0 \end{bmatrix} ; \ \mathbf{x}_V = \begin{bmatrix} \lambda \\ \beta \\ y_V \\ \psi_V \end{bmatrix} ; \ \mathbf{b}_V = \begin{bmatrix} k_\lambda \\ 0 \\ 0 \\ 0 \end{bmatrix} ; \ \mathbf{b}_C = \begin{bmatrix} 0 \\ 0 \\ 0 \\ -V \end{bmatrix}$$

with the elements $c_F = V/a$, $b_F = c_F - K$ and $a_F = -2K$.

These equations represent knowledge about the lateral motion behavior of a road vehicle under normal driving conditions. The first term on the right hand side of eq. (18.31) gives the state transition under zero control and curvature input; the second term indicates, that control action just turns the steering wheel which then through the first column in matrix $\mathbf{A}_V$ affects the slip angle β and the heading angle ψ after integration. The third term gives the influence of road curvature on the heading change relative to the road.

In the automotive literature much more elaborate motion models can be found, leading to system descriptions of more than twentieth order; they contain vehicle pitch, yaw and roll and the wheel suspension dynamics individually for each wheel. In our applications we are more interested in the basic trajectory dynamics in order, first, to reduce the search space for the evaluation of the next image, given the results of the previous evaluations, and secondly to reduce the combinatorial explosion of feature aggregation by exploiting basic temporal continuity conditions. Depending on the special task to be performed, some expansions of the model, for example for the inclusion of pitching motion, may be advantageous in the future.

18.5.9 The combined dynamical model for road recognition

The overall dynamical model for road and relative lateral state recognition consists of the two subsystems: 1. for the lateral dynamics of the vehicle, and 2. for the horizontal curvature dynamics. The following first order system with seven state components describes the differential equation constraints for guiding the interpretation exploiting knowledge about temporal processes in the real world. It can be seen that the two subsystems in the continuous form are almost completely decoupled; only the horizontal road curvature affects the lateral vehicle dynamics.

$$\begin{bmatrix} \dot{\lambda} \\ \dot{\beta} \\ \dot{y}_V \\ \dot{\psi}_V \\ \hline \dot{C}_{0hm} \\ \dot{C}_{1hm} \\ \dot{C}_{1h} \end{bmatrix} = \left[\begin{array}{cccc|ccc} 0 & 0 & 0 & 0 & 0 & 0 & 0 \\ b_F & a_F & 0 & 0 & 0 & 0 & 0 \\ 0 & V & 0 & V & 0 & 0 & 0 \\ c_F & 0 & 0 & 0 & -V & 0 & 0 \\ \hline 0 & 0 & 0 & 0 & 0 & V & 0 \\ 0 & 0 & 0 & 0 & 0 & -3\frac{V}{L} & 3\frac{V}{L} \\ 0 & 0 & 0 & 0 & 0 & 0 & 0 \end{array}\right] \begin{bmatrix} \lambda \\ \beta \\ y_V \\ \psi_V \\ C_{0hm} \\ C_{1hm} \\ C_{1h} \end{bmatrix}$$

$$+ \begin{bmatrix} k_\lambda \\ 0 \\ 0 \\ 0 \\ 0 \\ 0 \\ 0 \end{bmatrix} u_\lambda + \begin{bmatrix} 0 \\ 0 \\ 0 \\ 0 \\ 0 \\ 0 \\ n_{c1h} \end{bmatrix}. \qquad (18.32)$$

For sampled data systems in digital control with sampling period T, the corresponding state transition matrices and the control effect coefficient vector can be obtained by standard methods in systems dynamics theory (details are given in (Mysliwetz, 1990)). It should be noted, that most of the coefficients depend on vehicle speed. Since the recursive estimation technique requires linear models, the equations are locally linearized around the actual reference point.

18.5.10 Obstacle recognition

A second group of processors can be activated in parallel to group one for road recognition, in order to pick up and track features of an obstacle detected on the road. The detection process works with a long horizontal 16×256 pixel window in a line region in the image corresponding to the desired obstacle detection distance. This subprocess looks for inhomogeneities in the region evaluated and has been described in (Solder & Graefe, 1990). If an obstacle candidate has been detected, a second process is invoked searching in the same area with different feature extractors for groups of features indicative of an obstacle with upper/lower and left/right pairs of horizontal respectively vertical edge features (Regensburger & Graefe, 1990). If both processes find a likely candidate over several frames, a third process for spatio-temporal interpretation is invoked while the detection process stops working. The spatial interpretation process uses monocular motion stereo and the same 4D-approach as for road parameter and egomotion state estimation relative to the road (previous section).

Windows 5 to 8 in figure 18.4 may be evaluated by just one processor if the interpretation cycle time is set to 40 ms or more. 25 Hz interpretation rate is considered fast enough for speeds up to 100 km/h ($\approx$ 30 m/s). Since the information is most important for proper reaction, to know where on the road the obstacle is situated, windows 9 and 10 are placed to track the road boundaries at the point where the obstacle touches the road. This information may be fused with the road model derived from group 1. Sometimes, the road itself and the lower features of the obstacle cannot be seen due to occlusions. In this case, windows 5 to 7 allow us to track the object initially until the road becomes visible during the approach.

In the experiments, six PPs Intel 8086 and one GPP 80386/87 have been used. The window size was 48×48 pixel. For obstacle tracking, only vertical and horizontal line elements have been used as features, coordinated in a cross-like pattern. Four candidate feature positions for each real feature have been passed to the higher interpretation level. Using thresholds around the predicted feature position, a model driven measurement selection has been implemented. In the following subsections, the 4D model components are discussed in turn.

18.5.11 Geometric model

This model combines the geometric properties of the scene (road and obstacle) with the laws of perspective projection in order to describe the positions of relevant scene features in the image as a function of the relative spatial state. The obstacle is modeled as a 2D object having vertical and horizontal contour outlines at the horizontal and vertical position of the centroid.

Figure 18.11 shows the coordinate systems and terms used for state description. Given parameters are the camera elevation h_K above the ground plane, its focal length f, the camera mapping parameters K_y, K_z and the width of the road b_R.

The road is assumed to be planar. In figure 18.12 the image geometry for scene analysis is given. The obstacle touches the ground in image line z_{BOu}. If the vertical viewing direction and the camera elevation above the ground are known, this datum is directly related to the distance in the assumed planar case. However, if the road width is known from the road vision group, the two feature positions of the left (y_{BRl}) and right (y_{BRr}) road boundary also yield a distance measurement. Half the sum of y_{BRl} and y_{BRr} yields the direction to the road centerline at the position of the obstacle. The lateral position of the obstacle is at $(y_{BOl} + y_{BOr})/2 = y_{BOS}$. The obstacle width relative to the road is obtained immediately from the difference

$$\frac{y_{BOr} - y_{BOl}}{y_{BRr} - y_{BRl}} = \frac{b_O}{b}. \tag{18.33}$$

Similarly the obstacle height is obtained from the z-components. By assuming a constant width-to-height ratio for the obstacle the interpretation may be further stabilized.

Except for inferencing using knowledge about the world as indicated above, no direct distance measurement is taken. However, since the ve-

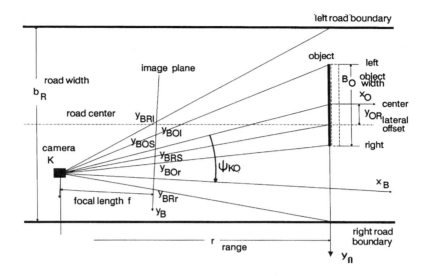

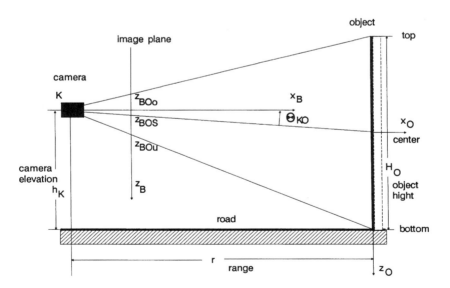

Figure 18.11
Measurement and relative state variables camera to object; (upper figure) top down view,
(lower figure) side view.

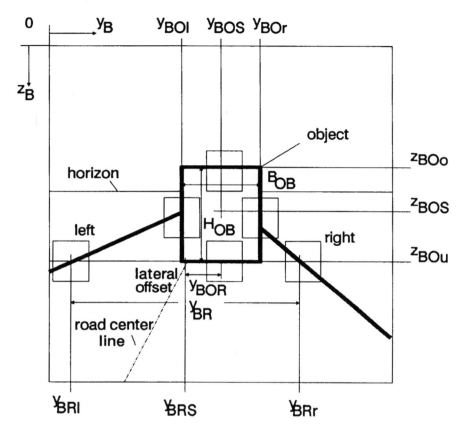

Figure 18.12
Feature based obstacle recognition, nomenclature.

hicle has an odometer, distances to a stationary object can be derived over
time using the dynamical model for egomotion. For moving obstacles, this
approach has been developed to determine the motion parameters for these
objects by recursive relative state estimation.

18.5.12 The dynamical model for relative state estimation

Of prime interest are the range r and the range rate $\dot{r} = v_r$ to the obstacle;
the former is the integral of the latter. Then, the lateral motion of the object
relative to the road v_{OR} is important for deriving the proper reaction for the
own vehicle. Since the control inputs to the observed object are not known
in general, they are modeled by stochastic disturbance variables s_i. This

yields the dynamical model

$$\dot{r} = v_O - v + s_r; \qquad \dot{y}_{OR} = v_{OR}$$
$$\dot{v}_O = s_{vO}; \qquad \dot{v}_{OR} = s_{yOR}. \tag{18.34}$$

In addition, for determining the obstacle size and the viewing direction relative to the road centerline at the distance of the obstacle, the following four state variables are added

$$\dot{H}_O = s_{HO} \qquad \dot{\psi}_{KO} = s_{\psi KO}$$
$$\dot{B}_O = s_{BO} \qquad \dot{\Theta}_{KO} = s_{\Theta KO} \tag{18.35}$$

where again the s_i are assumed to be unknown Gaussian random noise. In shorthand vector notation these eqs are written in the form of equation 18.31 with the state variables

$$\mathbf{x}^\top = (r, v_O, \psi_{KO}, \Theta_{KO}, B_O, H_O, y_{OR}, v_{OR}).$$

After transformation into discrete state transition form, the standard methods for state estimation are applied (see e.g. (Wuensche, 1986; Wuensche, 1988)).

18.6 System integration

Replicating the left processor group in figure 18.4 n times for n objects to be tracked, also requires the upper levels to be expanded. In a usual road scene, there may be several lanes (to be tracked by one more powerful road recognition group, right part in figure 18.4) and several independently moving objects on each lane.

In order to be able to understand situations correctly, the functional module M4 had to be expanded into a knowledge processing multiprocessor system as shown in the upper half of figure 18.13. This is being implemented at present on a transputer network added to the system. From each of the "2D object processor" feature extraction groups, there is a transputer link into the network for parallel data-communication between the higher and the lower levels. The 4D object processors are all T800-transputers at present. Once transputers had been integrated into the system, they also started to take over lower level functions. Therefore, the system is likely to become an all-transputer system in the near future.

Feature extraction and its control from the higher levels has remained unchanged, in essence. For the task of 4D object recognition, specialists for certain classes of objects have emerged (4D-OP, formerly GPP); at this level, time is introduced into the interpretation process and exploited for avoiding the combinatorial explosion during feature aggregation to objects. A large amount of implicit knowledge about the appearance of real world objects in perspective images is coded at this level.

	activity level	processors	operation	result
scene understanding	control level	MPS	compute expectations ⌐↓ control viewing direction apply vehicle control	→ action ⌐↓
	↑		↑	
	task level	MPS	relative goal state ←⌐ evaluation	→ planning, decisions
	↑		↑	↑
	object level	MPS	→ situation assessment ←⌐ parameter adaption	→ situation ←
state estimation	↑		↑	↑
	feature level	4D-OP	→ feature aggregation	→ objects in ← space/time
	↑		↑	↑
	pel level	PP	→ feature extraction	→ features in ←⌐ image plane

Figure 18.13
Modular processing structure for complex tasks.

A dynamical object data base collecting all information on actual objects constitutes the interface to the higher levels. There, the situation is assessed taking the own task into account; decisions are being made whether to continue with the control mode running or to switch to a different maneuver element. Note that though these high levels do not directly act on the controls there is a special control level implemented which closes the loop. In order to incur as little time delay as possible in the actuation process, feedback control works directly upon data in the dynamical data base. This way, the higher levels are somewhat decoupled from direct actuation, alleviating them from hard cycle time constraints. The control output is, however, fed back to all internal state representation and prediction instances in order to compute corresponding expectations.

Figure 18.14 shows an overall block diagram which better indicates the signal flow in the system. The inner core represents the lower two levels and the uppermost one of figure 18.13. The shaded areas implement the recursive estimation and single step prediction of object center of gravity states (engineering type methods) while the "geometric reasoning" block (lower right center) adds the shape aspects. Together with the peripheral functions (outer inverted U-shape) this might be called the artificial intelligence parts of the system.

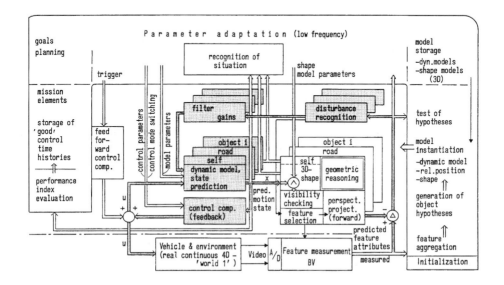

Block diagram of dynamic vision; control oriented AI
(4D prediction error minimization)

Figure 18.14
Block Diagram.

Initialisation (right bar in figure 18.14) is achieved by matching feature groups with projections of an hypothesized object. Three ingredients are always necessary for instantiation of an object model: the dynamical model for the temporal evolution of motion, the shape model for feature distribution around the center of the body, and the aspect conditions for computing the perspective projection. The generic object models will be kept in an object data base under development (upper right corner).

The upper bar of the inverted U in figure 18.14 represents the real-time monitoring and decision making part of the system. If prediction errors (arrow upwards between the inner and outer blocks) are consistently large, object hypotheses will have to be adjusted; this may be done by parameter changes or by switching to a completely different model. In (Schick & Dickmanns, 1991; Schick, 1992) a method has been presented which allows us to perform the parameter adjustment for known generic objects in a recursive way similar to and with the same methods as for state estimation.

Since the scene is time varying and new features belonging to yet unknown objects may occur, a steady monitoring has to be done in order to detect those and to come up with proper object hypotheses. In ambivalent cases, several object hypotheses may have to be started in parallel; they will be pruned over time when enough information has been collected for dropping the less likely ones.

The main task of the situation recognition level is to trigger proper use of the generic control procedures in the inner block for transforming measurements into actuator outputs. This may be done by either feedback or feedforward modes. The regulatory control tasks like lane keeping and convoy driving are realized by state feedback (lowest shaded block); maneuvering control tasks like lane change and turning off are realized by parameterized feedforward control time histories (block attached to the right of the left vertical bar in figure 18.14). All control outputs are sent to both the real-world vehicle and the internal models (lower center left).

The left vertical bar is reserved for future autonomous learning capabilities based on state time histories experienced (lower input), caused by control time history inputs (attached block to the right) both evaluated in conjunction with respect to some performance index (goal function for mission elements). More information on the intelligent control aspects may be found in (Dickmanns, 1991).

18.7   Experimental results

The approach described above has matured during half a decade of experimentation with three experimental vehicles: 1. VaMoRs, our experimental vehicle for autonomous mobility and machine vision, a 5-ton van; 2. a 10-ton bus of Daimler-Benz, our industry partner in the framework of the German information technology program for "Autonomous Mobile Systems" (BMFT), and 3. VITA, an autonomous vehicle of Daimler-Benz AG in the EUREKA project PROMETHEUS. Different sets of computers have been used over the years; in (Dickmanns & Graefe, 1988b; Dickmanns & Graefe, 1988a) the development of the custom made image sequence processing systems BVV_i has been sketched. Recent developments are tending towards Transputer hardware for easy expandability and, in the meantime, video-busses have become standard .

Inexpensive PC-type computers have always been used for the higher levels: initially, one PC based on the Intel 80286 microprocessor in addition to the BVV_2 with 8086 single board computers sufficed for guiding VaMoRs at its maximum speed of 96 km/h on an empty Autobahn in 1987 exploiting the 4D approach. Only through the powerful and intelligent interpretation constraints introduced by the integrated spatio-temporal models has it been possible to achieve these results with the low computing power on board.

Since 1989 the Intel 80386 single board computer has been introduced on an intermediate hierarchical level in the BVV_2 (Dickmanns & Mysliwetz, 1992) resulting in a much more robust road recognition under strongly perturbed environmental conditions through shadows of trees; here, the newly introduced "Gestalt"-idea of perspectively mapped curved roads was essential for achieving the performance level demonstrated.

At this stage, the module for obstacle recognition has also been introduced forming a second processor group as shown in figure 18.4 (see (Dickmanns & Christians, 1989)).

In 1991 all application software developed up to that point in different computer languages was translated into C and ported onto transputers. In a transition phase, both BVV_3 and transputers are used jointly.

Since 1984 active viewing direction control has been applied in the framework of our vision systems (Mysliwetz, 1984). In 1986 it has been implemented for better recognition of curved roads (Mysliwetz & Dickmanns, 1986). The microprocessor for viewing direction control is since integrated in the BVV_2. Especially with the introduction of a bifocal camera pair for better resolution further away this automatic viewing direction control became essential.

The performance level achieved and demonstrated at the PROMETHEUS-display at Torino in September 1991 encompasses the following capabilities of the autonomous vehicles:

1. lane keeping on roads with heavy shadows from trees under hard sunshine conditions; speed adjustment to road curvature in order not to exceed a preset lateral acceleration limit (for example 0.2 Earth-g)

2. driving at night with normal headlights switched on

3. detection of obstacles at distances up to about 90 m; monocular distance estimation through motion stereo (an inherent property of the 4D-approach) with sufficient accuracy up to about 50 m (with 25 mm focal length; the introduction of inertial gaze stabilization will allow greater focal lengths with correspondingly improved viewing ranges)

4. stopping in front of an obstacle at a preset distance from speeds up to 50 km/h

5. convoy driving behind another vehicle at a speed-dependent distance (2 seconds rule)

6. "stop-and-go" maneuvers behind a preceding vehicle utilising the capabilities quoted above

7. lane changes to the left and right triggered by the human operator who has to take care for other vehicles in the neighboring lanes.

With the increased computing power available on board, work is now under progress for coping simultaneously with several other objects and for recognizing object classes from more detailed spatial shape understanding under changing aspect conditions.

18.8   Other application areas

The same basic method, the expectation-based dynamic scene understanding 4D approach, has been applied to four more task domains over the last decade:

1.   balancing of an inverted pendulum on an electro-cart (Meissner & Dickmanns, 1983).

2.   reaction jet controlled autonomous vehicle docking (satellite model plant) (Wuensche, 1986).

3.   autonomous landing approach of aircraft (Eberl, 1987; Dickmanns, 1988; Schell, 1992).

4.   landmark navigation for autonomously guided vehicles (AGV) on the factory floor (Hock, 1991).

The complete spatial state estimation of a real aircraft (Dornier Do 128 twin turboprop of the Technical University of Braunschweig) relative to a rectangular landing strip from more than 1 km distance till close to touchdown has been the most complex task solved up to now. All six state variables of both the longitudinal and the lateral degrees of freedom (12 in total) have been estimated with 60 ms cycle time (16.67 Hz) using only a BVV_2 and one PC 386. Figure 18.15 shows the image areas tracked. Since space does not permit further details here, the interested reader is referred to (Schell, 1992).

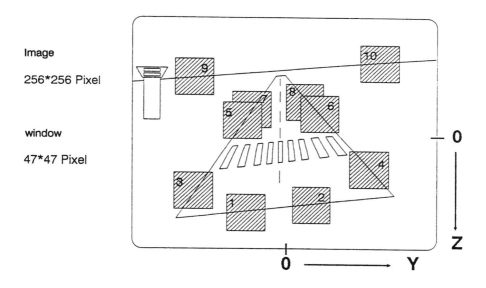

Figure 18.15
Tracked and evaluated image areas in the landing approach experiments. Image: 256×256 Pixel, Window: 47×47 Pixel.

Acknowledgements

Chapter 1: Terzopoulos and Szeliski

This research was supported by Digital Equipment Corporation and the Natural Sciences and Engineering Research Council of Canada. DT thanks Dimitri Metaxas for valuable discussions.

Chapter 2: Yuille and Hallinan

We acknowledge the financial support of the NSF for Grant No. IRI-9002141 and of DARPA for contract AFOSR-89-0506. We have benefitted greatly from the help and advice of members of the Harvard Robotics Group, especially Professor David Mumford. We also appreciate ideas and comments from Carsten Peterson, Mattias Ohlsson and Ko Honda.

Chapter 3: Curwen and Blake

We acknowledge the financial support of the SERC and of the EEC Esprit programme. We have benefitted greatly from the help and advice of members of the Robotics Research Group, University of Oxford, especially M. Brady, R. Cipolla, Z. Xie and A. Zisserman.

Chapter 5: Terzopoulos and Metaxas

This research was supported by the Natural Sciences and Engineering Research Council of Canada. The authors thank Richard Szeliski for valuable discussions.

Chapter 6: Rao

Part of this work was the result of a collaboration between Oxford University Robotics Research Group and British Aerospace Sowerby Research Centre, Bristol.

Chapter 7: Crisman

Much of the work presented here was completed while the author was at Carnegie Mellon University. We wish to thank Dr. Charles E. Thorpe and Dr. Takeo Kanade at Carnegie Mellon University who supervised the Navlab project. We would also like to thank the numerous members of the Navlab and related projects at Carnegie Mellon, without whom this work would not have been possible. This research was supported by the DARPA Road Following contracts DACA 76-89-C-0014 and DACA 76-85-C-0003.

Chapter 8: Brown, Coombs and Soong

This material is based upon work supported by the National Science Foundation under Grants numbered IRI-8903582, CDA-8822724, and IRI-89220771.

Chapter 9: Clark and Ferrier

The mechanical components of the Harvard Head system were designed and constructed by J. Page, W. Labossier, and M. Cohn, with input from R. Brockett, J. Clark and E. Rak. M. Cohn reverse engineered the Canon electronic focus controls (details can be found in (Ferrier, 1991)). The electronics for the motor drivers and associated systems was put together by J. Page. Software for the motion control systems was written by N. Ferrier, and P. Newman. Software for the visual processing modules was written by N. Ferrier with some assistance from M. Lee and E. Rak. Ideas and enthusiasm concerning the development of the head and its motion control were supplied in great abundance by R. Brockett. The authors would like to thank J. Daugman for bringing to our attention some of the psychophysiological work concerning attention.

This research was supported in part by the Office of Naval Research under grant N0014-84-K0504, the NSF University of Maryland/Harvard University Systems Research Center funded through grant CDR-88-03012, and by the Harvard-MIT-Brown Center for Intelligent Control Systems.

Chapter 10: Murray, Du, McLauchlan, Reid, Sharkey and Brady

This work has been funded by SERC Project GR/G30003 and EC Esprit Project 5390. We have benefited greatly from timely help and advice from other members of the Robotics Research Group, University of Oxford, Andrew Blake, Ron Daniel, Andrew Zisserman, Han Wang, Philip Torr and Rupert Curwen; and from discussions with European collaborators Thierry Viéville and Donald Weir. We express our gratitude to GEC Research for permission to include Figure 10.2.

Chapter 11: Blake, Zisserman and Cipolla

We acknowledge the financial support of the SERC and of the EEC Esprit programme. We have benefitted greatly from the help and advice of members of the Robotics Research Group at Oxford, especially M. Brady, A. Cox and Z. Xie.

Chapter 12: Cipolla and Blake

We acknowledge discussions with Professor Mike Brady, Kenichi Kanatani, Christopher Longuet-Higgins, and Andrew Zisserman. This work was partially funded by Esprit BRA 3274 (FIRST) and the SERC. Roberto Cipolla also gratefully acknowledges the support of the IBM UK Scientific Centre, St. Hugh's College, Oxford and the Toshiba Research and Development Center, Japan.

Chapter 13: Prescott and Mayhew

This work was supported by the Science and Engineering Research Council Grant 89317044. We wish to thank Neil Thacker, John Porrill, and John Frisby for their help and advice.

Chapter 14: Rimey and Brown

Peter von Kaenel worked on the Hough transform for circles and is currently building the modules that match models using straight lines. He also built several of the visual actions.

This material is based upon work supported by the National Science Foundation under Grants numbered IRI-8920771 and IRI-8903582. The Government has certain rights in this material.

Chapter 15: Rygol, Pollard, Brown and Mayhew

Grateful thanks are due to the AIVRU vision community, especially P. Courtney, J. P. Frisby, J. E. W. Mayhew, J. Porrill, T. Pridmore and N. Thacker.

This research was supported by SERC grant no. GR/E 64497 awarded to Professors J. E. W. Mayhew and J. P. Frisby under the ACME programme in collaboration with GEC Hirst Research Centre.

Chapter 16: Harris

The DROID 3D vision system has been developed at Roke Manor Research, currently with the aid of Esprit funding in the VOILA project, P2502.

Chapter 17: Ayache, Cohen and Herlin

Part of this work was partially supported by Digital Equipment Corporation, and by a MS2I-Matra Contract. The authors wish to aknowledge Gabriel Pelle (at Inserm, CHU Henri Mondor, France) for providing the ultrasound data and for helpful discussions, as well as L. Cohen who contributed actively to the work on active contours. Also, Andre Guéziec provided the programs to compute the curvature on digital curves, and P. Sulger implemented the point tracking algorithm. Finally Bob Hummel made extremely valuable comments on the first part of this work.

Chapter 18: Dickmanns

Part of this work has been externally funded by the Federal Ministry of Research and Technology (BMFT), the industrial partner Daimler Benz AG and the German Science Foundation DFG. Major contributions to the state of development are due to the Ph.D. students H. G. Meissner, H. J. Wünsche, A. Zapp, B. Mysliwetz, G. Eberl and R. Schnell. Over many years, the cooperation with my colleague V. Graefe and his students G. Haas, K. Kuhnert, U. Regensburger, U. Solder has advanced image sequence processing hardware and feature extraction methods.

References

Abbott, A. L. and Ahuja, N. (1988). Surface reconstruction by dynamic integration of focus, camera vergence, and stereo. In *Proceedings: International Conference on Computer Vision*. IEEE.

Agogino, A. M. and Ramamurthi, K. (1990). Real time influence diagrams for monitoring and controlling mechanical systems. In Oliver, R. M. and Smith, J. Q., editors, *Influence Diagrams, Belief Nets and Decision Analysis*, 199–228. John Wiley and Sons.

Agosta, J. M. (1990). The structure of Bayes networks for visual recognition. In *Uncertainty in AI*, 397–405. North-Holland.

Cameron,A.J. and Durrant-Whyte,H. (1990). A bayesian approach to optimal sensor placement. *Int. J. Robotics Research* **9**(5), 70–88.

Albus, J. S. (1971). A theory of cerebellar function. *Math Biosci* **10**, 25–61.

Aloimonos, J., Weiss, I., and Bandyopadhyay, A. (1987). Active vision. In *Proc. 1st Int. Conf. on Computer Vision*, 35–54.

Amini, A., Owen, R., Staib, L., Anandan, P., and Duncan, J. (1991). *Non-rigid motion models for tracking the left ventricular wall*. Lecture notes in computer science: Information processing in medical images. Springer-Verlag.

Amini, A. A., Weymouth, T. E., and Jain, R. C. (1990). Using dynamic programming for solving variational problems in vision. *IEEE Trans. Pattern Analysis and Machine Intell.* **12**(9), 855–867.

Anderson, R. (1988). *The design of ping-pong playing robot*. MIT Press, Cambridge.

Arbogast, E. and Mohr, R. (1990). 3D structure inference from images sequences. In Baird, H. S., editor, *Proceedings of the Syntactical and Structural Pattern Recognition Workshop*, 21–37, Murray-Hill, NJ.

Ayache, N., Boissonat, J. D., Brunet, E., Cohen, L. D., Chièze, J. P., Geiger, B., Monga, O., Rocchisani, J. M., and Sander, P. (1989). Building highly structured volume representations in 3D medical images. In *Proc. 3rd Symposium Computer Assisted Radiology*, 765–772, Berlin.

Ayache, N., Boissonnat, J. D., Cohen, L., Geiger, B., Levy-Vehel, J., Monga, O., and Sander, P. (1990). Steps toward the automatic interpretation of 3D images. In K. Hohne, H. F. and Pizer, S., editors, *3D Imaging in Medicine*, 107–120. NATO ASI Series, Springer-Verlag.

Ayache, N. and Faugeras, O. (1987). Registrating and fusing noisy visual maps. In *Proc. 1st Int. Conf. on Computer Vision*, 73–82.

Ballard, D. H. (1991). Animate vision. *Artificial Intelligence* **48**, 57–86.

Ballard, D. H. and Brown, C. M. (1982). *Computer Vision*. Prentice-Hall, Englewood Cliffs, New Jersey.

Ballard, D. H. and Ozcandarli, A. (1988). Eye fixation and early vision: kinetic depth. In *Proceedings of the 2nd International Conference on Computer Vision*, 524–531, Tampa, FL. IEEE Computer Society Press, Washington DC.

Bar-Shalom, Y. (1990). *Multi-Target Multi-Sensor Tracking*. Artec House.

Bar-Shalom, Y. and Fortmann, T. E. (1988). *Tracking and Data Association*. Academic Press.

Bartels, R. H., Beatty, J. C., and Barsky, B. A. (1987). *An Introduction to the Use of Splines in Computer Graphics and Geometric Modeling*. Morgan Kaufmann, Los Altos, CA.

Barto, A. G., Sutton, R. S., and Anderson, C. W. (1983). Neuronlike adaptive elements that can solve difficult learning control problems. *IEEE Transactions on Systems, Man, and Cybernbetics* **SMC-13**, 834–846.

Barto, A. G., Sutton, R. S., and Watkins, C. J. H. C. (1990). Learning and sequential decision making. In Moore, J. W. and Gabriel, M., editors, *Learning and Computational*

Neuroscience. MIT Press, Cambridge, MA.

Bathe, K.-J. and Wilson, E. L. (1976). *Numerical Methods in Finite Element Analysis.* Prentice-Hall, Inc., Englewood Cliffs, NJ.

Baumgarte, J. (1972). Stabilization of constraints and integrals of motion in dynamical systems. *Computer Methods in Applied Mechanics and Engineering* **1**, 1–16.

Beck, J. and Ambler, B. (1973). The effects of concentrated and distributed attention on peripheral acuity. *Perception and Psychophysics* **14**, 225–230.

Bennett, A. and Craw, I. (1991). Finding image features for deformable templates and detailed prior statistical knowledge. In Mowforth, P., editor, *Proc. British Machine Vision Conference*, 233–239, Glasgow. Springer-Verlag, London.

Berger, M.-O. (1990). Snake growing. In Faugeras, O., editor, *Proc. First European Conf. on Computer Vision*, 570–572, Antibes, France.

Bergholm, F. (1989). Motion from flow along contours: a note on robustness and ambiguous case. *Int. Journal of Computer Vision* **3**, 395–415.

Besag, J. (1974). Spatial interaction and statistical analysis of lattice systems. *J. Roy. Stat. Soc. Lond. B.* **36**, 192–225.

Besl, P. and Jain, R. (1982). Segmentation through variable-order surface fitting. *IEEE Trans. Pattern Analysis and Machine Intell.* **10**(2), 167–192.

Bierman, E. J. (1975). Measurement updating using the U-D factorization. In *Proc. IEEE Control and Decision Conf.*, 337–346, Houston, TX.

Bierman, E. J. (1977). *Factorization Methods for Discrete Sequential Estimation.* Academic Press, New York.

Blake, A. (1992). Computational modelling of hand-eye coordination. *Phil. Trans. Royal Soc. London* in press.

Blake, A., Brady, J. M., Cipolla, R., Xie, Z., and Zisserman, A. (1991). Visual navigation around curved obstacles. In *Proc. IEEE Int. Conf. Robotics and Automation*, volume 3, 2490–2499.

Blake, A. and Bulthoff, H. (1991). Shape from specularities: Computation and psychophysics. *Phil. Trans. Royal Soc. London* **331**, 237–252.

Blake, A. and Cipolla, R. C. (1990). Robust estimation of surface curvature from deformation of apparent contours. In Faugeras, O., editor, *Proc. 1st European Conference on Computer Vision*, 465–474. Springer–Verlag.

Blake, A. and Zisserman, A. (1987). *Visual Reconstruction.* MIT Press, Cambridge, USA.

Bogert, B. P., Healy, M. J. R., and Tukey, J. W. (1963). The quefrency alanysis of time series for echoes: Cepstrum, pseudo-autoco variance, cross-cepstrum, and saphe cracking. In Rosenblatt, M., editor, *Proc. Symp. Time Series Analysis*, 209–243, New York. John Wiley and Sons.

Bolle, R. M., Califano, A., and Kjeldsen, R. (1990). Data and model driven foveation. In *Proceedings: IEEE International Conference on Pattern Recognition*, 1–7.

Bolles, R. C. (1977). Verification vision for programmable assembly. In *Proceedings: International Joint Conference on Artificial Intelligence*, 569–575.

Bolles, R. C., Baker, H. H., and Marimont, D. H. (1987). Epipolar-plane image analysis: An approach to determining structure. *International Journal of Computer Vision* **1**, 7–55.

Bolles, R. C., Horaud, P., and Hannah, M. J. (1983). 3DPO: A three dimensional part orientation system. *Procs. IJCAI* **9**, 116–120.

Bookstein, F. L. (1989). Principal warps: Thin-plate splines and the decomposition of deformations. *IEEE Transactions on Pattern Analysis and Machine Intelligence* **PAMI-11**(6), 567–585.

Brady, J. M. (1987). Seeds of perception. In *Proc. 3rd Alvey Vision Conference*, 259–266.

Braitenberg, V. (1986). *Vehicles: experiments in synthetic psychology*. MIT Press, Cambridge, MA.

Bray, A. J. (1989). Tracking objects using image disparities. In *Proceedings of the Alvey Vision Conference*, 79–84.

Brockett, R. W. (1988). On the computer control of movement. In *Proceedings of the 1988 IEEE Robotics and Automation Conference*, Philadelphia.

Broida, T. J. and Chellappa, R. (1986). Kinematics and structure of a rigid object from a sequence of noisy images. In *Proc. Workshop on Motion: Representation and Analysis*, 95–100. IEEE.

Brooks, R. A. (1983). Solving path planning by representation of freespace. *IEEE Trans. Sys. Man. Cyb.* **13**, 190–197.

Brown, C. M. (1989). Gaze controls with interactions and delays. In *Image Understanding Workshop*, 200–218, Palo Alto, CA. Morgan Kaufmann.

Brown, C. M. (1990a). Gaze control with interactions and delays. *IEEE Trans. Sys. Man and Cyb* **63**, 61–70.

Brown, C. M. (1990b). Prediction and cooperation in gaze control. *Biological Cybernetics* **63**, 61–70.

Brown, C. M. and Coombs, D. J. (1991). Notes on control with delay. Technical Report TR 387, University of Rochester, Computer Science Department.

Brown, C. M. and Rimey, R. (1988). Kinematics, coordinate systems and conversions for the rochester robot. Technical Report 255, University of Rochester.

Brown, C. R. and Rygol, M. (1989). MARVIN: Multiprocessor architecture for vision. In *Applying Transputer Based Parallel Machines*. Proceedings oUG-10.

Brown, C. R. and Rygol, M. (1990). An environment for the development of large applications in Parallel C. In *Applications of Transputers 2*. IOS Press. Proceedings Transputer Applications.

Buda, A. J., Delp, E. J., Meyer, J. M., Jenkins, J. M., Smith, D. N., Bookstein, F. L., and Pitt, B. (1983). Automatic computer processing of digital 2-dimensional echocardiograms. *Amer. J. Cardiol.* **51**, 383–389.

Burr, D. and Ross, J. (1986). Visual processing of motion. *Trends in Neuroscience* **9**.

Burr, D. J. (1981). Elastic matching of line drawings. *IEEE Trans. Pattern Analysis and Machine Intell.* **PAMI-3**(6), 708–713.

Burt, P. J. (1988). Smart sensing within a pyramid vision machine. *IEEE Proceedings* **76**(8), 1006–1015.

Campani, M. and Verri, A. (1990). Computing optical flow from an overconstrained system of linear algebraic equations. In *Proc. 3rd Int. Conf. on Computer Vision*, 22–26.

Canny, J. (1986). A computational approach to edge detection. *IEEE Trans. Pattern Analysis and Machine Intell.* **PAMI-8**(6), 679–698.

Carlbom, I., Terzopoulos, D., and Harris, K. M. (1991). Reconstructing and visualizing models of neuronal dendrites. In Patrikalakis, N. M., editor, *Scientific Visualization of Physical Phenomena*, 623–638. Springer-Verlag, New York.

Carpenter, R. H. S. (1988). *Movements of the Eyes*. Pion.

Charniak, E. and McDermott, D. (1985). *Artificial Intelligence*. Addison-Wesley.

Chou, P. B. and Brown, C. M. (1990). The theory and practice of Bayesian image labeling. *Int. Journal of Computer Vision* **4**(3), 185–210.

Choudhary, A. N., Das, S., Ahuja, N., and Patel, J. H. (1990). A reconfigurable and hierarchical parallel processing architecture: Performance results for stereo vision. In *Proceedings IEEE 10th International Conference on Pattern Recognition*, volume 2, 389–

383.

Ciarlet, P. G. (1987). *The finite element methods for elliptic problems*. NORTH-HOLLAND.

Cipolla, R. (1991). *Active Visual Inference of Surface Shape*. PhD thesis, University of Oxford.

Cipolla, R. and Blake, A. (1990). The dynamic analysis of apparent contours. In *Proc. Third International Conference on Computer Vision*, 616–623, Osaka.

Clark, J. J. and Ferrier, N. J. (1988). Modal control of an attentive vision system. In *Proceedings of the 2nd International Conference on Computer Vision*, 514–523, Tampa, FL. IEEE Computer Society Press.

Clark, J. J. and Yuille, A. (1990). *Data Fusion For Sensory Information Processing Systems*. Kluwer Academic Publishers, Boston.

Cohen, I., Ayache, N., and Sulger, P. (1992a). Tracking points on deformables objects. In *Proceedings of the Second European Conference on Computer Vision*, Santa Margherita Ligure, Italy.

Cohen, I., Ayache, N., and Sulger, P. (1992b). Tracking points on deformables objects. Technical report, INRIA.

Cohen, I., Cohen, L. D., and Ayache., N. (1992c). Using deformable surfaces to segment 3D images and infer differential structures. *Computer Vision, Graphics, and Image Processing*.

Cohen, L. D. (1991). On active contour models and balloons. *CVGIP: Image Understanding* 53(2), 211–218.

Cohen, L. D. and Cohen, I. (1990). A finite element method applied to new active contour models and 3D reconstruction from cross sections. In *Proc. Third International Conference on Computer Vision*, 587–591. IEEE Computer Society Conference. Osaka, Japan.

Collewijn, H. and Tamminga, E. (1984). Human smooth and saccadic eye movements during voluntary pursuit of different target motions on different backgrounds. *Journal of Physiology* 351, 217–250.

Coombs, D. J. (1991). *Real-time gaze holding in binocular robot vision*. PhD thesis, University of Rochester.

Coombs, D. J. and Brown, C. M. (1991). Cooperative gaze holding in binocular vision. *IEEE Control Systems Magazine*.

Courant, R. and Hilbert, D. (1953). *Methods of Mathematical Physics*, volume I. Interscience, New York.

Cox, I. J. and Leonard, J. J. (1991). Probabilistic data association for dynamic world modeling: A multiple hypothesis approach. In *International Conference on Advanced Robotics*, Pisa, Italy.

Crisman, J. D. (1990). *Color Vision for the Detection of Unstructured Roads and Intersections*. PhD thesis, Carnegie Mellon University, Dept. of Electrical and Computer Engineering.

Curwen, R. M., Blake, A., and Cipolla, R. (1991). Parallel implementation of Lagrangian dynamics for real-time snakes. In Mowforth, P., editor, *British Machine Vision Conference*, 29–35, Glasgow. Springer-Verlag, London.

Cutting, C. B. (1989). Applications of computer graphics to the evaluation and treatment of major craniofacial malformation. In Udupa, J. K. and Herman, G. T., editors, *3D Imaging in Medicine*. CRC Press.

Dallos, P. J. and Jones, R. W. (1963). Learning behavior of the eye fixation control system. *IRE Transactions on Automatic Control* 8, 218–227.

David, C. and Zucker, S. W. (1990). Potentials, valleys, and dynamic global coverings.

Int. Journal of Computer Vision **5**(3), 219–238.

Davis, H. F. and Snider, A. D. (1979). *Introduction to vector analysis.* Allyn and Bacon.

Dean, T., Camus, T., and Kirman, J. (1990). Sequential decision making for active perception. In *Proceedings: DARPA Image Understanding Workshop*, 889–894.

Dean, T. L. and Wellman, M. P. (1991). *Planning and Control.* Morgan Kaufmann.

Deriche, R. (1987). Using Canny's criteria to derive a recursively implemented optimal edge detector. *International Journal of Computer Vision* **1**(2).

Dickmanns, E. D. (1985). 2D-object recognition and representation using normalized curvature functions. In Hamza, editor, *IASTED Conference on Robotics and Automation,* Santa Barbara. Acta Press.

Dickmanns, E. D. (1988). Computer vision for flight vehicles. *Zeitschrift fuer Flugwissenschaft und Weltraumforschung.*

Dickmanns, E. D. (1991). 4D dynamic vision for intelligent motion control. *Int. Journal for Engineering Applications of AI.* Special issue on Intelligent Autonomous Vehicles Research.

Dickmanns, E. D. and Christians, T. (1989). Relative 3D-state estimation for autonomous visual guidance of road vehicles. *Intelligent Autonomous Systems* **2**, 683–693.

Dickmanns, E. D. and Graefe, V. (1988a). Application of dynamic monocular machine vision. *J. Machine Vision Application* 240–261.

Dickmanns, E. D. and Graefe, V. (1988b). Dynamic monocular machine vision. *J. Machine Vision Application* 223–240.

Dickmanns, E. D. and Mysliwetz, B. (1992). Recursive 3D road and relative ego-state recognition. *IEEE Trans. Pattern Analysis and Machine Intell..* Special Issue on Interpretation of 3D Scenes. To Appear.

Dickmanns, E. D., Mysliwetz, B., and Christians, T. (1990). An integrated spatio-temporal approach to automated visual guidance of autonomous vehicles. *IEEE Trans. on Systems, Man, and Cybernetics* **20**(6), 1273–1284.

DoCarmo, M. P. (1976). *Differential Geometry of Curves and Surfaces.* Prentice-Hall.

Dorf, R. C. (1980). *Modern control systems.* Addison-Wesley, 3rd edition.

Du, F. and Brady, J. M. (1991). The kinematics and eye movements for a two-eyed robot head. In Mowforth, P., editor, *Proceedings of the 2nd British Machine Vision Conference,* Glasgow. Springer-Verlag, London.

Du, F., Brady, J. M., and Murray, D. W. (1991). Gaze control for a two-eyed robot head. In Mowforth, P., editor, *Proceedings of the 2nd British Machine Vision Conference,* Glasgow. Springer-Verlag, London.

Duda, R. and Hart, P. (1973). *Pattern Classification and Scene Analysis.* John Wiley and Sons, Inc.

Duncan, J. S., Owen, R. L., Staib, L. H., and Anandan, P. (1991). Measurement of non-rigid motion using contour shape descriptors. In *Proc. Computer Vision and Pattern Recognition*, 318–324. IEEE Computer Society Conference. Lahaina, Maui, Hawaii.

Durbin, R., Szeliski, R., and Yuille, A. (1989). An analysis of the elastic net approach to the travelling salesman problem. *Neural Computation* **1**(3), 348–358.

Durbin, R. and Willshaw, D. (1987). An analogue approach to the traveling salesman problem using an elastic net method. *Nature* **326**, 689–691.

Durrant-Whyte, H. F. (1988). *Integration, Coordination, and Control of Multi-Sensor Robot Systems.* Kluwer Academic.

E. R. Kandel and J. H. Schwartz (1981). *Principles of Neural Science*, chapter 34. Elsevier/North-Holland, New York.

Eberl, G. (1987). *Automatischer Landeanflug durch Rechnersehen.* Dissertation, Fakultat fur Luft- und Raumfahrttechnik der Universitat der Bundeswehr, Munschen.

Edge, P. (1991). Real-time gaze control: mount control system specification. Technical Report Y-216-6211, GEC Marconi Research Centre, Sensors and Avionic Research Laboratory.

Evans, R. J. (1990). Filtering of pose estimates generated by the RAPiD tracker in applications. In *Proceedings of the British Machine Vision Conference*, 79–84.

Faugeras, O., Lustman, F., and Toscani, G. (1987). Motion and structure from motion from point and line matches. In *Proc. 1st Int. Conf. on Computer Vision*, 25–34.

Faugeras, O. D. (1990). On the motion of 3-D curves and its relationship to optical flow. In *Proceedings of 1st European Conference on Computer Vision*.

Faugeras, O. D., Ayache, N., and Faverjon, B. (1986). Building visual maps by combining noisy stereo measurements. In *Proceedings: IEEE International Conference on Robotics and Automation*, 1433–1438, San Francisco, California. IEEE Computer Society Press.

Faugeras, O. D. and Hebert, M. (1986). The representation, recognition and positioning of 3D shapes from range data. *Int. Journal of Robotics Research* 5(3), 27–52.

Faure, F., Gambotto, J. P., Montserrat, G., and Patat, F. (1988). Space medical facility study. Technical report, ESA. final report, 6961/86/NL/PB.

Feldman, J. and Sproull, R. (1977). Decision theory and artificial intelligence II: The hungry monkey. *Cognitive Science* 1, 158–192.

Ferrie, F. P., Lagarde, J., and Whaite, P. (1989). Darboux frames, snakes, and superquadrics: Geometry from the bottom up. In *Proc. Workshop on Interpretation of 3D Scenes*, 170–176, Austin, TX.

Ferrier, N. (1991). The harvard binocular robotic head. Technical report, Harvard Robotics Laboratory.

Ferrier, N. (1992). *Trajectory control of active vision systems*. PhD thesis, Division of Applied Sciences, Harvard University.

Ferrier, N. and Clark, J. (1990). Optimal motions for active sensing. In *International Symposium on Robotics and Manufacturing*, Burnaby, BC, Canada.

Fischler, M. A. and Elschlager, R. A. (1973). The representation and matching of pictorial structures. *IEEE. Trans. Computers* C-22(1).

Fitzgerald, R. J. (1990). Development of practical PDA logic for multitarget tracking by microprocessor. In Bar-Shalom, Y., editor, *Multi-Target Multi-Sensor Tracking*. Artec House.

Fortmann, T. E., Bar-Shalom, Y., and Scheffe, M. (1983). Sonar tracking of multiple targets using joint probabilistic data association. *IEEE Journal of Oceanic Engineering* 8(3), 173–183.

Francois, E. and Bouthemy, P. (1990). Derivation of qualitative information in motion analysis. *Image and Vision Computing* 8(4), 279–288.

Freeman, H. and Chakravarti, I. (1980). The use of characteristic views in the recognition of three-dimensional objects. In *Pattern Recognition in Practice*, 277–288. North-Holland.

Frisby, J. P. and Mayhew, J. E. W. (1980). Spatial frequency tuned channels: implications for structure and function from psychophysical and compuatational studies of stereopsis. *Phil. Trans. R. Soc. Lond. B* 290, 95–116.

Fua, P. and Leclerc, Y. G. (1990). Model driven edge detection. *Machine Vision and Applications* 3, 45–56.

Garvey, T. (1976). Perceptual strategies for purposive vision. Technical Report 117, SRI AI Center.

Geiger, D. and Yuille, A. (1987). Stereopsis and eye movement. In *Proceedings of the First IEEE Conference on Computer Vision*, 306–314, London. IEEE.

Gelb, A., editor (1974). *Applied Optimal Estimation*. MIT Press, Cambridge, MA.

Geman, S. and Geman, D. (1984). Stochastic relaxation, Gibbs distribution, and the Bayesian restoration of images. *IEEE Trans. Pattern Analysis and Machine Intell.* **PAMI-6**(6), 721–741.

Giblin, P. and Weiss, R. (1987). Reconstruction of surfaces from profiles. In *Proc. 1st Int. Conf. on Computer Vision*, 136–144, London.

Gibson, J. J. (1979). *The Ecological Approach to Visual Perception*. Houghton Mifflin.

Goto, Y., Matsuzaki, K., Kweon, I., and Obatake, T. (1986). CMU sidewalk navigation system: A blackboard-based outdoor navigation system using sensor fusion with color-range images. In *Proc. First Joint Conf. ACM/IEEE*.

Grenander, U. (1989). The 1985 Rietz lecture: Advances in pattern theory. *The Annals of Statistics* **17**(1), 1–30.

Grenander, U., Chow, Y., and Keenan, D. M. (1991). *HANDS. A Pattern Theoretical Study of Biological Shapes*. Springer-Verlag. New York.

Grimson, W. E. L. and Lozano-Perez, T. (1984). Model based recognition from sparse range or tactile data. *Int. Journal of Robotics Research* **3**(3), 3–35.

Gross, A. D. and Boult, T. E. (1988). Error of Fit Measures for Recovering Parametric Solids. In *Second International Conference on Computer Vision*, 690–694.

Guéziec, A. and Ayache, N. (1991). Smoothing and matching of 3D space curves. Technical report, INRIA. Accepted at ECCV'92.

Haenny, P. E., Maunsell, J. H. R., and Schiller, P. H. (1985). State dependent activity in monkey visual cortex: visual and non-visual factors in V4. Preprint.

Hallam, J. (1983). Resolving observer motion by object tracking. In *Procs. of 8th International Joint Conference on Artificial Intelligence*, volume 2, 792–798.

Hallinan, P. W. (1991). Recognizing human eyes. In *SPIE Proc. Geometric Methods in Computer Vision*, volume 1570, 214–226, San Diego.

Hallinan, P. W. (1992). A robust deformable template for human eyes. Technical report, Robotics Labotatory, Harvard University.

Harris, C. G. (1987). Determination of ego-motion from matched points. In *Proc. 3rd Alvey Vision Conference*, 189–192.

Harris, C. G. (1990). Structure from motion under orthographic projection. In Faugeras, O., editor, *Proc. 1st European Conference on Computer Vision*, 118–123. Springer–Verlag.

Harris, C. G. (1992). Camera calibration. In *ECCV92*. Submitted.

Harris, C. G. and Pike, J. M. (1987). 3D positional integration from image sequences. In *Proc. 3rd Alvey Vision Conference*, 233–236.

Harris, C. G. and Stennett, C. (1990). 3D object tracking at video rate — RAPiD. In *Proceedings of the British Machine Vision Conference*, 73–78.

Harris, C. G. and Stephens, M. J. (1988). A combined corner and edge detector. In *Proc. 4rd Alvey Vision Conference*, 147–152.

Henrion, M. (1990). An introduction to algorithms for inference in belief nets. In *Uncertainty in AI*, 129–138. North-Holland.

Herlin, I. L. and Ayache, N. (1992a). Features extraction and analysis methods for sequences of ultrasound images. *Proceedings of the Second European Conference on Computer Vision*, in press, Santa Margherita Ligure, Italy.

Herlin, I. L. and Ayache, N. (1992b). Sequences of echocardiographic images. *IEEE Transaction on Medical Imaging*. Accepted for publication in November 1991.

Hildreth, E. C. (1984). *The Measurement of Visual Motion*. The MIT press, Cambridge, Massachusetts.

Hoare, C. A. R. (1985). *Communicating Sequential Processes*. Prentice Hall.

Hock, C. (1991). Landmark navigation with ATHENE. In *Proc. Int. Conf. on Advanced Robotics*, Pisa.

Horn, B. K. P. (1986). *Robot Vision*. MIT Press.

Horn, B. K. P. and Schunck, B. G. (1981). Determining optical flow. *Artificial Intelligence* **17**, 185–203.

Horowitz, B. and Pentland, A. (1991). Recovery of non-rigid motion and structures. In *Proc. Computer Vision and Pattern Recognition*, 325–330. IEEE Computer Society Conference. Lahaina, Maui, Hawaii.

Huang, T. and Tsai, R. (1981). Image sequence analysis : Motion estimation. In T.S.Huang, editor, *Image sequence analysis*. Springer-Verlag, New York.

Huber, P. J. (1981). *Robust Statistics*. John Wiley and Sons. New York.

Humphreys, G. W. and Bruce, V. (1989). *Visual Cognition: Computational, Experimental, and Neuropsychological Perspectives*. Lawrence Erlbaum.

Hurlbert, A. and Poggio, T. (1986). Do computers need attention? *Nature* **321**(12).

Hwang, T. and Clark, J. J. (1990). A spatio-temporal generalization of Canny's edge detector. In *10th International Conference on Pattern Recognition*, Atlantic City, New Jersey, USA.

Hwang, T. L., Clark, J. J., and Yuille, A. L. (1989). A depth recovery algorithm using defocus information. Technical report, Harvard Robotics Laboratory.

Inoue, H. and Mizoguchi, H. (1985). A flexible multi window vision system for robots. In *Proc. 2nd Int. Symp. on Robotics Research*, 95–102.

Jacobsen, S. C., Smith, C. C., Biggers, K. B., and Iversen, E. (1989). Behaviour based design of robot end effectors. In Brady, J. M., editor, *Robotics Science*. MIT Press, Cambridge MA.

Jarvis, R. (1983). A perspective on range finding techniques for computer vision. *IEEE Trans. PAMI* **5**(5), 122–139.

Jenkins, J. M., Qian, O., Besozzi, M., Delp, E. J., and Buda, A. J. (1981). Computer processing of echocardiographic images for automated edge detection of left ventricular boundaries. In *Computers in Cardiology*, volume 8.

Jensen, F. V., Lauritzen, S. L., and Olesen, K. G. (1990). Bayesian updating in recursive graphical models by local computations. *Computational Statistics Quarterly*. Also TR R-89-15, Institute for Electronic Systems, Department of Math and Computer Science, University of Aalborg, Denmark, 1989.

Johnson, L. W. and Reiss, R. D. (1982). *Numerical Analysis*. Addison-Wesley.

J.R.Quinlan (1986). Induction of decision trees. *Machine Learning* **1**(1), 81–106.

Kalman, R. E. (1960). A new approach to linear filtering and prediction problems. *Trans. ASME J. of Basic Engineering*.

Kanatani, K. (1986). Structure and motion from optical flow under orthographic projection. *Computer Vision, Graphics and Image Processing* **35**, 181–199.

Kass, M., Witkin, A., and Terzopoulos, D. (1987a). Snakes: Active contour models. In *Proc. 1st Int. Conf. on Computer Vision*, 259–268, London.

Kass, M., Witkin, A., and Terzopoulos, D. (1987b). Snakes: Active contour models. *Int. Journal of Computer Vision* **1**(4), 321–331.

Kastleman, K. (1979). *Digital Image Processing*. Prentice-Hall, Inc.

Kenue, S. (1989). Lanelok: Detection of lane boundaries and vehicle tracking using image processing techniques: Parts I and II. In *Mobile Robots IV*, Proc. SPIE.

Kitchen, L. and Rosenfeld, A. (1982). Grey level corner detection. *Pattern Recognition Letters* **1**, 95–102.

Kluge, K. and Thorpe, C. (1988). Explicit models for robot road following. In *Proc. IEEE*

Conf. on Robotics and Automation.

Koch, C. and Ullman, S. (1984). Selecting one among the many: A simple network implementing shifts in selective visual attention. Technical report, MIT AI Laboratory.

Koenderink, J. and Van Doorn, A. (1975). Invariant properties of the motion parallax field due to the movement of rigid bodies relative to an observer. *Optica Acta* **22**(9), 773–791.

Koenderink, J. and Van Doorn, A. (1978). How an ambulant observer can construct a model of the environment from the geometrical structure of the visual inflow. In Hauske, G. and Butenandt, E., editors, *Kybernetik*. Oldenburg, Munchen.

Koenderink, J. J. (1984). What does the occluding contour tell us about solid shape? *Perception* **13**, 321–330.

Koenderink, J. J. (1986). Optic flow. *Vision Research* **26**(1), 161–179.

Koenderink, J. J. (1990). *Solid Shape*. MIT Press.

Koenderink, J. J. and van Doorn, A. J. (1975). Invariant properties of the motion parallax field due to the movement of rigid bodies relative to an observer. *Optica Acta* **22**(9), 773–791.

Krotkov, E. (1987). Focussing. *Internation Journal of Computer Vision* **1**(3).

Krotkov, E. P. (1989). *Active computer vision by cooperative focus and stereo*. Springer-Verlag.

Kuan, D., Phipps, G., and Hsueh, A. (1987). Autonomous land vehicle road following. In *Proc. First Inter. Conf. on Computer Vision*, 557–566, London, England.

Kuan, D., Phipps, G., and Hsueh, A. C. (1986). A real time road following vision system for autonomous vehicles. *Proc. SPIE Mobile Robots Conf. Vol. 727. Cambridge. MA.* 152–160.

Kuhn, T. (1962). *The structure of scientific revolution*. The University of Chicago Press, Chicago.

Kuhnert, K. D. and Graefe, V. (1985). *Komponenten fuer die modellgestuetzte Interpretation dynamischer Szenen*. Final Report of BMFT-Project 08IT 15113, Aerospace Dept., Universitaet der Bundeswehr Muenchen.

Kurien, T. (1990). Issues in the design of practical multitarget tracking algorithms. In Bar-Shalom, Y., editor, *Multitarget-Multisensor Tracking*. Artec House.

Kushner, T. and Puri, S. (1987). Progress in road intersection detection for autonomous vehicle navigation. In *Mobile Robots II*, Proc. SPIE, 19–24.

Landau, L. D. and Lifshitz, E. M. (1972). *Mechanics and Electrodynamics*, volume 1 of *A Shorter Course of Theoretical Physics*. Pergamon Press.

Landau, L. D. and Lifshitz, E. M. (1986). *Theory of elasticity*. Pergamon Press, Oxford.

Lauritzen, S. L. and Spiegelhalter, D. J. (1988). Local computations with probabilities on graphical structures and their application to expert systems. *Journal of the Royal Statistical Society* **50**(2), 157–194.

Lee, D. N. (1980). The optic flow field: the foundation of vision. *Phil. Trans. R. Soc. Lond.* **290**.

Leitner, F., Marque, I., Lavallée, S., and Cinquin, P. (1990). Dynamic segmentation: Finding the edge with differential equations and 'spline snakes'. Technical Report TIMB-TIM 3-IMAG, Faculte de Medecine, La Tronche, France.

Levitt, T., Binford, T., Ettinger, G., and Gelband, P. (1989). Probability-based control for computer vision. In *Proceedings: DARPA Image Understanding Workshop*, 355–369.

Leymaire, F. (1990). Tracking and describing deformable objects using active contour models. Technical Report TR-CIM-90-9, McGill Research Center for Intelligent Machines, McGill University, Montreal.

Leymaire, F. and Levine, M. D. (1989). Snakes and skeletons. Technical Report TR-CIM-89-3, McGill Research Center for Intelligent Machines, McGill University, Montreal.

Liou, S. and Jain, R. (1986). Road following using vanishing points. In *Proc. Conf on Computer Vision and Pattern Recognition*, 41–46, Miami Beach, Florida.

Lipson, P., Yuille, A., Keefe, D. O., Cavanauch, J., Taffe, J., and Rosenthal, D. (1990). Deformable templates for feature extraction from medical images. In Faugeras, O., editor, *Proc. First European Conf. on Computer Vision*, 413–417, Antibes, France.

Listing, J. B. (1855). In *Ruete's Lehrbuch der Opthalmologie*, volume 1.

Longuet-Higgins, H. C. and Pradzny, K. (1980). The interpretation of a moving retinal image. *Proc. R. Soc. Lond.* **B208**, 385–397.

Lowe, D. G. (1990). Stabilized solution for 3D model parameters. In *Proceedings of the European Conference on Computer Vision*, 408–412.

Lumelsky, V. (1986). Continuous motion planning unknown environment for a 3D cartesian arm. In *Proc. IEEE Robotics and Automation*, 1050–1055.

Lumelsky, V. and Skewis, T. (1990). Incorporating range sensing in the robot navigation function. *Trans. IEEE SMC*.

Maragos, P. (1987). Tutorial on advances in morphological image processing and analysis. *Optical Engineering* **26**, 623–632.

Marr, D. (1982). *Vision*. W. H. Freeman and Co., San Francisco.

Marr, D. and Ullman, S. (1981). Directional selectivity and its use in early visual processing. *Proc. R. Soc. Lond. B* **211**, 151–180.

Marshall, J. E. (1979). *Control of Time-delay Systems*. Peter Peregrinus Ltd.

Martelli, A. (1972). Edge detection using heuristic search methods. *Computer Graphics and Image Processing* **1**, 169–182.

Matthies, L. H., Kanade, T., and Szeliski, R. (1989). Kalman filter-based algorithms for estimating depth from image sequences. *Int. Journal of Computer Vision* **3**, 209–236.

Matthies, L. H. and Shafer, S. A. (1987). Error modeling in stereo navigation. *IEEE Transactions of Robotics and Automation* 239–248.

Maybank, S. J. (1985). The angular velocity associated with the optical flow field arising from motion through a rigid environment. *Proc. Royal Society, London* **A401**, 317–326.

Maybank, S. J. (1987). Apparent area of a rigid moving body. *Image and Vision Computing* **5**(2), 111–113.

Maybeck, P. S. (1979). *Stochastic models, estimation and control*, volume 1. Academic Press.

Mayhew, J. E. W. (1986). Review of YASA project: February 1986. AIVRU memo 24, University of Sheffield.

McLauchlan, P. F. and Murray, D. W. (1991). Coarse image motion for saccade control. Technical report, Robotics Research Group, Dept of Engineering Science, University of Oxford.

Meissner, H. G. and Dickmanns, E. D. (1983). Control of an unstable plant by computer vision. In Huang, T. S., editor, *Image Sequence Processing and Dynamic Scene Analysis*. Springer Verlag.

Menet, S., Saint-Marc, P., and Medioni, G. (1990). B-snakes: Implementations and applications to stereo. In *Proc. DARPA Image Understanding Workshop*, 720–726, Pittsburgh, PA.

Metaxas, D. and Terzopoulos, D. (1991a). Constrained deformable superquadrics and nonrigid motion tracking. In *Proc. Computer Vision and Pattern Recognition*, 337–343, Lahaina, HI. IEEE Computer Society Press.

Metaxas, D. and Terzopoulos, D. (1991b). Shape representation and nonrigid motion tracking using deformable superquadrics. In Vemuri, B. C., editor, *Proc. SPIE 1570, Geometric Methods in Computer Vision*, 12–20, San Diego, CA. Society of Photo-Optical Instrumentation Engineers.

Meyer, P. L. (1970). *Introductory Probability and Statistical Applications*. Addison-Wesley, Reading, MA, 2nd edition.

Mishra, S. K., Goldgof, D. B., and Huang, T. S. (1991). Motion analysis and epicardial deformation estimation from angiography data. In *Proc. Computer Vision and Pattern Recognition*, 331–336. IEEE Computer Society Conference. Lahaina, Maui, Hawaii.

Monga, O., Benayoun, S., and Faugeras, O. D. (1992). Using third order derivatives to extract ridge lines in 3D images. In *IEEE Conference on Vision and Pattern Recognition*, Urbana Champaign. Submitted.

Monga, O. and Deriche, R. (1988). 3D edge detection using recursive filtering: application to scanner images. Technical Report 930, INRIA.

Montanari, U. (1971). On the optimal detection of curves in noisy pictures. *Commun. ACM* **14**(5), 335–345.

Moore, A. W. (1991). Variable resolution dynamic programming: efficiently learning action maps in multivariate real-valued state-spaces. In *Proceedings of the Eighth International Workshop on Machine Learning*. Morgan Kaufmann.

Moran, J. and Desimone, R. (1985). Selective attention gates visual processing in the extrastriate cortex. *Science* **229**, 782–784.

Murray, D. and Buxton, B. (1990). *Experiments in the machine interpretation of visual motion*. MIT Press.

Murray, D. W. (1992). Stereo for gazing and converging cameras. Technical Report OUEL 1915/92, Robotics Research Group, Dept of Engineering Science, University of Oxford.

Murray, D. W. and Buxton, B. F. (1991). *Experiments in the Machine Interpretation of Visual Motion*. MIT Press, Cambridge MA.

Mysliwetz, B. (1984). *Mikroprozessor-basierte Blickrichtungssteuerung durch eine Zwei-achs-Plattform*. Diploma thesis Techn, University of Munich.

Mysliwetz, B. (1990). *Parallelrechner-basierte Bildfolgeninterpretation zur autonomen Fahrzeugsteuerung*. Dissertation, Universitaet der Bundeswehr Muenchen, LRT.

Mysliwetz, B. and Dickmanns, E. D. (1986). A vision system with active gaze control for real-time interpretation of well structured scenes. In Hertzberger, L. O., editor, *Proc. 1st Conference on Intelligent Autonomous Systems*, 477–483, Amsterdam.

Neapolitan, R. E. (1990). *Probabilistic Reasoning in Expert Systems: Theory and Algorithms*. John Wiley and Sons.

Nelson, R. C. and Aloimonos, J. (1988). Using flow field divergence for obstacle avoidance: towards qualitative vision. In *Proc. 2nd Int. Conf. on Computer Vision*, 188–196.

Nudd, G. R., Atherton, T. J., Francis, N. D., Howarth, R. M., Kerbyson, D. J., Packwood, R. A., and Vaudin, G. J. (1990). A hierarchical multiple-SIMD architecture for image analysis. In *Procs. IEEE 10th International Conference on Pattern Recognition*, volume 2, 642–647.

Ohlsson, M., Peterson, C., and Yuille, A. L. (1992). Track finding with deformable templates – the elastic arms approach. *Computer Physics Communications*. In Press. Also: Harvard Robotics Group Techical Report 91-20.

Ohta, Y. and Kanade, T. (1985). Stereo by intra- and inter-scan line search using dynamic programming. *IEEE Trans. on Pattern Analysis and Machine Intelligence* **7**(2), 139–154.

Olson, T. J. and Coombs, D. J. (1991). Real-time vergence control for binocular robots. *Int. Journal of Computer Vision* **7**(1), 67–89.

Pahlavan, K. and Eklundh, J.-O. (1991). A head-eye system for active purposive computer vision. Technical Report CVAP-80, Dept of Numerical Analysis and Computing Science,

Royal Inst of Tech, Stockholm.

Parisi, G. (1988). *Statistical Field Theory*. Addison-Wesley, Reading. MA.

Pavlidis, T. and Liow, Y.-T. (1990). Integrated region growing and edge detection. *IEEE Trans. Pattern Analysis and Machine Intell.* **12**(3), 225–233.

Pearl, J. (1988). *Probabilistic Reasoning in Intelligent Systems: Networks of Plausible Inference*. Morgan Kaufman.

Pentland, A. (1986). Perceptual organization and the representation of natural form. *Artificial Intelligence* **28**, 293–331.

Pentland, A. (1987). A new sense for depth of field. *IEEE Transactions on Pattern Analysis and Machine Intelligence* **9**(4), 523–531.

Pentland, A. and Horowitz, B. (1991). Recovery of non-rigid motion and structure. *IEEE Trans. Pattern Analysis and Machine Intelligence* **13**(7), 730–742.

Peot, M. A. and Shachter, R. D. (1991). Fusion and propagation with multiple observations in belief networks. *Artificial Intelligence* **48**, 299–318.

Petersen, S. E., Robinson, D. L., and Keys, W. (1985). Pulvinar nuclei of the behaving rhesus monkey: visual responses and their modulation. *Journal of Neurophysiology* **54**, 867–886.

Peterson, C. (1990). Parallel distributed approaches to combinatorial optimization problems – benchmark studies on the TSP. *Neural Computation* **2**, 261–269.

Pollard, S., Mayhew, J., and Frisby, J. (1985a). PMF:A Stereo Correspondence Algorithm Using A Disparity Gradient. *Perception* **14**, 449–470.

Pollard, S. B., Mayhew, J. E. W., and Frisby, J. P. (1985b). PMF: A stereo correspondence algorithm using a disparity gradient limit. *Perception* **14**, 449–470.

Pollard, S. B., Porrill, J., and Mayhew, J. E. W. (1990). Experiments in vehicle control using predictive feed forward stereo. *Image and Vision Computing* **8**(1), 63–70.

Pollard, S. B., Porrill, J., Mayhew, J. E. W., and Frisby, J. P. (1987). Matching geometrical descriptions in three space. *Image and Vision Computing* **2**(5), 73–78.

Porrill, J., Pollard, S. B., Pridmore, T. P., Bowen, J., Mayhew, J. E. W., and Frisby, J. P. (1987a). TINA: The Sheffield AIVRU vision system. In *Procs. IJCAI 9*, 1138–1144.

Porrill, J., Pollard, S. B., Pridmore, T. P., Bowen, J. B., and Mayhew, J. E. W. M. (1987b). TINA: A 3D vision system for pick and place. In *Proc. 3rd Alvey Vision Conference*, 65–72.

Proakis, J. G. (1983). *Digital Communications*. McGraw-Hill, Inc.

Rao, B. S. Y. (1991). *Data Fusion Methods in Decentralized Sensing Systems*. PhD thesis, University of Oxford, Robotics Research Group.

Regensburger, U. and Graefe, V. (1990). Object classification for obstacle avoidance. *Proc. of the SPIE Symp. on Advances in Intelligent Systems. Boston*. 112–119.

Reid, D. B. (1979). An algorithm for tracking multiple targets. *IEEE Trans. Automatic Control* **24**(6).

Rimey, R. D. (1992). Where to look next using a Bayes net: An overview. In *Proceedings: DARPA Image Understanding Workshop*.

Robinson, D. A. (1965). The mechanics of human smooth pursuit eye movement. *Journal of Physiology* **180**, 569–591.

Robinson, D. A. (1968). The oculomotor motor control system: A review. *Proceedings of the IEEE* **56**(6), 1032–1049.

Robinson, D. A. (1987). Why visuomotor systems don't like negative feedback and how they avoid it. In Arbib, M. and Hanson, A., editors, *Vision, Brain and Cooperative Computation*, 89–107. MIT Press, Cambridge, MA.

Ross, S. (1983). *Introduction to stochastic dynamic programming*. Academic Press, New

York.

Rothwell, C. A., Zisserman, A., Forsyth, D. A., and Mundy, J. L. (1991). Using projective invariants for constant time library indexing in model based vision. In *Proceedings of the British Machine Vision Conference*, 62–70. Springer Verlag.

Rygol, M. (1991). *Exploitation of MIMD Architecture for 3D Machine Vision*. PhD thesis, University of Sheffield.

Rygol, M., McLauchlan, P., Courtney, P., Pollard, S. B., Porrill, J., Brown, C. R., and Mayhew, J. E. W. (1991). Parallel 3D vision for vehicle navigation and control. In *Procs. Transputing '91*. IOS Press.

Schell, R. (1992). *Bordautonomer automatischer Landeanflug aufgrund bildhafter und inertialer Messdatenauswertung*. Diss. UniBwM/LRT). To Appear.

Schick, J. (1992). *Gleichzeitige Erkennung von Form und Bewegung durch Rechnersehen*. Diss. UniBwM/LRT. To Appear.

Schick, J. and Dickmanns, E. D. (1991). Simultaneous estimation of 3D shape and motion of objects by computer vision. In *Proceedings IEEE Workshop on Visual Motion*, 256–261, Princeton, NJ. IEEE Computer Society Press.

Schunck, B. G. (1986). The image flow constraint equation. *Computer Vision, Graphics and Image Processing* **35**, 20–46.

Schunck, B. G. (1989). Image flow segmentation and estimation using constraint line clustering. *IEEE Transactions on Pattern Analysis and Machine Intelligence* **11**(10), 1010–1027.

Scott, G. L. (1987). The alternative snake – and other animals. In Eklundh, J.-O., editor, *The 1987 Stockholm Workshop on Computational Vision*, Stockholm. Dept. of Numerical Analysis and Computing Science, Royal Institute of Technology, TRITA-NA-P8714 CVAP 47.

Serra, J. (1982). *Image Analysis and Mathematical Morphology*. Academic Press, London.

Shabana, A. A. (1989). *Dynamics of Multibody Systems*. Wiley, New York.

Shachter, R. D. (1986). Evaluating influence diagrams. *Operations Research* **34**(6), 871–882.

Shackleton, M. A. and Welsh, W. J. (1991). Classification of facial features for recognition. *cvpr* 573–579.

Shafer, G. and Pearl, J., editors (1990). *Readings in Uncertain Reasoning*. Morgan Kaufmann.

Sharkey, P. M. and Murray, D. W. (1992). A modular versatile design for an active stereo head/eye platform. In *2nd Int Conf on Automation, Robotics and Computer Vision*, Singapore.

Shirai, Y. (1972). Recognition of polyhedrons with a rangefinder. *J. Artificial Intelligence* **4**(3), 243–250.

Shu, D. B., Nash, J. G., and Weems, C. C. (1990). A multiple-level heterogeneous architecture for image understanding. *Procs. IEEE 10th International Conference on Pattern Recognition* **2**, 629–634.

Simon, H. A. (1969). *The sciences of the artificial*. MIT Press, Cambridge, Massachusetts.

Smith, O. J. M. (1957). Closer control of loops with deadtime. *Chemical Eng Prog Trans* **53**, 217–219.

Smith, O. J. M. (1958). *Feedback Control Systems*. McGraw-Hill.

Solder, U. and Graefe, V. (1990). Object detection in real time. *Proc. of the SPIE Symp. on Advances in Intelligent Systems. Boston*. 104–111.

Solina, F. and Bajcsy, R. (1990). Recovery of parametric models from range images: The case for superquadrics with global deformations. *IEEE Trans. Pattern Analysis and*

Machine Intelligence **12**(2), 131–146.

Soong, J. and Brown, C. M. (1991). Inverse kinematics and gaze stabilizatoin for the rochester robot head. Technical Report 394, University of Rochester, Computer Science Department.

Sparks and Stephens, M. J. (1990). Integration of stereo and motion. In *Proc. 1st British Machine Vision Conference*, 127–132.

Staib, L. H. and Duncan, J. S. (1989). Parametrically deformable contour models. In *Proc. Computer Vision and Pattern Recognition*, 98–103, San Diego, CA. IEEE Computer Society Press.

Stephens, M. J. (1987). Matching features from edge-processed image sequences. In *Proc. 3rd Alvey Vision Conference*, 185–188.

Stephens, R. S. (1989). Real-time 3D object tracking. In *Proceedings of the Alvey Vision Conference*, 85–90.

Subbarao, M. (1990). Bounds on time–to–collision and rotational component from first-order derivatives of image flow. *Computer Vision, Graphics and Image Processing* **50**, 329–341.

Sullivan, G. (1992). Visual interpretation of known objects in constrained scenes. *Phil. Trans. Royal Soc. London* in press.

Sutton, R. S. (1988). Learning to predict by methods of temporal difference. *Machine Learning* **3**, 9–44.

Sutton, R. S. (1990). Integrated architectures for learning, planning and reacting based on approximate dynamic programming. In *Proceedings of The Seventh International Conference on Machine Learning*.

Swain, M. J. and Stricker, M. (1991). Promising directions in active vision. Technical report, University of Chicago.

Szeliski, R. (1989). *Bayesian Modeling of Uncertainty in Low-Level Vision*. Kluwer Academic Publishers, Boston, MA.

Szeliski, R. and Terzopoulos, D. (1991). Physically-based and probabilistic modeling for computer vision. In Vemuri, B. C., editor, *Proc. SPIE 1570, Geometric Methods in Computer Vision*, 140–152, San Diego, CA. Society of Photo-Optical Instrumentation Engineers.

Tanimoto, S. L. (1990). *The Elements of Artificial Intelligence*. Freeman.

Taxt, T., Lundervold, A., and Angelsen, B. (1990). Noise reduction and segmentation in time-varying ultrasound images. In *10th International Conference on Pattern Recognition*, Atlantic City, New Jersey, USA.

Terzopoulos, D. (1987). On matching deformable models to images: Direct and iterative solutions. In *Topical Meeting on Machine Vision, Technical Digest Series*, volume 12, 160–167, Washington, D. C. Optical Society of America.

Terzopoulos, D. and Metaxas, D. (1991). Dynamic 3D models with local and global deformations: Deformable superquadrics. *IEEE Trans. Pattern Analysis and Machine Intelligence* **13**(7), 703–714. See also Proc. Third International Conference on Computer Vision (ICCV'90), Osaka, Japan, Dec. 1990, pp. 606–615.

Terzopoulos, D. and Waters, K. (1990). Analysis of facial images using physical and anatomical models. In *Third International Conference on Computer Vision*, 727–732, Osaka, Japan.

Terzopoulos, D., Witkin, A., and Kass, M. (1988). Constraints on deformable models: Recovering 3D shape and nonrigid motion. *Artificial Intelligence* **36**(1), 91–123. See also Proc. Sixth National Conference on Artificial Intelligence (AAAI-87), Seattle, WA, July, 1987, pp. 755–760.

Thompson, D. W. and Mundy, J. L. (1987). Three-dimensional model matching from an unconstrained viewpoint. In *Proceedings of IEEE Conference on Robotics and Automa-*

tion.

Thorpe, C. E. (1991). Personal communication.

Torr, P. H. S., Wong, T., Murray, D. W., and Zisserman, A. (1991). Cooperating motion processes. In Mowforth, P., editor, *Proceedings of the 2nd British Machine Vision Conference*, 145–150, Glasgow. Springer-Verlag, London.

Treisman, A. M. and Gelade, G. (1980). A feature-integration theory of attention. *Cognitive Psychology* **12**, 97–136.

Tsai, R. Y. (1986). An efficient and accurate camera calibration technique for 3D machine vision. *IEEE Trans. Pattern Analysis and Machine Intell.* 364–374.

Tsugawa, S., Yatabe, T., Hirose, T., and Matsumoto, S. (1979). An automobile with artificial intelligence. In *Proc. 6th Inter. Joint Conf. on Artificial Intelligence*, volume IJCAI-6, 893–895, Tokyo, Japan.

Turk, M., Morgenthaler, D., Gremban, K., and Marra, M. (1988). VITS: A vision system for autonomous land vehicle navigation. *IEEE Trans. Pattern Analysis and Machine Intelligence* **PAMI-10**(3), 342–361.

Turk, M. A., Morgenthaler, D. G., Gremban, K. D., and Marra, M. (1987). Video road-following for the autonomous land vehicle. In *Proc. IEEE Int. Conf. Robotics and Automation*, 273–280, Raleigh, NC.

Ullman, S. (1979). *The interpretation of visual motion*. MIT Press, Cambridge,USA.

Ullman, S. (1984). Visual routines. *Cognition* **18**, 97–159.

Unser, M., Dong, L., Pelle, G., Brun, P., and Eden, M. (1989). Restoration on echocardiagrams using time warping and periodic averaging on a normalized time scale. In *Medical Imaging*, volume III. January 29 – February 3, Newport Beach.

Vaillant, R. (1990). Using occluding contours for 3D object modelling. In Faugeras, O., editor, *Proc. 1st European Conference on Computer Vision*, 454–464. Springer–Verlag.

Valkenburg, R. J. and Bowman, C. C. (1989). Kiwivision 2 – a hybrid pipelined / multi-transputer architecture for machine vision. In Chen, M. J. W., editor, *Proc. SPIE 1004*, 91–96.

Viéville, T. and Faugeras, O. D. (1991). Real time gaze control: architecture for sensing behaviors. In *Proceedings of the 5th Workshop on Computational Vision*, Rosenon, Sweden.

Wallace, R. and Howard, M. D. (1989). HBA vision architecture: built and benchmarked. *IEEE Trans. Pattern Analysis and Machine Intell.* 222–232.

Wallace, R., Matsuzaki, K., Goto, Y., Crisman, J., Webb, J., and Kanade, T. (1986). Progress in robot road following. In *Proc. IEEE Inter. Conf. Robotics and Automation*, 1615–1621, San Francisco, CA.

Wallace, R., Stentz, A., Thorpe, C., Moravec, H., Whittaker, W., and Kanade, T. (1985). First results in robot road following. In *Proc. IEEE Inter. Joint Conf. on Artificial Intelligence*.

Wang, H., Bowman, C., Brady, M., and Harris, C. G. (1992). A parallel implementation of a structure-from-motion algorithm. In *ECCV92*. Submitted.

Wang, H. and Brady, J. M. (1991). Corner detection for 3D vision using array processors. In *Proc BARNAIMAGE-91*, Barcelona, Spain. Springer-Verlag.

Watkins, C. J. H. C. (1989). *Learning from delayed rewards*. PhD thesis, King's College, Cambridge University, UK.

Waxman, A., LeMoigne, J., Davis, L., Srinivasan, B., Kusher, T., Liang, E., and Siddalingaiah, T. (1987). A visual navigation system for autonomous land vehicles. *IEEE Trans. on Robotics and Automation* **RA-3**(2), 124–141.

Waxman, A. M. and Ullman, S. (1985). Surface structure and three-dimensional motion from image flow kinematics. *Int. Journal of Robotics Research* **4**(3), 72–94.

Waxman, A. M. and Wohn, K. (1985). Contour evolution, neighbourhood deformation and global image flow: planar surfaces in motion. *Int. Journal of Robotics Research* **4**(3), 95–108.

Werbos, P. J. (1990). A menu for designs of reinforcement learning over time. In Miller III, W. T., Sutton, R. S., and Werbos, P. J., editors, *Neural networks for control*. MIT Press, Cambridge, MA.

Westheimer, G. (1957). Kinematics of the eye. *Journal of the Optical Society of America* **47**(10), 967–974.

Williams, D. J. and Shah, M. (1992). A fast algorithm for active contours and curvature estimation. *CVGIP: Image Understanding* **55**(1), 14–26.

Williams, R. J. (1988). Towards a theory of reinforcement-learning connectionist systems. Technical Report NU-CCS-88-3, College of computer science, Northeastern University, Boston, MA.

Wilson, H. R. and Bergen, J. R. (1979). A four mechanism model for threshold spatial vision. *Vision Research* **19**, 19–32.

Wolf, P. R. (1983). *Elements of Photogrammetry*. McGraw-Hill.

Wuensche, H. J. (1986). Detection and control of mobile robot motion by real-time computer vision. In N., M., editor, *Advances in Intelligent Robotics Systems*, volume 727 of *Proc. of the SPIE*, 100–109, Cambridge, Mass.

Wuensche, H. J. (1988). *Bewegungssteuerung durch Rechnersehen*. Springer-Verlag, Berlin, Fachberichte Messen, Steuern, Regeln Bd. 20.

Wurtz, R. H., Goldberg, M. E., and Robinson, D. L. (1980). Behavioral modulation of visual responses in the monkey: stimulus selection for attention and movement. *Progress in Psychobiology and Physiological Psychology* **9**, 43–83.

Wurtz, R. H., Richmond, B. J., and Newsome, W. T. (1984). Modulation of cortical visual processing by attention, perception, and movement. In *Dynamic Aspects of Neocortical Function*, 195–217. Wiley & Sons, New York.

Yarbus, A. (1967). *Eye Movements and Vision*. Plenum Press, New York.

Yeshurun, Y. and Schwartz, E. L. (1989a). Cepstral filtering on a columnar image architecture: a fast algorithm for binocular stereo segmentation. *IEEE Trans. Pattern Analysis and Machine Intell.* **11**(7).

Yeshurun, Y. and Schwartz, E. L. (1989b). Shape description with a space-variant sensor. *IEEE Trans. Pattern Analysis and Machine Intell.* **11**(11), 1217–1222.

Young, L. R. and Stark, L. (1963). Variable Feedback Experiments Testing a Sampled Data Model for Eye Tracking Movements. *IRE Transactions on Human Factors in Engineering* **4**, 38–51.

Yuille, A. L. (1990). Generalized deformable models, statistical physics, and matching problems. *Neural Computation* **2**, 1–24.

Yuille, A. L., Cohen, D. S., and Hallinan, P. W. (1989). Feature extraction from faces using deformable templates. In *Proc. CVPR*, 104–109.

Yuille, A. L., Hallinan, P. W., and Cohen, D. S. (1992). Detecting facial features using deformable templates. *International Journal of Computer Vision*. To Appear.

Yuille, A. L., Honda, K., and Peterson, C. (1991). Particle tracking by deformable templates. *Proceedings 1991 International Joint Conference on Neural Networks* **1**, 7–12.

Zhang, L. F. and Geiser, E. A. (1982). An approach to optimal threshold selection on a sequence of two-dimensional echocardiographic images. *IEEE Transactions on Biomedical Engineering* **BMB-29**(8).

Zucker, S. W., David, C., Dobbins, A., and Iverson, L. (1988). The organization of curve detection: Coarse tangent fields and fine spline coverings. In *Proc. 2nd Int. Conf. on Computer Vision*, 568–577, Tampa, FL.

Contributors

N. Ayache
I.N.R.I.A. BP 105, 78153 Le Chesnay, France

A. Blake
Robotics Research Group, Department of Engineering Science, University of Oxford,
Parks Road, Oxford, OX1 3PJ, United Kingdom

M. Brady
Robotics Research Group, Department of Engineering Science, University of Oxford,
Parks Road, Oxford, OX1 3PJ, United Kingdom

R. Brooks
MIT Artificial Intelligence Laboratory, 545 Technology Square, Cambridge. MA 02139,
U. S. A.

C. M. Brown
Department of Computer Science, 734 Computer Studies Building,
University of Rochester, Rochester, NY 14627 - 0226, U. S. A.

C. R. Brown
A.I. Vision Research Unit, Department of Psychology, University of Sheffield, Sheffield,
S10 2TN, United Kingdom

R. Cipolla
Robotics Research Group, Department of Engineering Science, University of Oxford,
Parks Road, Oxford, OX1 3PJ, United Kingdom

J.J. Clark
Division of Applied Sciences, G12d Pierce Hall, Harvard University, 29 Oxford Street,
Cambridge, MA 02138, U. S. A.

I. Cohen
I.N.R.I.A. BP 105, 78153 Le Chesnay, France

D. Coombs
National Institute of Standards and Technology, Robot Systems Division, Bldg. 220,
Rm. B12, Gaithersburg, MD 20899, U. S. A.

J. Crisman
Department of Electrical and Computer Engineering, 409 Dana Research Building,
Northeastern University, Boston, MA 02115, U. S. A.

R. Curwen
Robotics Research Group, Department of Engineering Science, University of Oxford,
Parks Road, Oxford, OX1 3PJ, United Kingdom

E. Dickmanns
Universität Bundeswehr München – LRT, W. Heisenberg Weg 39, D-8014 Neubiberg,
Germany

F. Du
Robotics Research Group, Department of Engineering Science, University of Oxford,
Parks Road, Oxford, OX1 3PJ, United Kingdom

N. Ferrier
Division of Applied Sciences, Pierce Hall G-14, Harvard University, Cambridge

MA 02138, U. S. A.

P. Hallinan
402 Cruft, Division of Applied Sciences, Harvard University, Cambridge, MA 02138,
U. S. A.

C. Harris
Roke Manor Research Limited, Romsey, Hampshire, SO51 0ZN, United Kingdom

I. Herlin
I.N.R.I.A. BP 105, 78153 Le Chesnay, France.

J. Mayhew
A.I. Vision Research Unit, Department of Psychology, University of Sheffield, Sheffield,
S10 2TN, United Kingdom.

P. McLauchlan
Robotics Research Group, Department of Engineering Science, University of Oxford,
Parks Road, Oxford, OX1 3PJ, United Kingdom.

D. Metaxas
University of Toronto, Department of Computer Science.

D. Murray
Robotics Research Group, Department of Engineering Science, University of Oxford,
Parks Road, Oxford, OX1 3PJ, United Kingdom

S. Pollard
A.I. Vision Research Unit, Department of Psychology, University of Sheffield, Sheffield,
S10 2TN, United Kingdom

T. Prescott
A.I. Vision Research Unit, Department of Psychology, University of Sheffield, Sheffield,
S10 2TN, United Kingdom

B. Rao
Robotics Research Group, Department of Engineering Science, University of Oxford,
Parks Road, Oxford, OX1 3PJ, United Kingdom

I. Reid
Robotics Research Group, Department of Engineering Science, University of Oxford,
Parks Road, Oxford, OX1 3PJ, United Kingdom

R. Rimey
Department of Computer Science, 734 Computer Studies Building,
University of Rochester, Rochester, NY 14627 - 0226, U. S. A.

M. Rygol
A.I. Vision Research Unit, Department of Psychology, University of Sheffield, Sheffield,
S10 2TN, United Kingdom

P. Sharkey
Robotics Research Group, Department of Engineering Science, University of Oxford,
Parks Road, Oxford, OX1 3PJ, United Kingdom

J. Soong
Department of Computer Science, Columbia University, New York, NY 10027, U. S. A.

R. Szeliski
Digital Equipment Corporation, Cambridge Research Laboratory, One Kendall Square, Bldg. 700, Cambridge MA 02139, U. S. A.

D. Terzopoulos
Dept. of Computer Science, University of Toronto, 10 King's College Road, Toronto, ON M5S 1A4 Canada.

A.L. Yuille
Division of Applied Sciences, G12e Pierce Hall, Harvard University, 29 Oxford Street, Cambridge, MA 02138, U. S. A.

A. Zisserman
Robotics Research Group, Department of Engineering Science, University of Oxford, Parks Road, Oxford, OX1 3PJ, United Kingdom

Index

$2\frac{1}{2}$D sketch, 278

accommodation, 141, 155, 158
accuracy
    sub-pixel, 266
action
    evaluation, 205, 209
    exploratory, 207
action integral, 6
adaptive module, 203
Adept robot, 198
Albus, J., 208
ambiguity
    bas–relief, 192
    speed–scale, 191, 192, 195, 273, 280
anatomical structure, 290
anisotropy, 285
annealing, 37, 207, 211, 212
    deterministic, 37
aperture problem, 60, 178
    in the large, 194
apparent contour, 176, 179, 181
    quantitative analysis, 177
    sidedness, 177, 181
    temporal derivative, 178
architecture
    distributed memory, 241
    general purpose, 239
    heterogeneous, 241
    hybrid parallel, 170
    mesh, 241
    MIMD, 170, 240
    parallel, 240
    pipeline, 170, 239, 247
        dataflow, 247
        length, 248
    processor farm, 248, 257, 259
    SIMD, 239, 240
Artificial Intelligence, 303, 331
attention
    modal control, 135
    servo model, 125
        open loop, 126
attribute vector, 266
Ayache, N., 285

B-spline, 3, 39–48, 52, 54, 193, 196
    contour, 196, 39, 190, 198
    coupled, 45
    template, 50
B-spline template, 40
backlash, 162
Barto, A., 203
Baumgarte, J., 82
Bayes net, 217, 219, 221, 222, 224, 230
    a priori belief, 227
    chance node, 224
    composite, 219, 222, 224
        TEA, see TEA

evidence, 219, 223, 224, 226
    instantiated node, 224
    link, 219
    node, 219
    revised polytree algorithm, 219
Bayes' rule, 13, 22, 29, 70, 109
Bayesian estimation, 11, 92, 95, 96
    posterior model, 11
    prior model, 11
    sensor model, 11, 12, 15
behaviour
    avoidance, 209
    reactive, 204
    tactical, 212
belief network
    temporal, 217
bending, see deformation
"best alignment" measure, 272
Bezier curve, 40, 47
binocular vision, 127, 195
Blake, A., 39, 175, 189
blind spot, 280
blur, 108
    artificial, 40
    Gaussian, 5, 143, 265
    motion, 153, 156, 267, 311, 314
Boltzmann distribution, see Gibbs
        distribution
boot mode, 269
boot-strap, 268
Brady, M., 155
Bray, A., 61
Bresenham method, 287
Brooks, R., 185
Brown, C., 141, 162, 217, 239

χ^2 test, 93, 184
CAD model
    ray-casting, 72
calibration, 267
camera
    acceleration, 156, 161
    bifocal pair, 333
    configuration, 157
    elevation, 317, 326
    focal length, 326
    motion, 309
    motor, 161
        DC servo, 161
        electric, 161
        hydraulic, 161
        stepper, 161
    pan, 151
        axis, 161
        motor, 153
    pin-hole, 267
    pitch angle, 322
    platform, 155
    tilt, 151, 157

motor, 153
tilt plane, 141
camera coordinate system, 267
camera model, 198, 247
  calibration, 64, 114, 245, 274
  linear, 114
camera motion, 124, 229
  prior estimate, 269
camera pan, 145
camera tilt, 145
Canny, J., 61, 245, 247, 258
centrifugal force, 81
centroid, 270–272
cerebellum, 208
chain rule, 282
Chakravarti, I., 253
characteristic view, 253, 256
Cipolla, R., 175, 189
Clark, J., 138, 141
client/server model, 244
clique, 253
clustering
  nearest mean, 108
clutter, 39, 60, 93–95, 99, 100, 151, 182,
      256
  high density, 97, 101, 105
  low density, 97, 105
  persistent, 102
Cohen, I., 285
coherence
  spatio-temporal, 256
collision, 198, 209
collision avoidance, 190, 197, 204
collisions
  distance between, 211
colour histogram, 224, 229
colour image, 108
colour model, 107
  Gaussian, 107–109
confidence level, 221
connectivity
  logical, 248
  spatial, 248
constraint
  disparity gradient, 246
  grouping, 246
contact
  time to, 191, 195, 198
continuity, 169
  local, 5
  temporal, 309
contour
  apparent, see apparent contour
  closed, 192
    divergence, 194
  coupled, 39, 41
  dynamic, see dynamic contour
  rigidity, 5
contour area

flux, 193
moment, 194
  first-order, 193
  higher, 194, 197
  temporal derivative, 193
  moment of, 193
  temporal derivative of, 192, 197
control law, 143
control system
  feed-forward, 304
  motor, 162
  oculomotor, 143, 155, 164
  PID, 143, 145, 151, 162, 163
    gain, 153
  predictive, 163
  second-order, 46, 143
  visuomotor, 141
convolution, 24, 40, 143, 170, 242, 245,
      266, 287
  discrete, 289
  separable, 245, 289
Coombs, D., 141
cooperation, 154, 169
Coriolis force, 81
corner detection, 266
corner response, 265
Crisman, J., 107
curse of dimensionality, 208
curvature
  extremal, 293
  geodesic, 180
  normal, 178, 181, 182
Curwen, R., 39
cyclotorsion, 157, 165

damping, 81, 84
  critical, 48, 54
damping constant, 46
  negative, 51
data association, 91–93, 101
  all neighbour, 95, 98
    JPDAF, 98–100, 102
    PDAF, 98, 100
  joint events, 99
  multiple hypothesis, 95, 96, 101, 105
  nearest neighbour, 95, 97
Datacube, 60, 134, 170, 242
decision rule, 217
deformable cylinder, 76
deformable model, 18, 75, 291
  dynamic, 4
deformable template, 21, 22, 293
  confidence criterion, 22
  geometric model, 22
  inertia, 25
  interaction energy, 25
  robustness, 27
  tracking, 31
deformation, 198

bending, 78
    energy of, 298
    global, 89
    local, 89
    of image, 189
    potential energy, 6, 291
    tapering, 78
deformation energy, 4
degrees of freedom, 39, 68, 80, 146, 157
depth from focus, 127
depth gradient, 191
diagnosis, 300
Dickmanns, E., 303
disparity space, 270, 271, 275, 276
distraction, 142, 150, 156
distributed mass, 40
divergence, 192, 195, 197
driving
    convoy, 333
    lane change, 333
    night, 333
DROID, 263
    real-time, 282
Du, F., 155
Duncan, J., 293
dynamic contour, 39, 185, 190
    control points, 42
    elasticity, 40
    forced oscillation, 47
    inertia, 42, 45
    modal eigenvalue, 47
    modal eigenvector, 47
    modes, 40
    rigid translation, 47
    shape matrix, 42
    steady state, 48
    transient response, 48
    unconstrained, 40
    velocity damping, 43
    viscosity, 40
dynamic model, 304, 306, 307, 309, 331
    eigen-characteristic, 304
    generic, 305
    response characteristic, 304
dynamic programming, 11, 203
dynamic vision
    4D approach, 303, 305, 316

echocardiograph, 286
edge
    connectivity, 246
    phase, 144
    rectified, 246
edge polarity, 72
efference copy, 132
ego-motion, 141, 142, 151, 268, 269,
        271, 308, 309, 314, 325
    drifting, 273
    feedback, 273

odometry, 273, 274
    roll-pitch-yaw, 273
elastic deformation, 298
elastic membrane, 43
elastic model, 21, 35
elastodynamic model, 3
EM photomicrograph, 5
environment
    crowded, 94
    man-made, 280
    natural, 304, 309
    technical, 304
    uncluttered, 61
    unconstrained, 264, 277
epipolar, 246
epipolar parameterisation, 178
Epipolar Plane Image, 183
estimator
    α-trimmed, 28, 30
    maximum *a posteriori*, 13
    maximum likelihood, 207
    non-maximum suppression, 29, 34
    recursive relative state, 328
EUCLID, 143
Euler equations, 9
    continuous, 52
Euler integration, 53
Euler method, 50, 85
    first-order, 83
    implicit, 51, 52
    semi-implicit, 10
    time step, 50
Euler-Lagrange equation, 43, 299–300
exploration, 141, 210
    active, 185
extremal boundary, 180, 181, 185

face recognition, 21
Faugeras, O., 254
feature, 265
    aggregation, 308, 329
    automatic extraction, 264
    beacon, 257, 259
    corner, 169, 189, 265
    easily visible, 307, 308
    global, 310
    line, 60, 246, 266
    linear, 313
    mis-positioned, 266
    point, 59, 189, 265, 271, 275
    vertical edge, 143
feature aggregation, 307
feature correspondence, 192
feature search
    basin of attraction, 34
    combinatorial explosion, 309
    diagonal, 65
    epipolar, 269, 276
    guided, 314

linear path, 40
match ambiguity, 269
normal, 41
radial, 41
range-gate mechanism, 54
recursive, 41
scale, 54
steepest descent, 25, 31
window, 54, 56
features
high curvature, 293
feedback control
linear, 82
Ferrier, N., 138, 141
FFT, 142
filter
cepstral, 142, 143
Deriche, 289, 292
disparity, 143
matched, 110
non-linear, 91
predictive, 146, 151
square root, 308
zero disparity, 143, 146, 150
finite difference, 9
finite element method, 3, 9, 80, 300
conforming, 293
stiffness matrix, 84
Fisher's linear discriminant, 27
fixation, 141, 142, 152, 155, 157, 165,
166, 168, 308
fixation point, 127
flux transport theorem, 193
focus, see accommodation
focus feature, 253
focus of expansion, 277, 280
force
virtual spring, 87
Fourier representation of curves, 3
foveal image, 169
foveation, 267
free-space, 181
freeway method
Brooks', 185
Frenet-Serret frame, 180

Gaussian
multi-class model, 110
gaze, 144, 159, 160
control, 148, 153, 156, 158, 162–164,
170
foveation, 141, 143, 150, 151, 168
motion, 166
shift, 156, 157
stabilization, 151
trajectory, 156, 164
gaze control, 141, 155
Geiger, 124
generalized coordinates, 82

geodesic, 175
extrapolation, 179
helical approximation, 180
geodesic path, 182
geodesic torsion, 178, 182
Gestalt, 309, 333
Gibbs distribution, 11, 13, 14, 24, 26,
36
grasp planning, 39, 176
greedy algorithm, 11
Green's theorem, 193, 196
Grenander, U., 21
Grimson, W., 253

Hallinan, P., 21, 28
Hamilton's principle, 6
Harris, C., 59, 263
Herlin, I., 285
Hildreth, E., 298
horopter, 143
Houbolt method, 10
Hough transform, 21, 37, 61, 223, 280
human eye, 155
human visual system, 168
hypothesis generation, 306
hypothesis search
candidate evaluation, 113
candidate generation, 112
candidate mask, 112
evaluation, 271
exhaustive, 111, 253
interpretation space, 111
limited, 111
robust minimisation, 272
hypothesis tree, 96, 253
exponential growth, 96
pruning, 96, 332

IBM PC, 311, 332
image
foreshortening, 198
foveal, 195, 219, 223, 310
peripheral, 219, 223, 224
reference, 101
warped, 249
image divergence, 192
image enhancement, 290
incorrect match, 272
industrial environment, 253
inference, 219
influence diagram, 217
integration
of vision modules, 244
interest operator, 142
interocular distance, 168, 169
interpolation matrix, 13
invariant, 190, 318
differential, 191–193
first-order, 189, 194, 195

second-order, 194
scalar, 190
spatial, 309
temporal, 309
irreversible decisions, 96

Kalman filter, 3, 4, 54, 68, 75, 86, 91,
        146, 163, 168–170, 268, 270,
        271, 274, 306, 315
    $\alpha\beta\gamma$, 145, 146
    continuous, 15, 16, 54
    extended, 13, 60, 270, 316
    first-order model, 102
    gain, 16, 56, 70
    gain matrix, 15, 69, 85, 86, 316, 317
    information matrix, 15
    initiation, 276
    non-linear, 75
    snake, 4, 5
    system model, 15
    three-dimensional, 69
    validation, 93, 184
Kalman snake, see Kalman filter
Kant, I., 303
kinematics, 166, 167
knowledge
    implicit, 329
Kuhnert's algorithm, 315

Lagrange multipliers, 82
Lagrangian dynamics, 6, 18, 40, 75, 81
    deformation potential energy, 6
    equations of motion, 7, 42, 44
    kinetic energy, 6, 41
    potential energy, 41
Lagrangian mechanics, 5
landing approach, 61, 334
LDU factorization, 11, 14
learning
    heuristic dynamic programming
        (HDP), 205
    adaptation, 212
    autonomous, 332
    credit assignment problem, 203
    dynamic programming (DP), 203
        HDP, 203
    effectiveness, 211
    eligibility trace, 206
    evaluation, 204
    evaluation function, 205, 211
        update rule, 206
    expected discounted return, 205
    gradient descent, 205, 206
    heuristic, 204
    heuristic dynamic programming
        (HDP), 204, 206, 208
    optimal policy, 204
    perception–action mapping, 203
    policy, 206

eligibility trace, 206, 207
policy function, 205, 209, 212
rate, 206, 207
reinforcement, 203, 204
return
    n-step corrected, 205
reward, 204, 205, 210
rule, 207
state transition, 204
least squares fit, 13, 46, 67, 169, 181,
        254, 308
Levitt, T., 217
likelihood map, 108, 110, 113
linear programming, 97
linear recursion, 91
Listing's law, 157, 165
Ljapunov, 82
looking, 156
Lowe, D., 60
Lumelsky, 179
Lumelsky, V., 185

manipulation, 190
manoeuvre
    n-point turn, 211
Markov random field , 12
Marr, D., 217
MARVIN, 240–244, 251, 256, 257
    slice-pair, 248
    vision coprocessor, 244
MARVIN video bus, 241
Masspar, 116
MaxVideo, 143
Maybank, S., 177
Mayhew, J., 203, 239, 253
McLauchlan, P., 155
membrane energy, 81
mental process, 303
message addressing, 243
Metaxas, D., 75
microprocessor, 240, 313, 315, 326, 332
modal analysis, 40, 46, 293
    feature inflection, 48
    feature rotation, 48
model
    client/server, 254
    free-space, 176
    geometric, 59
    integrated spatio-temporal, 332
model matching
    parallel, 252
morphological filter, 24, 27, 290
motion, 156
    background, 169
    compensation, 151
    constraint, 168, 303
    deliberate, 190, 198
    exploratory, 185
    nonrigid, 81

relative, 189, 192
segmentation, 169
soft constraints, 270, 272
speed–scale ambiguity, *see* ambiguity
stereo, 333
system requirements, 165
temporal evolution, 331
translational, 192
viewer, 191
motion parallax, 192, 195
motion planning, 176
multiprocessor, 311
    MIMD, 311
Murray, D., 155
mutual-exclusivity constraint, 221

nameserver, 243, 255
navigation, 107, 115, 156, 176, 178,
        181, 190, 197, 204, 208, 260,
        279, 334
adaptive, 203
map, 119
Navlab, 115, 119
neck, 158
Nelson, R., 197
neural network, 208
    CMAC, 208, 209
        tiling, 208, 209
Newmark method, 10
nodal variables, 13
nodal velocities, 16
noise, 27, 206, 245, 246, 275, 285, 314
additive, 207
Gaussian, 12, 15, 85, 92, 99
immunity to, 193
measurement, 190, 319
process, 316
salt and pepper, 28
sensor, 203
speckle, 289
numerical stability, 189
Nyquist limit, 54
Nyquist sampling, 52

object
articulated, 309
database, 331
detection, 168
hypothesis, 332
rigid, 59, 253, 309
object class, 253
obstacle, 211
avoidance, 333
range, 328
tracking, 326
obstacle avoidance, 213
occlusion, 17, 27, 28, 31, 81, 170, 175,
        184, 246, 326
sidedness, 185

oculomotor control, 126, 130
odometer, 328
optical flow, 265
outliers, 28, 308

parallax, 192
rate of, 187
parallel computing, 39, 52
parallelism
featural, 257
fine-grain, 240
spatial, 248
particle tracks, 21, 36
path
extremal, 181
path planning, 39, 279
pure pursuit, 107, 114
path- planning
obstacle detection, 183
path-planning
active exploration, 182
back-tracking, 187
exploratory motion, 179
safe clearance, 181
perception, 203
planar facet interpolation, 264
planning
grasp, 176
motion, 176
PMF stereo, 246, 252
Poisson distribution, 99, 100
Pollard, S., 239
polynomial fitting
dynamic, 46
Popper, K., 307
pose, 60, 268
estimate, 68
potential energy surface, 7
precategorical vision, 144
prediction, 304
positive feedback, 304
predictive feed-forward, 257
Prescott, T., 203
processor utilisation, 256
projection
central, 314
orthographic, 142
perspective, 59, 113, 142, 176, 192,
        267, 271, 307–309, 322, 326
inversion, 308, 316
Puma robot, 150
pursuit, 125, 126, 129, 142, 144, 161

quaternion, 68, 84, 254, 259

rank deficiency, 70
Rao, B., 91
RAPiD, 59–72
control point, 61, 64

profile edges, 71
view-potential table, 72
Rayleigh dissipation, 7
recognition, 156, 240, 279, 311
reconstruction
    image, 285
reconstructionist paradigm, 156, 217
rectification, 183
reflex
    optokinetic, 155, 161, 164
    vestibulo-ocular, 155, 161
reflex action, 211, 312
region of interest, 169, 172, 249
regression
    linear, 91
    orthogonal, 246, 249
    quadratic recursive, 183
Reid, I., 155
reliability, 165
representation
    cartesian, 289
    ego-centric, 278
    proprioceptive, 156
response latency, 248
retinal velocity, 130
Riccati equation, 15, 17, 85
rigidity, 18, 263, 285
Rimey, R., 217
road, 107, 114, 314
    Autobahn, 332
    boundary tracking, 313
    clothoid, 319
    curvature, 318, 319
        change, 319
        horizontal, 324
        piecewise linear, 319
        vertical, 322
    curved, 333
    intersection, 107, 110–114, 119
    kernel location, 110, 111, 114
    planar, 326
    recognition, 317
    structured, 116
    structured features, 107, 116
    unstructured, 107, 115, 116, 119
    vehicle guidance, 304
    width, 319, 326
road detection method
    gradient based, 116
    histogram and threshold, 116
    robustness, 115
    Shadow Boxing System, 116
robot
    Adept, 175
    robustness, 168, 170, 230, 245, 269, 272
router, 243
Rygol, M., 239

saccade, 124, 129, 145, 155, 161, 164,
        169
saliency measure, 125
scan conversion, 286
SCARA robot, 185
SCARF, 107, 108, 112–119
scene understanding
    3D, 306
second-order dynamics, 81
sensor
    laser range-finder, 209
    touch, 210
sensor model, 18
shadow, 313, 333
shadow boundary, 309
Shannon mutual information, 225
shape
    apparent, 192
    estimation, 87
shape from shading, 125
shape knowledge, 116
shape selectivity, 39
Sharkey, P., 155
signal dropout, 146
silhouette, 175, 185
    sidedness, 185
Skewis, 179
Smith predictor, 162, 163
smoothing, 289, 298
    temporal, 68, 292
snake, 21, 39, 40, 169, 190, 197, 291
    control point, 190
    elasticity, 18
    first-order Kalman filter, 17
    Kalman, see Kalman filter
    second-order Kalman filter, 17
    unconstrained, 39
Sobel edge operator, 116, 223
sonar-space filter, 287, 289
Soong, J., 141
specular surface, 187
state decoupling, 86
state estimate, 93
    coalesced, 100
Stephens, R., 61
stereo, 141, 190, 198, 280, 281
    correspondence, 167, 246
    disparity, 154, 164
    disparity space, 142
    triangulation, 245
    vergence, 141, 155, 161, 164
        axis, 161, 165
    vergence error, 142
stereo disparity, 141, 142, 247
    histogram, 142
stereo image-pair, 244
stereo vergence, 146
    symmetric, 143
stereo vision, 325

stiffness matrix, 9, 17, 81
strain energy, 81
sub-sampling, 143
Subbarao, M., 196
SUN, 61, 115, 143, 151, 171, 241, 256, 266
SUN computer, 132
superquadric
    deformable, 78
    ellipsoid, 78, 80
support feature, 253
surface
    extrapolation, 179
    fronto-parallel, 196
surface deformation, 293
surface orientation, 195, 198
surface sensor, 178
surface slant, 191
surface texture, 198, 314
surface tilt, 191
surveillance, 39, 156, 158, 159, 164, 168
    platform, 156
symmetry
    left–right, 213
symmetry-seeking model, 76
system
    latency, 160
    model matching, 254
Szeliski, R., 3

table
    pairwise relationships, 253
tapering, *see* deformation
task-oriented system, 217
TEA, 217–230
    action, *see* visual action
    BEL, 220–222, 225
        transport, 222
        weighting, 221
    evidence gathering, 222
    expected area, 220, 221, 229
    expected area net, 220, 224, 227
        link, 220
        node, 220
    IS-A tree, 221, 222, 224
        leaf, 221, 224
    PART-OF net, 220, 222, 224
    relation map, 220
    task net, 222, 224
    utility function, 229
        lookahead, 226
    vision module, 223
template matching, 22
tension
    of contour, 5
Terzopoulos, D., 3, 75
TINA, 245, 248, 250
TMAX, 241–242
tracking, 146, 168, 293, 311

alpha-beta ($\alpha\beta$), 60, 68, 146
    dynamic contour, 181
    force based, 7
    model based, 59
    non-rigid, 87
    real-time, 3, 39, 240
    repetition rate, 161
    rigid structure, 40
    smooth pursuit, 130
tracking dynamics, 39
transformation
    affine, 190
    geometric, 190
    relief, 195
transputer, 171, 239–241, 261, 311, 313, 315, 333
    concurrency model, 53
    link, 171, 329
    network, 329
    process, 53
transputer link, 241
transputer network, 39, 52, 61, 266
triangulation, 263, 270
    Delauney, 279
Tsai, R., 245

ultrasound, 285, 300
uncertainty, 12, 13, 54, 92, 181, 198, 203, 271, 274, 314
under-damped response, 143
utility
    expected
        maximising, 217

VAL, 151–153
validation, 54, 92, 93
    region, 93–100, 104
    gate, 184
validation region,
VaMoRs, 310, 323, 332
vanishing point, 111, 113
variational method, 299
VAX, 61
vehicle
    autonomous, 260, 309, 310
    docking, 334
    front-wheel steering, 322
    guidance, 312
    heading angle, 322
    slipping, 323
    steering angle, 322
    suspension dynamics, 324
    trajectory, 322, 323
    tyre, 323
velocity field, 190, 192
    deformation, 196
    dense, 192
    differential invariant
        first-order, 189

    second-order, 189
  differential invariant of, 189
  divergence, 192, 194, 196
  invariant, 192
  virtual, 308
vergence, 126, 129
vergence system, 132
Vestibular System, 130
vibration
  of robot, 181
video bus, 171
  distributed, 260, 261, 311
virtual process, 244
viscous drag, 40, 54
vision
  foveal, 280
  peripheral, 168, 280
visual action, 223, 225
  foveal, 229
  precondition, 224
  utility, 225, 227
  value, 225
  viewing direction control, 333
visual attention, 217, 313
visual routines, 126

Watkins, C., 203, 206, 208
WATSMART, 88
Werbos, P., 203
Wilson method, 10
world model
  4D, 308

Yuille, 124
Yuille, A., 21

Zisserman, A., 175
zoom, 158

Artificial Intelligence

Patrick Henry Winston, founding editor
J. Michael Brady, Daniel G. Bobrow, and Randall Davis, current editors

Artificial Intelligence: An MIT Perspective, Volume I: Expert Problem Solving, Natural Language Understanding, Intelligent Computer Coaches, Representation and Learning, edited by Patrick Henry Winston and Richard Henry Brown, 1979

Artificial Intelligence: An MIT Perspective, Volume II: Understanding Vision, Manipulation, Computer Design, Symbol Manipulation, edited by Patrick Henry Winston and Richard Henry Brown, 1979

NETL: A System for Representing and Using Real-World Knowledge, Scott Fahlman, 1979

The Interpretation of Visual Motion, by Shimon Ullman, 1979

A Theory of Syntactic Recognition for Natural Language, Mitchell P. Marcus, 1980

Turtle Geometry: The Computer as a Medium for Exploring Mathematics, Harold Abelson and Andrea di Sessa, 1981

From Images to Surfaces: A Computational Study of the Human Visual System, William Eric Leifur Grimson, 1981

Robot Manipulators: Mathematics, Programming, and Control, Richard P. Paul, 1981

Computational Models of Discourse, edited by Michael Brady and Robert C. Berwick, 1982

Robot Motion: Planning and Control, edited by Michael Brady, John M. Hollerbach, Timothy Johnson, Tomás Lozano-Pérez, and Matthew T. Mason, 1982

In-Depth Understanding: A Computer Model of Integrated Processing for Narrative Comprehension, Michael G. Dyer, 1983

Robotic Research: The First International Symposium, edited by Hideo Hanafusa and Hirochika Inoue, 1985

Robot Hands and the Mechanics of Manipulation, Matthew T. Mason and J. Kenneth Salisbury, Jr., 1985

The Acquisition of Syntactic Knowledge, Robert C. Berwick, 1985

The Connection Machine, W. Daniel Hillis, 1985

Legged Robots that Balance, Marc H. Raibert, 1986

Robotics Research: The Third International Symposium, edited by O.D. Faugeras and Georges Giralt, 1986

Machine Interpretation of Line Drawings, Kokichi Sugihara, 1986

ACTORS: A Model of Concurrent Computation in Distributed Systems, Gul A. Agha, 1986

Knowledge-Based Tutoring: The GUIDON Program, William Clancey, 1987

AI in the 1980s and Beyond: An MIT Survey, edited by W. Eric L. Grimson and Ramesh S. Patil, 1987

Visual Reconstruction, Andrew Blake and Andrew Zisserman, 1987

Reasoning about Change: Time and Causation from the Standpoint of Artificial Intelligence, Yoav Shoham, 1988

Model-Based Control of a Robot Manipulator, Chae H. An, Christopher G. Atkeson, and John M. Hollerbach, 1988

A Robot Ping-Pong Player: Experiment in Real-Time Intelligent Control, Russell L. Andersson, 1988

Robotics Research: The Fourth International Symposium, edited by Robert C. Bolles and Bernard Roth, 1988

The Paralation Model: Architecture-Independent Parallel Programming, Gary Sabot, 1988

Concurrent System for Knowledge Processing: An Actor Perspective, edited by Carl Hewitt and Gul Agha, 1989

Automated Deduction in Nonclassical Logics: Efficient Matrix Proof Methods for Modal and Intuitionistic Logics, Lincoln Wallen, 1989

Shape from Shading, edited by Berthold K.P. Horn and Michael J. Brooks, 1989

Ontic: A Knowledge Representation System for Mathematics, David A. McAllester, 1989

Solid Shape, Jan J. Koenderink, 1990

Expert Systems: Human Issues, edited by Dianne Berry and Anna Hart, 1990

Artificial Intelligence: Concepts and Applications, edited by A. R. Mirzai, 1990

Robotics Research: The Fifth International Symposium, edited by Hirofumi Miura and Suguru Arimoto, 1990

Theories of Comparative Analysis, Daniel S. Weld, 1990

Artificial Intelligence at MIT: Expanding Frontiers, edited by Patrick Henry Winston and Sarah Alexandra Shellard, 1990

Vector Models for Data-Parallel Computing, Guy E. Blelloch, 1990

Experiments in the Machine Interpretation of Visual Motion, David W. Murray and Bernard F. Buxton, 1990

Object Recognition by Computer: The Role of Geometric Constraints, W. Eric L. Grimson, 1990

Representing and Reasoning With Probabilistic Knowledge: A Logical Approach to Probabilities, Fahiem Bacchus, 1990

3D Model Recognition from Stereoscopic Cues, edited by John E.W. Mayhew and John P. Frisby, 1991

Artificial Vision for Mobile Robots: Stereo Vision and Multisensory Perception, Nicholas Ayache, 1991

Truth and Modality for Knowledge Representation, Raymond Turner, 1991

Made-Up Minds: A Constructivist Approach to Artificial Intelligence, Gary L. Drescher, 1991

Vision, Instruction, and Action, David Chapman, 1991

Do the Right Thing: Studies in Limited Rationality, Stuart Russell and Eric Wefeld, 1991

KAM: A System for Intelligently Guiding Numerical Experimentation by Computer, Kenneth Man-Kam Yip, 1991

Solving Geometric Constraint Systems: A Case Study in Kinematics, Glenn A. Kramer, 1992

Geometric Invariants in Computer Vision, edited by Joseph Mundy and Andrew Zisserman, 1992

HANDEY: A Robot Task Planner, Tomás Lozano-Pérez, Joseph L. Jones, Emmanuel Mazer, and Patrick A. O'Donnell, 1992

Active Vision, edited by Andrew Blake and Alan Yuille, 1992

The MIT Press, with Peter Denning as general consulting editor, publishes computer science books in the following series:

ACL-MIT Press Series in Natural Language Processing
Aravind K. Joshi, Karen Sparck Jones, and Mark Y. Liberman, editors

ACM Doctoral Dissertation Award and Distinguished Dissertation Series

Artificial Intelligence
Patrick Winston, founding editor
J. Michael Brady, Daniel G. Bobrow, and Randall Davis, editors

Charles Babbage Institute Reprint Series for the History of Computing
Martin Campbell-Kelly, editor

Computer Systems
Herb Schwetman, editor

Explorations with Logo
E. Paul Goldenberg, editor

Foundations of Computing
Michael Garey and Albert Meyer, editors

History of Computing
I. Bernard Cohen and William Aspray, editors

Logic Programming
Ehud Shapiro, editor; Fernando Pereira, Koichi Furukawa, Jean-Louis Lassez, and David H. D. Warren, associate editors

The MIT Press Electrical Engineering and Computer Science Series

Research Monographs in Parallel and Distributed Processing
Christopher Jesshope and David Klappholz, editors

Scientific and Engineering Computation
Janusz Kowalik, editor

Technical Communication and Information Systems
Edward Barrett, editor